Italy

THE COUNTRY AND ITS CUISINE

Italy

THE COUNTRY AND ITS CUISINE

INGEBORG PILS • STEFAN PALLMER

MARTIN KURTENBACH • BUENAVISTA STUDIO
(PHOTOGRAPHY)

Production of original edition: ditter.projektagentur GmbH
Text: Ingeborg Pils, Johannes B. Bucej
Recipes: Stefan Pallmer
Design and layout: Sabine Vonderstein
Picture editor: Claudia Bettray
Maps: Burga Fillery

Production of English edition:
    APE International, Richmond, VA
Translation from German: Linda Marianiello, Franz Vote
    and Heustis Whiteside for APE International
Editing: Tammi Reichel and Dr Pirette Michelli for APE International

ISBN: 978-1-4075-4758-9

Printed in China

Quantities in the recipes:
Unless otherwise specified, recipes are calculated to serve four people.
So that the list of ingredients for each recipe can also be used as a
shopping list, quantities of ingredients that are used more than once
have been added together. For further information about abbreviations
and quantities, see the appendix, page 500.

Note to the reader:
Measurements in spoons refer to a level tablespoon (15 ml) and
a level teaspoon (5 ml). Unless otherwise specified in the recipes,
full-fat milk (3.5% fat) has been used. Eggs, vegetables and potatoes
are presumed to be medium-sized. The times given are to be understood as approximate guidelines.

Fresh herbs should always be chopped or snipped just before they
are used, and grated cheese should always be freshly grated. When
the peel of citrus fruits is called for, always use fruit that has not been
chemically treated with pesticides.

Young children, pregnant women, older people and anyone who is
ill or recovering from illness should not partake of foods that contain
raw or only lightly cooked eggs, as well as raw fish and seafood.

Pregnant and nursing women are advised to refrain from eating
peanuts. Anyone who is allergic to nuts is advised that ready-prepared
products called for in the recipes in this book could contain traces of
nuts. Please check the manufacturer's statements on the packaging
of foods you purchase.

All of the recipes and information in this book have been compiled and
verified by the authors and the publisher with the greatest possible
diligence. Nonetheless, neither the authors nor the publisher and its
employees are liable for any possible errors or inaccuracies.

Contents

Foreword

Italy is a richly laid table, not only for gourmets, but also for anyone who appreciates honest, down-to-earth, home-cooked fare. In no other country is there such a tantalizing variety of gastronomic delights, enticing aromas and sophisticated nuances of flavours. For more than two thousand years, the Italian people have understood how to use the best that bountiful Mother Nature has to offer and to transform even the simplest of ingredients into small delicacies. Between the Alps and the Mediterranean, the broad plains and gentle hills, this lovely land that is rightly also called *Bel Paese*, the 'beautiful country', has generation after generation been the birthplace of regional specialities that can only be found in Italy.

We invite you to join us at this opulent feast table and get to know the cuisine of Italy's twenty regions. A good meal, they say in Italy, also provides cultural nourishment and can in a thousand different ways introduce the history, the traditions and the everyday life of a region. In that spirit, we wish you *buon appetito* – a good appetite – and great pleasure on your delicious journey of discovery from the Alps to the southern reaches of Sicily.

Ingeborg Pils   Stefan Pallmer

La Cucina Italiana

THE CUISINE OF ITALY

Guide to Osterias

The first edition of *Osterie d'Italia*, a guide to Italian country fare that was assembled by Slow Food, was published in 1990. To this day, the updated editions continue to provide indispensable help in seeking out simple, honest, family-run inns, regardless of whether you are in Rome, Florence, Venice or a small mountain village in Abruzzo. The heartiness and integrity of the cuisine were and remain Slow Food's criteria for including a guest house in their gastronomic guide. The latest edition offers a one-of-a-kind selection of more than 1,700 osterias, tavernas, farmsteads and wine bars that still offer genuine Italian regional cooking and hospitality. Superb insight into the culinary traditions of Italy is provided in a series of short essays on regional specialities and tips about artisanal enterprises that, above and beyond the restaurant industry, offer local products of special quality.

Italy: Motherland of European Cuisine

To describe Italy as the motherland of European cuisine is surely no exaggeration. But how is it that the art of Italian cooking enjoys a reputation like that of no other European country, with the possible exception of France? The term 'motherland' already sheds considerable light on the secret of her success, as it conjures associations with family connections, a feeling of togetherness, and identification with a small community of people. This tradition could only have come about in agricultural and rural surroundings to which people have been deeply tied for centuries.

To speak of a single Italian cuisine would simply not do it justice. The gastronomic traditions of this 1,500-km (930-mile) long peninsula are too diverse, and the fact that Italy as we know it today is actually a product of the nineteenth and twentieth centuries should not be over-

looked. Keeping in mind the turbulent history of the country, one can perhaps better understand why Italian food has always been a little piece of 'home on a plate'. It cannot simply be preserved in documents, read about in books or studied; rather, it is something that is literally 'ingested' by Italians every day.

Looked at this way, it is understandable that in the mid-twentieth century, cries of 'Italian cuisine is dying' and laments that 'Mamma doesn't cook anymore' fell on fertile soil. Despite all the predictions of gloom and doom, however, Italian cuisine is still alive and well. Although there have been some changes in eating habits and lifestyle, Italy has largely been able to preserve its cordial hospitality and traditional country fare.

People frown on rushed meals in Italy. Even at midday, they make time for a tranquil meal with colleagues and friends (left).

For hundreds of years, cooking secrets large and small have been passed down in families from one generation to the next (below).

Cooking Traditions

In the aftermath of World War II, there was an initial flight to the cities. As a result, entire rural areas experienced dramatic population declines, particularly in the south, while wealthy northern cities and the industrial centres grew. Emigrants from Campania, Sicily and Apulia brought their cuisine with them, and the northern metropolises became acquainted with ingredients and traditions that seemed almost exotic to long-time residents. Many people tasted things like pizza or durum wheat pasta for the first time. Olive oil entered the scene, along with bacon and butter.

In the countryside, on the other hand, regional cuisine nearly faded into oblivion, for who was there to carry on the traditions? Conversely, Milan, Bologna and the rest of northern Italy experienced a spate of new restaurant openings, and the wave continued southwards from there. Italy did not escape the 'blessings of modernity', of course, nor was it spared the post-war fascination with all aspects of the Anglo-American lifestyle. Whether in the form of convenience products or fast food, industrial

food production also installed itself in the Italian landscape, and it would be remiss not to mention that pizza and pasta are now part of that trend.

An entire generation, now with children of its own, broke with tradition and some know-how was lost. But the situation was

For Italians, eating is much more than simply consuming food. A companionable get-together with friends and family is every bit as important at meal-time.

As in practically no other country, Italians know how to enjoy even simple dishes with abandon.

never as drastic in Italy as in other countries that adopted the Anglo-American lifestyle hook, line and sinker. Italian cuisine owes a debt of gratitude to the fact that Italy, particularly in the south, is still primarily an agrarian society and not an industrial one, with notable exceptions such as the automotive industry.

In recent decades, there has been a renewed interest among gourmets everywhere in honest, authentic *cucina casalinga* (traditional country fare). This has offered Italian young people the opportunity to establish themselves as culinary artists and to profit from the new tourist boom. In the wake of the search for the original Italian guesthouse, many osterias and much agritourism have sprung up within the past two decades.

A rural-based farming culture that exudes healthy self-confidence and pride in the products of the land is the best way to ensure that the agrarian lifestyle and culinary traditions will continue to be essential elements of everyday life throughout Italy. The history of Italian cuisine begins with the Sybarites, continues throughout the Roman Empire, the Middle

Ages and the Renaissance, and extends to the present day. Apart from its long history, Italian cooking has been trendsetting, notwithstanding occasional slumps over the course of millennia.

Pampered by the sun and mild climate, Italian tomatoes develop an unmistakable flavour.

La Rocca Restaurant in the Albergo Hotel in San Leo presents local specialities.

Cooking

Cooking constitutes one of the most important forms of cultural expression. The fruit of a long historical tradition among a country's inhabitants, cooking varies from region to region, city to city, and village to village. Dishes and customs express who we are, help us to understand our roots, and represent us to the outside world. Associated with a specific landscape and its characteristic products, we transform our natural surroundings into our cultural identity through cooking. For this reason, culinary traditions are not static entities, but are active processes that are constantly being renewed and passed on to future generations.

Cooking in Ancient Rome

The first true art of European cooking developed in ancient Rome. Even in those days, it was not just the food that occupied a central role in everyday life: social gatherings and the enjoyment of food among family and friends were equally important. Meals were an integral part of the day, providing an opportunity for discussion and companionship that strengthened people's sense of belonging to a particular social class. Unlike in ancient Greece, women were present at banquets and, if witnesses are to be believed, people sometimes indulged in more than food.

Banquets were seldom as opulent as described by some ancient writers, however. They normally began with appetizers served with mead, followed by three further courses accompanied by wine. Favourite main courses included cooked meats – young goat, lamb, poultry, cured meat, sausages and ham – as well as vegetable dishes. Fruit, baked goods or sweet omelettes were served for dessert. Just as now, the types of dishes depended on the occasion, as well as the size of the purse. After one banquet, Pliny the Elder noted with some displeasure that, 'He served himself and a few others all sorts of delicacies, while everyone else got cheap stuff in small portions . . .'

Four hundred years ago, dark cooking areas with open fireplaces were a far cry from modern-day, ergonomically designed kitchens (above).

This illustration, which appeared in a cookbook around the end of the 16th century, shows the busy goings-on in a large kitchen (right).

Renaissance Cuisine

After the rather modest food of the Middle Ages, the art of Italian cooking flourished once more as the Renaissance began. The revival of classical antiquity not only influenced the fine and practical arts, but the culinary arts as well. Venice had become wealthy through the spice trade. The aristocratic families in Florence, Milan and Naples outdid one another with lavish festivals and even more luxurious banquets. Even the popes in Rome were enamoured of carnal pleasures and cultivated the high art of cooking.

The most exquisite pleasures were dished up for the Medicis in Florence, especially during the lifetime of the legendary Lorenzo the Magnificent (1449–1492). The bountiful tables created through the culinary arts provided not only an opportunity to celebrate pure *joie de vivre*, but even more importantly, an opportunity to showcase the power and wealth of the host.

One of the most spectacular banquets was given in 1473 by the pope's nephew, Pietro Riario, for Eleonora of Aragon, daughter of the king of Naples. Historian Bernardino Corio reported that 'crystallized, gold-covered fruits and Malmsey wine were served. These snacks were eaten standing. Before everyone took their places at the tables, covered in four cloths, pages washed the guests' hands with rose water. Trumpets blared, then the first dishes were served: roast chicken and capon, various kinds of fish, veal, goat, rabbit, a total of over thirty dishes, accompanied by Corsican wine. Even the bread was covered in gold, and the family coat of arms of the host and his guests could be recognized on it.'

Doge Alvise Mocenigo and his guests gracefully await the coming delights of the table, which are being arranged with the highest of blessings in the adjoining room.

Slow Food

The history of Slow Food reads in part like a legend. One widely circulated story is an anecdote from 1986: on the occasion of the opening of the first fast food restaurant in Rome's historic district, journalists from the nearby offices of the daily newspaper *Il Manifesto* staged an open-air banquet. The Slow Food organization grew out of the Arcigola movement, which is headed by Piedmontese journalist Carlo Petri. Calling itself the 'International Movement for the Preservation of the Right to Enjoyment', Slow Food was officially brought to life in 1989 at the Opéra Comique in Paris.

Slow Food is currently an international association, headquartered about 50 km (30 miles) south of Turin in Bra, and now has more than 80,000 members worldwide. In addition to advocating for preservation of regional food cultures, the movement's central themes include maintaining the diversity of useful plant and animal species (biodiversity) and supporting rural farming and traditional artisanal foods. Slow Food lobbies worldwide in favour of equitable conditions for food producers who work on the basis of 'good – clean – fair'.

Numerous associations (Italian: *presidi*) have been founded to assist traditional food producers. They help products and production methods that are threatened with extinction to retain a place in the food product market. These include both processed foods and ventures, for example, nomadic sheep herding and supporting improvements in traditional, skilled production methods.

The *Salone del Gusto* takes place every two years in Turin, and with around 150,000 visitors, is the largest gastronomic trade fair in the world. The Terra Madre Congress, which takes place concurrently, brings together farmers, fishermen, shepherds, scientists and gastronomes from all over the world, a clear sign that the goals of Slow Food have become firmly lodged in public consciousness over the past two decades.

Carlo Petrini (inset photo) founded Slow Food in 1986. He coined the term 'ecogastronomy', which stands for responsible agribusiness and regional diversity of flavours.

The University of Gastronomic Sciences, located in Pollenzo near Bra (Piedmont), is housed in beautiful quarters: the former summer residence of the Royal House of Savoy.

The University of Gastronomic Sciences

The University of Gastronomic Sciences (UNISG), the very first college dedicated entirely to food culture, opened its doors on 4 October 2004. Future communications specialists, multimedia opinion makers and journalists in the wine and gastronomic sectors, marketing specialists for outstanding products, as well as managers of protection consortia, agrarian and food companies, and tourist associations are among those educated here. The university is open to students from all over the world with instruction in two languages, Italian and English. Admission is subject to a numerus clausus and limited to sixty openings per year. This private college, accredited by the Italian state, is supported by Slow Food in collaboration with the regions of Piedmont and Emilia-Romagna.

Italian Academy of Cooking

'Italian cooking is dying out.' Journalist Orio Vergani attracted lots of attention with this painful outcry concerning the state of affairs in the restless Italy of the 1950s. He and his intellectual comrades-in-arms felt a moral obligation to make fervent contributions to the preservation and advancement of Italian gastronomic traditions. This led to the founding of the *Accademia Italiana della Cucina* (Italian Academy of Cooking) on 29 July 1953.

Along with the study of the history of Italian gastronomy and a critical examination of prevailing culinary developments, the Academy's bylaws established consultation with public officials, organizations and private institutions, as well as the support of projects and initiatives, the goal being to preserve characteristic national, regional and local cuisines. The bylaws obligated the Academy to absolute independence and forbade actions of a profit-oriented nature by its members.

Choosing a Restaurant in Italy

In Italy there are vast numbers of restaurants with a great variety of characteristics and offering totally different selections of dishes. Many visitors have less difficulty finding a restaurant, but rather more of a problem in choosing just the right guesthouse from among the many offerings. First of all, the budget plays a decisive role in whether someone wishes to enjoy *cucina grande* (gourmet cuisine) in an upscale restaurant or chooses the informal atmosphere and *cucina casalinga* (hearty country fare) of a traditional *osteria*.

Quite apart from financial considerations, it is highly advisable from a culinary perspective to discover those small, out of the way taverns where local specialities can be eaten in peace and good wines can be sipped by the glass. A word to the wise: Italian restaurateurs have a tendency to understatement. Particularly in bigger cities, guests will find epicurean shrines that modestly call themselves *osterias* or *enotecas*, yet offer the cuisine and prices of fine dining establishments. One tried-and-true method is to follow the locals to their favourite eateries. Italians are not only passionate cooks; they also love to dine out regularly and are sure to know the best places.

The Osteria Barella in Lucca is a favourite meeting place for those who appreciate traditional cuisine, whether locals or tourists (right).

People enjoy Italy's culinary specialities in the open air, as pictured here at the Pietratorcia Restaurant on Ischia (opposite page).

Types of Restaurants

Il Bar
Italian bars are the ideal solution for a little something between meals. Especially in the bigger cities, they offer yummy smaller fare such as classic tramezzini, panini and mini pizzas. Nuts, biscuits, salami or bite-sized pieces of cheese are absolutely essential with a glass of wine or an aperitif.

L'Enoteca
At one time, *enotecas* were nothing more than wine shops in which you could drink good wines by the glass. But an increasing number of *enoteca* owners now offer hot and cold local specialities, sometimes even complete meals.

La Pizzeria
The name says it all. Everything revolves around these crisp flatbreads, which are ideally baked in a traditional wood-fired stone oven. And it is not only parents with children who appreciate the relaxed, sociable atmosphere. The reputations of good pizza bakers usually precede them, so it makes sense to ask locals for a recommendation.

Il Ristorante-Pizzeria
Alongside simple pizzerias, there are an increasing number of restaurants that offer their guests *primi*, or first courses such as pasta and risotto, as well. They also serve uncomplicated meat, fish and vegetable *secondi*, or second courses. But you should not have high expectations of the cuisine in a *ristorante-pizzeria*.

L'Osteria
Osterias are simple bars that also serve a select few simple, regional dishes and are mainly frequented by locals. In many small communities, they constitute the centre of village life. In larger cities, on the other hand, veritable upscale restaurants are occasionally hidden behind this seemingly modest name.

La Trattoria
Trattorias are simple inns whose local culinary specialities mainly attract natives. Truck drivers swap addresses of the best trattorias. Anyone can eat there for a modest price, and the food is often very good.

Il Ristorante
Classic restaurants offer the entire spectrum of Italian cuisine in the form of the characteristic order of courses, accompanied by a refined dining experience. Anyone looking for pizza on the menu is out of luck. A dignified atmosphere, high-quality dishes and wines predominate, resulting in correspondingly high cheques.

L'Agriturismo
What began in many parts of Italy as an opportunity to take a vacation on a working farm (*l'agriturismo*) has meanwhile expanded into an important branch of gastronomy as well. This is where a few products of excellent quality – most often home-grown – are made into regional specialities according to traditional recipes. Agritourism is perhaps the best and most economical way to experience more closely the people who live in a region and their cooking traditions.

The Menu

In an Italian restaurant, a proper meal usually consists of at least three courses: an appetizer, followed by a first course (*primi piatti*) and a second course (*secondi piatti*). At the end of a fine meal some fresh fruit is eaten, at the very least, although dessert or a little cheese is preferable. It is customary to drink a glass of wine with a meal. People like to order house wines, *rosso* or *bianco della casa*, especially at midday. These are mainly simple yet good regional wines that are not too heavy.

While most Italian restaurants have printed or handwritten menus, a chalk-board with the daily specials written on it still stands at the entrance to many small osterias and trattorias. Either way, the menus and boards still do not generally include everything available, so guests are well advised to ask the waiter about any daily specials and to take a little time to

Excerpt from the menu of a Sicilian trattoria that serves local pasta and fish specialities (right).

The Osteria Il Riffaioli in Florence, one of more than 1,700 restaurants recommended in the Slow Food osteria guide, is well worth visiting (below).

TRATTORIA AL PONTE

Insalate

Insalata verde cogli agrumi *Mixed salad with citrus fruits*	5,50
Insalate siciliana *Salad with tomato, cucumber, beans, potato, feta and olives*	7,40

Primi Piatti

Pasta e ceci *Pasta and chickpeas*	7,20
Spaghetti alla Trapanese *Trapani-style pasta with tomatoes*	8,60
Perciatelli con le sarde *Pasta with sardines*	8,90
Polenta sulla spianatoia con vongole *Polenta on a board with clams*	9,00

Secondi Piatti

Stocca alla Moda di Messina *Messina-style stockfish*	15,80
Tunnu auruduci *Sweet-and-sour tuna steaks*	17,40
Pesce spada ai ferri *Grilled swordfish*	8,00

Verdure e Contorni

Carote al Marsala *Carrots with Marsala*	4,00
Carciofi al tegame *Steamed artichokes*	5,00
Melanzane alla campagnola *Country-style aubergines*	5,00
Patate fritte *Fried potatoes*	4,50

Dolci

Latte fritto *Fried pudding*	5,50
Cassata siciliana *Sicilian cassata*	6,20
Coperto	3,00

OSTERIA PONTE VECCHIO

Antipasti e Zuppe

Crostini misti *Toasted Tuscan bread with a variety of toppings*	6,70
Antipasto misto della casa *Mixed antipasto platter*	10,50
Insalata di rucola *Rocket salad with fried forest mushrooms*	4,80
Acquacotta *Tuscan soup with bread*	4,40
Cacciucco *Tuscan fish soup*	7,90

Primi Piatti

Paglia e fieno „Ponte Vecchio" *Ribbon noodles with cheese sauce*	8,20
Pappardelle sulla lepre *Wide noodles with rabbit ragout*	10,40
Panzerotti salvia e burro *Stuffed pasta pockets with sage and butter*	9,70

Secondi Piatti

Lombata di manzo alla griglia *Fillet of beef from the grill*	16,20
Brasato di cinghiale al vino rosso *Wild boar roast in red wine*	15,80
Spezzatino di agnello alle erbe *Lamb ragout with herbs*	14,50

Dolci

Crostata di mele *Tuscan apple pie*	4,20
Tiramisù	4,50

Chalkboards still take the place of printed menus in some places, especially at the entrances to smaller osterias and trattorias (above).

Excerpt from the menu of a Tuscan osteria that mainly offers traditional meat specialities (left).

discuss the various dishes with the staff. It is usually worth your while to seek and accept the waiter's advice.

In the meantime, there are also multilingual menus available in many restaurants that are often frequented by tourists. Nonetheless, it is still advisable to master a certain amount of 'culinary Italian', because not every waiter will be able to provide additional help in a guest's native language. Especially when it comes to more expensive dishes such as lobster, whole fish or *bistecca fiorentina*, it is a good idea to inquire about the price up front: the price listed on the menu is often per 100 grams, rather than for an entire portion.

The Courses

In Italy, a meal consisting of multiple courses begins with hot or cold appetizers called *antipasti*. Not only do they stimulate the appetite, they also provide diners with a first insight into the quality of the food. *Antipasti misti*, a plate of various small appetizers, are very popular. Guests can either choose their own or have the waiter put together a selection. Alternatively, one can also start off with a salad (*insalata*) or a soup (*zuppa* or *minestra*).

The *primo piatto* (first course) customarily consists of pasta, risotto or gnocchi. As with appetizers, it is also possible to order samples of two (*bis*) or three (*tris*) different dishes. In the case of *primi piatti*, portions tend to be smaller, because the main course is yet to come.

Main courses are listed under *secondi di pesce* (fish dishes) or *secondi di carne* (meat dishes). The second course is not usually served with *contorni* (side dishes). Vegetables, potatoes or polenta (a favourite in northern Italy), therefore, must be ordered separately. Pasta or rice will not be found listed under *contorni* in restaurants, because they have already been served as a first course.

Restaurants that cater to tourists also now offer a *piatto unico*, which is a course of meat or fish served with side dishes. These places also frequently offer a *menu turistico*, a fixed menu put together by the host. Anyone in search of authentic Italian cuisine should certainly avoid these kinds of restaurants.

Dolci (sweets) and *formaggi* (cheeses) complete a fine Italian meal. The classic desserts are not the only sweet finishes you have to choose from: special cakes, fresh fruits or fruit salads are also frequently available. Guests would do well to consult the waiter when selecting the cheese. An espresso, with or without liqueurs added, adds the final, crowning touch. Anyone who orders a cappuccino after dinner risks exposing himself or herself as a tourist: Italians only drink cappuccino for breakfast or in the morning.

Restaurant Etiquette

Different countries, different customs. This saying also holds true for dining in restaurants. Upon entering an Italian restaurant, it is not customary to walk right over to a coveted window table, as one might do in other European countries; the custom is to wait for the waiter at the entrance instead. The guest then tells her or him how many people are in the party and politely requests the desired window seat.

According to tradition, meals in Italy consist of several courses. In the past, especially in the best restaurants, guests were more or less compelled to order at least three courses. By now, though, things have relaxed and it is permissible to omit a course or to share a risotto or *primo piatto* with someone else without attracting the displeasure of the owner.

In many guesthouses, particularly in rural areas, it is still expected that guests will pay an additional amount for the *coperto* (bread and cover charge). This amount, however, must be clearly and visibly stated on the menu. The tip is now included in the price (*servizio compreso*). Waiters no longer expect an additional tip, even though many travel guides may say otherwise. Nonetheless, satisfied guests still leave a small amount on the table as a token of appreciation.

The easiest way to become unpopular with a waiter is to insist on separate cheques for each person in your party. The Italian custom is to present one cheque per table. After the cheque is paid, guests simply divide the total among themselves. To

Vinegar, oil, salt and pepper will almost always be on the table in restaurants, since in Italy guests can often dress their salad themselves.

consult the menu and painstakingly calculate who ate what is considered impolite.

In order to call a halt to tax evasion, which was jokingly referred to as a popular sport by some, it became compulsory to pocket the *ricevuta fiscale* (receipt), which could then be presented to tax investigators upon request. Many people still feel it is still advisable to save restaurant receipts at least temporarily.

Even in outdoor restaurants, as here in the Via di Arco de San Callisto in Rome, people wait until a server shows them to their table.

A meal without the finishing touch of an espresso is practically unthinkable to most Italians (below).

Paolo Lopriore, chef at the Il Canto Restaurant in the Hotel Certosa di Maggiano (Siena), and a colleague arrange a seafood plate.

Culinary Lexicon

A

abbacchio	suckling lamb
acciuga	anchovy
aceto	vinegar
aceto balsamico	balsamic vinegar
acido	sharp, acidic
affettato	cured meats, cold cuts
affumicato	smoked
aglio	garlic
agnello	lamb
agro	sour
agrodolce	sweet & sour
albicocca	apricot
alimentari	food
alimentarista	grocer
alloro	laurel
amarena	sour cherries/ cherries
amaretti	almond macaroons
amaro	bitter
aneto	fennel seed
anguilla	eel
antara	duck
antipasto	appetizer
aragosta	lobster
arancia	orange
aranciata	orangeade
asparago	asparagus
astice	spiny lobster

B

barbabietola	beetroot
barba di frate	monk's beard (leafy greens)
biscotto	biscuit
bistecca	steak
branzino	sea bass
brasato	roast
brodetto di pesce	fish stew
brodo	vegetable, meat or fish stock
burro	butter

C

calamaro	squid
caldo	hot
calzone	calzone
candito	crystallized fruit
canederli	bread dumplings
cannella	cinnamon
cantucci	Tuscan almond biscuit

cappero	capers
cappone	capon
capra	goat
carciofo	artichoke
carne	meat
carota	carrot
carpa, carpione	carp
cavolfiore	cauliflower
cavolini di Bruxelles	Brussels sprouts
cavolo	cabbage
cece	chickpea, garbanzo bean
cereali	grain
cernia	grouper
cervo	venison
cetriolo	cucumber
cime di rapa	broccoli rabe
cinghiale	wild boar
cioccolato	chocolate
cipolla	onion
cocomero	watermelon
coda di rospo	monkfish tail
coniglio	rabbit
coniglio selvatico	wild rabbit
contorno	side dish
coriandolo	coriander
cornetto	croissant
costata di manzo	rump steak
costoletta	cutlet
cotoletta	escalope
crostacei	crustaceans

D

dentice	dentex (Mediterranean fish)
dolce	sweet, sweet dish
dolcificante	sweetener
dragoncello	tarragon

E

erba cipollina	chives
erbe	herbs

F

fagiano	pheasant
fagiolino	green or wax beans
fagiolo	beans
faraona	guinea fowl
farina	flour
fegato	liver
fico	fig
filetto	fillet
finocchio	fennel

formaggio	cheese
fragola	strawberry
freddo	cold
frutta	fruit
frutti di bosco	mixed berries
frutti di mare	seafood
fungo	mushroom

G

galetto	small chicken
gallo	rooster
gamberetto	shrimp, prawn
gambero	many types of prawns and crayfish
gamberone	king prawn
gelato	ice, ice cream
grasso	fatty, rich
gusto	taste, flavour

I

indivia	endive
insalata	salad
integrale	whole grain
interiora	offal
involtino	roulade

L

lampone	raspberry
lardo	lard, pork fat
latte	milk
lattuga	lettuce
lauro	bay leaf
legumi	pulses
lenticchia	lentils
lepre	hare
limone	lemon
lingua	tongue
luccio	pike

M

macedonia	fruit salad
maggiorana	marjoram
magro	lean
maiale	pork
maionese	mayonnaise
mandorla	almond
manzo	beef
marrone	sweet chestnut
mela	apple
melanzana	aubergine
menta	peppermint
merluzzo	codfish
miele	honey
minestra	soup
mora	blackberries

N

nocciola	hazelnut
noce	walnut
noce moscata	nutmeg

O

oca	goose
olio	oil
oliva	olive
orata	gilthead sea bream
origano	oregano
osso	bone
ostrica	oyster

P

pancetta	Italian bacon
pan di spagna	sponge
pane	bread
pangrattato	breadcrumbs
panino	sandwich
panna	cream
pasta	pasta
pasta brisee	short pastry
pasta frolla	shortbread
patata	potato
pepe	pepper
peperoncino	chilli
peperone	pepper
pera	pear
pernice	partridge
pesca	peach
pesce	fish
pesce persico	freshwater fish
pesce spada	swordfish
piccante	spicy
piccione	dove, pigeon
piedino	hock
pinolo	pine kernel
pisello	pea
pistacchio	pistachio nut
pollame	poultry
pollo	chicken
polpetta	meatball
pomodoro	tomato
porcino	cep
prugna	plum

Q

quaglia	quail

R

rafano	horseradish
ravanello	radish
ribes	currant
riccio di mare	sea urchin
ripieno	stuffed
riso	rice
rombo	turbot
rosmarino	rosemary

A glass of Prosecco is always a lovely way to begin an evening meal.

S

sale	salt
salmone	salmon
salsa	sauce
salume	salami
salvia	sage
sambuco	elderberry
sanguinello	blood orange
sardina	sardine
scampo	scampi, Dublin Bay prawn
sedano	celery
selvaggina	wild game
semifreddo	semi-frozen dessert
semolino	hard wheat
senape	mustard

seppia — squid, octopus

seppia	squid, octopus
sformato	pudding
sgombro	herring
siluro	wels catfish
sogliola	sole
sorbetto	sorbet
spezzatino	stew
spinacio	spinach
spugnola	morel
surgelato	deep frozen

T

tacchino	turkey
tartufo	truffle
tonno	tuna
torta	cake
trota	trout

U

uovo	egg
uva	grape
uva spina	gooseberry
uvetta	raisin

V

vaniglia	vanilla
verdura	greens
vitello	veal
vongola	clam

Z

zafferano	saffron
zenzero	ginger
zucca	squash
zucchero	sugar

The Osteria Vini da Pinto in Venice posts its selection of antipasti on little signs (opposite page).

Very finely sliced salami and cured ham specialities are popular antipasti (below).

Methods of Preparation

ai ferri	grilled		
al cartoccio	en papillote	ripieno	stuffed
al dente	al dente	salmi	wild game prepared in liquid
al forno	oven baked	sott'olio	preserved in oil
all'amatriciana	pasta sauce with onions, bacon, tomatoes and chilli	sottaceto	pickled in vinegar
		(in) umido	prepared in aromatic liquid
alla cacciatora	hunter style		
alla carbonara	carbonara	**Drinks**	
alla griglia	from the grill		
alla marinara	prepared with tomatoes, oregano, olives, anchovies and capers	acqua	water
		acqua minerale	mineral water
alla norma	pasta sauce with aubergine and tomato	aranciata	orangeade
alla parmigiana	prepared with grated Parmesan	birra	beer
alla pescatora	prepared with shellfish and crustaceans	birra alla spina	beer on tap
		cioccolata	chocolate
all'arrabbiata	prepared with a spicy sauce	limonata	lemonade
arrosto	roast	liquore	liqueur
bollito	boiled	spremuta	drink made from squeezed fruit
casalinga	home-made	spumante	sparkling wine
cotto	cooked	succo	juice made from fruit or vegetables
crudo	raw	vino	wine
fritto	fried	vino bianco	white wine
marinata	marinated	vino rosso	red wine

Culinary Regions

Italy is divided into twenty regions that extend from the Alps southwards to Sicily. They differ greatly from one another in terms of natural features and soil configuration, and what's more, they were also subject to entirely different cultural influences in the course of history. So it is no wonder that the traditional foods of these individual regions, based on local agricultural products, differ considerably from one another in some respects. Over the course of centuries, each has developed characteristic dishes and methods of preparation that are found only in that region, and are protected like valuable treasures.

The next few pages provide an initial overview of the culinary features, agricultural products, specialities and gastronomic festivals of each region. Throughout the book, regional cuisines are discussed more fully in connection with a traditional dish or characteristic products.

Roads wind their way between cypresses and traverse the Tuscan countryside, as here in Monticchiello.

SWITZERLAND

AUSTRIA

**TRENTINO-
ALTO ADIGE**
P. 159

**FRIULI-
VENEZIA
GIULIA**
P. 270

SLOVENIA

VALLE D'AOSTA P. 158

Aosta

LOMBARDY
P. 182

Trento

Milan

Lake
Garda

Etsch

VENETO
P. 174

Triest

Turin

Po

Venice

PIEDMONT
P. 76

EMILIA–ROMAGNA
P. 410

LIGURIA P. 138

Genoa

Bologna

Arno

Florence

Ligurian Sea

TUSCANY
P. 122

Ancona

THE MARCHE
P. 164

Perugia

UMBRIA
P. 314

Adriatic Sea

Tiber

L'Aquila

ABRUZZO
P. 396

Rome

MOLISE
P. 326

LAZIO
P. 364

Campobasso

APULIA
P. 258

CAMPANIA
P. 386

Bari

SARDINIA
P. 295

Naples

Potenza

BASILICATA
P. 382

Tyrrhenian Sea

Cagliari

CALABRIA
P. 426

Catanzaro

Ionian Sea

Palermo

SICILY
P. 232

Mediterranean Sea

Valle d'Aosta

Fontina cheese, the most famous product of Valle d'Aosta, is made from the milk of cows that graze on the slopes of Italy's most mountainous areas. Other well-known products are *lardo di Arnad*, an aromatic bacon with herbs and spices, *jambon de Bosses*, a mild raw ham with an aftertaste of wild game, and *boudin*, a black pudding made from pork and beetroots. Saint-Rhemy-en-Bosses celebrates its ham festival in July, while Arnad's bacon festival is in August.

Piedmont/Piemonte

Piedmont is a culinary gold mine: from white truffles found in Alba to numerous varieties of cheese with protected guarantees of origin, spicy sausages such as donkey salami, and the meat of a special breed of Piedmontese cattle, all the way to sweet temptations including *amaretti, biscotti, torcetti*, nougat and *gianduiotti*, which are hazelnut pralines from Turin. In addition to the many folk festivals devoted to famous red wines such as Barolo, Barbaresco and Barbera, the *Mostra Mercato del Tartufo*, a national white truffle trade fair, takes place every October in Alba.

Liguria

Fresh basil, vegetables and fish are leading symbols of Ligurian cuisine. Added to these are flavourful, cold-pressed taggiasca olive oil, pastas such as *trenette* and *trofie*, Genoese *pandolce* and *amaretti di Sassello*. Sought-after treasures include Conio beans and Quarantina potatoes from Pigna. The *Sagra del Pesce*, a fish festival at which fresh fish is fried up in a gigantic pan, takes place every year in Camogli.

Lombardy/Lombardia

Lombardy has an astonishing variety of specialities to offer, including *panettone*, Milanese risotto, *bresaola*, *torrone alle mandorle* (almond nougat), Gorgonzola, pumpkin tortelli, *pizzocheri* (buckwheat pasta) and *viulin*, a delicious alpine ham. The region is also the birthplace of a famous, dry sparkling wine called *Franciacorta*. Not to be missed is the annual *Sagra dell'oca* (Goose Festival) in Motara in September, which features unique goose salami, among other things.

Trentino-Alto Adige

The close proximity of Austria is still in evidence today, particularly in South Tyrol, in the gastronomy of Trentino-Alto Adige, a region that stretches from the shores of Lago di Garda to the Dolomite Alps. Wine and apples are cultivated on a large scale, and the region's Alpine specialities clearly bear a strong resemblance to north-eastern European cuisine. In Trentino, on the other hand, the influence of the former Venetian Republic is still evident. Many little towns hold small wine festivals in the autumn, and the famous Speck Festival held in Bolzano each May is dedicated to the famous bacon of the Alto Adige.

Veneto

Four main products shape the cuisine of Veneto: rice, polenta, pulses and dried codfish. Whereas rice and polenta combined with fresh fish and seafood predominate in the former maritime metropolis of Venice, vegetables, including asparagus, broccoli and radicchio, and sausage specialities such as *soppressata* predominate in the more rural areas of Veneto. Regional delicacies can be sampled in September at the *Sagra del Sedano* (Celery Festival) in Rubbio di Conco.

Friuli-Venezia Giulia

Austrian, Hungarian, Slovenian and Croatian cultural and culinary influences melded in this region from early on. Its most famous products are undoubtedly mild, air-dried *prosciutto di San Daniele* and Montasio cheese. Outstanding white wines come from Collio and Grave del Friuli. Grappa and Maraschino are known the world over. San Daniele honours its special cured ham with the *Aria di Festa*, a lively festival with music and food tastings that takes place every August.

Emilia-Romagna

Emilia-Romagna has introduced the epicurean world to pork, tortelli, Parmesan and, last but not least, one of the premium vinegars of the world, *aceto balsamico tradizionale*. The town of Parma is home to the air-dried ham that carries its name, mortadella comes from Bologna and a spicy salami hails from Felino. Other cured meat specialities include *culatello di Zibello* and Langhirano ham. The *Sagra del Fungo Porcino* (Cep Festival) takes place in Borgotaro each September.

Tuscany/Toscana

Tuscany is a favourite vacation spot for epicures. Its simple cuisine is based on high quality raw ingredients. Particularly delicious examples are Tuscany's world-famous olive oil, sausage products made from Cinta Senese pigs, flavourful *lardo di Colonnata* bacon and Chianina beef from Maremma. Of course, the wines of the Chianti region must be added, the finest of which are Brunello di Montalcino and Vino Nobile di Montepulciano.

Umbria

Black truffles and Norcia sausages have made Umbria famous well beyond its borders. Gourmets are also familiar with Castelluccio lentils, Colfiorito potatoes and green, cold-pressed olive oil. The most well-known wines are Orvieto, a white wine, and Sangrantino di Montefalco, one of Italy's best reds. The *Eurochocolate Perugia*, a chocolate festival, takes place each year in October.

The Marche

The diverse cuisine of the Marche, a region that lies between the Adriatic Sea and the Apennines, is based on outstanding products from land and sea: Acqualagna truffles, Fabriano sausage and ham, meat and fresh fish. Local Ascolana Tenera olive trees yield particularly large and flavourful fruit. Particularly noteworthy among the regional wines are Verdicchio del castelli di Jesi, a white, and two reds, Rosso Conero and Lacrima di Morro.

Lazio/Latium

In Lazio and around the Eternal City of Rome, hearty rural cooking predominates. Its roots go back thousands of years to an agricultural tradition that includes tender, milk-fed Easter lamb, as well as nutritious pasta dishes and offal. The most important vegetables are artichokes, beans, peas, courgettes, celery, potatoes, lentils and olives. The strawberry festival held in Nemi is one of the region's loveliest culinary celebrations. In June, at the height of the strawberry season, you can sample the sweet fruit, as well as ices, ice cream, wines and liqueurs made from it.

Abruzzo

Raising livestock and planting crops still characterize this craggy, mountainous region where pasta, vegetables and meat are the staples of the cuisine. *Peperoncini*, the small, very spicy chillies that season just about everything, reign supreme. Among the most important regional products are saffron, hand-crafted pasta, olive oil and cheese, especially *pecorino* and *scamorza*. The full-bodied red wine Montepulciano d'Abruzzo is a must.

The Ligurian coast near Genoa offers picturesque sights and cultural attractions.

Molise

The tiny, narrow region of Molise – the second smallest in Italy – stretches from the Apennine mountain chain to the sea. Sheep and goats are herded traditionally here, and are raised mainly for their milk. The sharp sheep's and goat's cheeses from Agone are known outside of the region, as are hearty sausage specialities such as *salsiccia ferrazzanese*, which is flavoured with chillies and fennel seeds. Special healing properties were previously attributed to onions, and Isernia celebrates the bulbous plant each June at its onion festival.

Campania

In the fertile, volcanic soils around Mount Vesuvius, tomatoes, peppers, artichokes, fennel and citrus fruits ripen under the best climatic conditions. They shape the cuisine of Campania every bit as much as fish and seafood, Neapolitan pizza and the famous *mozzarella di bufala*, made from the flavourful milk of water buffaloes. *Limoncello*, at once a refreshing and full-flavoured lemon liqueur, is becoming more and more popular.

Apulia/Puglia

Vegetables, olive oil, pasta and wine are the staples of the food found in the Apulian region. Italy's bread basket, as the region has come to be known today, produces the majority of the semolina (hard wheat) that is used in making pasta. Apulia is also the country's largest producer of olive oil. High-quality preserved vegetable and sausage specialities are made according to traditional recipes. Each June you can sample the full-bodied red wines, headed up by *primitivo* and *malvasia*, at the traditional wine festival in Orsara.

Basilicata

Surrounded by the regions of Campania, Apulia and Calabria, Basilicata has not yet become a major tourist destination. It is supposedly the birthplace of *salsiccia*, which, along with a second sausage speciality called *soperzata*, was already produced in antiquity. Other famous regional products include oyster mushrooms and *peperoncini*. Aglianico del Vulture, a red wine extolled as the 'Barolo of the south', is one of Italy's most important wines.

In several regions of Italy, truffle trade fairs are a high point on the culinary calendar (right).

In many regions, flavourful olive oil is one of the most important products.

Calabria

Calabria is strategically situated between the Tyrrhenian and Ionian seas, and has attracted foreign conquerors from time immemorial: Greeks, Teutons, Arabs, the French and Spaniards. Today some of the best Italian citrus fruits, figs, apricots, plums, almonds and bergamots, a type of bitter orange from which an essential oil is extracted for use in making perfume, thrive here under the intense southern sun. Aubergines and red onions from Tropea are also famous.

Sicily/Sicilia

The largest island in the Mediterranean is a fish lover's paradise: tuna and lobsters from Trapani, swordfish from Messina . . . But it has a lot more to offer than 'just' Neptune's treasures. Citrus fruits and flavourful vegetables including pumpkin and courgette are cultivated, and sea salt is extracted by means of large saltworks along the salt road between Trapani and Marsala. Additional specialities include *frutta martorana* (marzipan fruits from Martorana) and sweet dessert wines such as Marsala.

Sardinia/Sardegna

The culinary specialities of this island are based on livestock and the previously rather modest lifestyle of the farmers and shepherds. There are supposedly around a thousand different kinds of sheep's cheese in Sardinia. Other foods that should not be missed are the crisp, wafer-thin Sardinian bread called *pane frattau*, air-dried sausages such as wild boar salami, and Asfodelo honey. The best-known wines are a full-bodied red, Cannonau, and a light white, Vermentino.

The Valle d'Aosta lies in north-western Italy. Italy's smallest region borders Switzerland to the north and France to the west (right).

To a certain extent, time seems to have stood still at the market in Maratea, Basilicata. Here, fruits and vegetables are still weighed by hand.

Italian Markets

For many travellers to Italy, one of the greatest pleasures is a stroll around one of the ubiquitous and colourful markets that are held in every village and every city district. Nowhere else are *alimentari* (foods) presented so appetizingly, appealingly and animatedly as on the streets, plazas and in the covered markets of Italy. Whatever is on sale in these markets arrives fresh from local producers: vegetables, fish, meat, home-made pasta, cheese, sausage, bread and wine, some of which even comes directly from farmers, fishermen and vintners. There is hardly a better or more beautiful way to get an overview of the local products.

Unlike a quick trip to the supermarket, shopping at these markets is a leisurely affair. The quality and prices of the mainly regional products must be compared. Furthermore, you don't always find the items on your shopping list right away, because what is for sale at a farmer's market depends upon the time of year. Needless to say, local fruits and vegetables are not always in season. But Italian home cooks are flexible; their meal plans are based on whatever they have just bought at the local market.

Unlike some other markets, where the merchants often sell their wares until late in the evening, albeit with a long break for the midday meal, fresh produce markets are usually only open from about 8 am until 1 pm.

The open trucks used by fruit and vegetable farmers are a daily sight on the streets of Italy (above).

The owner of a delicatessen proudly presents his salami specialities (below left).

The nicest part of shopping is taking a break at a small osteria (below right).

a cibo delicato
olio prelibato

OLIO PURO D'OLIVA
ISNARDI
PIETRO ISNARDI – PRODUTTORE
IMPERIA – ONEGLIA

High quality, cold-pressed olive oil helped make the treasures of Italian cooking famous around the world.

Italy's Culinary Ambassadors

Pizza, pasta, Parmesan, salami, prosciutto, olive oil and wine are the most famous ambassadors of Italian cuisine, known almost everywhere in the world. Pasta, for example, is the soul of Italian cooking. There are countless variations, shapes and colours, and the methods of preparation are just as numerous. The most famous pasta worldwide is surely spaghetti, served in the classic way with tomato sauce and freshly grated Parmesan, Italy's most internationally celebrated hard cheese.

Salami and prosciutto definitely occupy the number two spot. With great skill and patience, butchers still make ham and sausage specialities according to the old recipes. The gentle production methods virtually guarantee the outstanding flavour and unmistakable character of hams and salamis. Eighteen Italian ham and sausage specialities already bear the EU Protected Designation of Origin (DOP in Italian) status, which ensures their extraordinary quality.

Olive oil was already used in antiquity as both a foodstuff and a remedy. Connoisseurs everywhere still swear by cold-pressed oil made from hand-picked olives.

Along with pizza, Italy's most famous culinary product must surely be ice cream – the essence of vacation, sun and sea. There are supposedly around 1,500 flavours of ice cream in the *Bel Paese*, and new ones are invented each year. Just one more reason to enjoy the good life in the place where it originated.

Italy is a pasta paradise: spaghetti with meat sauce helps many children appreciate Italian cuisine early on (opposite, top).

Parmigiano Reggiano, a typical Italian product from Reggio Emilia, is enormously popular worldwide and is commonly known as Parmesan cheese.

There are about 1,500 different flavours of ice cream in Italy, and new ones are being invented all the time (below).

Aperitivi

The Aperitivo: Cult and Culture

The aperitivo, a little drink before the evening meal, has long since become an institution, especially in northern and central Italy. It is both a ritual and an element of the joy of living. People meet with friends or associates in one of the countless little bars in order to make new personal or business contacts, to nourish ongoing ones or simply to take a little break between the business day and family life – as well as to be seen socially, and show off the *bella figura*, a ubiquitous Italian phrase that means you are entirely up-to-date and know the right people and places.

This festive start to evening leisure time is particularly popular in Milan, the elegant, glamorous capital of Lombardy. Italy's second largest city is a business, fashion and media centre. What is trendy here is sure to become part of life in the nation's other metropolises soon. And, incidentally, Milan is said to be the birthplace of the aperitivo. The fact is that in the bars and cafés around the cathedral, anyone who is important – or wants to be(long) – shows up for a little glass of something. Whether standing or sitting on a comfortable stool in front of a café in Italy's most beautiful shopping district, the Galleria Vittorio Emanuele II, the Milanese partake in the national sport of people-watching, and not only at aperitivo time.

Bars are favourite places to see and be seen, while allowing oneself to be pampered by waiters serving drinks.

The Galleria Vittorio Emanuele II is considered to be Italy's most beautiful shopping gallery.

Galleria Vittorio Emanuele II

Ever since its grand opening in 1867, the Galleria Vittorio Emanuele II has connected the plaza in front of Milan Cathedral with that of Milan's world-famous La Scala opera house. The arcade consists of two shopping passages, each 14 metres (46 ft) wide and paved with marble floors, covered by an arching steel-and-glass roof. A glass dome 47 metres (154 ft) high, with internal dimensions equal to those of St Peter's Basilica in Rome, curves over the point where the lanes intersect. Sadly, Giuseppe Mengoni, the architect of this monumental structure, did not live to see its completion. Shortly before the construction was completed, he fell from the scaffolding to his death.

The elegant Zucca in Galleria, formerly known as the Caffè Camparino, stands at the corner of the Piazza del Duomo (Cathedral Plaza). Not long before the Galleria was completed, Gaspare Davide Campari fulfilled a lifelong dream by purchasing a little bar where he served his Bitter d'Olanda, or Dutch bitters. He was strongly supported by his wife Letizia, a talented saleswoman, who popularized the Dutch bitters under the name of Campari.

To prepare a classic Campari, you first need a tall, thin glass to preserve the aroma. Secondly, Campari should not 'offend the throat', meaning it should be neither too cold nor too warm. Thirdly, it is served with a splash of soda water. In Italy and elsewhere around the world, Campari Soda is also available premixed in small, conical bottles, a trademark shape dating from the 1930s that has become a highly recognizable, classic design.

Punt e Mes

Cinzano rosso

Cynar

Campari

Campari (called Campari Bitter in Italy, or simply Bitter) was created in Milan in 1862 and is the registered brand name for a red, herbal liqueur with a bittersweet taste. Its slightly bitter taste and ruby red colour soon made Campari a favourite ingredient for mixed drinks.

Originally, though, it was invented as a type of bitters. A Swedish herbalist named Fernet was living in Italy at the time and assisted with the formulation.

To this day, Campari is made according to the original recipe, which is a well-guarded family secret. It is said that eighty-six different roots, herbs, spices and fruits form the basis of this bitters. The colour comes from a natural dye, Cochineal E 120, which is taken from female insects that live on cacti. The insects are dried in the sun and subsequently ground. The ingredients for Campari are steeped in distilled water and combined with alcohol (ethanol). After resting for a few days, the mixture goes through many stages of filtering to remove impurities. It is then poured into large, glass-lined containers and brought to drinking strength with water and sugar syrup (25 per cent alcohol by volume). After resting for thirty days, the drink is again filtered and bottled.

Tramezzini al prosciutto e rucola

Sandwich bread is the best to use for tramezzini. The first step is to cut off all the crusts.

Place eight slices of bread next to one another and evenly spread with mayonnaise.

Remove any coarse stalks from the rocket and arrange the leaves evenly on four slices of bread.

Place cooked ham and tomato slices on the rocket, then add salt and pepper.

Garnish the tomatoes with basil leaves, then top with the other four slices of bread.

Slice each sandwich diagonally and arrange the *tramezzini* in portions on plates.

Tramezzini al prosciutto e rucola
Ham and Rocket Sandwiches

2 handfuls rocket
8 slices sandwich bread
2 tbsp mayonnaise
150 g/5 oz cooked ham, sliced
2 tomatoes, sliced
salt
freshly ground pepper
a few basil leaves

Wash the rocket, spin it dry and remove any coarse stalks. Remove the crust from the bread and spread mayonnaise on each slice. Place rocket on four of the bread slices, then layer with ham and tomatoes. Season with salt and pepper. Divide the basil leaves between the four sandwiches and top with the remaining bread slices. Slice each sandwich diagonally. Prosciutto, mortadella or sliced mozzarella can be substituted for the ham.

Tramezzini di tonno
Tuna Sandwiches

185 g/6½ oz canned tuna in oil
1 tbsp capers
2 eggs, hard boiled
8 lettuce leaves
8 slices sandwich bread
3–4 tbsp black olive paste

Drain the tuna thoroughly, then use a fork to flake it. Finely chop the capers and combine them with the tuna. Peel the eggs and cut them into even slices. Wash the lettuce leaves and spin them dry. Cut the crusts off the bread and spread each slice with a little of the olive paste. Divide the tuna–caper mixture among four of the pieces of bread. Top these with sliced egg and two lettuce leaves, then cover with the remaining slices of bread. Cut each sandwich diagonally.

Tramezzini di gamberi
Prawn Sandwiches

150 g/5 oz small prawns, cooked and shelled
1 tbsp lime juice
2 eggs, hard boiled
4 tbsp mayonnaise
4 lettuce leaves
8 slices sandwich bread
salt
freshly ground pepper

Season the prawns with the lime juice, salt and pepper. Peel and chop the eggs. Mix the prawns with the eggs and 2 tablespoons of mayonnaise. Wash the lettuce leaves and spin them dry. Remove the bread crusts and spread the rest of the mayonnaise on four of the slices. Spread the prawn mixture on the other four pieces of bread and top each one with a lettuce leaf. Cover with the remaining bread slices and cut each sandwich diagonally.

Spritz and Ombretta

By the end of the eighteenth century, aperitifs were already being celebrated in the big coffeehouses of Milan, Turin, Venice, Florence, Bologna, Rome and Naples. In Friuli-Venezia and in the better part of the Veneto region, they are now enjoyed in the early evening with wine and hors d'oeuvres. *Spritz* (*spriz* in the Venetian dialect, pronounced 'spreetz') is a very popular creation made of white wine from Veneto, soda water and a mixture (*correzione*) of bitters (Campari or Aperol) over ice, plus a slice of lemon or orange.

Venice is also the birthplace of the *ombra* or *ombretta*, the custom of drinking a small glass of wine in the morning. Equally suitable for an *ombra* are the light, delicate sparkling Prosecco wines, a medium sweet, cool Garda Cortese or a dry Verdicchio, with its pleasant notes of apricot and elderflower.

Shadows on the Canal Grande

Dai, andemo a bever un'ombra! ('Come on, let's go have a glass!') This kind of invitation is often heard on the streets and plazas of Venice beginning in the late hours of the morning. That is when the *bacari* – simply furnished stand-up bars that offer a modest selection of wines and sandwiches – begin to fill up with locals for the first time.

Ombra (Italian for 'shadow') is the Venetian word for a glass of wine – a small glass, to be precise, one that holds no more than 100 ml, or 3½ fluid ounces. Nonetheless, since approximately 50,000 *ombre* are imbibed each day, that still adds up to a substantial quantity.

As elder Venetians tell it, the term comes from the period when cool wine was still offered by vendors on the Piazza San Marco to refresh visitors and passersby in the hot summer months. In order to protect themselves from the sun, the wine sellers and their carts would follow the shadow of San Marco's bell tower (campanile) as it moved across the plaza. There haven't been any roaming wine sellers on the plaza for quite a long time, but the *ombra* tradition has remained.

Bars

For Italians, unlike the rest of the Western world, a bar is so much more than just a place to imbibe alcoholic beverages. In Italy, the word 'bar' refers mainly to small gastronomic establishments that are found on almost every city street. This is where people meet in the morning, mainly in stand-up cafés, to drink an espresso or cappuccino and to eat a brioche, a *cornetto* (sweet croissant) or a *panino* (sandwich). In the course of a day, labourers, office workers and housewives stop by to leaf through the newspapers that have been laid out or to exchange the latest neighbourhood gossip. In the afternoon, the bars fill with young people making plans for the evening and, a little later, with business people, who drop by for a quick *aperitivo*. In the evening, especially in rural areas, the older men then come to play cards at the little tables next to the bar. Weather permitting, the owner will put the stools out on the street so that guests can watch the activity on the piazza.

Italian bars have yet another distinctive feature. The cash register is most often found right by the door on the bar top. You place an order here, pay and get a receipt on a little strip of paper called a *scontrino*. Then you hand it to the bartender with your order. By the way, those who eat and drink while standing usually pay less than guests who sit at the tables. Throughout Italy, green and black olives in oil and herbs, as well as small bowls of nuts and salty snacks, are served gratis with aperitifs.

For a classic Bellini, peel a white peach and purée the fruit in a blender.

Put a spoonful of the puréed fruit in an ice-cold champagne glass and fill it with cold Prosecco.

Spremuta di frutta
Fruit Juice Cocktail

2 limes
4 tbsp brown cane sugar
crushed ice
600 ml/1 pint freshly squeezed orange juice
4 fresh mint leaves

Cut the limes into eight pieces, arrange in four glasses and crush them with the sugar. Fill the glasses two-thirds full with crushed ice and pour the orange juice over it. Garnish with mint leaves.

Bellini
by Giuseppe Cipriani, Harry's Bar, Venice, 1948

1 large white peach
400 ml/14 fl oz Prosecco or champagne

Peel the peach and cut it into sections. Purée the fruit and pour it into four tall, ice-cold champagne glasses. Pour the Prosecco over the fruit and serve immediately.

Spritz

60 ml/2 fl oz Aperol
100 ml/3½ fl oz ice-cold dry white wine
100 ml/3½ fl oz ice-cold soda water

Combine the Aperol and white wine in a wine glass, and fill with soda water.

Gingerino col Bianco

juice of ½ lemon
sugar
100 ml/3½ fl oz Gingerino (an alcohol-free soft drink)
100 ml/3½ fl oz white wine
1 lime slice

Moisten the rim of a cocktail glass with the lemon juice and dip it in the sugar, so that the glass has a sugar-covered rim. Pour the Gingerino and white wine into the glass and decorate with a slice of lime.

Ernest Hemingway and Harry's Bar

Harry's Bar is considered nothing less than the poster child of bar culture, not only in Venice, but internationally as well. It was founded in 1931 by a certain Giuseppe Arrigo Cipriani, thanks to a major injection of capital from his friend, Harry Pickering, the bar's namesake. It soon became famous, not only for the quality of the drinks, but also for various light meals, particularly their superb chicken sandwiches. What characterized Harry's Bar, above all else, was Giuseppe Cipriani's sixth sense for perfect hospitality, his fine grasp of his guests' wishes and his understanding of their whims. A concoction invented in-house by the name of Bellini, a drink consisting of puréed white peaches and sparkling wine, took the entire world by storm.

Shortly after World War II, Harry's Bar became the centre of attraction for the international jet set, including such luminaries as Orson Welles, Lauren Bacall, Truman Capote and Nobel Prize for Literature recipient Ernest Hemingway, who immortalized the place in his novel *Across the River and Into the Trees*. In 1980, Giuseppe's son, Arrigo, took over the running of the bar and changed … nothing. Even today, bar aficionados continue to make the pilgrimage to the local tavern behind St Mark's Cathedral.

The legendary Harry's Bar in the Calle Vallaresso is a must-see for every visitor to Venice, as are gondolas and the pigeons on Piazza San Marco.

Negroni Cocktail
Hotel Baglioni, Florence, 1920

20 ml/4 tsp Campari
20 ml/4 tsp sweet red vermouth
20 ml/4 tsp gin
3 dashes Angostura bitters
soda water
1 orange slice

Stir together the Campari, vermouth, gin and Angostura in a glass tumbler. Fill with a little soda water and decorate the cocktail with a slice of orange.

Americano

20 ml/4 tsp Campari
20 ml/4 tsp sweet red vermouth
20 ml/4 tsp dry vermouth
½ slice lemon
club soda

Fill a glass tumbler with the Campari, both kinds of vermouth, and some club soda. Add two ice cubes and the lemon slice.

Vermouth

Vermouth is the appellation for an aromatic sweet wine with herbs and spices that is often served as an aperitif. It derives its name from *wermut*, the German word for wormwood, or *Artemesia absinthium*, a herb whose bitter aroma gives vermouth its flavour. As early as the fifth century BCE, the famous physician Hippocrates recognized that wine prepared with wormwood was stimulating and beneficial to the stomach. The first vermouth was produced in the late eighteenth century by the Cinzano family of Piedmont. Cinzano celebrated its two-hundred-fiftieth anniversary in 2007 and is the oldest brand of Italian vermouth in existence today.

In Italy, the first official license for the production of vermouth, the *Licenza No. 1*, was awarded in 1863 to the Turin enterprise of Martini & Rossi. Even today, Martini remains the most popular, best-selling vermouth in Italy. Incidentally, authentic Italian vermouth is made from the Moscato Bianco grape, as required by law since 1933.

Drinking, Talking, Relaxing

There are lots of excellent reasons to enjoy an *aperitivo*. Before the meal, a pleasant drink can whet your appetite and help you let go of the stress of daily life, which is quickly replaced by pleasant anticipation of the upcoming fare and company at the table. For hosts, aperitifs are a nice welcoming gesture, because no one has to wait empty-handed until the last guests arrive. And gourmets love them precisely because they stimulate the appetite. In addition to a modest alcohol content, most *aperitivi* primarily contain ingredients that, whether sour or bitter, 'get the [stomach] juices flowing'. Like a small beer, certain herbal bitters, vermouth or fruit juices also serve this function. A young, sparkling white wine not only loosens the tongue, but also enlivens the palate with its tartness.

Both alcoholic and non-alcoholic beverages can be considered aperitifs. The drinks should be stimulating and attune the palate to the upcoming enjoyment, but they must never be permitted to satiate one's appetite. That is why concoctions that include egg or cream are taboo, especially in cocktails or long drinks, because these ingredients would overtax the taste buds. Freshly squeezed vegetable or fruit juices are ideally suited for alcohol-free aperitifs, whether they are served as pure juice, diluted with mineral water, or mixed into a refreshing cocktail.

Frizzante (semi-sparkling wine), *spumante* (sparkling wine) or *talento* (sparkling wine fermented in the bottle) all make great aperitifs, since their tingly, refreshing taste pleases the palate and is guaranteed to put you in a good mood. They should not be served too cold, so that their fine bouquet can optimally come to the fore. For a light, refreshing aperitif, fruit-based mixed drinks are usually prepared with a *spumante* or *frizzante*.

The subsequent meal and the wines that are paired with it play a role in selecting just the right aperitif. A sweet wine or liqueur, for example, would not be favourable in combination with a first course accompanied by a light, dry white wine. And if the first course is a hot soup, ice-cold drinks should be dispensed with.

According to an Italian adage, *Chi bene comincia è a metà dell'opera* ('What starts well is half accomplished'). And so the most important rule for a successful start to an evening is to enjoy your aperitif leisurely and, of course, in pleasant company.

The Rosa Rosae Bar in Bologna's Via Clavature is both traditional and trendy. People love to meet friends here for aperitifs.

Beer in the Land of Wine

For a long time, Italy was just a small speck on the world map of beer consumption, but that has changed in the last two decades. Italy is now the biggest importer of Bavarian beer, and nearly half of Bavaria's beer exports go there. In the chronicles of Italian beer, 2003 was a historic year: per capita consumption surpassed 30 litres (50 pints) for the first time. On the drink menu, German beers are often found alongside the major brands from northern Italy: Dreher (Trieste), Wührer (Brescia) and Forst (Meran). Statisticians have figured out that the typical Italian beer drinker is between twenty-five and forty-four years old and lives in one of the larger northern Italian cities. About half of all beer is consumed outside the home, and pizza is the preferred food to accompany it.

Antipasti e Salumi

Antipasti, Salami and Cured Meats

One of the most pleasing and delicious culinary traditions in Italy is antipasti, little hot and cold appetizers that are intended to whet one's appetite for the pleasures to come. There are many yarns spun around the origins of *antipasti* (literally, 'before the pasta'), and there is hardly a province anywhere in Italy that does not claim to be the true birthplace of antipasto.

As early as the first century CE, Marcus Gavius Apicius, author of the oldest extant collection of Italian recipes, recommended appetizers (Latin: *gustaciones*) such as ham with figs, eel marinated in rosemary, and song bird tongues in his cookbook. On the streets of Rome and Pompei, snack bars offered rice ball fritters and chickpea cakes to stave off hunger between meals.

The Renaissance also lays claim to having invented antipasto. Integral to the lush banquets of that time were artfully decorated buffets with cold foods, served with sweet and piquant sauces. As a rule, they were the beginning and end of a comparatively frugal meal. The arrangement of antipasti in many Italian restaurants is still reminiscent of that tradition. Display cases laden with enticing plates of cold appetizers are often located near the entrance or in the middle of the dining room. This allows guests to take their time selecting the culinary delights they would like to sample from among the rich offerings.

Not all antipasti, however, have their roots in luxury. Many delicacies that are now considered classics originated in the kitchens of the less well-to-do. Time and again, fantasy and ingenuity won out over humble provisions. Perhaps the best example of this is bruschetta, a thick slice of country bread flavoured with a clove of garlic and sprinkled with olive oil. Covered with ripe slices of tomato, this everyday peasant meal has become an international speciality. Crostini are favourites in southern Italy: these are toasted slices of bread that are brushed with pastes made from various vegetables such as artichokes, aubergines, olives, mushrooms or asparagus.

For a long time, antipasti were served primarily in restaurants and at large family gatherings. But eating habits have changed in Italy in recent years, and today antipasti are increasingly taking the place of large meals, above all in the major cities. And it

Antipasti are the cornerstone of Italian cuisine. The offerings are so varied and diversified that appetizers often make a complete meal.

is no wonder, because like no other course on the menu, antipasti make perfect little meals even when eaten 'solo'.

The Best of the Land and the Sea

The many kinds of antipasti are typically divided into three categories:

affettati (cold meats and cheeses)

antipasto misto (a platter of mixed appetizers, often without meat)

antipasto misto mare (a platter of mixed appetizers with fish and seafood).

Classic *affettati* are especially favoured in the northern and central regions of Italy. They most often consist of various types of ham and salami, complemented by various regional specialities that might include bresaola, mortadella, soppressate or zampone. Sliced very thin and served in combination with fruit or stuffed with marinated vegetables such as artichoke hearts, wild mushrooms, olives and pearl onions, they are timeless delicacies.

Antipasto misto was once a typical meal of leftovers for the servants, put together from the food that remained after an elaborate party. One of the important precepts of the Italian kitchen, *l'arte di arrangiarsi* ('the art of making do'), made necessity the mother of invention. Cooks were always inventing new creations in order to dress up leftover food, making it both delicious and elegant.

All along Italy's extensive 7,600 km (4,700 miles) of coastline, restaurants offer an impressive array of *antipasti misti mare* featuring fresh, baked and breaded seafood, marinated mussels and little deep-fried fish. According to gourmets, few dishes can be found that meld Neptune's flavourful treasures so harmoniously as the *insalata di frutti di mare* (seafood medley), which is often considered to be the measure of a chef's accomplishments.

Grilled aubergine slices with garlic in vinegar and oil

A small selection of typical antipasti

Favourite Antipasti

Olive ascolane
Fried Stuffed Olives

30 large, stoned green olives
150 g/5 oz salsiccia
(coarse, spicy sausage)
2 tbsp grated Parmesan
1 tbsp tomato purée
1 egg, beaten
oil for frying
flour for breading
breadcrumbs

Heat the oil in a deep fryer to 175°C/350°F. Rinse the olives with water and dry well. Press the sausage from its skin and combine the meat with the Parmesan and tomato purée. Fill the olives with the mixture and pinch them shut.

Dredge the olives in flour, then dip in the beaten egg and coat with breadcrumbs. Fry in the hot oil until golden brown, then place on paper towels. Serve hot or cold.

Melanzane alla campagnola
Country-style Marinated
Aubergine Slices

4 aubergines
6 tomatoes
2 garlic cloves
½ bunch parsley
4 tbsp olive oil, plus extra for greasing
salt
freshly ground pepper

Wash and trim the aubergines, then cut into slices 1 cm/½ inch thick. Salt them and place in a sieve to drain for 1 hour.

Preheat the oven to 200°C/390°F/gas mark 6. Meanwhile, peel and quarter the tomatoes, remove the seeds and finely dice the flesh. Peel the garlic and finely chop it along with the parsley. Add this mixture to the tomatoes, then season with salt and pepper to taste. Stir in 2 tablespoons of the olive oil and leave everything to marinate briefly.

Pat the aubergine slices dry with paper towels and arrange them next to each other on an oiled baking tray. Drizzle the remaining olive oil over them, then bake in the oven for 5 minutes on each side.

Brush the aubergine slices with the tomato mixture and stack them into little towers.

Pomodorini ciliegia ripieni
Stuffed Cherry Tomatoes

500 g/1 lb 2 oz cherry tomatoes
200 g/7 oz feta cheese, diced
2 tbsp olive oil
1 handful basil
salt
freshly ground pepper

Cut the tops off the tomatoes, discard them, then remove the seeds. Cut the feta cheese into small cubes.

Season the inside of the tomatoes with salt and pepper, then stuff them with the cheese cubes. Drizzle the olive oil over them and add more pepper.

Rinse and spin dry the basil. Garnish the tomatoes with individual basil leaves.

Vongole veraci marinate
Marinated Clams

1 kg/2 lb 4 oz fresh clams
1 onion
2 garlic cloves
100 ml/3½ fl oz olive oil
250 ml/9 fl oz dry white wine
1 tbsp finely chopped parsley
juice of ½ lemon
salt
freshly ground pepper
8 scallop shells
(available at fish markets)

Scrub the shells. Soak them in cold water for 1 hour, changing the water several times. Discard any clams that have open shells. Peel the onion and garlic and finely dice them.

Heat 2 tablespoons of the oil in a large saucepan and sauté the onions and garlic until translucent. Deglaze with the wine and bring to the boil. Add the clams, cover and cook on high heat for 3 to 4 minutes, shaking the pan several times.

Remove the clams from the pan with a slotted spoon, discarding any that have not opened. Cut the clam flesh out of the shells and place in a bowl.

Stir together the parsley, lemon juice and remaining olive oil, and season with salt and pepper. Pour over the clams and leave them to marinate for 30 minutes. Serve the marinated clams in the scallop shells.

Bruschetta con mozzarella
Bruschetta with
Mozzarella and Tomatoes

4 slices Tuscan country bread
2 garlic cloves
4 tbsp olive oil
150 g/5 oz buffalo mozzarella, sliced
2 tomatoes, sliced
salt
freshly ground pepper
basil leaves to garnish

Grill or toast the bread slices on both sides until golden brown.

Cut the garlic cloves in half. Rub each slice of toast with the cut side of a halved garlic clove, drizzle with 1 tablespoon of olive oil, then cut in half. Top the bread with sliced mozzarella and tomatoes, season with salt and pepper and garnish with basil leaves.

Salvia fritta
Fried Sage Leaves

2 eggs
4 tbsp flour
pinch of salt
⅛ tsp easy-blend dried yeast
125 ml/4 fl oz dry white wine
250 g/9 oz buffalo mozzarella
32 large sage leaves
olive oil for frying

Separate the eggs. Whisk the egg yolks together with the flour, salt, yeast and white wine until smooth. Leave the batter to rest for 30 minutes. Then beat the egg whites to very stiff peaks and fold into the batter.

Cut the mozzarella into eight slices, then cut each slice in half. Place a piece of mozzarella on 16 of the sage leaves, top with the remaining leaves and press down gently.

Heat olive oil in a deep frying pan or deep-fryer to 175°C/350°F. Dip the sage bundles into the batter one at a time. Fry a few of them at a time in the hot oil until golden brown. Before serving, briefly set on paper towels to remove excess oil.

Mozzarella

Mozzarella is a fresh, delicate white cheese with just a hint of sweetness. It is a *pasta filata*, or stretched-curd type of cheese (Italian: *filare*, to pull). As it is being made, the cheese curd is scalded and kneaded or stretched, then shaped into balls, plaits or other regionally typical configurations. It is most often sold fresh, packed in salt water. *Burrielli*, an exceptional delicacy, consists of little mozzarella balls that are stored in milk-filled clay amphoras. Mozzarella has experienced a similar culinary fate to that of Parmesan: both cheeses are famous in nearly every corner of the globe, yet it is mainly only cheap imitations of these Italian specialities that are sold. Authentic *mozzarella di bufala* is produced in the Aversa, Battipaglia, Capua, Eboli and Sessa Aurunca regions of Campania, and has carried the DOP (Protected Designation of Origin) certification mark since the 1990s. In order to claim DOP status, the cheese must be made from the milk of water buffalo cows that are raised on the open range and nourished with natural feed. Buffalo milk contains significantly more calcium, protein and fat than the milk of typical dairy cows.

Mozzarella di bufala is a speciality that comes at a price. That is why in many shops you will find the less expensive variety, *mozzarella fior di latte*, which is made from cow's milk and cannot come close to the flavour of the original. The two kinds of mozzarella differ not only in flavour: *mozzarella di bufala* contains over 50 per cent more fat, has 45 per cent less water than its cow's milk cousin and when sliced reveals a finely layered texture. It is best suited for fillings or for the famous *insalata caprese*, tomato slices with buffalo mozzarella and basil.

Basil

Basil has been cultivated for over 4,000 years. The ancient Greeks called the intensely aromatic plant 'the royal herb', and treasured not only its powerful fragrance, but also its healing properties. Basil originally came from Asia. Today there are at least sixty varieties of basil, the most familiar of which are small-leaf Greek basil, and sweet or Italian basil, also called *Basilico genovese*. Both of these have a distinctly different flavour than the Asian and African varieties. When used fresh, delicate green basil leaves from the Mediterranean regions have a slightly peppery, spicy-sweet flavour. These sensitive plants need a lot of sun and plentiful moisture. Liguria has nearly ideal climatic conditions for optimal cultivation, as does Piedmont. When using basil in cooking, it should not be cooked with the rest of the ingredients, but instead should be added at the end of the cooking process. Apropos, basil is a symbol of love in Italy.

Insalata caprese di bufala
Mozzarella with Tomatoes and Basil

500 g/1 lb 2 oz vine tomatoes, sliced
1 buffalo mozzarella, ca. 300 g/11 oz, sliced
1 bunch basil
4 tbsp olive oil
salt
freshly ground pepper

Arrange the tomato and mozzarella slices on four plates. Rinse the basil and shake it dry. Tear off the leaves and sprinkle them over the tomatoes and mozzarella slices.

Whisk the olive oil with salt and pepper and drizzle over the salad. Traditionally, *insalata caprese* is made without vinegar, but more and more often balsamic vinegar is added to the dressing.

Mozzarella in carozza
Breaded Mozzarella Sandwich

1 buffalo mozzarella, ca. 300 g/11 oz
8 thin slices white bread, with crusts removed
125 ml/4 fl oz milk
2 eggs
salt
freshly ground pepper
flour for breading
olive oil for frying

Cut the mozzarella into four slices slightly smaller than the bread. Arrange the cheese on four slices of bread, season with salt and pepper, then cover with the remaining bread and press down lightly. Pour the milk into a flat bowl, briefly turn each sandwich in it and press the bread firmly against the side of the bowl. Whisk the eggs in a deep dish. Turn the bread in the eggs to coat thoroughly, then coat in flour. Heat an ample amount of olive oil in a deep pan and fry the sandwiches on each side until golden brown. Serve very hot.

Only 'happy' water buffalo deliver milk for authentic mozzarella. The largest population of these animals lives in Campania on the Gulf of Naples.

To produce mozzarella, buffalo milk is first combined with rennet. The resulting cheese curd is cut into pieces and placed in a kettle.

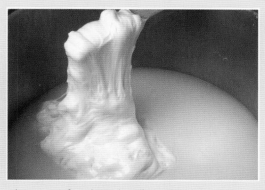

The pieces of curd are then doused with hot water and pulled into strands by hand, using a wooden stick, until they be come a doughy, elastic paste.

The uniform pieces are separated, then pulled into shape, kneaded and dunked again in hot whey until the desired consistency is achieved.

Crostini, Bruschetta and Fettunta

Crostini, at least according to the residents of Florence, are distinctly Florentine appetizers, and there are countless varieties of them. Nonetheless, they are very popular in southern Italy as well. Each and every household, trattoria and restaurant has a particular house recipe for the topping, which is spread on thick slices of white toast, and differs only slightly in the combination of ingredients and accompanying herbs.

In any event, it is an indisputable fact that crostini are just plain good food. In Tuscany, the classic topping is made from chicken or wild game liver pâté, while in Campania they use juicy, ripe tomatoes. Olive and artichoke pastes are preferred in Apulia, and a fine truffle cream in Piedmont. But there are no limits to a cook's fantasy. Tuscan country bread has not been obligatory for some time now: baguette, focaccia, and corn and rye breads are also used to make crostini.

Traditional Tuscan cuisine is country style. The distinctive regional products from this area for centuries have been olive oil and unsalted white bread. There have been many attempts to explain why, even today, salt is not used in baking bread here. Culinary historians believe it is due to the Tuscan preference for highly spiced ham and salami, as well as the intense flavours of the foods often eaten. Bread, therefore, is simply meant to highlight the quality of the slightly piquant olive oil or the unique flavours of the famous chicken liver pâté and aromatic pastes, rather than to mask them.

When the season for pressing olives begins in late autumn, festive celebrations are held in many little villages to taste the new oil. When it comes straight out of the oil press, it has a sharp flavour that develops best on toast. As far back as ancient Rome, the senate distributed flatbreads dipped in olive oil to the people on important feast days in December and January. Bruschetta – or *fettunta*, as it is called in Tuscany – still tastes best at this time of year.

Crostini con erbe e pomodori
Crostini with Herbs and Tomatoes

6 plum tomatoes
1 small bunch basil
2 garlic cloves, minced
3 tbsp olive oil
1 tbsp finely chopped parsley
½ tsp finely chopped oregano
12 small slices Tuscan white bread (or ciabatta)
salt
freshly ground pepper

Skin the tomatoes, quarter them, core and cut into small dice. Rinse the basil, shake it dry and cut the leaves into fine strips. Combine the tomatoes with the garlic, olive oil, salt, pepper and herbs, and allow to stand briefly.

Toast, grill or oven-bake the slices of bread on both sides until golden brown. Top each slice with some of the tomato mixture.

Bruschetta
Bruschetta with Garlic and Oil

4 slices Tuscan country bread
2 garlic cloves
4 tbsp olive oil
salt
freshly ground pepper

Toast, grill or oven-bake the slices of bread on both sides until golden brown.

Cut the garlic in half. Rub each slice with half a clove of garlic and drizzle with 1 tablespoon of the olive oil. Season to taste with salt and pepper.

Among the Italian antipasti there are countless varieties of crostini (opposite).

To this day, saltless Tuscan country bread is still made exclusively from flour and water and baked in wood-burning ovens.

Crostini neri
Crostini with Olive Paste

200 g/7 oz black olives, stoned

3 anchovy fillets in oil

1 tbsp capers

3–4 tbsp olive oil

12 small slices Tuscan white bread (or ciabatta)

12 basil leaves

salt

cayenne pepper

Roughly chop the olives and anchovy fillets. Then purée them together with the capers and as much olive oil as needed to make a thick paste. Season to taste with salt and cayenne pepper.

Toast, grill or oven-bake the slices of bread on both sides until golden brown. Spread each slice with olive paste and garnish with a basil leaf.

Crostini al pomodoro
Crostini with Tomatoes

12 small slices Tuscan white bread (or ciabatta)

2 garlic cloves

2–3 tbsp olive oil

4 small beef tomatoes, sliced

50 g/1¾ oz Parmesan (whole piece, not grated)

salt

freshly ground pepper

a few basil leaves

Toast, grill or oven-bake the slices of bread on both sides until golden brown. Peel the garlic cloves and cut them in half. Rub the toast with garlic and drizzle with the olive oil. Top each piece with tomato slices, season with salt and pepper, and finely grate the Parmesan over the tomatoes.

Cut the basil into fine strips and garnish the crostini with them.

Crostini alla toscana
Crostini with Chicken Liver Pâté

200 g/7 oz chicken liver

2 tbsp olive oil

1 shallot, finely chopped

100 ml/3½ fl oz Vin Santo

1 tbsp finely chopped thyme

12 small slices of Tuscan white bread (or ciabatta)

salt

freshly ground pepper

Rinse and dry the chicken livers, remove the membranes, then chop into small pieces.

Heat the olive oil and sauté the shallot in it until translucent. Add the livers and sauté while stirring. Deglaze with the wine, add the thyme and cook until the wine has nearly evaporated. Remove from the heat, cool slightly, then purée. Season the chicken liver pâté with salt and pepper.

Toast, grill or oven-bake the slices of bread on both sides until golden brown. Cool slightly, then spread with pâté and serve immediately.

Pickling Vegetables

Home-bottled vegetables are the pride of every Italian housewife. Next to salting and drying, the oldest method of preserving vegetables is pickling. While people in other parts of Europe mainly use lactic acid fermentation to preserve raw vegetables, in Italy, vegetables are dried, fried or grilled prior to pickling. That imparts additional flavours, which, together with fresh herbs and spices, give the vegetables their special taste.

To make the very best pickles, use ripe (but not over-ripe) vegetables from the family garden or an organic farm. They should be thoroughly washed, dried and, depending upon the recipe, cut into slices or strips, diced or pickled whole. Vinegar fermentation lowers the natural pH of foods and thus inhibits the growth of micro-organisms. The more acidic the food, the fewer bacteria and moulds will be able to grow in it. What's more, acidity not only inhibits the growth of bacteria, but also destroys bacteria altogether. Carrots, peppers, gherkins, baby onions, mushrooms and cauliflower are ideal, and can be pickled separately or in a colourful mix of everything you especially enjoy.

To preserve vegetables in oil, cooking oil is poured over the food; in Italy this is predominantly olive oil. The foods are submerged in oil, making them airtight and preventing the growth of harmful micro-organisms. Even in antiquity, cheese and olives were preserved in this way.

Producing home-made pickles requires a certain amount of time and attention, but is well worth the effort. First of all, it is important to use the right containers. Glass jars that seal well are best suited for this purpose. They can easily be cleaned, and glass does not affect the flavour of foods stored in it. A further advantage is that you can see what is inside at a glance.

Before the jars are filled with prepared vegetables, they need to be thoroughly sterilized. For this purpose, the jars are first washed and then placed in a large pot of boiling water for ten minutes. After that, they are placed inside a hot oven for a few minutes. After they are filled, glass jars must be firmly sealed. The ideal storage room is cool, dry and as dark as possible. These home-made specialities will store for up to ten months, which is long enough to bridge the gap between the end of the growing season and when fresh produce is available again in the spring.

Flavoured vinegar that has been boiled with herbs and spices forms the basis for many pickled vegetable specialities.

Vegetables such as courgette, Romanesco cauliflower, spring onions and carrots are cleaned, chopped into bite-sized pieces and blanched.

The blanched vegetables are then placed in a clean, sterilized container. Glass jars that seal well are best suited for this.

In the final step, the boiling vinegar is poured over the vegetables and the container firmly sealed.

Verdure miste sott'olio
Mixed Vegetables in Oil

2 aubergines
2 large courgettes
200 g/7 oz oyster mushrooms
250 ml/9 fl oz olive oil, plus extra to grease the pan
2 garlic cloves, finely sliced
leaves of 4–5 thyme sprigs
2 bay leaves
125 ml/4 fl oz red wine vinegar
salt
freshly ground pepper

Wash and trim the aubergines and courgettes and cut them into slices. Clean the oyster mushrooms and halve or quarter them, depending on their size. Coat a griddle pan with olive oil and grill the vegetables in portions for 2 to 3 minutes on each side. Place the grilled slices in a bowl and season with salt and pepper.

Sprinkle the garlic and thyme leaves over the vegetables, and place the bay leaves in between them. Whisk the olive oil, vinegar, salt and pepper into a marinade and pour over the hot vegetables. Leave to cool, then cover with clingfilm and chill overnight in the refrigerator. Bring the vegetables to room temperature 30 minutes before serving.

Dried Tomatoes

For centuries, Italian tomatoes have been preserved for the winter by traditional means. Following the harvest, the most perfect tomatoes are chosen and washed before they are set out to dry. Protected by fly netting, the halved fruits are placed on palettes near the front door to dry in the intense summer sunshine. Approximately 11 kg (24 lb) of fresh tomatoes yield 1 kg (2 lb) of sun-dried fruit. Many of the dried tomatoes are preserved in flavoured oils. As *pomodori secchi*, they make a classic appetizer.

Funghi sott'olio
Mushrooms Preserved in Oil

1 kg/2 lb 4 oz small mushrooms
(champignons, ceps, chantarelles,
honey mushrooms)

1 fresh red chilli

250 ml/9 fl oz olive oil

100 ml/3½ fl oz white balsamic vinegar

salt

1 small sprig oregano or rosemary

Clean the mushrooms and pat dry with paper towels. Cut the chilli in half, remove the core and cut the flesh into fine strips.

Heat 5 tablespoons of the olive oil in a large frying pan and brown the mushrooms on all sides until the liquid has evaporated.

Add the chilli to the pan and sauté briefly. Deglaze the pan with the vinegar, add salt, then transfer the mushrooms to a bowl. Add the herb and remaining olive oil. Cover and leave the mushrooms to marinate overnight.

Verdure sottaceto
Vegetables Pickled in Vinegar

For the marinade:

250 ml/9 fl oz dry white wine

200 ml/7 fl oz white wine vinegar

100 ml/3½ fl oz olive oil

1 piece lemon peel

5 sprigs parsley

1 celery stick, diced

1 sprig thyme

1 bay leaf

1 garlic clove

10 peppercorns

½ tsp salt

1 kg/2 lb 4 oz vegetables (carrots, celery,
green beans, asparagus, courgette,
cauliflower, peppers, leeks, onions)

1 tbsp sugar

juice of 1 lemon

salt

In a saucepan, bring to the boil 500 ml/ 18 fl oz of water and all the ingredients for the marinade. Simmer for 15 minutes.

Cut the vegetables into chunks of equal size. Fill another pan with salted water, add the sugar and lemon juice, and bring to the boil. Cook each vegetable in the water, separately, for 3 to 7 minutes depending on kind and size. Remove the vegetables, drain well and layer them inside a large bottling jar. Pour the boiling marinade over them and seal the jar. Marinate the vegetables in the refrigerator for at least two days.

Funghi sott'olio

Cipolle all'agrodolce
Pearl Onions in Balsamico

500 g/1 lb 2 oz pearl onions
1 garlic clove
2 sprigs thyme
2 bay leaves
2 cloves
5 black peppercorns
250 ml/9 fl oz red wine
125 ml/4 fl oz balsamic vinegar
1 tsp thyme honey
2 tbsp olive oil

Place the pearl onions and garlic in a saucepan. Add the thyme, bay leaves, cloves and peppercorns. Pour on the red wine and vinegar, and stir in the honey. Bring to the boil and simmer for approximately 25 minutes or until the pearl onions are soft.

Remove the pan from the stove and leave the onions to cool in the stock. Discard the thyme, bay leaves and cloves, then stir in the olive oil.

Fagioli all'agrodolce
Marinated White Beans

250 g/9 oz dried white beans
1 bay leaf
1 garlic clove
4 spring onions
1 tbsp lemon juice
3 tbsp white wine vinegar
5 tbsp olive oil
1 tbsp finely chopped parsley
50 g/1¾ oz grated Parmesan
salt and pepper

Soak the beans overnight in plenty of water. The next day, simmer the beans in the soaking water, adding the bay leaf and garlic to the pan. Bring to the boil, then skim off and cook on low heat until the beans are tender.

Remove the beans from the stove. Discard the garlic and bay leaf, then leave the beans to cool in the cooking liquid until lukewarm. Trim the spring onions and cut them into fine strips. Whisk the lemon juice, vinegar, oil, and salt and pepper to make a dressing.

Pour off the liquid from the beans and drain well. Combine the beans with the spring onions and dressing and leave to marinate for at least 15 minutes. Sprinkle with the parsley and grated Parmesan before serving.

Bay Leaves

The evergreen bay laurel tree, whose leaves were woven into victory crowns in ancient Roman times, originally came from the Middle East. Bay leaves were equally important for cooking in those days. Fresh or dried bay leaves flavoured soups, meat and fish dishes, sauces and pastas, lending them a tart and slightly bitter taste. But one should refrain from eating the leaves, and not only because of their intense flavour. The leathery leaf is no delicacy, and is therefore most often removed before serving. It is preferable not to use ground bay leaves because, like most spices, they lose much of their flavour once they are cut, leaving nothing but a bitter taste. For pickling vegetables, fresh bay leaves are far superior to dried ones, because they have a more intense flavour.

Fagioli all'agrodolce

Vegetable Antipasti

For vegetarians, as well, the Italian antipasto buffet is a veritable gourmet's paradise. The Italians have perfected the art of turning flavourful vegetables and just a few other high-quality ingredients into Lucullan delights. Wild mushrooms (which are briefly sautéed with fresh herbs), breaded and fried vegetables, and sweet-and-sour pickled peppers or aubergines are very popular throughout the country. All of these dishes derive their incomparable taste from top-quality, perfectly ripe vegetables, as well as fresh, flavourful herbs and, of course, the very best olive oil.

Special Vegetable Antipasto Favourites

Sweet-and-sour carrots (*carote in agro*) come from the Piedmont region. To make them, slice carrots and simmer them in equal parts of wine, vinegar and water. Season them with chopped garlic, bay leaf, rosemary, sugar, salt and pepper, and cook just until tender crisp (al dente). When the carrots have cooled slightly, stir in olive oil and leave them overnight.

A speciality from Lombardy is hot bean salad (*fagioli in insalata*). Soak dried white beans overnight. The next day, bring the soaking liquid to the boil and cook the beans until tender, then drain well. While they are still hot, combine the beans with diced onion, finely chopped parsley, olive oil, vinegar, salt and pepper.

Funghi porcini all'ambrosiana
Ceps with Herbs

500 g/1 lb 2 oz ceps
2–3 garlic cloves
4 tbsp olive oil
1 tbsp rosemary leaves
1 bay leaf
75 ml/2½ fl oz white wine
salt
freshly ground pepper

Clean the ceps and cut them into slices approximately 1 cm/½ inch thick. Peel the garlic and cut it into small slivers.

Heat the olive oil in a deep pan. Add the ceps, garlic, rosemary and bay leaf, and sauté while stirring. Deglaze the pan with the white wine and season with salt. Simmer on low heat for 10 minutes.

Remove from the stove and leave the ceps to cool slightly in the pan juices. Season with pepper before serving.

Peperonata
Pickled Peppers

2 each: red, green and yellow peppers
500 g/1 lb 2 oz tomatoes
4 tbsp olive oil
2 onions, finely chopped
2 garlic cloves, minced
1 bay leaf
1 dried chilli
3 tbsp balsamic vinegar
1 pinch sugar
1 small sprig rosemary
salt
freshly ground pepper

Wash and trim the peppers, cut them in half, then cut into bite-sized pieces.

Peel, core and roughly chop the tomatoes. Heat the olive oil in a large pan and sauté the onions. Add the peppers and garlic, salt lightly and gently simmer them in the juices for 5 minutes.

Add the tomatoes, bay leaf and crumbled chilli to the pan. Stir in the vinegar and sugar, cover the pan and simmer for 15 minutes on very low heat. Season to taste with black pepper and add the rosemary. Pour the peppers into a bottling jar while still hot and leave overnight or longer before serving.

Funghi porcini all'ambrosiana

Peperonata

Chargrilled Vegetables

Around the world, food has been prepared over an open fire for millennia. To this day, the unique flavour of barbecued or charcoal-grilled fish or meat cannot be replaced, not even by the latest in culinary technology. Yet while people in other countries mainly barbecue protein foods, Italians also love the distinctive flavour of chargrilled vegetables, polenta and bread. This flavour is enhanced by taking chargrilled vegetables, drizzling a little of the best olive oil over them and limiting seasonings to lemon juice, salt and freshly ground pepper. Thus served, even plain radicchio or aubergine become special treats.

This technique of cooking vegetables also has a long history. Years ago, field workers built fires in the autumn not only to warm themselves, but also as a means to prepare small meals. The workers took field crops such as beetroot or onions, wrapped them in several layers of moist paper and placed them in the fire. By the time the next break came around, their food was ready.

Funghi alla griglia
Chargrilled Ceps

8 large cep caps
juice of 1 lemon
100 ml/3½ fl oz olive oil
1 tbsp finely chopped parsley
1 garlic clove, minced
salt
freshly ground pepper
lemon wedges to garnish

Clean the cep caps and place them in a bowl. Make a marinade of the lemon juice, olive oil, parsley, garlic, salt and pepper. Pour over the mushroom caps and marinate for 30 minutes at room temperature, turning frequently.

Remove the ceps from their marinade, drain and cook on a hot barbecue or under a grill on medium heat for about 5 minutes on each side. Arrange the caps on a platter, drizzle with the marinade and garnish with lemon wedges.

Peperoni alla griglia
Roasted Peppers

2 red peppers
2 green peppers
2 yellow peppers
olive oil for the baking tray

Preheat the oven to 250°C/480°F/gas mark 9. Clean the peppers, cut them in half lengthways, trim and pat dry with paper towels.

Thoroughly grease a baking tray with olive oil. Place the peppers on it with the cut side facing down. Roast them in the oven for 25 to 30 minutes, or until the skin blisters. Remove from the oven and cover the baking tray with a damp tea towel.

Leave the peppers to rest for about 10 minutes, then remove the skins with a kitchen knife and cut the peppers into strips or dice, depending on the recipe.

Green asparagus spears (below), grilled with a little olive oil on low heat for 10 minutes, are a favourite delicacy.

Artichokes (right) are sometimes cut in half and grilled over medium heat. Only the tender inner leaves and bases are edible.

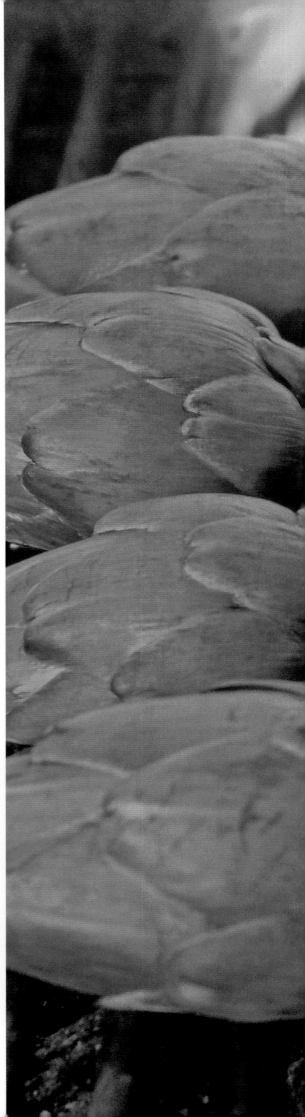

To skin peppers, first cut them in half and remove the cores. Then roast them in a very hot oven.

After cooling briefly, you can remove the skin from the peppers without difficulty.

Radicchio Trevisano

In the provinces of Treviso, Padua and Venice, a very special kind of radicchio is cultivated. It has long, smooth, white-veined, wine-red leaves and a slight touch of bitterness. Because of its al dente consistency, this kind of radicchio is not only great for salads, but is also excellent for grilling and roasting. The growing areas are limited to only a few hamlets, where radicchio is planted in the traditional way with no more than six to eight plants per square metre. Devotees reverently call radicchio, which is the emblem of Treviso, the 'King of Winter Fare'. Two kinds are offered: 'early' Treviso is available in stores from the first of September, while the more expensive 'late' version is found from December through March. Late radicchio has a smaller head, and the ends of the leaves curve slightly towards the centre. The name *radicchio di Treviso* has been protected by IGP (*Indicazione Geografica Protetta*) status since 1966, and a consortium has watched over the production and marketing of this much-loved vegetable ever since.

Radicchio ai ferri
Chargrilled Radicchio

4 firm Trevisano radicchios
2 tbsp olive oil
salt
freshly ground pepper

Wash the radicchio and pat completely dry. Whisk salt and pepper into the olive oil. Brush the radicchio with the olive oil and cook on a hot barbecue or under a hot grill until evenly browned, turning constantly. While cooking, drizzle with the spiced oil several times. Serve hot as a side dish.

Stuffed Vegetables

Throughout the Mediterranean region, stuffed vegetables are very popular everyday fare. Fleshy vegetables with firm skins or rinds that can be thoroughly scooped out are best suited for this purpose. They should not be over-ripe, so that they hold their shape when filled and cooked.

The sky is the limit when it comes to the fillings. Raw vegetables such as tomatoes and cucumbers make excellent, flavourful 'packaging' for salads with mayonnaise. On the other hand, braised vegetables such as aubergine or courgette make delicious shells for mince or seasoned rice.

Stuffed vegetables are not only suitable as main dishes, but also as antipasti. When served as appetizers, they are often cut into bite-sized portions, and can be enjoyed hot or cold.

Pomodori ripieni di tonno
Stuffed Tomatoes

4 large, firm beef tomatoes
150 g/5 oz canned tuna in oil
2 eggs, hard boiled
1 small white onion, finely chopped
4 tbsp mayonnaise
1 tbsp finely chopped parsley
4 lettuce leaves
salt
freshly ground pepper

Wash the tomatoes and cut off the tops, including the stalks, for use as lids. Scoop out the core and seeds with a spoon.

Salt the insides of the tomatoes, place upside down in a sieve and drain.

Drain the tuna and flake with a fork. Peel and chop the eggs. Combine the onions, tuna and egg with the mayonnaise and parsley, then add salt and pepper to taste.

Put the filling in the tomatoes, set the tops back on and arrange the filled tomatoes on the lettuce leaves.

First remove the tops from the washed tomatoes and scoop out the core and seeds with a spoon. Only the firm flesh should remain.

Lightly salt the tomatoes to draw out some of the liquid. Place them upside down in a sieve and drain for 10 minutes.

For the stuffing, mix drained canned tuna with mayonnaise, finely chopped hard-boiled eggs and finely chopped parsley. Season the mixture with salt and pepper.

Finally, stuff the hollow tomatoes with the tuna filling and place the tops over the stuffing to garnish. Arrange the stuffed vegetables on a plate and serve.

Funghi porcini ripieni
Stuffed Ceps

500 g/1 lb 2 oz ceps
100 ml/3½ fl oz olive oil,
plus extra for greasing
1 small white onion, finely chopped
1 garlic clove, minced
100 ml/3½ fl oz white wine
2 tbsp finely chopped parsley
50 g/1¾ oz grated Pecorino Romano
1 tbsp breadcrumbs
salt
freshly ground pepper

Grease a baking dish with olive oil. Clean the ceps. Remove the stalks from the caps and finely chop the stalks.

Heat half of the olive oil in a large frying pan and sauté the cep caps over low heat for about 5 minutes. Remove the mushroom caps from the pan and place them face down in the baking dish.

Sauté the onion, garlic and chopped cep stalks in the pan juices for 5 minutes, stirring continuously. Deglaze with the wine, then stir in the parsley. Season with salt and pepper, and simmer for another 5 minutes.

Use the mixture to stuff the mushroom caps. Mix the Pecorino Romano and bread-crumbs and sprinkle over the stuffed caps. Drizzle with the remaining olive oil and brown for a few minutes under the grill.

Cipolle ripiene
Stuffed Onions

4 large onions
50 g/1¾ oz prosciutto,
cut into fine strips
1 tbsp finely chopped sage
1 tbsp finely chopped oregano
200 g/7 oz fresh goat's cheese
1 egg
125 ml/4 fl oz white wine
60 g/2 oz grated Parmesan
salt
freshly ground pepper

Preheat the oven to 175°C/350°F/gas mark 4. Peel the onions. Bring a saucepan of salted water to the boil and cook the onions for 10 to 15 minutes. Then refresh them in cold water, cool a little longer, and cut off the top third for use as a lid. Carefully scoop out the onions with a spoon, leaving a shell about 1 cm/¼ inch thick. Finely dice the scooped-out flesh.

Combine the diced onion, ham and herbs with the cheese and egg. Season with salt and pepper. Fill the onion shells with this mixture and top them with the onion lids.

Place the stuffed onions close together in a baking dish and pour the wine over them. Cover the dish with aluminium foil and bake for 30 to 40 minutes. Sprinkle the stuffed onions with the grated Parmesan before serving.

Cipolle ripiene

Fish and Seafood

It should come as no surprise that seafood is a firm fixture of antipasto buffets all along the Italian coastline, even if the crustaceans are no longer coming exclusively from the Mediterranean, but are farmed in Central America and Asia as well. What endures is the Italians' love of Neptune's treasures, accompanied by the ability to conjure up a wealth of delicious dishes with mussels, prawns and small fish, ranging from simple to elaborate, with just a few carefully selected ingredients.

A visit to the local fish markets in the small coastal villages of a morning is a must. Not only will you be astonished to discover that there are indeed still fish in Italian waters, you can also enjoy mussels and other seafood in one of the small, local restaurants. Nowhere do they taste as good, for this is where they land in the pot fresh from the sea and are prepared without gimmicks. Add a piece of bread and a glass of wine, and little else is needed for a feeling of all-round well-being.

Bianchetti

Bianchetti, young anchovies and sardines, are a connoisseur's speciality. They are not only tasty, they are healthy as well, because they are high in omega-3 fatty acids. In Liguria and the Veneto region, the little fish are deep-fried and eaten whole. In the Maremma area, they are cooked with eggs into a frittata or with a thin batter in *frittele* (fritters). In southern Italy, *bianchetti* are thickened into a paste with tomatoes and chilli, and spread on slices of toast.

Insalata di mare
Seafood Medley

500 g/1 lb 2 oz live clams
1 small onion
2 garlic cloves
1 bunch soup vegetables (mixed root vegetables and herbs)
100 ml/3½ fl oz olive oil
250 ml/9 fl oz white wine
400 g/14 oz small squid, ready to cook
200 g/7 oz prawns, shelled
1 celery stick
2 tbsp finely chopped parsley
4 tbsp lemon juice
salt
freshly ground black pepper

Clean the clams under flowing cold water and discard any that are already open. Peel and chop the onions and garlic. Finely dice the soup vegetables (for example, onion, carrot, turnip and parsley).

Heat 3 tablespoons of the olive oil in a deep pan and lightly sauté the onion, garlic and soup vegetables. Pour in the white wine, add the clams and simmer for 10 minutes.

Then remove the clams and discard any that have not opened.

Strain the clam stock, bring it to the boil and cook the squid in it for about 20 minutes. Then add the prawns to the pot and cook for 2 to 3 minutes longer. Strain and drain well.

Chop the celery into thin slices. Scoop out the clam flesh and combine it with the squid, prawns, celery and parsley. Season the remaining olive oil with the lemon juice, salt and pepper, and pour over the salad.

Stir well, cover, and chill in the refrigerator for 2 hours. Remove the Seafood Medley from the refrigerator 10 minutes before serving.

Sarde in saor
Venetian-style Sardines

2 tbsp currants
1 litre/1¾ pints dry white wine
750 g/1 lb 10 oz fresh small sardines, ready to cook
150 ml/5 fl oz olive oil
4 onions, cut in thin rings
1 tbsp mixed spice seeds (black pepper, allspice, coriander)
4 bay leaves
250 ml/9 fl oz white wine vinegar
2 tbsp sugar
salt and pepper
flour for coating

Soak the currants in 100 ml/3½ fl oz of the wine for about 10 minutes. Wash the sardines and pat them dry. Season inside and out with salt and pepper, coat with flour and shake off the excess.

Heat 100 ml/3½ fl oz of the olive oil in a deep pan and fry the fish on both sides, in portions, until golden brown. Remove from the pan and drain on paper towels.

Gently sauté the onion in the remaining olive oil, pour on the rest of the wine, add the seeds and bay leaves and bring to the boil. Stir in the vinegar, currants and sugar and simmer the stock for 10 minutes on low heat.

Turn half of the sardines into a ceramic bowl and pour on a little of the onion-currant stock. Add the remaining sardines and spread the rest of the stock over them. Cover the bowl with clingfilm and leave the sardines in a cool place for at least 2 days before serving.

Wash the fresh sardines, pat dry and coat with flour. Shake off the extra flour.

Fry the sardines on both sides in olive oil on medium heat until golden brown.

Gently simmer the onion rings with bay leaves in olive oil, then cook al dente in white wine.

Season the hot onion stock with vinegar, currants and sugar, and pour over the fried sardines.

Cozze e vongole passate ai ferri
Grilled Mussels

1 kg/2 lb 4 oz live blue mussels
500 g/1 lb 2 oz live cockles
3 tbsp olive oil
1 bunch soup vegetables
(mixed root vegetables and herbs),
roughly chopped
1 onion, chopped
2 garlic cloves, chopped
coarse sea salt
2 tbsp pine kernels
25 g/1 oz soft butter
2 tbsp grated Parmesan
1 tbsp finely chopped parsley
salt
freshly ground pepper

Clean the mussels and cockles thoroughly under cold running water and dispense with any beards. Discard any open cockles.

Heat the olive oil in a large saucepan and fry the soup vegetables, onion and garlic in it. Add the clams, cover the pan and simmer for about 5 minutes, shaking the pan several times during that time. Take the cockles out of the pan and leave them to cool. Discard any cockles that are still closed.

Spread a generous amount of sea salt inside a deep baking dish. Break off one half of each blue mussel shell, scoop out the flesh, return it to the shell and place in the bed of salt. Remove the cockle flesh and purée it in a blender with the pine kernels, butter and Parmesan. Stir in the parsley, then season with salt and pepper.

Cover the mussels with the mixture and place under a hot grill for approximately 5 minutes.

Carciofi e frutti di mare
Artichokes with Seafood

4–6 small young artichokes
juice of 2 lemons
3 garlic cloves
60 ml/2 fl oz olive oil
125 ml/4 fl oz white wine
450 g/1 lb frozen, pre-cooked
mixed seafood (thawed)
300 g/11 oz buffalo mozzarella, sliced
salt
freshly ground pepper
butter for greasing

Clean the artichokes, cut the stalks to a length of 4 cm/1½ inches, and peel. Remove the tough outer leaves and slice off the thistles from the inner leaves.

Fill a bowl with 1 litre/1¾ pints of water and add the lemon juice. Cut the artichokes lengthways into thin slices and immediately drop them into the lemon water. Soak them for 10 minutes, then pour off the water and drain well.

Slice the garlic. Heat the olive oil in a non-stick frying pan and fry the garlic until it is golden brown, then remove and discard it.

Sauté the artichoke slices in the olive oil, stirring constantly. Season with salt and pepper, then add the white wine. Cover the pan and gently braise the artichokes on medium heat for about 30 minutes, shaking the pan several times as they cook. During that time, preheat the oven to 225°C/440°F/ gas mark 7 and butter a baking dish.

Place the artichoke slices in the baking dish and pour on the cooking juices. Add the seafood to the artichokes and top with mozzarella slices. Bake for 20 to 25 minutes until the mozzarella starts to brown.

Carciofi e frutti di mare

Gamberetti olio e limone
Prawns in Lemon Dressing

500 g/1 lb 2 oz cooked prawns
100 ml/3½ fl oz lemon juice
150 ml/5 fl oz olive oil
4 lettuce leaves
4 lemon slices
salt
freshly ground white pepper
cayenne pepper

Put the prawns in a sieve, rinse briefly with running water, then drain. Whisk salt, white pepper and a pinch of cayenne into the lemon juice and olive oil. Toss the prawns in it and marinate briefly. Place the lettuce in four glass bowls and arrange the prawns on top. Garnish each bowl with one slice of lemon.

Favourite Fish Antipasti

Acciughe al verde (Piedmont): Pickled anchovies with garlic, parsley, lemon juice and olive oil.
Baccala mantecato (Veneto): Dried cod with chives, garlic and oil.
Bottarga (Sardinia): Thin slices of dried, salted tuna roe served with olive oil and lemon juice.
Moscardini (Liguria): Tiny squid braised with tomatoes, rosemary and garlic.
Mussoli in insalata (Friuli-Venezia Giulia): Steamed mussels in lemon juice and olive oil with parsley.
Mustica (Calabria): Salted anchovies in a spicy chilli marinade.
Pesce scabecciau (Sardinia): Small fish baked in vinegar marinade with garlic, parsley and tomatoes.
Sfogie in saor (Veneto): Small baked sole, pickled in sweet-and-sour vinegar with raisins and spices.

Carpaccio

Approximately fifty years ago, the legendary Giuseppe Cipriani created the first carpaccio at Harry's Bar in Venice in honour of the countess Amalia Nani Mocenigo. The noblewoman, a regular guest at his bar, had anaemia, and as a result her doctor had recommended that she eat a diet rich in raw meat. Because of the colours that prevail on the plate – red (meat) and white (mayonnaise) – Cipriani named his creation after the renowned Renaissance painter Vittore Carpaccio, who especially prized these colours and used them frequently in his paintings.

These days carpaccio signifies extremely thin slices of raw meat, fish or vegetables marinated in a little olive oil, lemon, salt and pepper. Because it is not cooked, it is particularly important that only ingredients of the highest quality be used for carpaccio, ones that have ripened into their own distinctive flavours. If you are not a purist, you can lend additional flavour to carpaccio with rocket, Parmesan, herbs and garlic.

Carpaccio di finocchi con finocchiona

Carpaccio di finocchi con finocchiona
Fennel Salami Carpaccio

2 large fennel bulbs

100 g/3½ oz fennel salami, finely sliced

juice of 1 lemon and 1 orange

1 tsp flower blossom honey

1 tsp mustard

1 tbsp white wine vinegar

3½ tbsp olive oil

salt and pepper

Trim the fennel and slice it very thin with a mandolin or a food slicer. Decoratively arrange the sliced salami on four plates.

Whisk together the remaining ingredients and pour this dressing over the fennel-salami carpaccio. Marinate for 10 minutes or longer before serving.

Carpaccio cipriani
Fillet of Beef Carpaccio

200 g/7 oz fillet of beef

3 tbsp mayonnaise

1–2 tsp lemon juice

1 tbsp milk

Worcestershire sauce

salt

freshly ground pepper

Wrap the beef fillet in clingfilm and place it in the freezer to harden.

Stir the mayonnaise, lemon juice and milk into a thick cream and season with the Worcestershire sauce, salt and pepper. Cut the frozen fillet into wafer-thin slices and lay them on a chilled serving platter. Use a spoon to drizzle the mayonnaise sauce over the meat in a grid-like pattern.

Carpaccio di porcini

Carpaccio di porcini
Cep Carpaccio

2 bunches rocket

400 g/14 oz small ceps

juice of 2 lemons

5 tbsp olive oil

2 tbsp balsamic vinegar

50 g/1¾ oz piece of Parmesan

salt

freshly ground pepper

Wash the rocket, removing any wilted leaves and thick stalks, then shake dry. Place it on four plates.

Clean the ceps, slice them finely lengthways, and immediately place in the lemon juice, turning to coat both sides. Arrange the sliced mushrooms on the rocket. Whisk the olive oil with the vinegar, add salt and pepper and drizzle over the ceps. Top with finely shaved Parmesan.

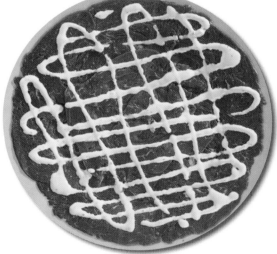

Carpaccio cipriani

Carpaccio di pesce spada
Swordfish Carpaccio

100 g/3½ oz seaweed

1 avocado

juice of 3 lemons

1 tsp red peppercorns

500 g/1 lb 2 oz swordfish fillet, frozen

4 tbsp olive oil

salt

freshly ground white pepper

Wash the seaweed, discarding any hard stalks, then break it into bite-sized pieces and set on paper towels to dry. Cut the avocado in half lengthways. Twist the halves in opposite directions to separate the flesh from the stone. With a spoon, scoop the flesh from the skin in one piece, cut it into thin slices and immediately sprinkle with some of the lemon juice. Crush the peppercorns in a mortar.

With a food slicer, cut the frozen swordfish into wafer-thin slices and place them on four plates. Season with the remaining lemon juice, crushed peppercorns, salt and white pepper. Arrange the seaweed and avocado slices decoratively on the fish, drizzle with the olive oil and serve immediately.

Anchovies

Little anchovy fillets are used often and enthusiastically as a condiment in Italian cuisine, giving sauces, salads and meat dishes a very special taste.

The ancient Romans used small anchovies cooked in brine with oregano and freshly pressed grape juice to make a clear, spicy sauce called *liquamen*. Like many of today's prepared sauces, it added flavour to many dishes.

After being pickled and preserved in brine or oil, the fillets are called anchovies. Some anchovies are matured for two years or even longer, and they have a crumbly consistency. The quality of the anchovies depends on how long they mature, as well as the quality of the oil used.

The starting point for producing preserved anchovies is catching them fresh.

In order to draw out water, the fish are packed in ample salt and stored for at least three months.

The cured fish are then filleted by hand, filled into jars and covered with oil.

PIEDMONT

The cuisine of the Piedmont region counts among Italy's finest and most diverse. While the recipes originated in country kitchens, many of them have been refined over the course of centuries, and although it would be vehemently denied by patriots, have drawn a little inspiration from neighbouring France. A most fitting description of the Piedmontese and their eating habits comes from the words of author Oscar Wilde: 'They have simple taste – the best is just right for them.'

Characteristics of the cuisine include the extravagant use of butter and bacon, and a distinct preference for rice, raw vegetables and veal. Fresh seafood has hardly ever played a role in classic Piedmontese cuisine. One reason for this is surely Liguria, the small yet very mountainous strip of land that separates Piedmont from the sea. As a result, pickled and dried fish occupied a firm place on their menus from very early on. Although anchovies were considered food for the poor in earlier times, one of Piedmont's national dishes, *bagna cauda*, would not taste nearly as good without them.

Isola Bella with its baroque gardens lies at the centre of Lake Maggiore. Laid out by Count Carlo Borromeo beginning in 1632, even today, these are among the most beautiful gardens in Italy.

Bagna cauda
Vegetable Fondue

2 red peppers	
1 bunch young carrots	
8 celery sticks	
1 large fennel bulb	
50 g/1¾ oz anchovy fillets in oil	
6–8 garlic cloves	
100 g/3½ oz butter	
150 ml/5 fl oz olive oil	

Wash, peel and trim the vegetables as needed. Cut the peppers in half, remove the cores, and cut into slices 2 cm/³/₄ inch wide. Quarter the carrots lengthways and cut the celery sticks in half. Thinly slice the fennel bulb. Arrange the vegetables on a large platter or in individual portions in bowls.

Rinse the anchovy fillets in cold water, pat them dry and chop finely. Peel the garlic and chop it finely as well. Melt the butter in a small frying pan and gently fry the garlic, but do not brown it. Stir in the anchovies and olive oil and heat to simmering point. Then simmer the sauce gently on low heat for 10 minutes. Place the pan on a food warmer on the table, but do not cook any further. Dip the vegetable strips in the anchovy sauce by hand or with a fork.

The vegetables used vary according to what is in season. Among the best suited for dipping are young spring onions, chicory leaves, broccoli florets and courgette sticks.

Vitello Tonnato

A classic of the Italian appetizer buffet table is *vitello tonnato*, which is thinly sliced, cooked veal in a tuna mayonnaise with capers. The original recipe presumably stems from eighteenth-century Piedmontese or Lombard kitchens, where preserved tuna was not yet available. In those days, veal roasts were stewed with salted anchovies for several hours. They were then sliced, covered with pan juices, garnished with capers and served hot. Considering the method of preparation, the dish was more akin to a *brasato* (roast), but the addition of anchovies already gave it an entirely unique flavour.

Over time, the Piedmontese varied this recipe and boiled the meat instead of stewing it. After it had cooked, they marinated it overnight in a sauce made from olive oil, tuna, anchovies, parsley, lemon juice and soft-boiled egg yolk. This same *vitello tonnato alla maniera rustica antica* (traditional style) is still offered in many osterias today. Since the beginning of the last century, *vitello tonnato* has been prepared with tuna mayonnaise.

Carne cruda all'albese
Veal Tartar

400 g/14 oz veal fillet
4 tbsp olive oil
1 tbsp lemon juice
100 g/3½ oz wild herbs
salt
cayenne pepper
freshly ground pepper

Using a large, sharp knife or a meat mincer, chop the veal very finely. Season it with a little salt and cayenne pepper, and mix in half of the olive oil.

Stir in the lemon juice, remaining olive oil, and salt and pepper. Wash the wild herbs, discarding any that are wilted, and spin dry. Arrange the meat on a serving plate and place the wild herbs around it. Drizzle the olive oil dressing over the herbs.

The Church of Saints Nazario and Celso is a landmark of the old Piedmontese village of Montechiaro d'Asti. It was built from sandstone and brick at the beginning of the 7th century.

Capers

Since ancient times, capers have been among the staples of Italian cuisine. During the spring caper harvest, the unopened buds are picked by hand before dawn. They are then cleaned and pickled in salt, brine, wine vinegar or oil. This gives them their distinctive, bitter-spicy taste. The most intensely flavoured capers are the salted ones, and these are preferred by Italian cooks. Raw capers are inedible. The smaller the caper, the milder its flavour. Flavourful caper berries, the fruit of the caper, are also pickled in salt and vinegar brine and served as *antipasti*.

Vitello tonnato
Veal in Tuna Sauce

600 g/1 lb 5 oz veal (loin)
750 ml/1⅓ pints dry white wine
2 tbsp white wine vinegar
1 celery stick
1 small onion
1 bay leaf, crumbled
2 cloves
5 black peppercorns
150 g/5 oz canned tuna in oil
3 anchovy fillets in oil
2 tbsp capers
2 egg yolks
2 tbsp lemon juice
200 ml/7 fl oz olive oil
salt and freshly ground pepper

Remove any tendons and skin from the veal. Wash the meat, pat it dry and tie the loin together with kitchen twine. Place the meat in a ceramic bowl.

In a separate bowl, combine the white wine and vinegar. Dice the celery and onion and stir them into the wine and vinegar along with the bay leaf, cloves and peppercorns. Pour this marinade over the meat.

Marinate the meat in the refrigerator for 24 hours, turning it several times. The next day, place the meat and its marinade in a large saucepan, add enough water to fully cover the meat, salt lightly and simmer for about 1 hour.

Drain the tuna and purée it in a mixer with the anchovies and capers. Whisk the egg yoke with the lemon juice, salt and pepper. Then pour the oil into the egg yolk in a thin stream and stir vigorously until the mayonnaise firms up. Mix in the puréed tuna.

Remove the meat from the stock and leave it to cool. Remove the twine and cut the meat into thin slices. Arrange on a serving platter and spread the tuna mayonnaise over it.

Prosciutto di Parma

The mild flavour, spicy aroma and coppery colour of prosciutto di Parma are unmistakable. Only four things are required to create it: a fresh Large White, Landrace or Duroc pork leg weighing between 12 and 15 kg (26–33 lb), sea salt, the extraordinary climatic conditions of the region surrounding Parma and enough time for maturing, no less than twelve months. After this amount of time, an inspector from the independent *Istituto Parma Qualità* comes calling. Only after passing this inspection is the prosciutto branded with the Ducal Crown or trademark. Almost ten million hams receive this stamp of quality each year.

Prosciutto is produced from pork legs, which are rubbed lightly with sea salt, especially on the meaty surface and all around the hip joint.

They are put in cold storage for a hundred days, during which they absorb the salt. They are then washed and hung up to air dry. Now and then, the meaty side is brushed with lard.

The Ducal Crown is trademark of the Consorzio del Prosciutto di Parma. It is the reward for a year of processing and for centuries of experience in the production of ham.

Ham

Ham is the best part of the pig, and it is not only Italian producers and consumers who are of that opinion. The flavourful, air-dried hindquarters of the pig have been treasured since ancient times. The Italian word *prosciutto* comes from the Latin *perexsutum*, which means 'dried'. The Romans were intimately familiar with the secrets of producing fine ham. They also knew that the low humidity, wind and climate at the outskirts of the northern Italian Alps were ideal for the preservation of meats, and even improved the quality of the meat itself.

To this very day, the time-tested method of preparing cured ham has not changed very much in Italy. The back leg or haunch (with or without the bone) is first cured in salt and herbs for a period of time, and then air dried (not smoked). The tangy air circulates throughout the drying rooms and lends the ham its unique flavour, which, like the climate, differs slightly from region to region.

The most famous Italian cured raw hams are undoubtedly *prosciutto di Parma* and *prosciutto di San Daniele*. As DOP hams (*Denominazione d'Origine Protetta*, or Protected Designation of Origin), both have enjoyed protected status within the European Union for years, and a consortium oversees them to maintain the high quality standards of these specialities.

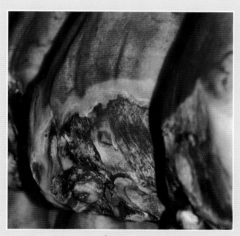

Prosciutto di San Daniele

San Daniele ham can look back on a long and illustrious history. It was the Celts who laid the foundations for fruitful agriculture at this location in the region of Friuli. And the ancient gravestone of a butcher, found in Portogruaro near Venice, bears a perfectly depicted San Daniele ham, including the hoof. To this day, this very special prosciutto is made from pork legs with the entire leg bone intact. In order to bear the designation *prosciutto di San Daniele*, the pigs must be born in specific regions of Italy, and they must be raised, fed and slaughtered according to regulations. Only sea salt is rubbed on the fresh pork legs, which are then air dried. The ageing process takes at least twelve months. Finished hams have an intense flavour and distinct aftertaste. Wrapped around grissini breadsticks, the very finely sliced ham is shown to best advantage.

Prosciutto con melone e fichi
Prosciutto with Figs and Melon

½ *honeydew melon*
8 fresh figs
200 g/7 oz prosciutto

Quarter the melon, remove the seeds and peel, and cut into slices. Wash and pat dry the figs, then cut them crossways, so that they open like flowers.

Place the figs in the middle of a plate and add the melon slices. Arrange the prosciutto decoratively around the fruit.

Bresaola

Bresaola is a special kind of air-dried beef made from certain meaty, high-quality cuts of beef in Valtellina, a valley in the northern Italian Alps. The meat is cured with a little salt and spices such as pepper, cinnamon, nutmeg, garlic, bay leaf and juniper berries, and then left to age in the cool air. Thanks to favourable climatic conditions, the meat remains tender and moist even after the drying process is completed. It has a distinctive dark red colour, and is exceptionally soft and mild. In 1998, a consortium was founded to safeguard the name *Bresaola della Valtellina*, to protect its traditional production, and to support marketing and distribution efforts.

Bresaola is cut into gossamer-thin slices and usually served as an appetizer, either on its own or with olive oil and pepper in the style of carpaccio.

Bresaola con rucola
Bresaola with Rocket

1 handful rocket
300 g/11 oz bresaola, finely sliced
80 ml/3 fl oz olive oil
coarsely ground pepper
1 lemon, cut into wedges

Wash the rocket, removing any coarse stalks, and spin it dry. Cut the leaves into fine strips.

Lay out the bresaola slices on four plates. Drizzle the olive oil over them, turning the plates as you do to distribute the oil evenly.

Grind pepper over the bresaola and sprinkle with the rocket strips. Garnish with lemon wedges.

Selected pieces of beef are cut and then rubbed with seasonings and salt.

The meat is air cured for an entire month, during which it is turned in the seasonings every two days.

The meat is then tied up like a rolled roast and left to air dry for a few months.

During the ageing process, a natural, protective layer of white mould develops on the bresaola.

Grissini

40 g/1½ oz compressed fresh yeast or
2 sachets easy-blend dried yeast
1 pinch sugar
400 g/14 oz flour, plus extra for dusting
1 tsp salt
3 tbsp olive oil

Crumble or sprinkle the yeast in 250 ml/
9 fl oz lukewarm water and dissolve it with
the sugar. Stir in 4 tablespoons of the flour,
cover, and leave the resulting sponge in a
warm place to prove for 15 minutes.

Sift the remaining flour into a bowl, make
a hollow in the middle and pour the sponge
into it. Knead into a silky dough, along with
the salt and olive oil. Form the dough into a
ball, cover and set it aside for 1 hour, or until it
has doubled in volume.

Cover two baking trays with baking
paper and preheat the oven to 200°C/390°F/
gas mark 6. Knead the dough vigorously, then
divide it into about 30 equal portions. Roll
out each piece on a floured surface into thin
sticks about 30 cm/12 inches long. Place the
sticks of dough next to each other on a baking
tray and bake for about 15 minutes or until
golden brown. Halfway through the baking
time, brush the grissini with water. Leave the
breadsticks on the trays to cool.

Salumi

First, a little theory: *salumi* is the generic Italian term used for all sausage products that are made from salted or dried cuts of meat, whether whole or ground. The centuries-old tradition of preserving meat by curing it dates back to the period of tenant farming. In those days, farmers paid land owners half or more of their autumn harvest in exchange for use of the land and a house. This often included pigs, which had to be slaughtered and preserved.

The most important *salumi*, both in Italy and abroad, are raw, cured ham and various salami specialities. But there is also a whole range of delicious sausage varieties that are often important only locally.

In central and southern Italy, *capocollo calabrese* is made from the meat of the neck and head of the pig. The meat is first pickled in brine for a few days, then placed in red wine, seasoned with peppercorns and stuffed into casings. These are are suspended between two thin strips of wood. The sausages are then air dried or smoked. After that, the wooden slats are removed and the sausages are tied together with string. In Apulia, these sausages are smaller and spicier. They are dried in the cool smoke of green oak branches and have an intensely smoked flavour.

Cinta Senese

Cinta senese are free-range pigs, almost totally black in colour, instantly recognizable by the white belt (*cinta*) that surrounds their ribs, shoulders and front legs. Since the Middle Ages, this breed has lived in a semi-wild state throughout the Chianti region. In the middle of the last century, these simple country swine were almost displaced by meatier and more prolific breeds. About twenty years ago there were only a few of the animals left, and the *cinta senese* were placed on the list of endangered breeds. They are now being bred again, and a consortium oversees their marketing. This breed is not only used for flavourful Tuscan raw ham, but also for traditional sausage varieties such as *salsicce* (small raw sausages), salami and *rigatino*, a kind of bacon with a thin layer of fat. In order to protect against imitations, the consortium provides genuine *cinta senese* sausages with a quality control number.

For many varieties of salami, the first step is to put pork with a fat content of about 30 per cent through a meat mincer.

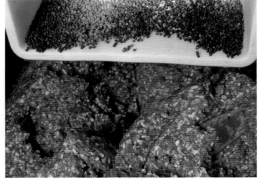

The pork mince is mixed with salt, sugar, pepper and other spices. In addition, raw bacon is often added.

Finocchiona is a Tuscan speciality that is shaped similar to a salami. To make it, a combination of beef and pork are put through the meat mincer, then seasoned with wild fennel seeds, pepper, salt, garlic and red wine. This mixture is stuffed into casings and must mature for some time before its flavour fully develops.

Luganega or *lucanica* are hearty sausages from Venice, something like bratwurst. They are made from the neck and cheek of the pig. The main seasoning is pepper, while other seasonings differ from maker to maker.

Soppressata, speciality sausages from southern Italy and the Veneto region, consist of up to 70 per cent lean pork, and the rest comes from the fattier meat of the back and belly. Before it is stuffed into casings, the meat is chopped roughly with a knife and seasoned with chilli powder, salt, pepper and red wine. These sausages are first smoked and dried, then matured for up to fifteen months in cool, well-ventilated rooms. Soppressata are appreciably larger than salami and often rectangular. They are eaten sliced with fruit or slightly hot and served as a side dish with polenta.

Zampone are stuffed pig's trotters, an integral element of the cuisine in Emilia-Romagna. The skin of the boned and pickled pig's trotter is stuffed with a sausage meat mixture, tongue and pistachio nuts, then dried in special ovens. Finally, the sausages are cooked for several hours at a low temperature. They are eaten sliced, usually while still hot, with vegetables.

Italian delicatessens are a veritable paradise for gourmets. The selection of ham, bacon and salami specialities is dizzying at first glance, but also full of promise.

Pancetta

Pancetta is a slightly marbled bacon, usually cured with the skin. In northern Italy, it is used to season meat dishes and also served finely sliced as an antipasto. Traditionally, the raw bacon is salted and seasoned with pepper, garlic, cloves, rosemary and fennel seeds before being smoked.

Pancetta made from leaner pigs is an especially tender and tasty dry-cured meat that is flavoured with spices, rolled and stuffed into casings to air dry for several months.

The salami meat is stuffed into natural casings, and experienced butchers shape them by hand into the characteristic form of a particular salami.

The raw sausages are then air dried in special rooms for 60 to 90 days, depending on their size.

Italian Meats and Sausages

Milano Salami
Fine-grained salame di Milano are the best known and most Italian salami. During the maturation period, the approximately 30-cm (12-inch) long sausages are traditionally tied with sausage twine and covered with straw. That is how they derive their distinctive shape.

Salametto
These small, fine-grained raw sausages mature for at least thirty days in natural casings. They belong to the salami macinati fini, which are a finely chopped variety of salami that come in various shapes and sizes.

Salsiccia stagionata di cinghiale
These spicy little wild boar salami are made in Tuscany and Umbria. Whole chains of them linked together are air dried.

Prosciutto di Guarcino
This traditional ham, produced in the Lazio region, matures for at least fifteen months. Its spicy flavour comes from full-bodied red wine that is seasoned with chilli, among other things.

Pancetta
Delicate pancetta is an Italian speciality that is spiced with different herbs from region to region and is usually cured complete with the rind.

Lardo di Colonnata

The little town of Colonnata lies right next to the Tuscan marble quarries in the Apuan Alps and, naturally, is also home to a bacon speciality of the same name. Its amazing history extends all the way from providing quarry workers with a filling meal to becoming a speciality attraction on gourmets' tables all around the world.

In spite of this, European Union bureaucracy almost deprived the Italians of their favourite bacon. Traditionally, the pieces of pork fat matured under a layer of fragrant sea salt and wild herbs for six months in a total of five hundred marble tubs in underground cellars. EU bureaucrats declared this practice unsanitary and wanted to stop production. Today, the ageing cellars are tiled, but the marble tubs remain and the manufacturing method has not changed. Meanwhile, outside of Colonnata, attempts are being made to produce a similar type of bacon in plastic tubs. Anyone who has eaten genuine *lardo di Colonnata*, however, will immediately recognize the melt-in-your-mouth quality of the original. 'When you eat Colonnata bacon, you have to be able to taste the bread and tomatoes at the same time. The bacon should never overpower any other flavour.' That is how the locals describe the unique taste of *lardo*, which alternates a little between sweet and delicate.

Coppa
Coppa is made from the collar of the pig. The meat is pickled in brine for ten to eighteen days, then stuffed into beef casings and air dried.

Cotechino
Cotechino comes from Modena and is made of bacon rind, lean pork, fat and spices. During cooking, the bacon rind turns gelatinous, giving these sausages their special consistency and incomparable flavour.

Indugghia
These raw sausages are a speciality of Calabria. They are made of pork, bacon, liver and lung, and usually served as part of an antipasto platter.

Salami di Varzi
Lombard salami di Varzi, Italy's premier salami, carries the DOP trademark. This salami has a refined taste and exceptional flavour thanks to a long period of maturation.

Pancetta supermagra
To make this speciality sausage, lean bacon is rolled up and stuffed into casings, air dried and served as a cold meat.

Norcinetto
A special delicacy for salami lovers, this small, firm salami matures in fresh mountain air.

Mortadella
Mortadella, from Bologna, is the most famous Italian cooked sausage. It is made of finely ground pork with roughly diced bacon, salt, sugar and peppercorns. The sausage meat is filled into natural casings, formed into large, heavy sausages, and then cooked at 90°C (200°F).

Soppressata
Made from cubes of lean pork, bacon, salt and peppercorns, these spicy sausages are pressed in natural casings for a while before being dried. Their name is derived from this method of preparation.

Pizza e Pane

Pizza
and
Bread

Senza il pane tutto divento orfano. This Italian proverb says, 'Without bread, everyone is an orphan.' A basket of bread – or at least a jar of thin *grissini* (breadsticks) – is an integral part of every Italian table. It is mainly white bread, which is eaten practically around the clock, and in substantial quantities, or so it would seem to foreigners. But appearances can be deceiving. Although it is true that some form of bread must accompany a meal, Italians consume no more bread than do the French, Germans or Spanish. Italians eat mainly white bread, and it comes in every imaginable shape and size. That is probably because white bread used to be reserved for people with higher incomes, while the poor had to settle for darker breads made from maize, rye and chestnut flours. Today, it is just the opposite, although wheat is still the most important grain for bread-making.

Bread, in whatever form, has been a staple food in Italy since antiquity. Even in Roman times, the baker's craft was a major industry. In 100 BCE, there were some 258 bakeries and one baking school in Rome. The Roman emperors also recognized early on that the population could be kept happy with *panem et circenses* (bread and circuses), at least for a while.

'The ratio of bread to drink should be two to one, of bread to eggs one-and-a-half to one, of bread to meat three to one, and of bread to moist fish, green vegetables and fruit, four to one.' Fifteenth-century philosopher Marsilio Ficino established this principle for the ideal consumption of bread in his pamphlet entitled *De longa vita* ('On Long Life'). In the Renaissance, bread was handed out with each course at the feast tables of the Medici family, as well as at the more modest repasts eaten in Leonardo da Vinci's workshops. And according to legend, Michelangelo is said to have nourished himself on bread alone when he worked.

One of the oldest types of bread is *pane di padula*, which is still baked today in the province of Salerno, and is made from a mixture of durum semolina and soft wheat flour. The tops of the round loaves are engraved with squares, and thus resemble the breads depicted on mosaics found in Pompeii. The distinctive bread of the Basilicata region, *pane di matera*, also has a long tradition. Even the Roman poet Horace praised its tasty dough and beguiling scent, for *pane di matera* is made from twice-ground durum semolina and baked in wooden ovens.

Bread is an important staple food throughout Italy, and it is served with every meal. White bread, in particular, is available in every shape and size imaginable. Each region has its own bread recipes and specialities.

The Significance of Bread

Bread is the symbol of life and occupies a central place not only in Christendom. Even in ancient times, it was a symbol of fertility and was offered to the gods during religious ceremonies. Grain symbolized the fertility of the soil, and the bread baked on hot stones was considered sacred.

In the first centuries of Christianity, loaves of bread were very large and ring-shaped. Only from the eleventh century onwards did loaves became smaller and round. In the mid-thirteenth century, eucharistic bread was converted into the Host, which was initially made from the finest wheat and baked only by priests on special grills.

To this day, special breads are baked for certain religious celebrations in Italy. In Basilicata, a ring-shaped bread flavoured with lard and fennel seeds is prepared for the Feast of the Immaculate Conception on 8 December. On Corpus Christi, people in Calabria bake a ring-shaped wholemeal bread that can be hung over people's arms during their procession. And in many regions, ritual speciality breads appear on the table at Easter, on the Feast of Saint Nicholas (6 December) and on the Feast of Saint Lucia (13 December).

Italians rarely throw bread away, not least due to its great symbolic importance. Bread crusts can be used to thicken soups, breadcrumbs to thicken sauces and hardened leftover bread is added to soups and salads.

Regional Breads

On any trip through Italy, you will soon discover that every region has its own speciality breads that are made from different ingredients. There are over 200 types of Italian bread, which, given the diversity of shapes and local names, proudly add up to 1,500 different kinds of bread and rolls.

Depending on the flour used, they can be categorized as regular white bread, rye bread, granary bread or speciality bread made from mixed flours. In the Abruzzo region, the traditional *pane cappelli* is still made from durum wheat semolina. In the province of Teramo, a speciality is *parruozzo*, a soft cornbread that is eaten with boiled vegetables. And the Sicilian province of Messina is home to *pane a birra*, made with brewer's yeast, then plaited and strewn with sesame seeds.

Panino classico

Panino condito

Crocetta

Panino di soia

Pane siciliano

Rosetta

Ciabatta

Pane sardo

Coccia

Frisella casareccia

Frustina

Michetta

Marsigliese

Frisella integrale

Tarallo sugna e pepe

Miciarella

Sfilatino

Pane napoletano

Panello canole

Baking Bread

The ingredients for good bread have remained the same for millennia: flour, water, yeast and usually a little salt. In addition to these fundamental components, the approximately 35,000 Italian bakers are allowed to enrich their breads with many other natural ingredients: butter, olive oil, lard, milk, grape must, grapes, raisins, figs, olives, nuts, almonds, rosemary, aniseed, oregano, caraway, sesame, flaxseed, malt, sucrose or dextrose, pumpkin and honey are all permitted. Thus, in addition to traditional classic breads, there are delicious *panini dolci*, sweet breads with raisins (*all'u vetta pane*), almond bread (*pane con le mandorle*) and nut bread (*pane con le noci*), to name just a few.

Pane casalingo alle olive
Home-made Olive Bread

Ingredients for 3 small loaves:
500 g/1 lb 2 oz plain flour,
plus extra for dusting
1 sachet easy-blend dried yeast
1 tsp salt
1 pinch sugar
300 ml/11 fl oz lukewarm water
250 g/9 oz chard, chopped
100 g/3½ oz black olives,
stoned and chopped
2 tbsp olive oil,
plus extra for greasing

Sift the flour into a bowl and make a hollow in the middle. Place the yeast, salt and sugar in the hollow, then add the water. Knead the mixture into a smooth, silky dough. Leave it to rise, covered, for about 1 hour or until it has doubled in size.

Grease a baking tray with olive oil and preheat the oven to 220°C/430°F/gas mark 7. Knead the chard and olives into the dough, then divide it into thirds. Form each third into a rounded rectangular loaf and place on a greased baking tray. Cover the loaves with a flour-dusted tea towel and leave them to rise again for 1 hour.

Brush the loaves with olive oil and bake for 20 to 25 minutes. Cool thoroughly on a metal rack.

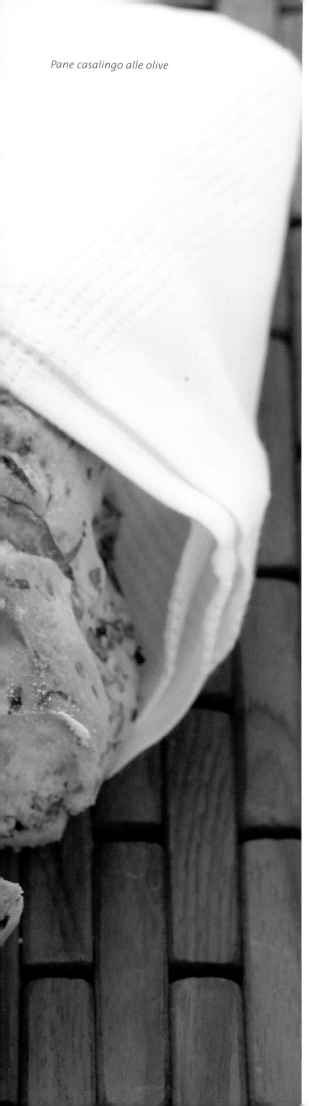

Pane casalingo alle olive

Taralli
Bread Rings

40 g/1½ oz compressed fresh yeast or
2 sachets easy-blend dried yeast

1 pinch sugar

500 g/1 lb 2 oz flour,
plus extra for dusting

1 tsp salt

1 tsp fennel seeds, crushed

120 g/4 oz soft lard

olive oil

Crumble the yeast into 250 ml/9 fl oz luke-warm water and dissolve it along with the sugar. Stir in 4 tablespoons of the flour, cover and leave the resulting sponge to prove in a warm place for 15 minutes.

Sift the remaining flour into a bowl, make a hollow in the centre, and pour the sponge into it. Add the salt, fennel seeds and lard and knead everything into a smooth, silky dough. Shape it into a ball, cover, and leave in a warm spot to rise for 1 hour or until it has doubled in volume.

Vigorously knead the dough. On a floured surface, form it into a roll and cut it into 10 equal pieces. Roll each piece into a thin coil and shape into a ring. Place the dough rings on a baking tray covered with baking paper, brush with a little olive oil, cover with a tea towel and leave them to rise for 1 hour. Preheat the oven to 160°C/320°F/gas mark 3. Bake the bread rings for 50 to 60 minutes, then cool completely on a metal rack.

The raw materials for all white breads and rolls are wheat flour, yeast, water and usually a little salt.

First, a sponge is made from a portion of the flour, crumbled yeast and lukewarm water.

Once the sponge has risen, it is thoroughly kneaded with the remaining flour and other ingredients.

Shaped into a ball, the dough is covered and set in a warm place to rise until doubled in volume.

Then the dough is vigorously pulled and kneaded by hand again for a few minutes.

Finally, the finished dough is formed into a loaf and left to rise a second time before baking.

Focaccia alla salvia

Focaccia

Focaccia is a very popular flatbread in Liguria. When baked to perfection, it is soft inside and crisp outside. In earlier times, it used to be eaten as a meal in itself with fresh figs. Today it is available around the clock, an indispensable part of breakfast, snack time, or a savoury bite to eat with aperitifs. In Genoa and the surrounding area, numerous *panetterie* and *focaccerie* offer this delicious flatbread from the early hours of the morning onwards. And many locals eat the bread directly from the bag while walking down the street.

The medieval town of Recco in Liguria is considered the birthplace of cheese focaccia. Long ago, a certain Mr Manuelina Maggio is supposed to have baked this special flatbread for the first time. His recipe: a simple yeast dough with oil produced in the Ligurian Riviera, filled with *stracchino*, the rich, soft cheese native to this region.

Since 1976, the gastronomic consortium of Recco has organized events featuring *focaccia col formaggio*, which has been a protected trademark since 1995. Each year on the fourth Sunday in May, Recco celebrates the Focaccia Festival, called the *Sagra della focaccia*. Throughout the day bakers hand out their delicious flatbread free of charge.

Focaccia alla salvia
Focaccia with Sage

40 g/1½ oz compressed fresh yeast or 2 sachets easy-blend dried yeast
1 pinch sugar
400 g/14 oz flour, plus extra for dusting
1 tsp salt
125 ml/4 fl oz olive oil, plus extra for greasing
12 fresh sage leaves, finely chopped
2 tbsp coarse sea salt

Crumble the yeast into 250 ml/9 fl oz lukewarm water and dissolve it along with the sugar. Stir in 4 tablespoons of the flour, cover and leave the resulting sponge to prove in a warm place for 15 minutes.

Sift the remaining flour into a bowl, make a hollow in the centre and pour the sponge into it. Add the salt and 3–4 tablespoons of the olive oil and knead into a silky dough. Shape it into a ball, cover and leave it to rise in a warm spot for 1 hour or until doubled in volume.

Grease a baking tray with olive oil and preheat the oven to 250°C/480°F/gas mark 9. Vigorously knead the dough again, working in the sage leaves. On a floured surface, roll out the dough to a thickness of about 2 cm/¾ inch, then place it on the baking tray. Gently press down on the dough with your fingers to form many little indentations. Brush it with the remaining olive oil, scatter sea salt over the top and bake for 20 to 25 minutes. Cut into squares to serve.

Focaccia con cipolle
Focaccia with Onions

40 g/1½ oz compressed fresh yeast or 2 sachets easy-blend dried yeast
1 pinch sugar
400 g/14 oz flour, plus extra for dusting
1 tsp salt
125 ml/4 fl oz olive oil, plus extra for greasing
2 onions, cut into thin rings
100 g/3½ oz black olives, stoned
2–3 garlic cloves, finely chopped
1 tbsp coarse sea salt
2 tsp crushed peppercorns

Crumble the yeast into 250 ml/9 fl oz lukewarm water and dissolve it along with the sugar. Stir in 4 tablespoons of the flour, cover and leave the resulting sponge to prove in a warm place for 15 minutes.

Sift the remaining flour into a bowl, make a hollow in the centre and pour the sponge into it. Add the salt and 3–4 tablespoons olive oil and knead into a silky dough. Shape it into a ball, cover and leave to rise for 1 hour or until doubled in volume.

Grease a baking tray with olive oil and preheat the oven to 250°C/480°F/gas mark 9. Vigorously knead the dough. On a floured surface, roll it out to a thickness of about 2 cm/¾ inch, then place on the baking tray and prick with a fork. Cover with the onions and olives and sprinkle with garlic. Drizzle on the remaining olive oil, season with sea salt and pepper, and bake for about 20 minutes.

To make focaccia dough, first dissolve the yeast in lukewarm water along with a little sugar.

Stir in a small amount of flour, cover and leave the sponge to rise in a warm, draught-free spot.

Then knead the sponge with the other ingredients by hand or a food processor.

Put the dough in a bowl, cover it and leave it to rise until it has doubled in volume.

On a floured surface, roll out the dough into an oval about 2 cm (¾ inch) thick.

Place it on a greased baking tray and cover with onion rings and olives.

Pizza

There is probably no other dish that is as internationally synonymous with Italian cuisine as the *pizza*, although Italians principally understand it to mean Neapolitan pizza. This is all the more remarkable since pizza is the offspring of peasants' kitchens. Born of necessity, it was the means to concoct a flavourful, satisfying meal from a few very simple ingredients.

The first written pizza recipe dates back to 1858, but Neapolitans were already familiar with it at the beginning of the eighteenth century. Pizza dough with tomatoes was first documented in Naples at the end of the seventeenth century. Pizza's triumphal journey around the globe did not start in Naples, but rather in far away New York City. In 1905, Signore Lombardi opened the first pizzeria in New York's Little Italy neighbourhood. American pizzas, unlike those from pizza's hometown of Naples, were lavishly decked out with a variety of ingredients and soon became a smash hit. Indeed, pizza is one of the Americans' favourite foods: 40 hectares of pizza is consumed every day in the United States!

The thin, flat dough is first covered with flavourful tomato sauce.

Then the pizza is topped with buffalo mozzarella cut into small pieces.

Marinara and Margherita

When King Umberto I of Italy and his wife, Margaret of Savoy, visited the city of Naples on 11 June 1889, she expressed the desire to try a local speciality. In the royal kitchen, pizza baker Raffaele Esposito created a new variation on the ordinary *pizza marinara* for them. *Pizza marinara*, made with garlic, oregano and oil, was chiefly popular among fishermen coming ashore in the early morning after a night at sea. Raffaele regarded this simple garlic pizza as inappropriate and chose ingredients representing the Italian national colours instead: green (basil), white (mozzarella) and red (tomatoes). It was named *pizza margherita* in honour of the queen. She must have been very pleased, because from then on Raffaele was known by the title *Fornitore della Real Casa*, Purveyor to the Royal Court. One of the oldest pizzerias in Naples, the Pizzeria Da Michele, to this day serves nothing but *pizza marinara* and *pizza margherita*.

The One and Only Authentic Neapolitan Pizza

The *Associazione Vera Pizza Napoletana* endeavours to defend Neapolitan pizza against cheap imitations. This organization has established standards for a genuine pizza. An authentic pizza must be made of dough that is kneaded by hand, its crust must be formed and flattened solely by hand, and it must be round. Pizza dough may consist only of flour, yeast, salt and water.

A genuine Neopolitan pizza has a maximum diameter of 30 cm (12 inches), and it must be baked directly on the stone floor of the pizza oven. All deviations from this original recipe 'must lie within the limits of good taste and culinary responsibility'.

Fresh basil leaves and rich, fruity olive oil lend pizzas colour and flavour.

The Pizza Oven

When asked why their pizzas taste so much better than pizzas anywhere else, Italians do not have to think for long before responding. It is still the wood-fired ovens that lend the dough its very special flavour. A genuine pizza oven is dome shaped, and its interior walls are lined with ovenproof (heat-resistant) tiles. In the small village of Maiano near Naples, these ovens have been handmade out of clay from the Sorrento Peninsula since the fifteenth century, using a special technique.

On the stone floor of the pizza oven, a wood fire burns directly on the baking surface. But the fire hardly produces any smoke, because cherry or olive wood are burnt. The flames heat up the tile walls, while the distinctive shape of the oven provides for even distribution of the heat. When fully heated, the burning wood is pushed to the rear of the oven to make room for the pizzas. The glowing embers keep the temperature of the oven at a minimum of 400°C (750°F). At this incredible temperature, the pizza bakes very quickly. In less than a minute, the base of the dough is crisp, the tomatoes are not yet dry, the mozzarella is perfectly melted and the healthy fatty acids in the olive oil have not yet been destroyed.

Piadina

Piadina is to Emilia-Romagna and the northern Marche provinces what pizza is to Naples: a simple and inexpensive dish, eaten in the fingers and enthusiastically accompanied by a small glass of table wine. Piadina consists of wheat flour, lard, salt, bicarbonate of soda and water. Using a rolling pin, the dough is rolled out into thin circles about 20 cm (8 inches) in diameter and then baked, traditionally in a terracotta pan. The finished *piadina* are folded over and cut into four pieces, or rolled up. They are eaten hot with cheese, ham, sausage or salad, and can also be stuffed with sautéed vegetables.

Basic Pizza Dough

40 g/1½ oz compressed fresh yeast or
2 sachets easy-blend dried yeast

½ tsp sugar

400 g/14 oz flour,
plus extra for dusting

1 tsp salt

3 tbsp olive oil

Crumble the yeast into a small bowl and sprinkle with the sugar. Add 125 ml/4 fl oz lukewarm water, then stir to dissolve the yeast and sugar. Cover with a clean tea towel and prove in a warm spot for 30 minutes. Sift the flour into a large bowl. Make a hollow in the centre and pour the yeast mixture, salt, olive oil and 5–7 tablespoons of water into it. Knead everything into a smooth, silky dough, then shape it into a ball. Dust the ball with a little flour, cover and set aside in a warm place to rise for an additional hour, or until doubled in volume.

Pizzette

Pizzette
Small Pizzas

40 g/1½ oz compressed fresh yeast or
2 sachets easy-blend dried yeast

½ tsp sugar

400 g/14 oz flour, plus extra for dusting

1 tsp salt

60 ml/2 fl oz olive oil,
plus extra for greasing

500 g/1 lb 2 oz tomatoes

1 radicchio

100 g/3½ oz bacon, cut into strips

50 g/1¾ oz pine kernels

Crumble the yeast into a small bowl and sprinkle with the sugar. Add 125 ml/4 fl oz lukewarm water, then stir to dissolve the yeast and sugar. Cover with a clean tea towel and prove in a warm spot for 30 minutes. Sift the flour into a large bowl. Make a hollow in the centre and pour the yeast mixture, salt, 3 tablespoons of olive oil and 5–7 tablespoons of water into it. Knead everything into a smooth, silky dough, then shape it into a ball. Dust the ball with a little flour, cover and set aside in a warm place to rise for about 1 hour or until doubled in volume.

Grease two baking sheets with olive oil and preheat the oven to 200°C/390°F/ gas mark 6. Peel and quarter the tomatoes, remove the seeds, and cut into small dice. Trim the radicchio and break it into bite-sized pieces.

Divide the dough into 12 equal pieces. Form each into a ball, flatten and place the rounds on the baking sheets. Top with the diced tomato and bacon and drizzle on the remaining oil. Bake for 15 minutes, then sprinkle the radicchio and pine kernels over the *pizzette* and bake for another 5 minutes.

Pizza di patate
Apulian Potato Pizza

750 g/1 lb 10 oz potatoes

1 tsp salt

3 tbsp flour

70 ml/2½ fl oz olive oil,
plus extra for greasing

400 g/14 oz canned peeled tomatoes

100 g/3½ oz black olives

12 anchovies in oil

150 g/5 oz feta cheese, diced

1 onion, cut into rings

2 garlic cloves, finely chopped

½ tsp rosemary

½ tsp dried oregano

freshly ground pepper

Bring a saucepan of salted water to the boil and cook the potatoes. Drain, rinse them in cold water, peel, and put through a potato press while still hot. Stir in the salt, flour and 2 tablespoons of the olive oil and leave the mixture to cool.

Grease a springform cake tin (28 cm/ 11 inches in diameter) with olive oil and pre- heat the oven to 220°C/430°F/gas mark 7. Drain the tomatoes and cut them into small pieces. Press the potato dough into the pan, creating a rim. Spread the tomatoes, olives, anchovies, feta cheese, onion and garlic on the dough. Sprinkle with rosemary, oregano and pepper, then bake for approximately 30 minutes.

The Most Popular Pizzas

Pizza con gamberi
Prawn Pizza

1 pizza dough
(see recipe on page 101)
750 g/1 lb 10 oz tomatoes
600 g/1 lb 5 oz cooked prawns, shelled
100 g/3½ oz black olives
2 tsp fennel seeds
4 tbsp olive oil, plus extra for greasing
1 handful rocket
flour for dusting
salt and pepper

Preheat the oven to 225°C/435°F/gas mark 7 and grease four round pizza pans. Peel and quarter the tomatoes, remove the seeds, and cut into small dice. Rinse the prawns and drain well.

Divide the dough into four equal portions and roll them into circles on a floured surface. Place the dough on the pizza pans and top with the tomatoes, prawns and olives. Season with the fennel seeds, salt and pepper and drizzle with the olive oil. Bake for about 20 minutes.

Wash the rocket and remove any coarse stalks. Shortly before serving, distribute the rocket leaves on top of the pizzas.

Pizza Margherita

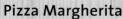

1 pizza dough
(see recipe on page 101)
75 ml/2½ fl oz olive oil,
plus extra for greasing
2 small onions, diced
400 g/14 oz canned diced tomatoes
50 g/1¾ oz canned tomato sauce
1 tsp oregano
400 g/14 oz mozzarella
salt and pepper
flour for dusting
basil leaves to garnish

Heat 4 tablespoons of the olive oil and sauté the onions until translucent. Add both kinds of tomatoes and the oregano, and season with salt and pepper. Cook the sauce for about 30 minutes on medium heat.

Preheat the oven to 225°C/435°F/gas mark 7 and grease four round pizza pans with olive oil. Divide the dough into four equal portions and roll them into circles on a floured surface. Place the circles of dough on the pizza pans.

Thinly slice the mozzarella. Brush the dough with the tomato sauce, cover with mozzarella slices, and drizzle on the remaining olive oil. Bake for about 20 minutes, then garnish with basil leaves and serve immediately.

Pizza alla marinara
Mariner's Pizza

1 pizza dough
(see recipe on page 101)
800 g/1 lb 12 oz canned diced tomatoes
3–4 garlic cloves, finely chopped
1 tbsp oregano
50 g/1¾ oz capers
100 g/3½ oz black olives
200 g/7 oz Bel Paese cheese, grated
3 tbsp olive oil, plus extra for greasing
flour for dusting
salt
freshly ground pepper

Preheat the oven to 225°C/435°F/gas mark 7 and grease four round pizza pans with olive oil. Divide the dough into four equal portions and roll them into circles on a floured surface. Place the circles of dough on the pizza pans.

Distribute the tomatoes on the dough. Season with the garlic, oregano, salt and pepper. Scatter on the capers and olives and sprinkle with the grated cheese. Drizzle on the olive oil, then bake the pizzas for about 20 minutes.

Pizza quattro stagioni
Four Seasons Pizza

1 pizza dough
(see recipe on page 101)
1 tbsp butter
200 g/7 oz mushrooms, sliced
4 tomatoes
200 g/7 oz cooked ham
200 g/7 oz mozzarella
4 artichoke hearts in oil
16 black olives
1 tsp oregano
4 tbsp olive oil, plus extra for greasing
flour for dusting
salt and pepper

Preheat the oven to 225°C/435°F/gas mark 7 and grease four round pizza pans with olive oil. Heat the butter and sauté the mushrooms for 10 minutes. Peel and quarter the tomatoes, remove the seeds, and cut into small dice. Cut the ham into small pieces. Thinly slice the mozzarella. Quarter the artichoke hearts.

Divide the dough into four equal portions and roll them into circles on a floured surface. Place the circles of dough on the pizza pans.

Distribute the tomatoes and mozzarella evenly on the pizzas. Cover one quarter of each of the pizzas with one of the following toppings: mushrooms, ham, artichokes and olives. Season with the oregano, salt and pepper and drizzle with the olive oil. Bake for about 20 minutes.

Sardenaira
Onion Pizza

1 pizza dough
(see recipe on page 101)
500 g/1 lb 2 oz onions
4 garlic cloves
6 tbsp olive oil,
plus extra for greasing
2 tbsp finely chopped fresh oregano
400 g/14 oz canned diced tomatoes
50 g/1¾ oz salted anchovies
100 g/3½ oz black olives,
stoned and halved
flour for dusting
salt and pepper

Preheat the oven to 225°C/435°F/gas mark 7 and grease four round pizza pans with a little olive oil.

Slice the onions into very fine rings and finely slice the garlic. Heat 4 tablespoons of the olive oil in a deep frying pan and fry the onions and garlic. Stir in the oregano. Remove from the heat and cool slightly.

Divide the dough into four equal portions and roll them into circles on a floured surface. Place the circles of dough on the pizza pans. Top the dough with the onions and tomatoes. Season with salt and pepper.

Rinse the anchovies in cold water, then drain. Distribute the anchovies and olives on the pizzas and drizzle with the remaining olive oil. Bake for about 20 minutes.

Sfinciuni
Sicilian Pizza

1 pizza dough
(see recipe on page 101)
75 ml/2½ fl oz olive oil,
plus extra for greasing
1 small onion, finely chopped
800 g/1 lb 12 oz canned diced tomatoes
300 g/11 oz salted sprats (sardines)
150 g/5 oz caciocavallo cheese (cascaval)
2 tbsp breadcrumbs
flour for dusting
salt and pepper

Preheat the oven to 175°C/350°F/gas mark 4 and grease a springform cake tin (26 cm/10 inches in diameter) with olive oil.

Heat 2 tablespoons of the olive oil and sauté the onions. Add the tomatoes, season with salt and pepper, and leave the sauce to thicken for about 20 minutes.

Rinse the sprats under running cold water and pat dry. Remove the heads and bone the fish. Finely dice the cheese.

Roll out the pizza dough on a floured surface and place it in the springform tin, pressing the dough about 5 cm/2 inches up the side. Brush it with half of the tomato sauce, cover with half of the sprats and add half of the cheese. Then bake for 20 minutes.

Remove the pizza from the oven and top it with the remaining tomato sauce, cheese and sprats. Sprinkle with the breadcrumbs and drizzle on the remaining olive oil. Bake for another 10 minutes.

Pizza alla napoletana
Neapolitan Pizza

1 pizza dough
(see recipe on page 101)
800 g/1 lb 12 oz tomatoes
200 g/7 oz mozzarella
8 anchovies in oil
2 tsp dried oregano
4 tbsp olive oil, plus extra
to grease the pan
flour for dusting
salt and pepper

Preheat the oven to 225°C/435°F/gas mark 7 and grease four round pizza pans with olive oil. Peel and quarter the tomatoes, remove the seeds, and cut into small dice. Thinly slice the mozzarella. Finely chop the anchovies.

Divide the dough into four equal portions and roll them into circles on a floured surface. Place the circles of dough on the pizza pans. Top the dough with the tomatoes, mozzarella and anchovies. Season with the oregano, salt and pepper. Drizzle with the olive oil and bake for about 20 minutes.

Pizza con carciofi
Pizza with Artichokes

1 pizza dough
(see recipe on page 101)
400 g/14 oz artichoke hearts in oil
200 g/7 oz mozzarella
4 tbsp olive oil,
plus extra for greasing
flour for dusting
8 mild chillies in oil
4 garlic cloves, finely chopped
2 tbsp finely chopped parsley
salt and pepper

Preheat the oven to 225°C/435°F/gas mark 7 and grease four round pizza pans with a little olive oil.

Slice the artichoke hearts lengthways and finely dice the mozzarella.

Divide the dough into four equal portions and roll them into circles on a floured surface. Place the circles of dough on the pizza pans. Distribute the artichokes and peppers on top. Sprinkle with garlic and half the parsley. Season with salt and pepper and drizzle on the olive oil. Put the mozzarella on top of the pizzas and bake for about 20 minutes. Sprinkle with the remaining parsley before serving.

Pizza con carciofi

Insalate e Minestre

Salads
and
Soups

SALADS

Colourful salads grace the table at nearly every meal in Italy. Crisp salad leaves, wild herbs and fresh vegetables that are ideal for making delicious salads in very little time are found practically year round at every market. But mushrooms, poultry, fish and pulses also combine perfectly with the right dressing, enriching the classic selection of salads.

The word 'salad' comes from the Latin *salata* and literally means 'brined'. This refers to the original method of preparation. Raw vegetable salads were usually flavoured with a very salty dressing. The proper seasoning of salad was a highly regarded art in ancient Rome. There were special chefs who were responsible solely for the salads at large banquets.

An old proverb says that you need four people to make a successful salad: a spendthrift to pour on the oil, a miser for the vinegar, a wise man to add the salt and a fool to toss the salad vigorously. Except for the fool, the expression is still valid today. After all, to avoid damaging the delicate leaves, tender leaf lettuce needs to be carefully tossed by hand or with salad servers made of olive wood. And the dressing is not added until shortly before serving so that the salad stays crisp.

In addition to their preparation, leaf lettuces are delicate in other ways: the fresher they are, the more valuable nutrients they contain. Only hardy types such as endive, cos lettuce and radicchio keep at all well. Since some of the vitamins in lettuce are water soluble, it is best to rinse it briefly under cold running water, and lettuce should never be left sitting in water for any length of time. The leaves should either be spun in a salad spinner or dried with a clean tea towel, because you do not want to dilute the dressing. Depending on the recipe, the leaves can be torn into bite-sized pieces or cut into strips.

Batavia *originally comes from France and is a relative of iceberg lettuce. It is green inside and the leaf edges are reddish. Batavia is mainly grown in hothouses and is used like lettuce.*

Oakleaf lettuce, foglia di quercia, *a type of looseleaf lettuce, takes its name from the shape of the leaf edges that resemble oak leaves. The reddish leaves are very tender, wilt quickly and taste slightly nutty.*

Endive, indivia scarola, *does not form a tight head. The wide, undivided leaves are more robust than those of lettuce and have a slightly bitter taste. They are cut into strips.*

Frisee, indivia riccia, *is a curly endive with deeply slit leaves. Its flavour is somewhat more bitter than that of its unfledged relatives, but it also has more bite. The individual leaves are pulled apart.*

Bibb lettuce, lattuga, *is available year round in Italy. The leaves are detached singly from the stalk with the exception of the heart and torn into bite-sized pieces. In winter, this lettuce is grown in greenhouses and has a fairly neutral flavour.*

Dandelions, dente di leone (also insalata matta, sofione, tarassaco), grow wild in meadows. The leaves are tender, bitter-sweet and serrated like radicchio. Dandelions grown outdoors have sturdy green leaves; you can spot the hothouse variety by its bright yellow-green leaves.

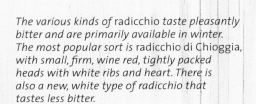

The various kinds of radicchio taste pleasantly bitter and are primarily available in winter. The most popular sort is radicchio di Chioggia, with small, firm, wine red, tightly packed heads with white ribs and heart. There is also a new, white type of radicchio that tastes less bitter.

Belgian Endive

Indivia belga, or Belgian endive, is grown in darkened places or beneath opaque foil so that the leaves remain white. About 200 years ago, a gardener in Brussels discovered chicory roots that had begun to sprout in a dark basement corner of the botanical gardens. They were the original impetus for what has today become a worldwide love of Belgian endive. The flavour is fresh and slightly spicy. Only the stalk is bitter, and is thus cut out in a wedge. The leaves can either be cut into strips or used whole for dipping.

Even if Belgium is considered the home of Belgian endive today, you can glean from Pliny the Elder, one of the most famous naturalists of antiquity, that the Romans already knew about bleached chicory leaves in salads. He described the healing powers of this herbaceous perennial. Chicory is particularly rich in carotene, phosphorus and calcium. From Italy comes red chicory, a cross between white chicory and red radicchio.

Cos lettuce, romana, has a flavour similar to Bibb lettuce, but also has a markedly sweet and distinctive taste. The robust outer leaves are cut into strips; the lighter heart is very tender. In earlier times, the leaves were tied together while the lettuce was growing in order to keep the heart pale. New varieties that grow up to 40 cm high can take care of this on their own .

Lollo rosso lettuce is the crinkled version of Batavia, a red variety of lettuce from France. It tastes a little nutty and adds visual contrast to the salad plate. Lollo verde or lollo bianco is its green cousin. It has very curly, wavy leaves with bright green or yellow-toned edges.

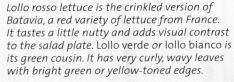

Olive Oil

The olive harvest takes place in November and December. Traditionally, the ripe olives are either knocked down from the trees with wooden poles, picked by hand or carefully stripped from the branches with a special kind of small rake. They are then caught in nets or tarpaulins that have been laid out beneath the trees. On average, a single tree bears between 50 and 70 kg (110–155 lb) of olives, from which about 8 litres (14 pints) of olive oil are produced.

Even though new methods have come about in the meantime, most oil presses are still operated with hydraulic pressure. First of all, heavy millstones crush the fruit and stones into a paste. The paste, spread on discs and hydraulically pressed at a temperature corresponding to that of the human body, yields an emulsion consisting of oil and vegetable water. This mixture is separated by means of a vertical centrifuge, and the impurities are then removed from the extracted olive oil by filtering it. One modern method works via centrifugation, which uses a 'decanter' that separates the oil from the vegetable liquid and pomace before it is filtered. Systems such as this are gradually beginning to replace traditional hydraulic presses.

Regardless of the pressing method, no heat can be applied to the fruit, for that could harm the quality of the final product.

In the old days, when the presses were still run by hand or powered by animals, the paste usually had to be squeezed two or as even three times to extract every last bit of oil from the olives. Prior to the second and third pressings, hot water was poured over the previously pressed paste. If ripe olives are not properly pressed, the proportion of free fatty acids in the oil increases. They are the result of a natural chemical process that greatly influences the quality of an olive oil's flavour. The fewer oleic acids an olive oil contains, the better its quality.

As a rule, today olives are mechanically pressed, and only once. This results in various grades of oil with differing flavours, depending on the country of origin, location, climate and ripeness of the fruit. A series of chemophysical parameters are measured in order to be able to divide them into grades. In the end, the sensibilities and the sense of taste and smell of eight to twelve experts determine how the oil is actually classified. They check the flavour and smell of the olive oil and ascertain whether the products are defective.

Since 1 November 2003, extra virgin olive oil may only carry the annotation 'cold-pressed' or 'cold-extracted' if the oil was pressed at a temperature of less than 27°C (80.6°F). Admittedly, warm water is sometimes used in modern presses, due to the different kinds of olives and rather variable consistency of the paste.

Olive trees can live for several hundred years. With advancing age, they become ever more gnarled.

For the production of the highest quality oils, the ripe olives are still harvested by hand today.

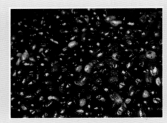

The undamaged, healthy fruit is stored in well-ventilated rooms until processing.

Whole olives are washed and ground into a thick paste using large millstones.

The olive paste is then spread on fibre discs that are stacked on top of one another.

The discs are firmly compressed so that an emulsion of vegetable water and oil flows out of them.

There are legally established classifications for olive oil that inform consumers about what they are buying:

Extra Virgin Olive Oil, or *extra vergine*: This is the highest grade of olive oil. It is extracted directly from the olives exclusively by mechanical means. Its oleic acid content may not exceed 0.8 grams per 100 grams of oil.

Virgin Olive Oil: This oil is also mechanically pressed directly from the olives. Its oleic acid content may be up to a maximum of 3 grams per 100 grams of oil.

Olive Oil: Oil that has not been classified as virgin olive oil is further processed and refined, then some virgin olive oil is blended in to restore the characteristic flavour of olive oil. It is sold simply as olive oil. Its oleic acid content may exceed 3 grams per 100 grams of oil.

The indication 'from Italy' means that the oil must come from olives that were grown and pressed in Italy. If the label contains the name of the producer and the words '*prodotto e confenzionato da*', then you can be certain that particular olive oil was produced and bottled in the place or region mentioned. Olive oils that are so labelled come mainly from smaller, family-owned businesses. The same applies even more strictly to olive oils that come from protected regions of origin or protected geographical areas of cultivation.

Oil and olives were already daily foodstuffs in ancient Rome. Their own olive trees were not sufficient to meet the Roman's needs, not by a long shot. They imported oil from the empire's provinces, particularly from Spain and North Africa. Mount Testaccio near Ostia is proof of how much that amounted to: it is an artificial hill that consists exclusively of the shards of broken oil vessels.

Italian Olive Oils

When it comes to olive oils, about 250 different types of olive trees produce a wide palette of flavours. Broadly speaking, Italy can be divided into four cultivation zones:

Liguria, Sardinia and the Coastal Zones of Tuscany Due to the particular marine climate, the oils from here have a rather light and delicate flavour.

Central Italy The oils from Tuscany and Umbria are, above all, highly aromatic, especially when freshly pressed, and have a strong 'bite' in the aftertaste.

Southern Italy These are very pungent oils with an intense, almost 'fatty' olive flavour that results from the hot climate.

Sicily Various microclimates on the island generate a rich variety of oils, found nowhere else in Italy.

Aceto Balsamico & Co.

In the Italian provinces of Modena and Reggio Emilia, an extraordinary flavoured vinegar, *aceto balsamico*, is produced from white Trebbiano and Sauvignon grape must, which is the juice and skins left after grapes are pressed. In Reggio Emilia, the must of Lambrusco grapes is also used. The incomparable flavour of balsamic vinegar is not due to herbs or any other ingredients, but rather solely to the fact that it matures in various wooden casks without preservatives or artificial colouring for many years.

First, about half of the grape must is boiled for several hours and placed in wooden casks, where it undergoes fermentation. During its maturation, which lasts at least twelve years, it is decanted into smaller and smaller containers that are made of different woods: oak, chestnut, cherry, ash, and mulberry. In the end, between 2.5 and 5 litres (4–9 pints) of balsamic vinegar result from every 100 kg (220 lb) of grapes. Some of the evaporated vinegar is added to younger vinegar, and a portion of the mature vinegar is returned to the 'youngest' cask containing grape must. This is why no age is given on the label of *aceto balsamico tradizionale*. The designation *extravecchio* (or occasionally *stravecchio*) may only adorn vinegar that has been aged for twenty-five years or more. Just 10,000 litres (17,600 pints) of *aceto balsamico tradizionale* are produced annually.

The name balsamico is not protected. Any vinegar can be called *aceto balsamico*, no matter where it is manufactured. Generic balsamic vinegars are most often high-quality fruit and wine vinegars. Through the addition of flavourings and caramel syrup, they become well-balanced, delicate, fruity vinegar creations. *Balsamico bianco,* or white balsamic vinegar, is milder than the average wine vinegar. The various flavours of white balsamic are shown to perfection and no acidity interferes with them.

Aceto balsamco di Modena is a mixture of regular wine vinegar and concentrated grape juice that gets its brown colour from spirit caramel. The better brands add a little genuine *balsamico tradizionale*.

A view of Modena (above)

In Italy, there are a range of aromatic vinegars used for various purposes and with various ingredients. From left to right:

Giusti aceto stravecchio, Aceto di vino cabernet, Giusti aceto balsamico DOP, Giusti aceto balsamico, Giusti aceto balsamico banda rossa

Genuine aceto balsamico tradizionale *matures for at least twelve years in wooden casks.*

A linen cloth covers the tap opening and prevents dust and dirt entering.

During maturation, the balsamico is decanted into another, smaller wooden cask every year.

At the end of the long maturation period, no more than 5 litres (9 pints) of balsamic vinegar, at best, remain from the original 100 kg (220 lb) of grapes.

Favourite Salads

Insalata di arance
Orange Salad

4 oranges
1 red onion
2 tbsp finely chopped parsley
4 tbsp olive oil
salt
freshly ground pepper

Peel the oranges and remove the pith, then slice in rounds. Lay them out in a fan pattern on a plate. Peel and halve the onion, and thinly slice one half. Finely chop the other and combine with the parsley.

Sprinkle the sliced and chopped onions over the orange slices, season with a little salt and pepper, and drizzle olive oil over the salad. Cover with clingfilm and marinate for 1 hour in the refrigerator. Remove from the refrigerator 5 minutes before serving.

Insalata di tonno e fagioli
Bean Salad with Tuna

400 g/14 oz white beans, cooked
4 spring onions, finely chopped
1 fresh red chilli, finely chopped
2 celery sticks, finely diced
2 tbsp lemon juice
6 tbsp olive oil
170 g/6 oz canned tuna in oil
1 tbsp finely chopped parsley
salt
freshly ground pepper

Mix together the cooked beans, spring onions, chilli and celery. Whisk together the lemon juice and olive oil to make a dressing, season with salt and pepper, and pour it over the salad. Set aside to marinate for 15 minutes.

Drain the tuna fish and break into bite-sized chunks. Stir the tuna and parsley into the bean salad.

Olio e sale alla barese
Tomato Salad with Cucumber, Onion and Bread

1 small cucumber, peeled
2 beef tomatoes
1 white onion
4 tbsp olive oil
2 tbsp white wine vinegar
2 slices of white country bread
salt
freshly ground pepper

Slice the cucumber and tomatoes and place them in a salad bowl. Slice the onion into fine rings, then toss them with the cucumber and tomatoes.

Whisk together the olive oil and vinegar, season with salt and pepper, and pour over the salad. Marinate for 20 minutes.

Toast the bread slices on both sides under a grill or in the oven until golden brown, then cut into bite-sized pieces. Toss them into the salad and serve immediately.

Insalata di carciofi
Artichoke Salad

8 small purple artichokes
3 tbsp lemon juice
250 ml/9 fl oz white wine
½ tsp salt, plus extra to season
100 ml/3½ fl oz olive oil
2 garlic cloves, finely chopped
1 small red onion, finely chopped
2 tbsp tarragon vinegar
6 basil leaves
freshly ground pepper

Remove the hard outer leaves from the artichokes and cut away the upper half of the tender inner leaves. Shorten the stalks to 5 cm and peel them. Immediately place the artichokes in a saucepan with water and the lemon juice.

Add the white wine, salt and 2 tablespoons of the olive oil to the pan and bring to the boil. Cover and simmer on medium heat for 20 to 25 minutes. Then take the artichokes out of the water, cool slightly, then cut them in half lengthways.

Stir the garlic and onion with 2 tablespoons of the artichoke cooking water, the tarragon vinegar, and salt and pepper to taste. Mix in the remaining olive oil. Cut the basil leaves into fine strips. Lay the artichoke halves face up in a bowl, pour the dressing over them and sprinkle the basil on top. Serve while moderately hot.

Radicchio alla vicentina
Radicchio Salad

400 g/14 oz radicchio di Chioggia
100 g/3½ oz pancetta
1 tbsp olive oil
2 tbsp balsamic vinegar
salt
freshly ground pepper

Trim and wash the radicchio, then spin it dry. Tear the leaves into bite-sized pieces and arrange them on four plates. Finely dice the pancetta.

Heat the olive oil in a frying pan and fry the pancetta until crisp. Deglaze with the vinegar and season with salt and pepper. Pour the pancetta and pan juices over the radicchio and serve immediately.

Panzanella
Bread Salad

400 g/14 oz day-old
Tuscan country bread
1 small cucumber
2 small white onions
100 ml/3½ fl oz olive oil
2–3 tbsp red wine vinegar
500 g/1 lb 2 oz tomatoes, sliced
1 handful rocket
salt
freshly ground pepper

Cut the bread into slices about 2 cm/³/₄ inch thick and soak them in a bowl of cold water for no more than 10 minutes.

Peel the cucumber, cut it in half lengthways, and deseed. Thinly slice the cucumber halves. Slice the onions into fine rings. Thoroughly squeeze the water from the bread slices and tear into bite-sized pieces.

Heat half the olive oil in a non-stick frying pan and sauté the bread, turning it constantly. Remove from the heat and leave to cool.

Whisk together the remaining olive oil, the vinegar, salt and pepper. In a larger bowl, combine the cucumbers, tomatoes, onions, toast and dressing.

Wash the rocket, removing any wilted leaves or coarse stalks, and pat it dry. Line four bowls with the rocket and arrange the bread salad on it. In the original version, bread salad was covered and left to marinate in a cool place for several hours. Nowadays, it is usually served immediately so that the toast remains crisp.

Asparagi all'olio e aceto balsamico
Asparagus Salad
with Balsamic Vinegar

400 g/14 oz each: green asparagus,
white asparagus
75 ml/2½ fl oz olive oil
2 tbsp balsamic vinegar
salt
freshly ground pepper
parsley leaves to garnish

Wash and trim the asparagus. Lightly peel the white asparagus and remove the woody ends from both kinds. Cut all the asparagus stalks to the same length, bundle them in portions and place in a deep, narrow saucepan. Fill the pan two-thirds full with cold water, add a little salt, cover the pan and bring to the boil. Cook until the asparagus is tender yet still crisp.

Remove the asparagus from the water and drain well. Whisk together the olive oil, vinegar, salt and pepper to make a dressing. Lay the asparagus on a serving plate, pour the dressing over it and garnish with parsley. Serve while moderately hot.

Rucola

Rucola is an annual wild herb with long, dark green leaves that is known by many names in English: rocket, Italian cress, arugula or rucola. The variety with delicate leaves is a familiar salad ingredient, whereas the broad-leaved version is mainly used to produce oil. The more mature types of rocket taste slightly sour and a little peppery. Most cultivated types of rocket that are available today have a predominantly nutty, mild flavour. Although it looks robust at first glance, rocket is very delicate and wilts easily. It is most often used in combination with other salad leaves, often with fruit. Rocket with bresaola or prosciutto and Parmesan is a very popular appetizer, but rocket is being used more and more on pizzas, or finely cut and mixed into pasta dishes.

Insalata con rucola e parmigiano
Rocket and Parmesan Salad

2 handfuls rocket
1 small fennel bulb
75 ml/2½ fl oz olive oil
2 tbsp balsamic vinegar
100 g/3½ oz Parmesan
50 g/1¾ oz pine kernels
salt
freshly ground pepper

Wash the rocket, removing any wilted leaves or coarse stalks, and pat it dry. Divide the leaves among four plates. Halve the fennel bulb, slice it finely and spread some over the rocket on each plate.

Whisk together the olive oil, balsamic vinegar, salt and pepper and drizzle over the salad. Top the salad with shaved Parmesan. Dry-roast the pine kernels in an ungreased frying pan until golden brown, then sprinkle over each serving of salad.

Insalata con rucola e parmigiano

SOUPS

The Italians often say that soups are the true test for aficionados of great food. To prepare a good soup requires time, care and attention, beginning with shopping for just the right ingredients. The ingredients that go into the soup kettle vary from region to region, but one thing is the same throughout Italy: the stock is made from a piece of meat and never from a stock cube. Every home maker and every butcher knows the best cuts of meat for a hearty stock: breast, back, stomach, shoulder and tongue. Poultry stock is made not only from soup chickens, but also from duck, goose and capon meat.

All soups are based on two basic recipes: *minestra in brodo*, which is a broth with vegetables, noodles or rice; and *zuppa*, a thick soup that is frequently poured over a slice of bread. *Minestrone* is the most famous Italian soup, and it can be found in countless variations. In the northern regions of Italy it is prepared with rice and Parmesan, in Tuscany with beans and fresh olive oil, and in the south with tomatoes and garlic.

Zuppa has peasant roots. It was made from whatever was in season, as well as leftovers from slaughtering or fishing. Some delicious, filling examples are spelt soup, Tuscan cabbage soup, hearty tripe stew and fish soup, which is often served as a main course.

Minestrone

200 g/7 oz dried white beans
2 potatoes
2 carrots
1 celery stick
1 onion, finely chopped
1 garlic clove, finely chopped
4 tbsp olive oil
2 small courgettes
2 small tomatoes
150 g/5 oz peas
125 g/4½ oz pearl barley
125 g/4½ oz smoked bacon, cut in fine strips (optional)
50 g/1¾ oz grated Parmesan
1 tbsp finely chopped basil
salt
freshly ground pepper

Soak the beans overnight. Wash, trim and peel the potatoes, carrots and celery, then cut into small dice. Heat the olive oil in a large soup kettle and fry the onion and garlic until translucent. Add the diced vegetables to the pot and brown briefly.

Pour the soaking water off the beans. Add the beans and 2 litres/3½ pints of water to the kettle, cover and simmer on low heat for 1 hour.

Thinly slice the courgettes. Peel and quarter the tomatoes, remove the seeds, and dice. Add the courgettes, tomatoes, peas, pearl barley and the bacon (if using) to the soup. Season with salt and pepper and cook for an additional 20 to 25 minutes, stirring occasionally. Prior to serving, sprinkle on the Parmesan and basil. Older recipes called for minestrone to be simmered for up to 4 hours, but today many people prefer their vegetables a little crisper.

Zolfino Beans

Zolfino beans, also called *burrino* beans because of their luxurious texture, come from the Arno Valley in Tuscany. The tiny, bulbous, pale yellow beans grow on diminutive bushes. They have a thin pod that melts on the tongue 'like a communion wafer'. The pulp has a uniform texture, almost like a purée.

For a long time, they were grown exclusively around the hamlet of La Penna and were almost unknown outside of the area. They were a peasant food that neither made it into the kitchens of the wealthy nor on to priests' tables. The beans were cooked in spring water for hours and eaten with fresh onions dipped in salt. in the meantime, however, the Slow Food Movement has discovered the beans, making this local speciality famous far beyond Tuscany. A distinctive feature of these beans is that they must be cooked for at least four hours in order for their full flavour to develop.

Pulses

Pulses, whether lentils, beans or chick-peas, play an important role in Italian cuisine. In many cultures, pulses have traditionally been associated with 'peasant' cooking. In Italy, however, they have always been found on gourmet's tables, and happily so. Today, nutrition experts advise us to replace meat with protein-rich pulses – and it is ideal to do so in accompaniment with pasta dishes.

High-grade vegetable protein is not the only plus point with regard to pulses. They also contain B vitamins and minerals such as iron, calcium, magnesium, phosphorous and lecithin (an important component in cellular metabolism), as well as all-important fibre, making pulses indispensable to healthy nutrition.

The most famous lentils in Italy are those from Castelluccio in Umbria. One thousand of these tiny lentils, which are less than 2 mm (1/16 inch) across, weigh only 23 grams (3/4 oz)! They grow 1,400 metres (4,600 ft) above sea level, and have extremely thin skins and an outstanding flavour.

The most familiar of the Italian beans is probably the borlotti bean, also known as the cranberry bean, which made their way to Italy via the subtropical forests of Central and South America. They are primarily cultivated in central and southern Italy. These beans have red flecks and turn greenish during cooking.

The little *fagiolina del Trasimeno*, a bean that comes from the Lake Trasimeno region, tastes delicate and spicy at the same time. These tiny beans are about the size of a rice kernel. Somewhat larger, but not a bit less tasty, are the beans from the towns of Pigna, Conio and Badalucco in Liguria, also called 'the white treasure from the hills'. They are grown at 300 metres (1,000 ft) above sea level on southward-facing terraces in these three villages and their surrounding areas. They are small and kidney shaped, and have thin skins that are barely noticeable once the beans have been cooked. This gives the beans their incomparable, very subtle flavour.

Favourite Soups

Canederli allo speck in brodo
Bacon Dumpling Soup

5 day-old rolls
125 ml/4 fl oz lukewarm milk
100 g/3½ oz smoked bacon, diced
1 small onion, diced
2 tbsp finely chopped parsley
2 eggs
1 litre/1¾ pints hearty meat stock
salt
freshly ground pepper
freshly grated nutmeg

Cut the rolls into fine slices, pour the warm milk over them and soak for 10 minutes.

Render the bacon in an ungreased frying pan, then add the onions and sauté. Stir in half of the parsley. Remove from the heat and set aside to cool. Then add the bacon and onions to the bread, add the eggs and knead well. Season the dumpling mixture to taste with salt, pepper and nutmeg and set it aside for 30 minutes.

With wet hands, form small dumplings from the dough. Bring a large saucepan of salted water to the boil. Add the dumplings and simmer for 10 minutes on low heat until done. Bring the meat stock to the boil. Transfer the dumplings to the stock and steep them briefly, but do not cook further. Sprinkle with the remaining chopped parsley before serving.

Zuppa di pesce
Fish Soup

750 g/1 lb 10 oz mixed fresh fish,
ready to cook
2 tbsp olive oil
1 onion, finely chopped
2 garlic cloves, finely chopped
1 leek, cut into thin rings
1 tbsp tomato purée
4 tomatoes
1 tsp fennel seeds
1 tbsp finely chopped parsley
salt
freshly ground pepper

Wash the fish thoroughly. Bring 1 litre/ 1¾ pints of water with 1 teaspoon salt to the boil, add the fish and simmer on low heat for 10 minutes, but do not cook any longer than that. Remove the fish from the stock, pat it dry and set aside to cool.

Heat the olive oil in a soup kettle and sauté the onion, garlic and leek until the onions are translucent. Stir in the tomato purée, then add the fish stock and bring to the boil.

Peel and quarter the tomatoes, remove the seeds, and dice. Crush the fennel seeds with a mortar and pestle. Add the tomatoes and ground fennel seeds to the soup and simmer for 10 minutes. Skin the fish, fillet it, and cut into bite-sized pieces. Heat the fish in the soup. Season with salt and pepper to taste. Serve the soup sprinkled with parsley.

Cipollata
Onion Soup

5 tbsp olive oil
50 g/1¼ oz smoked bacon, diced
750 g/1 lb 10 oz white onions,
cut into thin rings
500 g/1 lb 2 oz canned tomato purée
2 eggs
40 g/1½ oz grated Parmesan
8 basil leaves, cut into strips
salt
freshly ground pepper

Heat the olive oil in a saucepan and render the bacon in it. Add the onions and sauté on low heat, stirring continuously, until they are translucent but do not allow to brown. Stir in the tomato purée and add 500 ml/18 fl oz water. Season with salt and pepper, cover, and simmer for about 1 hour. Stir frequently and add water as needed, but be careful that the soup does not become too thin.

Whisk the eggs with the Parmesan. Remove the onion soup from the stove and stir in the egg-and-cheese mixture. Serve sprinkled with the basil.

Minestra di farro
Spelt Soup

2 tbsp olive oil
1 small onion, finely chopped
1 carrot, diced
1 celery stick, diced
3 tomatoes, peeled and diced
1.5 litres meat stock
200 g/7 oz spelt flour
100 g/3½ oz cooked ham
1 tbsp each: grated Parmesan, pecorino
salt
freshly ground pepper

Heat the olive oil in a soup kettle and sauté the onion and vegetables in it, then pour in the meat stock. Bring to the boil and cook for about 1 hour.

Pass the soup through a sieve and bring to the boil once more. Season with salt and stir in the spelt flour. Simmer for another 25 minutes on low heat, stirring frequently.

Cut the ham into narrow strips, then stir the ham and cheeses into the soup. Add salt and pepper to taste and serve immediately.

Tuscany

TUSCANY

Tuscan food is simple, down-home cooking, and has renounced none of its peasant roots. It relies on the unique flavours of freshly harvested products that are in most cases underscored simply by a few herbs and flavourful olive oil. Meat, pulses, pecorino cheese and saltless bread are the pillars of Tuscan cuisine. Pork, beef, lamb and wild boar are traditionally grilled. For a long time, open fireplaces were the only source of heat on farms, and meat was also cooked in them. The farmers of Tuscany were poor and could not afford to throw away old bread. It was made into thick, hearty soups that are still regional specialities.

The Etruscans were the pioneers of Tuscan cuisine. They planted fruit trees, pulses and grain. The Romans gave this fertile land to legionaries as fiefdoms in return for their service to the homeland. Even in those days, a hearty grain soup made from emmer, an older strain of wheat, was widely disseminated among all social classes. Pulses were commonplace, as were milk and milk products. Meat was reserved for the well-to-do. Long before the birth of Christ, the Etruscans cultivated grapes for wine in Tuscany, making it one of the oldest wine-growing regions in Europe.

Panata
Bread Soup

200 g/7 oz plum tomatoes
1 celery stick
100 ml/3½ fl oz olive oil
1 garlic clove, finely chopped
2 bay leaves
4 slices day-old Tuscan country bread
4 eggs
50 g/1¾ oz grated Parmesan
1 tbsp finely chopped parsley
salt
freshly ground pepper

Peel and quarter the tomatoes, remove the seeds, and dice. Finely dice the celery. Heat 4 tablespoons of the olive oil in a saucepan and sauté the vegetables and garlic. Add 1 litre/1¾ pints of water and the bay leaves and season with salt and pepper. Simmer the stock for about 30 minutes, then pour it through a sieve into a larger saucepan.

Remove the crusts from the bread. Cut the bread into bite-sized pieces and sauté in the remaining olive oil. Divide the cubes among four soup bowls. Bring the vegetable stock to the boil once more, crack the eggs into it one at a time, and cook them in the hot stock. Place 1 poached egg in each bowl and pour hot stock over it. Sprinkle with Parmesan and parsley and serve immediately.

Pappa al pomodoro
Tomato Soup

1 kg/2 lb 4 oz tomatoes
4 tbsp olive oil
4 garlic cloves, finely chopped
750 ml/1⅓ pints meat stock
4 slices Tuscan country bread
a few basil leaves to garnish
salt
freshly ground pepper

Peel and quarter the tomatoes, remove the seeds, and chop into cubes. Heat the olive oil and fry the garlic. Add the diced tomatoes and cook for 5 minutes. Pour in the meat stock and leave the mixture to thicken on medium heat until the desired consistency is reached. Season with salt and pepper.

Toast the bread slices on both sides under a hot grill or in the oven until golden brown, then cut them into cubes. Add the bread cubes to the soup just before serving and garnish with basil leaves.

Ribollita
Tuscan Bean Soup

150 g/5 oz dried white beans
100 g/3½ oz pancetta
½ Savoy cabbage, cut into strips
2 carrots, sliced
400 g/14 oz canned peeled tomatoes
1 litre/1¾ pints meat stock
1 tbsp chopped oregano
1 onion
4 slices day-old Tuscan country bread
50 g/1¾ oz grated Parmesan
2 tbsp olive oil
salt
freshly ground pepper

Soak the beans overnight in 1 litre/1¾ pints of water. The next day, bring to the boil in the soaking water and simmer for 1 hour.

Finely dice the pancetta and render it in a soup kettle, then sauté the cabbage and carrots in the fat. Mash the tomatoes with a fork and add them to the pot. Pour in the stock and season with the oregano and salt and pepper.

When the beans have cooked, pour off the cooking water, add the beans to the soup and simmer for another 15 minutes. Slice the onion into very thin rings. Preheat the oven to 250°C/480°F/gas mark 9.

Toast the bread, cut it in half and place in four ovenproof soup bowls. Pour the soup over the bread and top with onion rings. Sprinkle with Parmesan and drizzle with the olive oil. Bake until the onion rings are brown.

Primi Piatti

The First Course

PASTA

Even today, it is not clear who actually invented the noodle. It is likely that any culture that had mastered the art of baking bread would have also made noodle-like foods from flour and water. But in no other country does *pasta* (literally, 'dough') have such significance as in Italy. Statistically speaking, every Italian enjoys an average of 27 kg (60 lb) of pasta per year. Italians devote more time and attention to it than to any other foodstuff, and no other product in the world better represents a country's cuisine. Pasta combines all the virtues of the Italian kitchen. It is made from simple, but very good ingredients and cooked with dedication, ingenuity and love.

Archaeologists have found the earliest references to the preparation of pasta in Etruscan hillside tombs dating from the fourth century BCE. Reliefs on the gravestones included equipment for making noodles as well as illustrations of flour sacks, pastry boards, pastry tongs, rolling pins and pasta cutters. Many people believe this was the birthplace of pasta.

A major contribution to the further development of pasta was made more than a thousand years later by the Arabs, who 'invented' the drying of fresh noodles and the production of tube-shaped pastas. When they conquered Sicily in the ninth century, they brought this technique with them to the island. The Arabs also introduced new and highly sophisticated forms of irrigation. So it was that grain cultivation flourished in grand style on the once-dry Sicilian soil.

The earliest surviving pasta recipes date back to the Renaissance. In the fifteenth century, Maestro Martino da Como, the famous personal chef to the patriarch of Aquileia, described several ways of making pasta in his *Libro de Arte Coquinaria* ('Book of Culinary Arts'). The cookbook was not written in Latin, as had been the custom heretofore, but rather in colloquial Italian. It contains, among other things, recipes for 'noodles made from the finest flour, egg white and rose water' that were as thin as straw, rolled by hand and dried in the sun. Another recipe describes how to make *con siciliani*, for which the dough is wrapped around a small metal rod so that the noodles remain hollow inside.

Pasta was not a staple at that time, but rather a luxury food for the well-to-do. Pasta cost three times as much as bread and thus was reserved for the privileged classes: refined with sugar and spices (which were also expensive imported goods), it was prepared according to recipes that sound like they would take some getting used to nowadays. Although tomatoes are

As recently as one hundred years ago in Naples, noodles were hung in long strands on wooden poles in the open air to dry.

inextricably linked to pasta in most people's minds today, they were still unknown in Europe at that time.

But pasta's triumphal march was unstoppable. In the eighteenth century, it was poised to overcome class barriers. Naples was the centre of the pasta movement. Not only did durum wheat flourish in the province of Campania; its climate, characterized by sunshine, gentle breezes around the Gulf of Naples and hot winds from Vesuvius, was ideally suited for the production of dried noodles. Here, pasta could dry slowly enough so that it did not become brittle, yet fast enough to avoid becoming mouldy. By the end of the eighteenth century, hundreds of pasta shops lined the streets of Naples. The pasta was cooked at open stalls over charcoal fires, and people ate it on the spot with their fingers.

Then politics entered the picture: the great Italian freedom fighter Giuseppe Garibaldi, who wanted to free Italy from foreign rule, supposedly liberated Naples with the battle cry, 'It will be macaroni, I swear to you, that will unite Italy.'

At the beginning of the 20th century, pasta dough was pressed into long spaghetti or macaroni and cut by hand using machines like this (left).

In the past, pasta was cooked and sold by street vendors and eaten right on the spot, with the fingers, while standing (below).

Primi Piatti | 127

Making Pasta

Pasta is made from ground durum wheat and water. Depending on the region, eggs may also be added. It is based on semolina, a ground meal that is somewhat more coarse-grained than flour. Producing good pasta begins with the selection of the right kind of durum wheat. Among connoisseurs, Capelli durum wheat is considered the best. This variety originated in the 1920s and is regarded as the forbearer of many of today's durum wheats.

In addition to the major, world-famous Italian pasta producers, there are still a number of small artisan *pastifici* (pasta manufacturers) such as the Lucchese and Latini enterprises, which are still devoted to producing pasta according to the old, traditional methods. With these pastas, the strong flavour of the grain is in the foreground.

The wheat grains are separated from the outer layers during milling. Some producers grind only the innermost part of the grain into coarse semolina; others mill the whole grain, including the wheat germ. The semolina is kneaded with cold water.

The dough is prepared slowly and gently, so that the gluten in the semolina has sufficient time to develop, which is what will later give the pasta its firm consistency. Whereas home cooks must repeatedly knead the pasta dough, press it flat, pound it and then press it again until it becomes smooth and elastic, in the factory any air that interferes with the pasta dough is removed inside a vacuum chamber in order to make it malleable.

Factory-made dough is then placed in a press and squeezed through nozzles or moulds under high pressure to shape it into the various types of pasta, or it is rolled flat and cut into ribbons of different thicknesses. In handmade artisan factories, the noodles are drawn through bronze dies. Bronze has a rough surface and passes on this texture to the pasta. Teflon-coated dies are used in the larger factories, resulting in noodles with a very smooth surface. However, these noodles don't absorb the sauce nearly as well as handmade, slightly porous pasta.

The final stage is drying, a process in which the pasta is evenly dehydrated from the inside out. If this occurs too quickly, the noodles become brittle. They lose not only some of their nutritive value and taste, but also their appetizing appearance when they are eventually cooked. The gentlest

In Italy there are more than 600 different types, shapes and sizes of pasta. Imaginative new creations are introduced all the time.

drying takes place at 35–50°C (95–120°F), depending on the type of pasta, and lasts between twelve and forty-eight hours.

In old granite flour mills, the durum wheat grain is ground into a coarse meal, semolina, the basis for good, handmade artisan pasta (right).

In a factory, the dough is rolled out into large, thin sheets, then cut into ribbon-style pasta.

Durum Wheat

Pasta is made from semolina, which is produced from coarsely ground durum wheat. Golden durum wheat has a higher gluten content and a different structure than soft wheat, which is better suited for baking. The higher gluten content makes pasta dough elastic and malleable, yet with a firm consistency, which ensures that the pasta retains its shape during cooking.

As early as 1574, the Genoese guild of pasta producers decreed in their bylaws that only durum wheat, *semola*, and water were to be used for their pasta. According to present-day Italian food law, authentic pasta must still be made from durum wheat semolina. When that is the case, the label reads '*pasta di semola di grano duro*'.

After foreign competitors had successfully marketed egg noodles with Italian names and shapes, the Italians themselves started to produce *pasta all'uovo*. They can be purchased fresh or dried, mainly as stuffed or ribbon-style pasta.

Wheat grain

Italian flour

Pasta with Tradition

In Italy there are still a number of *pastifici* (pasta producers) whose pasta is made in traditional, artisan style from high-quality durum wheat and fresh spring water, drawn by old machines with bronze dies and gently dried at a low temperature for up to fifty hours. These producers include Cavalier Giuseppe Cocco from Abruzzo, Leonardo Saltarelli (Perugia), the Martelli family from Lari in the province of Pisa, Pastificio Fabbri from Strada in Chianti, Pasta Lucchese (Tuscany), La Fabbrica della Pasta Gragnano near Naples and the Latini family (the Marche), who, in addition to growing the durum wheat for their pasta, also cultivate the old Senatore Capelli strain of wheat.

The great pasta manufacturer De Cecco started over 120 years ago with a stone mill in Fara San Martino, where the firm produced 'the best flour in the region'. A pasta factory was built next door in which the noodles were not dried in the sun but, for the first time, in a low temperature drying facility. This better preserved the texture of the starch, and the fleeting aromatic compounds could no longer escape.

Home-made Pasta

For Italian home cooks, starting with fresh ingredients is a given, so naturally *pasta fresca* (fresh pasta) is still made at home today. Generally, a distinction is made between *pasta liscia* (smooth and flat such as ribbon noodles) and *pasta ripiena* (shapes that are stuffed). Golden ribbon noodles were allegedly invented in 1503 by a cook from Bologna, who was inspired by Lucrezia Borgia's long blond curls.

As is the case with the use of butter versus olive oil for cooking, there is a kind of border drawn through the country with regard to their use in pasta dough. In Emilia-Romagna, noodle dough is traditionally made with many eggs and flour, but without any water or salt. In Piedmont, cooks reckon on using eight fresh eggs or three whole eggs and nine egg yolks per kilogram of fine wheat flour, known in Britain as Italian flour. Here and there, similar recipes can also be found in Abruzzo, the Marche, Lazio, Umbria and Tuscany. In Liguria and Veneto, on the other hand, the dough contains fewer eggs but more flour, and olive oil is sometimes added. In the southern part of Italy, only durum wheat semolina and water belong in classic pasta dough.

Pasta fatta in casa (pasta fresca)
Fresh Home-made Pasta

400 g/14 oz Italian flour, plus extra for dusting

1 pinch salt
1 egg
2 tbsp olive oil

Sift the flour on to a work surface and press a hollow in the centre. Stir together 8 tablespoons of water with the salt, egg and olive oil and pour the mixture into the hollow. Stir everything together until it forms a smooth, supple dough. Shape the dough into a ball and leave it to rest under a damp cloth for 40 minutes.

Separate the dough into small portions. Using a pasta machine, roll out to the desired thickness according to the manufacturer's instructions.

Cut the dough sheets to the desired width with the appropriate attachment. Roll the noodles into loose nests with a fork, place them side by side on a board or baking tray and leave to dry a little.

For egg noodle dough, first sift the flour on to a work surface, press a hollow in the centre, then add eggs, salt, water and olive oil.

With a wooden spoon, stir in part of the flour from the edge towards the centre. Then knead all the ingredients into a silky, smooth dough by hand.

Leave the dough to rest beneath a damp cloth for 40 minutes. After that, use a rolling pin to roll it out into the thinnest possible rectangular sheet.

Pasta rossa
Red Pasta

400 g/14 oz Italian flour,
plus extra for dusting

1 pinch salt

3 tbsp tomato purée

1 tbsp olive oil

3 eggs

Sift the flour on to a work surface and press a hollow in the centre. Stir together the salt, tomato purée, olive oil and 1 tablespoon of water and pour into the hollow. Add the eggs and knead everything into a silky, smooth dough for 10 minutes. Add 1–2 tablespoons of water, as needed. Shape the dough into a ball and leave it to rest under a damp cloth for 40 minutes.

Pasta verde
Green Pasta

200 g/7 oz frozen spinach, thawed

1 pinch salt

400 g/14 oz Italian flour,
plus extra for dusting

3 eggs

1 tbsp olive oil

Drain the spinach well, purée it with the salt and steam in a non-stick pan until thickened. Remove from the heat and set aside to cool.

Sift the flour on to a work surface and press a hollow in the centre. Place the eggs, olive oil and puréed spinach in the hollow and knead everything into a silky, smooth dough. Add 1–2 tablespoons of water, as needed. Shape the dough into a ball and leave it to rest under a damp cloth for 40 minutes.

Pasta nera
Black Pasta

400 g/14 oz Italian flour,
plus extra for dusting

1 pinch salt

8 g squid ink
(2 sachets of 0.15-oz)

1 tbsp olive oil

3 eggs

Sift the flour on to the work surface and press a hollow in the centre. Stir together the salt, squid ink, olive oil and 1 tablespoon of water and pour into the hollow. Add the eggs and knead everything into a silky, smooth dough. Add 1–2 tablespoons of water, as needed. Shape the dough into a ball and leave it to rest under a damp cloth for 40 minutes.

For ribbon noodles, dust the sheet of dough with flour and loosely roll it up lengthways. Cut it into thin strips with a large, sharp knife.

Unroll the noodle strands, then roll them up with a fork into small, loose nests and place them side by side on a lightly floured board.

Leave the noodles to dry a little before cooking. The longer the noodles dry, the longer they take to cook. Fully dried, they will keep for weeks.

Pasta al Dente

If a few basic guidelines are followed, cooking pasta to perfection is child's play. The most important one is to prepare and serve the pasta immediately after pouring off the cooking water. That explains why, in Italy, one asks guests who come for a meal, 'Si butta?' ('To the table?'), which roughly means, 'Should I put the pasta on to cook?'

A pasta kettle should be generously sized and as wide as possible so that the heat is distributed evenly. In general, use 1 litre (1¾ pints) of water and 10 grams (⅓ oz) of salt, preferably sea salt, for every 100 grams (3½ oz) of pasta. Heat the water first, and when the water comes to the boil, add the salt and then the noodles. Stir briefly at this point so that the pasta does not stick together. Cook the pasta for the length of time indicated on the packet, stirring occasionally. Shortly before the end of the cooking time, test for doneness by simply taking a noodle from the pot and splitting it with a fork. If the inside has a white circle or white dots, the pasta needs to cook a little longer. If the pasta has an even colour, it is *al dente*, and ready to eat. Translated literally as 'to the tooth', *al dente* means that the pasta is still firm, and not too soft or mushy. Now the pasta is ready to be drained, mixed with the sauce and served. There is nothing more needed in order to cook pasta perfectly.

In Italy, perfectly cooked spaghetti must be al dente, *literally, 'to the tooth' – soft, yet with a bit of bite.*

Pasta and Sauce

The perfect combination of pasta and sauce – in Italian, *sugo* – is an art in itself. Indeed, it is only with the right sauce that pasta can develop its full flavour.

Of course, the choice of sauce is also a matter of personal taste. Nevertheless, there are a few culinary standards: fresh egg noodles and stuffed pasta harmonize nicely with cream and butter sauces, while dried pasta goes well with olive oil-based sauces. The larger the cavity or surface area of the pasta, the more sauce it can absorb and the richer the sauce may be. Thin pasta should never be overwhelmed by too powerful a sauce. A rule of thumb is: the heavier the sauce, the broader the pasta. Tomato sauce, *sugo al pomodoro*, is a classic. It goes with any pasta, provided it is made from flavourful tomatoes and good olive oil and tastefully rounded off with herbs or vegetables.

Meat sauce, *ragù*, stands a close second. In Italy, there are allegedly as many recipes for it as there are stoves. *Ragù* is ideal for tubular pasta, spaghetti and other ribbon-style noodles.

Fish and seafood sauces are ideally suited for long, thin noodles. *Pesto* can be served with spaghetti or ribbon pasta, and even with stuffed pasta.

Salsa al Gorgonzola
Gorgonzola Sauce

1 tbsp butter
100 g/3½ oz Gorgonzola
150 ml/5 fl oz double cream
150 ml/5 fl oz milk
2 sage leaves, finely chopped
salt
freshly ground pepper

Heat the butter, Gorgonzola, double cream and milk in the top of a double boiler, stirring slowly until the cheese is melted. Season the sauce with the sage, and salt and pepper to taste.

Sugo ai carciofi e speck
Artichoke and Bacon Sauce

8 small purple artichokes
4 tbsp lemon juice
4 garlic cloves
150 g/5 oz pancetta
5 tbsp olive oil
250 ml/9 fl oz dry white wine
400 ml/14 fl oz stock
(or according to taste)
salt
freshly ground pepper

Trim the artichokes, shorten the stalks to about 4 cm/1½ inches and peel them. Remove the tough outer leaves as well as the hard thorns from the remaining leaves. Combine the lemon juice and some water in a bowl. Slice the artichokes lengthways and immediately place them in the bowl of lemon water. Leave them to soak a little, then pour off the liquid and pat dry.

Peel the garlic and cut into thin slices. Dice the bacon. Heat the olive oil in a large frying pan and sauté the bacon and artichokes. Add the garlic and fry until golden brown. Deglaze with the wine. Pour in the stock, bring to the boil, and season with salt and pepper. Cover the vegetables and cook on low heat for about 15 minutes until the artichokes are done.

Salsa alla cacciatora
Hunter's Sauce

50 g/1¾ oz dried ceps
4 tbsp olive oil
1 onion, finely chopped
1 garlic clove, finely chopped
50 g/1¾ oz smoked pancetta, diced
1 celery stick, finely diced
50 g/1¾ oz dry-cured
or smoked ham, diced
100 ml/3½ fl oz red wine
1 bay leaf
150 ml/5 fl oz double cream
salt
freshly ground pepper

Soak the ceps in 250 ml/9 fl oz lukewarm water for 30 minutes. Then drain the mushrooms through a fine sieve, retaining the soaking water, and roughly chop the ceps. Heat the olive oil in a deep frying pan. Fry the onion, garlic and pancetta in the oil until the onions are translucent. Add the celery and ham, and season with salt and pepper. Pour in the red wine and reduce.

Add the ceps, soaking water and bay leaf to the pan. Simmer the sauce for 10 minutes. Stir in the cream and leave the sauce to reduce for another 10 minutes. Remove the bay leaf and season the sauce to taste with salt and pepper.

Sugo con le conchiglie
Shellfish Sauce

1 kg/2 lb 4 oz mixed shellfish
1 kg/2 lb 4 oz plum tomatoes
5 tbsp olive oil
1 large onion, finely chopped
2 garlic cloves, finely chopped
2 celery sticks, diced
2 carrots, diced
2 tbsp finely chopped parsley
salt
freshly ground pepper

Thoroughly wash the shellfish, brushing the shells and removing the beards as needed, and discard any shells that are open. Peel the tomatoes, cut them into wedges, remove the seeds, and cut into fine dice. Heat the olive oil in a large saucepan and sauté the onion and garlic until the onion is translucent. Add the celery and carrots and cook briefly. Stir in the shellfish, cover the pan and cook on high heat for about 5 minutes, shaking the pan a few times.

Remove the shellfish from the pot and discard any shells that are still closed. Add the tomatoes to the vegetable mixture, season with salt and pepper and reduce slightly.

Add the shellfish to the tomato sauce and simmer briefly on low heat. Stir in the chopped parsley.

Salsa all'amatriciana
Tomato and Bacon Sauce

150 g/5 oz pancetta
500 g/1 lb 2 oz tomatoes
2 tbsp olive oil
1 small onion, finely chopped
1 fresh red chilli, finely chopped
salt
freshly ground pepper

Chop the pancetta into fine dice. Peel and quarter the tomatoes, remove the seeds, and chop roughly.

Heat the olive oil in a pan and render the pancetta. Add the onion and chilli to the pan and fry until the onions are translucent. Stir in the tomatoes and simmer the sauce for 15 to 20 minutes. Season with salt and pepper to taste.

Sugo con le conchiglie

Ragù alla bolognese
Bolognese Sauce

25 g/1 oz dried ceps
1 tbsp butter
50 g/1¾ oz pancetta, diced
1 small onion, minced
1 garlic clove, minced
2 small carrots, minced
2 celery sticks, minced
300 g/11 oz minced beef
1 pinch sugar
1 tbsp tomato purée
125 ml/4 fl oz red wine
250 g/9 oz canned tomato purée
salt
freshly ground pepper
freshly grated nutmeg

Soak the ceps in 125 ml/4 fl oz lukewarm water for 20 minutes.

Melt the butter in a frying pan and fry the pancetta in it. Add the onion and garlic and fry until the onion is translucent. Stir in the carrots and celery and cook for a few minutes, stirring frequently.

Mix in the mince and brown it, stirring constantly. Season with salt, pepper, nutmeg and a pinch of sugar. Stir in the tomato purée and cook for a minute or two, then add the red wine. Mix in the tomato purée.

Finely slice the ceps and add them to the sauce. Pour the soaking water through a fine sieve into the sauce. Thicken the sauce by cooking it on low heat for 1 hour.

Ragù

Some critics claim that there are as many recipes for *ragù* in Italy as there are stoves on which the meat sauce is cooked. The types of meat, vegetables, spices and herbs certainly do vary by region, and the recipes are modified according to personal preferences and family traditions.

Ragù alla romagnola, made from minced beef, salsiccia, pancetta, carrots, celery, onion, tomatoes and white wine, comes from Piedmont. For *ragù alla napoletana*, pork is cooked in lard. In the Abruzzo region, lamb is stewed in white wine with tomatoes, peppers, garlic and bay leaves. All of these meat sauces have one thing in common: while the older generation, in particular, insists that a genuine *ragù* has to simmer for at least two hours, or better still three hours, the tendency nowadays is to leave the sauce to cook on the hob for a shorter period. This not only saves time, but also maintains the unique flavours of the individual ingredients.

For an authentic Bolognese sauce, first soak dried ceps in lukewarm water.

Then fry the pancetta and finely diced vegetables in olive oil.

The next step is to add the minced beef and brown it until it is crumbly.

Season the mixture with salt, pepper and nutmeg, stir in the tomato purée, and cook it briefly.

Add the finely chopped ceps and pour in the soaking water while straining it through a sieve.

LIGURIA AND PESTO

The Mediterranean Sea and fresh aromatic herbs are decisive elements for the flavours of Ligurian gastonomy. Liguria is one of Italy's smallest regions, but at the same time it has the highest population density. That explains why the cuisine is traditionally rather sparing. Only a few ingredients are used, but they are very good ones: fresh fish, vegetables from people's own gardens, pulses, wild and cultivated herbs and the finest olive oil. Genoese cuisine has been enhanced by spices and influences from the Orient, a legacy of the brisk trade that took place in the Middle Ages. Meat is consumed only in small quantities and mainly limited to light-coloured meats. Animal fats are rarely used; even cheese and cream are utilized only in small quantities for binding sauces and filling pasta.

The flagship of Ligurian cuisine is *pesto alla genovese*. By now, this aromatic green mixture of basil, olive oil, pine kernels, garlic and grated cheese has entered the realm of international cuisine. Depending on the village, mashed potatoes, fresh beans and local spices are added along with these basic ingredients. The quality of the ingredients is crucial: the best basil is supposed to come from Pra, a small town near Genoa. A number of home cooks also carry on the tradition of *pesto corto*, in which what remains in the mortar after making pesto is mixed with fresh tomatoes and served with pasta.

Pesto alla genovese
Pesto Sauce

2 tbsp pine kernels
3–4 garlic cloves
2 handfuls fresh basil
½ tsp salt
1 tbsp each: grated Parmesan and Pecorino Romano
100 ml/3½ fl oz olive oil

Dry-roast the pine kernels in an ungreased frying pan until golden brown. Cool slightly, then chop them roughly. Peel and roughly chop the garlic as well.

Rinse the basil, dry thoroughly and cut the leaves into strips. Put the pine kernels, garlic, basil and salt in a large mortar and crush everything to a paste.

Work the two cheeses into the paste gradually. Then pour in the olive oil in a thin stream and stir until the sauce has a creamy consistency, adding a little water if needed.

Finely chopped basil, pine kernels and garlic form the basis for pesto.

The ingredients are placed in a large mortar made of porcelain, granite or ceramic.

The mixture is ground to a paste and freshly grated cheese is added.

Flavourful olive oil is poured into the paste in a thin stream and blended in.

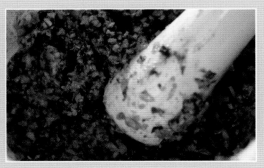
The pesto is mixed into a creamy sauce, with the addition of a little water, as needed.

Spaghetti & Co.

Spaghetti is just one kind of *pasta lunga*, or long noodle. The name is derived from *spago*, the Italian word for 'cord'. Spaghetti is often considered the quintessential Italian pasta abroad, and it is without question the most famous kind of pasta, but it is not the oldest. As a rule, today spaghetti is produced in factories.

The name *spaghetti* was originally a collective term for all forms of dried, cord-like pasta, regardless of its thickness. Today, the designations are more differentiated. Even so, all *vermicelli*, whether thick or thin, have one thing in common: they are eaten with a fork. It is immaterial if waiters give tourists a spoon to go with the fork, because the proper way to eat spaghetti is by wrapping it around the fork at the edge of one's plate. It is perfectly permissible to lean slightly forwards over your plate while doing so.

Spaghettini, also called *vermicelli* in Naples, is thinner than regular spaghetti. Some popular ways to serve it are with shellfish, seafood or simply *aglio, olio, e peperoncino* – that is, with garlic, olive oil and chillies.

Bucatini are very popular in central Italy. This thicker spaghetti with a hole (*buco*) in the centre goes wonderfully with hearty tomato sauces or rich sauces with bacon.

Linguine (literally, 'tongues') resemble rolled-out, flattened spaghetti. They have a somewhat coarse surface that sauces adhere to especially well.

The Royal Spaghetti Fork

Pasta not only brings happiness, but also fosters creativity. Ferdinand II, for example, king of Naples from 1830 to 1859, was a passionate spaghetti aficionado. Since this pasta could not be eaten with the sharp, three-pronged forks that were used at court in those days, and the king didn't want to eat pasta with his fingers like a commoner, he had his steward make a blunt, four-pronged fork, which is the precursor of today's fork design.

Spaghetti alla Chitarra

Spaghetti alla chitarra, also called *maccheroni alla chitarra*, is spaghetti that is about 2 mm thick with a square cross section. It is produced in Abruzzo using a *chitarra* (literally, 'guitar'), a frame that has thin wires stretched across it. The thinly rolled-out dough is laid on top of the strings, then pressed down on them with a rolling pin. And that is how long, thin pasta is made from the dough.

Spaghetti alla Carbonara

400 g/14 oz spaghetti
4 eggs
4 tbsp double cream
50 g/1¾ oz grated Parmesan
50 g/1¾ oz grated Pecorino Romano
1 tbsp butter
150 g/5 oz pancetta, finely diced
salt
freshly ground pepper

Bring a large saucepan of lightly salted water to the boil. Add the pasta and cook according to packet instructions until al dente.

Meanwhile, stir together the eggs, cream and cheeses in a bowl. Add salt and pepper.

Melt the butter in a large frying pan and fry the pancetta until crisp. Drain the spaghetti and add it to the pan while still dripping wet. Pour the cheese sauce over it. Remove the pan from the stove. Toss the pasta in the sauce until the eggs begin to thicken but are still creamy. Serve on heated plates, sprinkled with freshly ground pepper.

Spaghetti aglio, olio e peperoncino
Spaghetti with Garlic, Oil and Chillies

400 g/14 oz spaghetti
100 ml/3½ fl oz olive oil
4–6 garlic cloves, finely chopped
2–3 dried chilli peppers
2 tbsp finely chopped parsley
salt
freshly ground pepper
75 g/2½ oz grated Parmesan

Bring a large saucepan of lightly salted water to the boil. Add the pasta and cook according to packet instructions until al dente.

In a deep frying pan, heat the olive oil and sauté the garlic and whole chillies in it. As soon as the desired spiciness is reached, remove the chillies from the pan. For a very spicy dish, you can leave the chillies in the garlic oil.

Drain the spaghetti, add it to the deep frying pan while still dripping wet, and mix with the hot garlic oil and parsley. Season with pepper and serve on heated plates with the Parmesan on the side.

Spaghetti al pomodoro
Spaghetti with Tomato Sauce

600 g/1 lb 5 oz tomatoes
4 tbsp olive oil
1 pinch sugar
400 g/14 oz spaghetti
1 tbsp finely chopped basil leaves
salt
freshly ground pepper
75 g/2½ oz grated Parmesan
or pecorino cheese

Peel and quarter the tomatoes, remove the seeds and dice. Then heat the olive oil in a large frying pan and cook the tomatoes. Season with the sugar, salt and pepper, and simmer on low heat for about 20 minutes.

Bring a large saucepan of lightly salted water to the boil. Add the pasta and cook it according to packet instructions until al dente. Drain the spaghetti and combine it with the tomato sauce while still dripping wet. Serve on heated plates sprinkled with basil, with the cheese on the side.

Bucatini alla puttanesca
Bucatini with Tomatoes, Capers and Olives

100 g/3½ oz stoned black olives
5 anchovies in oil
4 tbsp olive oil
2 tbsp tomato purée
800 g/1 lb 12 oz canned peeled tomatoes
60 g/2 oz small capers
salt
freshly ground pepper
400 g/14 oz bucatini pasta

Cut the olives into quarters. Finely chop the anchovies. Heat the olive oil in a frying pan, stir in the tomato purée and cook it briefly. Crush the tomatoes with a fork, then add them to the pan. Stir in the olives, anchovies and capers and simmer the sauce on low heat for 20 minutes. Season to taste with salt and pepper.

Bring a large saucepan of lightly salted water to the boil. Add the pasta and cook according to packet instructions until al dente. Drain the bucatini and mix it into the sauce while still dripping wet. Serve immediately on heated plates.

Many Shapes and Sizes

In Italy, there are more than 600 different types and shapes of pasta on the market. They often differ from one another only minimally in terms of shape, size, diameter and type of dough. Pasta makers go to a great deal of trouble to constantly develop new shapes and fanciful names, and the pasta industry is very creative in this respect. Some of the classic types of pasta have beautiful and onomatopoeic names such as *conchiglie* (shells), *farfalle* (butterflies), *orecchiette* (little ears), *penne* (feather or quill), *ruote* (cartwheel), *strangolapreti* or *strozzapreti* (priest stranglers) and *capelli d'angelo* (angel hair).

In spite of the major pasta producers' marketing efforts, about a dozen standard types still make up over 90 per cent of the pasta market. The rest are regional specialities, new creations that disappear from the market in short order, or pasta created for special occasions such as millennium pasta or pasta in the shape of a tennis racket, produced especially for the world championships.

Pastasciutta

Outside of Italy, *pastasciutta* is one of the most misunderstood pastas, for this is not a matter of a recipe for pasta with meat sauce. *Pastasciutta* (literally, 'dry pasta') describes all kinds of pasta dishes that can be prepared with sauce or cheese, from simple spaghetti with tomato sauce to sophisticated pumpkin tortellini in butter to rich lasagne. Despite the sauce that adorns them, and unlike noodles in stock or soup, in Italian cuisine these pastas are considered 'dry'.

Pastasciutta, like risotto or gnocchi, is served as a first course in restaurants, and it is customarily followed by a meat or fish course. That is why the portions of pasta served are not all that generous. In Italy, it is still not the custom to order *pastasciutta* as a meal in itself. This puts off Italian gastronomes to the same degree as the habit many tourists have of sprinkling cheese over every pasta dish, even if it contains fish or seafood.

Quadrucci

Orecchiette

Malloreddus

Trofie

Fettuccine

Maltagliati

Spaghetti

Penne

Farfalle

Fusilli

Casareccia al Pomodoro

Cavatellucci

Rigatoni

Tagliatelle

Ruote tricolori

Tagliatelle verdi

Tofarelle

Cannelloni

Lasagne

Fusilli tricolori

Favourite Pasta Dishes

Tagliolini al tartufo
Tagliolini with White Truffles

400 g/14 oz tagliolini
100 g/3½ oz butter
1 small white truffle
salt

Bring a large saucepan of lightly salted water to the boil. Add the pasta and cook according to packet instructions until al dente.

Meanwhile, melt the butter, but be careful it does not turn brown.

Clean the truffle with a dry, soft brush. Drain the pasta thoroughly, then distribute it on four plates. Pour the melted butter over each serving. With a truffle grater, finely shave the truffle over the pasta.

Linguine con salsa di pesce
Linguine with Fish Sauce

400 g/14 oz fish fillets
such as perch or codfish
600 g/1 lb 5 oz tomatoes
1 onion
4 tbsp olive oil
350 g/12 oz linguine
1 tbsp finely chopped parsley
flour for coating
salt
freshly ground pepper
basil leaves to garnish

Wash the fish fillets, pat them dry and coat in flour. Peel and quarter the tomatoes, remove the seeds, and dice. Peel the onion, then cut it in half and slice.

Heat the olive oil in a pan and fry the fish on both sides until golden brown, then remove from the pan and keep warm. Sauté the onions in the oil until translucent, then add the tomatoes. Season with salt and pepper, cover the pan and simmer on low heat for about 10 minutes.

In the meantime, bring a large saucepan of lightly salted water to the boil. Add the pasta and cook according to packet instructions until al dente. Drain the pasta and toss it with the tomato sauce and parsley while the pasta is still dripping wet. Cut the fish into bite-sized pieces and blend into the pasta. Cover and briefly allow the flavours to mingle. Serve on heated plates garnished with basil leaves.

Tagliatelle

As if the numerous types of pasta were not confusing enough, the exact same pasta can also have up to ten different names, depending on the region and manufacturer! Luckily, classic tagliatelle have the same name throughout Italy. Often they are available as both dry and fresh egg noodle products.

Tuscan *pappardelle* are the widest tagliatelle. The linguistic origin of these delicious noodles is anything but genteel. This Tuscan word originally meant 'to fill one's gullet', and it is also used in this sense in Boccaccio's *Decameron*.

One of the most popular kinds of egg noodles, tagliatelle are about 8 mm wide. Their name comes from the Italian verb *tagliare*, 'to cut'. They are usually available rolled into small nests or spirals. They initially came from Bologna, and go perfectly with meat sauces.

In the vicinity of Rome, the somewhat more slender, thicker tagliatelle are called *fettuccine*, or *trenette* in Liguria. They are just as delightful with a flavourful pesto as with cream or butter sauces containing vegetables, fish or seafood.

Tagliarellini are about 4 mm wide. Green and white *tagliarellini* are the basis for the classic pasta dish *paglia e fieno* ('straw and hay').

Tagliolini, the most delicate of egg noodles, are just 1 mm wide and taste best with just a touch of butter and white truffles.

Pappardelle al sugo di lepre
Pappardelle with Rabbit Sauce

4 rabbit legs
4 tbsp olive oil
1 onion, finely diced
1 carrot, diced
1 celery stick, diced
250 ml/9 fl oz red wine
400 g/14 oz pappardelle
salt
freshly ground pepper
1 tbsp finely chopped parsley

Wash the rabbit legs, pat them dry, then vigorously rub them with salt and pepper.

Heat the olive oil in an iron casserole and sauté the diced vegetables in it. Add the rabbit legs and brown on both sides. Deglaze with the wine, cover and stew on low heat for about 40 minutes until the meat is done. Then take the legs out of the sauce. Remove the meat from the bones, cut it into small cubes and put the meat back into the sauce.

Bring a large saucepan of lightly salted water to the boil. Add the pasta and cook until al dente. Mix the pasta into the sauce while still dripping wet. Add salt and pepper to taste. Serve sprinkled with parsley.

Penne all'arrabbiata
Spicy Penne

500 g/1 lb 2 oz tomatoes
2 tbsp olive oil
100 g/3½ oz pancetta, diced
1 onion, finely chopped
2 garlic cloves, finely chopped
2–3 dried red chillies
400 g/14 oz penne rigate
75 g/2½ oz grated Pecorino Romano
salt

Peel and quarter the tomatoes, remove the seeds, and cut into small dice. Heat the olive oil in a deep frying pan and fry the pancetta in it. Add the onion and garlic and fry until the onions are translucent. Then add the diced tomatoes and whole chillies and leave the sauce to simmer on low heat for a while. As soon as it reaches the desired level of spiciness, remove the chillies from the pan.

Bring a large saucepan of lightly salted water to the boil. Add the pasta and cook for half the time stated in the packet instructions, then drain, reserving some of the pasta cooking water.

Mix the penne, 2 tablespoons of the Pecorino Romano and 3–4 tablespoons of pasta water into the tomato sauce and finish cooking the pasta in the sauce, stirring frequently. Serve on heated plates sprinkled with the remaining Pecorino Romano.

Rigatoni all'amatriciana
Rigatoni with Bacon and Onions

3 tomatoes
2 tbsp olive oil
100 g/3½ oz pancetta, diced
2 small white onions, minced
1 small, dried red chilli, minced
salt
350 g/12 oz rigatoni
60 g/2 oz grated Pecorino Romano

Peel and quarter the tomatoes, remove the seeds, and dice. Heat the olive oil in a large frying pan and fry the diced pancetta until crisp, then remove from the pan and keep warm. Sauté the onion and chilli in the bacon fat. Add the tomatoes, salt lightly and simmer for 10 minutes.

In the meantime, bring a large saucepan of lightly salted water to the boil. Add the pasta and cook according to packet instructions until al dente. Drain the water and tip the pasta into a preheated bowl. Combine it thoroughly with the pancetta, tomato sauce and Pecorino Romano. Serve immediately.

Ziti con salsiccia
Ziti with Sausage

250 g/9 oz salsiccia (Italian sausage)
2 yellow peppers
2 tomatoes
2 tbsp olive oil
1 white onion, finely chopped
2 garlic cloves, finely chopped
250 ml/9 fl oz white wine
1 tbsp oregano, finely chopped
350 g/12 oz ziti
salt
freshly ground pepper

Skin and slice the sausage. Cut the peppers in half, remove the cores, and cut into strips. Peel and quarter the tomatoes, remove the seeds, and cut into small dice.

Heat the olive oil in a deep frying pan and sauté the onions and garlic until the onions are translucent. Add the sliced sausage and peppers and continue to cook, stirring. Add the diced tomatoes, pour in the wine, then season with the oregano and pepper to taste. Simmer for 15 to 20 minutes on low heat.

In the meantime, break the pasta into bite-sized pieces. Bring a large saucepan of lightly salted water to the boil. Add the pasta and cook according to packet instructions until al dente. Drain the pasta and combine with the sauce. Cover and leave it to stand for 1 or 2 minutes. Serve on heated plates.

Naples

An old Neapolitan proverb says, 'Three things can ruin a family: sweets, fresh bread and *maccheroni*.' For a long time, pasta made from fine flour was a costly indulgence. People still sing folksongs that are full of longing for a far-away land in which the heavens rain *maccheroni*. Only with the advent of industrial production did pasta become an affordable food for everyday enjoyment.

In Naples, which is still the centre of pasta making today, factory production began in the nineteenth century with the invention of rolling and kneading machines. In those days, almost every packet of pasta was decorated with a view of the Gulf of Naples and a plume of smoke over Mount Vesuvius.

Neapolitans believe that none less than the god Vulcan could have been the first to convert a formless mass of semolina and water into graceful strands of pasta. After this fare had won over the hearts and palates of the gods, Ceres, the goddess of growing plants and motherly love, revealed the secret of pasta making to the Neapolitans, for whom she held a special fondness.

Pipe con rana pescatrice
Pipe with Monkfish

400 g/14 oz monkfish fillets
400 g/14 oz pipe pasta
60 ml/2 fl oz olive oil
1 small white onion, finely chopped
1 garlic clove, finely chopped
1 tbsp chopped capers
1 tbsp finely chopped parsley
salt
freshly ground pepper

Wash the fish, pat it dry and dice. Bring a large saucepan of lightly salted water to the boil. Add the pasta and cook according to packet instructions until al dente.

Meanwhile, heat the olive oil in a deep saucepan and sauté the onion and garlic in it. Add the fish to the pan and fry for 4 minutes, stirring continuously. Season with salt and pepper, then add the capers.

Drain the pasta and combine it with the fish while still dripping wet. Cover the pan and leave it to stand for a minute or two. Add the parsley. Serve the pasta on four heated plates.

Orecchiette con broccoli
Orecchiette with Broccoli

500 g/1 lb 2 oz broccoli florets
1 fresh red chilli
4 anchovy fillets in oil
100 ml/3½ fl oz olive oil
4 garlic cloves, finely chopped
25 g/1 oz pine kernels
400 g/14 oz canned peeled tomatoes
300 g/11 oz orecchiette
60 g/2 oz grated Pecorino Romano
salt
freshly ground pepper

Bring a saucepan of salted water to the boil and blanch the broccoli florets for 3 minutes. Drain the broccoli thoroughly, reserving the cooking water.

Halve and core the chilli. Rinse the anchovies under cold running water. Finely chop both. Heat the olive oil in a deep frying pan and fry the chilli, anchovies, garlic and pine kernels. Add the tomatoes, season with salt and pepper, and simmer for 15 minutes.

Meanwhile, bring the broccoli water to the boil once more and cook the orecchiette in it until al dente. Drain the pasta and add it to the tomato sauce while still dripping wet. Blend in the broccoli florets and 2 tablespoons of the Pecorino Romano. Cover the pan and heat for a few minutes on low heat. Sprinkle the remaining cheese on top and serve.

Farfalle con pomodori
secchi e basilico
Farfalle with Sun-dried Tomatoes
and Basil

30 g/1 oz sun-dried tomatoes
50 g/1¾ oz pine kernels
1 handful fresh basil
2 garlic cloves, chopped
½ tsp salt
100 ml/3½ fl oz olive oil
1 tbsp grated Parmesan
400 g/14 oz farfalle
salt
freshly ground pepper

Pour hot water over the sun-dried tomatoes and soak them for 25 minutes. Then pour off the water, squeeze out the liquid and chop.

Dry-roast the pine kernels in an ungreased frying pan until golden brown. Wash the basil and pat it dry, then pluck off the leaves. Crush half of the pine kernels with the basil leaves, garlic and salt in a large mortar. Gradually work in the olive oil, then add the Parmesan last. Stir the chopped tomatoes into the basil sauce.

Bring a large saucepan of lightly salted water to the boil. Add the pasta and cook according to packet instructions until al dente. Drain the pasta and combine it, still dripping wet, with the basil-tomato sauce in a heated bowl. Serve on warmed plates seasoned with pepper and sprinkled with the remaining pine kernels.

Trofie pesto rosso
Trofie with Red Pesto

For the dough:
300 g/11 oz durum wheat flour,
plus extra for dusting
1 tsp white wine vinegar
2 tbsp olive oil
1 pinch salt
3 tbsp semolina

For the pesto:
50 g/1¾ oz pine kernels
2 garlic cloves, chopped
1 fresh red chilli, chopped
150 g/5 oz sun-dried tomatoes in oil
1 tbsp tomato purée
freshly ground pepper
1 tbsp grated Parmesan

Sift the flour into a bowl and make a well in the centre. Pour in about 150 ml/5 fl oz water and the vinegar, olive oil and salt. Knead everything into a smooth, silky dough. Divide the dough into two portions. Roll both of them out thin on a floured work surface and leave it to dry a little. Sprinkle the dough with the semolina and, using a sharp knife or pastry wheel, cut into thin noodles and roll them by hand.

For the pesto, dry-roast the pine kernels in an ungreased frying pan on low heat until golden brown, stirring constantly. Purée the pine kernels, garlic, chilli and tomatoes (including the oil) in a blender. Mix in the tomato purée and as much water as needed to make a smooth paste. Season generously with salt and pepper.

Bring a large saucepan of lightly salted water to the boil. Add the pasta and cook until al dente. Stir the Parmesan and 3 tablespoons of the pasta cooking water into the pesto sauce. Drain the pasta, tip it into a heated bowl, combine with the pesto and serve immediately. Sprinkle with additional Parmesan, if desired.

Cut off thin strips from a sheet of pasta dough with a pastry wheel or a knife.

Fully purée the ingredients for the red pesto sauce in a food processor or blender.

Cook the pasta until al dente in plenty of salted water, then drain it and combine with the pesto.

Trofie pesto rosso

Valtellina Cuisine

Valtellina, a part of Lombardy, is actually the upper Adda River Valley and flows around 129 km from the Swiss border through north-eastern Italy. The cuisine of this region is rooted in the peasant soil and consists mainly of simple, regional ingredients: aromatic little hams, meat specialities such as bresaola (air-dried beef), full-flavoured cheeses, maize, buckwheat and last but not least, wine.

The most renowned Valtelline dish is *pizzocheri*, a kind of tagliatelle made from buckwheat that is cooked with potatoes and Savoy cabbage or spare ribs and dressed with Valtellina Casera cheese. This regional semi-fat cheese is made from partially cooked, semi-skimmed cow's milk. Savoy cabbage grows in every farmer's garden and is the most popular winter vegetable. Buckwheat also thrives in the cool climate of this Alpine valley. Admittedly, buckwheat flour has not always been held in very high regard. In the meantime, however, epicures value its pleasantly rich flavour.

Pasta e lenticchie
Pasta with Lentils

150 g/5 oz Castellucio lentils
50 g/1¾ oz pancetta, diced
4 tbsp olive oil
1 small onion, finely chopped
2 garlic cloves, finely chopped
1 celery stick, diced
1 carrot, diced
500 ml/18 fl oz vegetable stock
1 bay leaf
1 sprig rosemary
200 g/7 oz short macaroni
salt
freshly ground pepper
2 tbsp finely chopped parsley

Rinse the lentils and drain them. Heat the olive oil and render the bacon. Lightly sauté the onion and garlic in the oil and bacon fat. Add the celery and carrot to the pan, cook a few minutes, then add the lentils, stock, bay leaf and rosemary. Simmer on low heat for about 40 minutes. Discard the bay leaf and rosemary. Bring a large saucepan of lightly salted water to the boil. Add the macaroni and cook it until al dente. Drain the pasta and combine it with the lentils. Season with salt and pepper and sprinkle with the parsley.

The town of Bellagio, whose lakeside promenade is lined with stylish hotels and cafés, is considered 'the pearl of Lake Como'.

Pizzoccheri
Buckwheat Pasta
with Savoy Cabbage

100 g/3½ oz buckwheat flour

100 g/3½ oz wholemeal flour,
plus extra for dusting

1 egg

2 egg yolks

1 tsp salt

3–5 tbsp white wine

250 g/9 oz Savoy cabbage

2 potatoes

100 g/3½ oz butter

2 garlic cloves, finely sliced

6 sage leaves, cut into strips

250 g/9 oz Valtellina Casera cheese, diced

Sift both flours on to a work surface and make a well in the centre. Put the egg, egg yolks, salt and white wine in the hollow and knead everything into a smooth, silky dough. Wrap the dough in a damp cloth and set it aside for 1 hour at room temperature.

On a floured work surface, roll out the dough to a thickness of 5 mm/⅕ inch. Use a pastry wheel to cut out pieces of pasta approximately 5 x 2 cm/2 x ¾ inch. Cut the Savoy cabbage into thin strips and slice the potatoes. Bring a large saucepan of lightly salted water to the boil. Add the cabbage and potatoes and cook for 15 minutes. Then add the pasta and cook for another 10 minutes.

Meanwhile, melt the butter and stir in the garlic and sage. Drain the potatoes, cabbage and pasta and place them in a preheated bowl. Mix in the Valtellina Casera cheese and pour the sage butter over the dish.

Pasta Ripiena, Delicious and Much Loved

Pasta ripiena (stuffed or filled pasta) has captured the fancy and stimulated the creativity of Italian chefs for centuries. Even today, the starting point is pasta dough made with fresh eggs, filled with all sorts of delicious things and shaped into 'pockets', squares, rectangles, triangles, circles, rings, crescents, even 'hats'. *Pasta ripiena* is mainly found in northern and central Italy. This is

The basis of very popular northern and central Italian pasta ripiena is fresh egg noodle dough cut into various shapes and stuffed.

because fresh eggs, a prerequisite for supple, smooth dough that can be easily moulded, used to be a rarity in southern Italy.

Initially, the large selection of *pasta ripiena* can be confusing to non-Italians. Not only their shapes differ almost from city to city, but every region has its own tradition when it comes to the filling, too. In Romagna they use meat, in Emilia, herbs. Stew meat is the custom in Piedmont; herbs, fish or meat in Liguria, and meat or sausage in Tuscany. *Cappelletti*, the smallest stuffed pasta, come from Ferrara and are filled with a turkey mixture. If they are made with pumpkin, they are called *cappellacci*. Large *tortelloni* come from Piacenza and have a ricotta and herb filling. Small *tortellini* from Bologna are stuffed with a mixture of meat, mortadella and ham. *Ravioli* from Modena

contain roast meat, while Parma, the city of *anolini*, uses a meat and vegetable filling. In Piedmont, *agnolotti* are stuffed with meat and cabbage. Ligurian *pansoti* have wild herbs in them and, in the Marche, *cappelletti alla pescarese* have roast pork, cooked capon or turkey filling.

Tortellini

It is said that Venus herself, the goddess of love, served as a model for the beguiling pasta rings called *tortellini*. According to legend, Venus had stopped at a simple inn during a visit to the earth. When the innkeeper brought a refreshment to her room, the naked Venus suddenly stood across from him. Overcome by the perfect shape of her navel, he rushed immediately into the kitchen to replicate it in dough form.

The truth is, tortellini are the culinary emblem of Bologna. In the little lanes of the provincial capital, you can almost look over the shoulders of the tortellini makers while they work. Tortellini are served in a rich broth or with meat ragout. They taste best in one of the typical trattorias between the Piazza Maggiore and the pergolas of the historic old city centre, just a few steps away from the towers of the Asinelli and Garisenda families.

Tortellini are delicious little stuffed 'pasta pockets'. They are traditionally served with melted butter and Parmesan.

The triangle is curved around the forefinger and the tip of the triangle folded in. Finally, the ends of the dough are joined in a ring.

Venus' navel supposedly served as the model for shapely tortellini.

The pasta dough is rolled out thin and cut first into strips, then into squares.

Filling is placed in the centre of each square, which is then folded into a triangle.

Tortellini ai funghi
Mushroom Tortellini

For the dough:
1 g saffron strands
300 g/11 oz Italian flour,
plus extra for dusting
1 egg and 1 egg white
2 tbsp oil
½ tsp salt
1 tbsp vinegar

For the filling:
2 tbsp butter
2 shallots, finely chopped
1 garlic clove, finely chopped
300 g/11 oz button mushrooms
or wild mushrooms, finely chopped
2 tbsp finely chopped parsley
1 tsp dried thyme
2 tbsp grated Parmesan
salt and pepper

Soak the saffron in 2 tablespoons of hot water. Place the flour in a bowl, press a hollow in the centre and pour the saffron water into it through a sieve. Add the egg, egg white, oil, salt and vinegar and knead into a silky, smooth dough. Add a little water as needed. Wrap the dough in clingfilm and chill in the refrigerator for 1 hour.

For the filling, melt the butter in a frying pan, add the shallots, garlic and mushrooms, and sauté on medium heat until all the liquid evaporates. Blend in the parsley and season with the thyme, salt and pepper. Leave the mushroom mixture to cool slightly, then stir in the Parmesan. Put the mixture in the refrigerator to chill.

Thinly roll out the pasta dough. Cut it into 6-cm/2½-inch squares with a pastry wheel and place a little of the filling in the middle of each square. Fold each square into a triangle, being sure to securely close the edges of the dough over the filling.

Wind each triangle around your forefinger. Curve the tip and lay the other two corners over your finger. Clasp the ends into a ring and press them firmly together. Set the tortellini on a floured tea towel to dry for 30 minutes. Bring a large saucepan of lightly salted water to the boil. Add the tortellini and cook until al dente.

Ravioli al formaggio
Ravioli with Feta Cheese

For the dough:
300 g/11 oz Italian flour,
plus extra for dusting
2 eggs
1 tbsp oil
½ tsp salt
1 tsp vinegar
3–4 tbsp water

For the filling:
250 g/9 oz feta cheese
2 garlic cloves, finely chopped
2 tbsp finely chopped parsley
1 fresh red chilli,
cored and finely chopped
salt and pepper

Knead the flour, eggs, oil, salt, vinegar and water into a silky, smooth dough. Wrap the dough in clingfilm and chill in the refrigerator for 1 hour.

For the filling, crumble the cheese and combine it with the garlic, parsley and chilli. Season to taste with salt and pepper. Prepare the ravioli in the same way as for the following recipe, *Ravioli alla zucca*.

Ravioli alla zucca
Pumpkin-filled Ravioli

For the dough:
300 g/11 oz Italian flour,
plus extra for dusting
2 eggs
1 tbsp oil
½ tsp salt
1 tsp vinegar
3–4 tbsp water

For the filling:
1 tbsp olive oil
500 g/1 lb 2 oz pumpkin, cubed
1 shallot, finely diced
50 g/1¾ oz grated Parmesan
1 egg
1 tbsp finely chopped parsley
salt and pepper

Knead the flour, eggs, oil, salt, vinegar and water into a silky, smooth dough. Wrap the dough in clingfilm and chill in the refrigerator for 1 hour.

For the filling, heat the olive oil in a frying pan and sauté the pumpkin and shallot until the shallot is translucent. Add 125 ml/4 fl oz water and cook the pumpkin until the liquid evaporates. Cool slightly, then mix with the Parmesan, egg, parsley, and salt and pepper.

Divide the dough in half. Thinly roll out both pieces. Place small spoonfuls of the pumpkin mixture about 4 cm/1½ inches apart on one sheet of pasta. Brush a little water on the spaces in between. Lay the second sheet on top and press down around each piece of filling. Use a pastry wheel to cut out squares, then press their edges together with a fork. Set aside the ravioli to dry for 30 minutes, then bring a large saucepan of lightly salted water to the boil. Add the ravioli and cook over medium heat until al dente. Remove them with a slotted spoon and drain well on paper towels.

VALLE D'AOSTA

Valle d'Aosta & Alto Adige

The insurmountable chain of the Alps has shielded the residents of the Valle d'Aosta and their traditions from many outside influences for centuries. Nevertheless, Roman legionaries had left their culinary imprint behind. They not only brought the art of viticulture to this isolated region, but their barley soup as well. To this day, soup made from meat stock, polenta and *fonduta*, a kind of cheese fondue, are important parts of daily cooking.

The most well-known soup recipes date back to Roman times: *zuppa valdostana* and *zuppa alla valpellinetze*, made from Savoy cabbage, cabbage and stale rye bread. Soups are often served with bacon or sausage. Air-dried hams from Bosses, for which a Mass is said annually in July, are famous, as are *lardo di Arnad*, a kind of bacon flavoured with herbs and spices, and a beef speciality that is preserved in salt.

The Valle d'Aosta region borders Switzerland to the north. One of the most beautiful views of the Matterhorn is from idyllically situated Lake Blu, a glacial lake.

TRENTINO— ALTO ADIGE

Peasant culture and tradition characterize traditional Alto Adige home cooking, which artfully unites Mediterranean and Tyrolean cooking secrets. Wine, milk, cheese, vegetables, fruit, honey and bread: the palette of products is as diverse as the land itself, and most are still made using artisanal methods that have been handed down for generations. *Moretti*, sausages seasoned with wild herbs, are as much at home here as the famous bacon. With more than 300 sunny days and up to 2,000 hours of sunlight per year, conditions for growing fruit are simply heavenly. Apples and wine grapes, in particular, grow superbly.

The Speck Festival held in Bolzano in May is popular with tourists and natives alike, and the Consortium invites everyone to taste their bacon specialities. In the autumn, *törggelen* is a great attraction, when nearly every small restaurant offers hot chestnuts, *schüttelbrot* (an old Alto Adige speciality), bacon and cheese to go with the young wine. *Törggelen* is an old custom: after the grape harvest, when harvesting in the fields was over with, the farmers finally had time to taste the *nuien* (new, sweet and sweeter wines) with family and friends. Derived from the Latin *torculum*, the grape press is still called a *torkl* or *torggl* in the vernacular.

The Funes Valley lies in the province of Bolzano and is especially popular among nature-loving mountain climbers in the autumn.

Schlutzkrapfen
Filled Pasta Pockets

150 g/5 oz rye flour
100 g/3½ oz wholemeal flour
1 egg
1 tbsp olive oil
300 g/11 oz spinach
150 g/5 oz butter
1 small onion, finely chopped
1 garlic clove, finely chopped
100 g/3½ oz quark (curd cheese)
100 g/3½ oz Parmesan, grated
freshly grated nutmeg
salt and pepper
snipped chives to garnish

Knead together both flours, the egg, olive oil and 3–4 tablespoons of lukewarm water into a smooth dough. Form it into a ball, wrap in clingfilm and set aside for 30 minutes. Wash the spinach. While still dripping wet, heat it in a covered saucepan briefly until it wilts. Drain well, then chop finely. Heat 1 tablespoon of butter and sauté the onion and garlic. Remove from the heat and mix in the spinach, quark and 1 tablespoon of Parmesan. Season with nutmeg, salt and pepper.

Roll out the dough as thin as possible in a pasta machine. Cut out circles 7 cm/2¾ inch in diameter. Place a little spinach filling on each circle, moisten the edges with water and fold the dough over the filling to form a semicircle. Press the edges together. Cook until al dente in gently boiling salted water.

Brown the remaining butter and pour it over the *schultzkrapfen*. Sprinkle with the remaining Parmesan and the chives.

Panzerotti al gambero
Panzerotti Stuffed with Prawns

250 g/9 oz flour, plus extra for dusting
2 eggs
5 tbsp olive oil
1 tbsp wine vinegar
300 g/11 oz raw prawns
40 ml/2½ tbsp brandy
250 ml/9 fl oz white wine
300 g/11 oz tomatoes
1 onion, diced
1 garlic clove, finely chopped
1 tbsp balsamic vinegar
5 spring onions, chopped
1 celery stick, diced
2 tbsp finely chopped parsley
sugar
salt and pepper
celery leaves to garnish

Knead together the flour, eggs, 1 tablespoon of olive oil, vinegar, 1–2 tablespoons of water and a pinch of salt into a silky, smooth dough. Wrap the dough in clingfilm and chill in the refrigerator for 2 hours.

Wash the prawns and drain them. Heat 1 tablespoon of oil in a frying pan and fry the prawns briefly on all sides until they turn pink. Then remove from the pan and leave them to cool.

Shell and de-vein the prawns. Finely chop the heads and shells and brown in the pan for 2 minutes. Pour in the brandy and wine, then vigorously boil down the resulting stock. Pour off the liquid through a fine sieve and set it aside.

Peel and quarter the tomatoes, remove the seeds, and dice. Heat the remaining oil in a clean frying pan and sauté the onion and garlic. Add the tomatoes and cook briefly. Pour in the stock, stir, then season to taste with the vinegar, sugar, salt and pepper. Simmer on low heat until the sauce thickens.

Dice the prawns. Combine with the spring onions and celery, and add salt and pepper.

Thinly roll out the dough on a floured work surface. Cut out 10-cm/4-inch circles of dough. Use a teaspoon to place grape-sized portions of the filling on the dough circles. Fold half of the dough over the filling so that it forms a semicircle. With a fork, press the edges together around the filling.

Place portions of the panzerotti in boiling salted water and cook on medium heat for 3 to 4 minutes. Remove with a slotted spoon and transfer into the sauce. Sprinkle with the chopped parsley and garnish with celery leaves to serve.

Sauté the prawns briefly in olive oil until they turn pink. Then remove from the shells.

Stew the tomatoes with onion and garlic, then pour in the prawn stock.

Cut circles out of the sheet of dough. Put a little filling in the centre of each. Fold the dough over into semicircles.

Cook the panzerotti in boiling, salted water for several minutes, then remove with a slotted spoon.

Lasagne

As with so many Italian dishes, the most famous baked pasta, *lasagne*, has ancient Roman roots. The writer Horace raved about *lagani*, thin sheets of pasta made from water and flour. He enjoyed eating the pasta with chickpeas and leeks. *Lasagne e ceci*, lasagne with chickpeas, is still a very popular dish in Basilicata today.

Proficient home cooks and good restaurants prepare their lasagne with home-made pasta. The pasta dough is thinly rolled out, then cut into strips 10 cm (4 inches) wide and the same length as the baking dish in which the lasagne will be made. After letting the pasta dry for a while, it can be used uncooked. Store-bought lasagne is faster and easier, and it is also available ready to use without precooking.

Lasagne is a culinary delight. It consists of alternating layers of pasta, vegetables, meat or fish, and sauce. Tomato sauce provides a fresh, juicy taste, while a bechamel sauce makes the lasagne creamy and also gives it firmness. Mozzarella or Parmesan make for a crisp, cheesy crust when it is grilled.

Garlic

This aromatic, healthy bulb was long considered to be poor people's food. In fact, noblemen who smelled of garlic were denied entry at court. But in the end, the little white or red garlic bulb finally did find its way into fine cuisine, at least in Italy. Not only the pungent aroma, but also the health benefits of garlic are indisputable. Its intense odour, perceived by some to be unpleasant, comes from the essential oil that is released not only via the breath, but also through the pores of the skin after it is eaten.

Lasagne con verdure e coda di rospo
Vegetable Lasagne with Monkfish

100 g/3½ oz butter, plus extra for greasing
2 onions, diced
1 tbsp flour
150 ml/5 fl oz fish stock
125 ml/4 fl oz dry vermouth
500 ml/18 fl oz double cream
2 egg yolks
1 tbsp spicy mustard
juice of 1 lemon
2–3 leeks, sliced
3 courgettes, diced
4 carrots, diced
1 fennel bulb, diced
80 g/3 oz breadcrumbs
2 garlic cloves, finely chopped
2 tbsp finely chopped parsley
12 lasagne noodles
500 g/1 lb 2 oz monkfish fillets
1 handful fresh dill, finely chopped
salt and pepper

Heat half the butter and sauté the onion, then dust with the flour. Pour in the fish stock and vermouth and simmer for 10 minutes. Stir in the cream and cook 10 minutes more. Remove from the heat and bind with the egg yolk. Season with salt, pepper, mustard and lemon juice. Preheat the oven to 200°C/390°F/gas mark 6 and grease a baking dish with butter.

Blanch the vegetables and drain. In a bowl, mix them with half of the sauce. Fry the garlic and breadcrumbs in the remaining butter until golden brown. Mix in the parsley.

Cover the base of the baking dish with a thin layer of sauce. Layer lasagne noodles, half the vegetables and half the breadcrumbs. Top with another layer of pasta. Arrange the fish on the pasta, season with salt, pepper and dill, and pour a little sauce over it. Then cover with more lasagne noodles, the remainder of the vegetables and a little of the breadcrumb mixture, and finish with a layer of noodles. Pour the rest of the sauce over top, sprinkle on the left-over breadcrumbs and bake for 20 to 25 minutes.

Lasagne verde al forno
Green Lasagne with Minced Beef

2 tbsp olive oil,
plus extra for greasing
1 onion, diced
2 garlic cloves, finely chopped
1 carrot, diced
1 celery stick, diced
400 g/14 oz minced beef
500 g/1 lb 2 oz canned tomato purée
2 tsp dried oregano
600 ml/1 pint bechamel sauce
12 green lasagne noodles,
ready to use without precooking
300 g/11 oz mozzarella, thinly sliced
50 g/1¾ oz grated Parmesan
salt
freshly ground pepper

Preheat the oven to 200°C/390°F/gas mark 6 and grease a rectangular baking dish. Heat the olive oil in a frying pan and sauté the onion, garlic, carrots and celery, then add the mince and brown it, stirring often. When the meat has browned, mix in the tomatoes, season with salt, pepper and oregano, and simmer for 15 minutes.

Heat the bechamel sauce and cover the base of the baking dish with a thin layer of it. Alternate a layer of lasagne noodles with a layer of meat sauce, then mozzarella slices, followed by lasagne noodles and bechamel sauce until all the ingredients have been used. Finally, cover the top of the lasagne with bechamel sauce and sprinkle with the Parmesan. Bake for 25 to 30 minutes. Wait 5 minutes before cutting the lasagne.

Trenette al forno con tonno
Baked Trenette with Tuna Fish

370 g/13 oz canned tuna and vegetables
500 g/1 lb 2 oz canned tomato purée
1 tsp dried oregano
1 tbsp finely chopped parsley
350 g/12 oz trenette pasta
300 g/11 oz mozzarella, diced
2 tomatoes, sliced
salt
freshly ground pepper

Preheat the oven to 200°C/390°F/gas mark 6 and grease a baking dish. Drain the tuna and vegetables in a sieve, then use a fork to flake the fish. Heat the tomato purée in a saucepan, add the tuna and simmer for a few minutes. Remove the sauce from the heat and season with oregano, parsley, salt and pepper.

Bring a large saucepan of lightly salted water to the boil. Add the pasta and cook according to packet instructions until al dente. Drain well. Spread one-third of the sauce in the base of the baking dish. Layer half of the pasta and half the mozzarella on top, then pour in another third of the sauce and add the remaining pasta. Spread the remaining sauce over the pasta and cover with sliced tomatoes. Layer the remaining mozzarella on top and bake the casserole for approximately 30 minutes.

Cannelloni agli spinaci
Spinach Cannelloni

600 g/1 lb 5 oz spinach
1½ tbsp butter
1 small onion, finely chopped
200 g/7 oz ricotta cheese
12 cannelloni,
ready to use without precooking
600 ml/1 pint bechamel sauce
50 g/1¾ oz grated Parmesan
salt
freshly ground pepper
freshly grated nutmeg

Preheat the oven to 200°C/390°F/gas mark 6 and grease a baking dish. Wash the spinach thoroughly and remove any wilted leaves and coarse stalks. Heat the butter in a saucepan and sauté the onion until it is translucent. Add the spinach while still dripping wet, cover the pan and leave it to wilt. Drain the spinach well in a sieve, then chop it.

Combine the spinach and ricotta, then add salt, pepper and nutmeg to taste. Transfer the spinach mixture into a piping bag with a large nozzle and use it to fill the cannelloni.

Lay the filled cannelloni side by side in the baking dish, cover with the bechamel sauce and sprinkle with the Parmesan. Bake for 25 to 30 minutes.

THE MARCHE

The Marche

From a geographical perspective, the Marche region is a link between northern and southern Italy. The adjacent regions have strongly influenced its cuisine: Piedmont to the north, Tuscany and Umbria to the west along the Apennines, and Abruzzo to the south. But it was not the magnificent Renaissance cuisine of its neighbours that left a deep footprint here.

The classic cuisine of the Marche is not fancy, and regional agricultural products including grain, wine, honey, fruit, vegetables and milk shape it. Added to that are fish and seafood on its 180 km (112 miles) of Adriatic coastline and in the interior, pork, ham and sausage. *Porchetta*, grilled suckling pig seasoned with wild fennel, is a typical food of this region. According to natives, however, their greatest wealth comes from the earth. Along with highly coveted white truffles, these include wild mushrooms, herbs and the large olives that were already famous in antiquity. They produce a flavourful oil with very little acidity.

Apart from numerous shops and small restaurants, the city of Gradara also has a well-preserved medieval castle.

Vincisgrassi

The 'national' pasta dish of the Marche is *vincisgrassi*, a kind of lasagne that is prepared with chicken giblets and pancetta, but without tomato sauce. On major holidays, the classic recipe is enhanced with sliced truffles, whereby the amount of truffles used is based on financial considerations rather than any recipe requirements.

The name *vincisgrassi* supposedly goes back to the Prince of Windisch-Graetz, an Austrian field marshal who was in the Marche in 1799 during the Napoleonic Wars and, according to legend, prized this dish above all else. The recipe itself, however, must surely be considerably older.

Vincisgrassi
Marche-style Lasagne

100 g/3½ oz butter
100 g/3½ oz pancetta, diced
1 small onion, diced
1 carrot, diced
300 g/11 oz chicken giblets
50 ml/1½ fl oz white wine
1 tbsp tomato purée
100 ml/3½ fl oz meat stock
⅛ tsp cinnamon
20 g/¾ oz dried ceps
125 ml/4 fl oz milk
400 ml/14 fl oz bechamel sauce
12 lasagne noodles,
ready to use without precooking
75 g/2½ oz grated Parmesan
salt
freshly ground pepper

Heat the butter in a deep frying pan and render the pancetta. Add the onion and carrot and sauté. Chop the giblets, setting aside the liver. Add the other giblets to the pan, fry briefly, then deglaze with the wine. Stir the tomato purée into the stock and add to the meat in the pan. Season with the cinnamon, and salt and pepper to taste. Cover and simmer on low heat for about 1 hour. Soak the ceps in lukewarm water.

Pour the water off the ceps, squeeze out excess liquid and cut the mushrooms into small pieces. Add them to the pan along with the chopped chicken liver and milk. Mix everything well, then simmer for 30 minutes.

Grease a rectangular baking dish and preheat the oven to 200°C/390°F/gas mark 6. Heat the bechamel sauce and cover the base of the dish with a thin layer of it. Alternate lasagne noodles with chicken sauce, followed by noodles and bechamel sauce until all ingredients have been used. Spread bechamel sauce on top of the lasagne and sprinkle with Parmesan. Bake for 25 to 30 minutes. Wait 5 minutes before cutting the lasagne.

GNOCCHI

Gnocchi are a classic part of Italian cuisine and, particularly in northern and central Italy, a popular first course. Despite the simplicity of the ingredients from which they are made, they are a delicacy. Connoisseurs declare that they taste best *au naturel* with nothing more than a little melted butter and freshly grated Parmesan; yet it would be a shame to forego all the other delicious gnocchi dishes.

Gnocchi probably originated in Lombardy in association with the pre-Lenten carnival celebrations. Traditionally, gnocchi were prepared by the man of the house and eaten with butter, tomato sauce or with sugar and cinnamon.

Cooking perfect gnocchi is an art form that requires some time. They must be fluffy, yet retain their shape during cooking. Almost no one achieves this on their first try.

Preparation of the dough demands an instinctive feel, because there are no precise guidelines for the ingredients. The amount of flour needed for the dough depends on the amount of starch in the potatoes, and will range between 200 and 350 grams of flour per kilogram (3–5 oz per pound) of potatoes. To make the best possible gnocchi, use fully ripe baking potatoes and allow the steam escape from them before putting them through a potato press.

The shape of the gnocchi is just as important as the choice of the right potatoes. Genuine gnocchi must have grooves or indentations so they are better able to pick up the butter or sauce. This is accomplished either by rolling each gnocchi over the back of a fork or by pressing them against the inside of a cheese grater. Gnocchi that are made in factories generally have a smooth surface, which is a peccadillo in the eyes of traditionalists.

Basic Gnocchi Recipe

1 kg/2 lb 4 oz baking potatoes
1 egg
2 egg yolks
300 g/11 oz flour
salt

Bring a saucepan of salted water to the boil and cook the potatoes for about 25 minutes. Then pour off the water. Cool the potatoes slightly, peel them and put through a potato press while still hot. Leave them to cool further and salt lightly.

Knead together the potatoes, egg and egg yolks. Work in as much flour as needed to produce a smooth, supple dough that does not stick to your fingers. The amount of flour will vary depending on the type of potatoes used. On a floured work surface, form finger-width rolls or logs from the potato dough. Cut the logs into pieces 2–3 cm/¾–1 inch long and gently roll each one over the back of a fork to give the gnocchi their characteristic texture. Bring a large saucepan of salted water to the boil and cook the gnocchi, in portions, until they rise to the surface. Remove with a slotted spoon, drain and prepare according to the desired recipe.

Gnocchi di zucca mantovani
Mantua-style Pumpkin Gnocchi

500 g/1 lb 2 oz pumpkin flesh
150 g/5 oz flour
50 g/1¾ oz amaretti crumbs
2 eggs
1 pinch salt
75 g/2½ oz butter, melted
75 g/2½ oz grated Parmesan

Preheat the oven to 200°C/390°F/gas mark 6. Dice the pumpkin, place it in a baking dish and bake for 45 minutes. Press the pumpkin through a sieve while it is still hot. Add the flour, amaretti crumbs, eggs and a pinch of salt to the pumpkin and knead thoroughly into a smooth, supple dough. On a floured work surface, form finger-width rolls. Cut them into pieces about 2–3 cm/¾–1 inch long and gently roll each one over the back of a fork. Bring a large saucepan of salted water to the boil and cook the gnocchi, in portions, until they rise to the surface. Remove with a slotted spoon, drain and drizzle each serving with melted butter and sprinkle with grated Parmesan.

To make gnocchi dough, boil the potatoes, remove the skins and put through a potato press while still hot.

Knead the potato with egg, egg yolks and as much flour as needed to produce a smooth, supple dough.

Divide the dough into portions on a floured surface and form into finger-width rolls.

Cut off small pieces from the roll of potato dough with a sharp knife or a cleaver.

Roll the gnocchi over the back of a fork to give them texture, and cook in boiling salted water.

The gnocchi are done when they rise to the surface. Remove from the water with a slotted spoon.

Drain the gnocchi and when all are cooked toss them in a tomato sauce.

Simmer briefly in the sauce, then sprinkle with freshly grated Parmesan.

Verona and the Gnocchi Festival

The old city of Verona – cultured, renowned, lively and colourful – lies on a tongue of land formed by the river Adige. Romans, Ostrogoths, Franks, Saxons, Hohenstaufers and later the Venetians as well, have all left their mark on the cityscape of this northern Italian city, one of the most beautiful in Italy. It was named a World Heritage Centre by UNESCO in 2000. Tourist attractions include the *Casa di Giulietta*, the house at Via Cappello 23, where Juliet longingly awaited her Romeo in Shakespeare's version of the legend, as well as the Roman amphitheatre that forms the backdrop for a world-famous opera festival each summer.

The *Baccanale del gnocco*, also called the *Funzione dei gnocchi* and the *Festa dell'abbondanza*, is worth seeing during carnival time in Verona. On carnival Friday, a *Papa del Gnocho* (Pope of Bacchanalia) is chosen. He leads the festive carnival procession through the old city, riding on a donkey, outfitted with an artificial belly full of gnocchi and a giant fork for a sceptre, on which a colossal gnocco is skewered. After the procession, everyone present is served gnocchi, either with the traditional topping of melted butter and shaved cheese or with *pastissada de caval*, a flavourful ragout made with horsemeat. The custom dates back to the sixteenth century. Between 1520 and 1531, the Adige flooded frequently, causing famines. In those days, a doctor named Tommaso da Vico gave out free flour, cheese and wine to the needy in the vicinity of the Romanesque Basilica of San Zeno. *Pastissada de caval* has an even longer history, stretching back more than 1,500 years. The people of Verona were near starvation during wartime when, after a particularly gruesome battle, horses were left strewn over the battlefield. King Theodoric allowed the people have the horsemeat, and this dish was the result. Our recipe is prepared with beef, resulting in a somewhat different flavour.

Gnoccho literally means 'dumpling', but it also means 'dunce' in the vernacular. True to the motto, 'you are what you eat', the Veronese were first called *gnocchi* in a mocking line of poetry that dates from the nineteenth century.

The Ponte Pietra is among Verona's places of interest. Both of the arched bridges on the left bank of the Adige date back to Roman times.

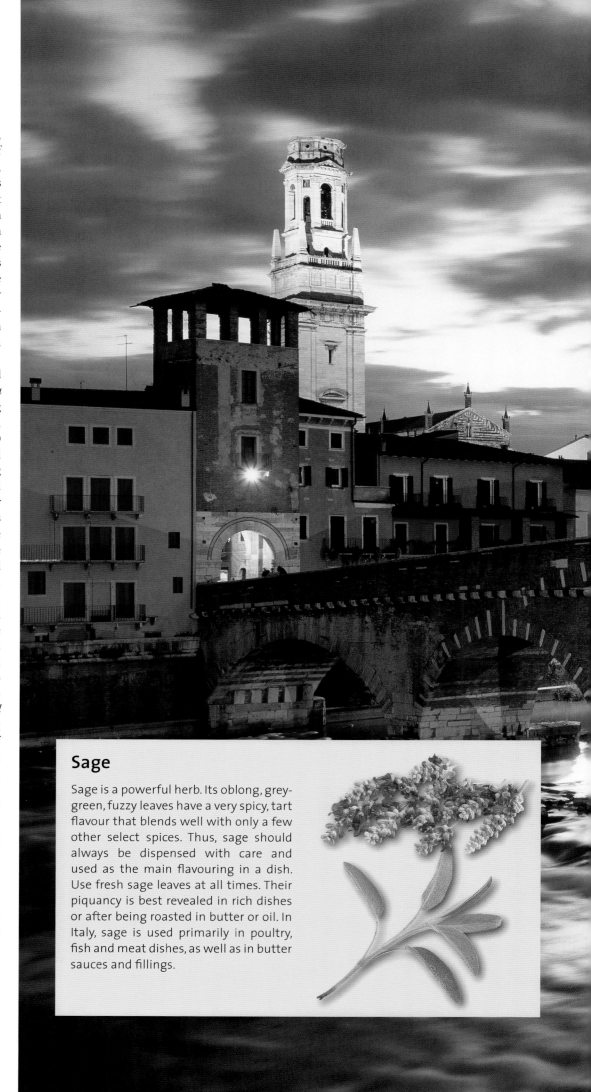

Sage

Sage is a powerful herb. Its oblong, grey-green, fuzzy leaves have a very spicy, tart flavour that blends well with only a few other select spices. Thus, sage should always be dispensed with care and used as the main flavouring in a dish. Use fresh sage leaves at all times. Their piquancy is best revealed in rich dishes or after being roasted in butter or oil. In Italy, sage is used primarily in poultry, fish and meat dishes, as well as in butter sauces and fillings.

Gnocchi del carnevale di Verona
Verona's Carnival Gnocchi

800 g/1 lb 12 oz beef
2 tbsp olive oil
1 tbsp butter
1 white onion, finely chopped
2 garlic cloves, finely chopped
1 tsp Hungarian paprika
250 ml/9 fl oz red wine
4 tomatoes, roughly chopped
1 bay leaf
1 handful fresh thyme
250 ml/9 fl oz meat stock
salt
freshly ground pepper
cooked gnocchi from 1 kg/2 lb 4 oz potatoes
(see basic gnocchi recipe on page 167)

Cut the meat into small cubes. Heat the olive oil and butter in a casserole and brown the meat in it. Add the onion and garlic and sauté them. Season with the paprika, salt and pepper, then deglaze the pot with the wine. Stir in the tomatoes and add the herbs, then the stock. Stew on low heat for about 2 hours, then remove the herbs. Season the ragout to taste with salt and pepper, and serve with freshly cooked gnocchi.

Varieties of Gnocchi

The gnocchi family is large. Depending on the region, these small dumplings may be made from potatoes, pumpkin, semolina, maize or chestnut flour. In Trentino, little gnocchi are prepared with potato dough and beetroots. Melted butter is then poured over them and they are sprinkled with poppy seeds. Potato gnocchi are also stuffed with a hefty cheese-and-bacon mixture.

Sweet *gnocchi di prugne* come from the area near the Austrian border, and are stuffed with dried plums. In Trieste, they also make sweet *gnocchi al cacao* from potato gnocchi with plain chocolate and crystallized fruit. These are not served as a dessert, but rather as a first course, even though they are sweet, and may be part of an antipasto buffet.

Gnocchi alla romana do not come from the Italian capital as their name suggests, but from Piedmont. Made from durum wheat semolina, these dumplings or slices are topped with cheese and baked in the oven. No one knows how they found their way from Piedmont to Rome or how the tradition of eating this dish on Thursdays originated.

The name of the gnocchi speciality from Lombardy is not very flattering: *malfatti* (badly made). These are tasty round pasta balls made from chopped spinach, ricotta and flour. Their name stems from their rather simple form as compared with that of classic gnocchi.

Sardinian *malloreddus*, however, resemble little ribbed shells and are seasoned with saffron. They are served with tomato sauce, diced spicy sausages and grated feta cheese.

Gnocchi are found throughout Italy in many different shapes and sizes. The ingredients also vary from one region to another.

Gnocchi con salsa all'astice
Venetian-style Gnocchi with Lobster Sauce

250 ml/9 fl oz double cream
125 ml/4 fl oz white wine
200 g/7 oz cooked lobster meat
salt
freshly ground pepper
freshly grated nutmeg
1 tbsp finely chopped fennel
cooked gnocchi from 1 kg/2 lb 4 oz potatoes (see basic gnocchi recipe on page 167)

Combine the cream and wine in a saucepan, heat and reduce a little. Remove the lobster meat from the shell(s) and cut into small pieces. Heat the lobster in the sauce, but do not boil the sauce. Season with salt, pepper and nutmeg, then add the fennel. Serve the cooked gnocchi topped with the lobster sauce.

Gnocchi alla romana

Gnocchi alla romana
Roman-style Gnocchi

500 ml/18 fl oz milk
125 g/4½ oz butter,
plus extra for greasing
½ tsp salt
250 g/9 oz durum wheat semolina
100 g/3½ oz grated Parmesan
2 egg yolks
2 tbsp grated fontina cheese
salt
freshly ground pepper
freshly grated nutmeg

Combine the milk, 400 ml/14 fl oz water, 2 tablespoons of the butter and the salt in a large saucepan and bring to the boil. Gradually sprinkle in the semolina and cook on low heat for 25 to 30 minutes, stirring continuously. Transfer the mixture to a bowl and stir in 2 tablespoons of the Parmesan and the egg yolks. Season the mixture with salt, pepper and nutmeg. Set aside to cool.

Grease a baking dish and preheat the oven to 200°C/390°F/gas mark 6. Use two spoons to form gnocchi from the semolina dough and set them in the baking dish. Mix the remaining Parmesan with the fontina and sprinkle over the gnocchi. Melt the rest of the butter and pour it over the cheese. Bake for about 20 minutes until golden brown.

Malfatti
Lombardian Gnocchi

500 g/1 lb 2 oz spinach
100 g/3½ oz butter
1 small onion, finely chopped
200 g/7 oz ricotta cheese
2 eggs
75 g/2½ oz freshly grated Parmesan
freshly grated nutmeg
salt
freshly ground white pepper
150 g/5 oz flour
2 tbsp cornflour
8 sage leaves

Wash the spinach thoroughly, removing any wilted leaves and coarse stalks. Place it in a saucepan while still dripping wet. Cover the pan and wilt the spinach on medium heat, then pour off the liquid and drain well. Melt 1 tablespoon of the butter in a frying pan and sauté the onion until translucent. Finely chop the spinach, add it to the onion, then remove from the heat and set aside to cool.

Blend together the ricotta, eggs and 2 tablespoons of the Parmesan until smooth. Add the chopped spinach and season with nutmeg, salt and pepper. Gradually work in the flour and cornflour. If the dough is too soft, knead in a little more flour.

Bring a large saucepan of lightly salted water to the boil. Form the dough into little balls and cook in the boiling salted water until they rise to the surface. Then remove the gnocchi with a slotted spoon and drain well. Melt the rest of the butter and toss the sage leaves in it. Divide the gnocchi among plates that have been heated. Sprinkle each serving with some of the remaining Parmesan and drizzle with the sage butter.

Malfatti

POLENTA

Grain porridge, called *puls* or *pulmentum*, was already an important staple in antiquity. It consisted of ground cereals, most often oats, buckwheat or spelt, that was cooked in water. Long before rice, maize or potatoes arrived in Italy, grain porridge, the original version of *polenta*, nourished countless Roman legionaries, simple craftsmen and peasants.

With the discovery of the New World, maize was brought to Europe, initially as an imported good. Starting with Venice, it spread throughout northern and central Italy. Leonardo Emo Capodilista, a patrician, was supposedly the first to plant maize in Italy as an economical provision for his household servants. The adept Venetian merchants soon recognized the value of the new crop: the crop yield added up to eighty times that of the seed rate.

Later on, polenta became a food for people who were too poor to buy bread. It was eaten for breakfast. According to legend, farmers in Piedmont dipped slices of polenta in salted anchovies to give them

Maize is principally cultivated in northern Italy. The kernels are ground into corn semolina, the finished product used to make popular polenta, which is much more than simple maize flour.

some flavour. The anchovies were not eaten along with the polenta, but were used to flavour several servings instead. In Venice, mortadella or pickled fish is still eaten on cold slices of polenta today.

Over the course of centuries, polenta followed the same culinary path as many other dishes of humble origins. It has evolved from a poor people's meal to classic cuisine, winning a permanent place for itself on the menus of upscale dining establishments.

Southern Italians still mockingly call their northern countrymen *polentoni* ('polenta eaters') because of their taste for golden yellow or white polenta. In the countryside, polenta is still cooked traditionally in a copper kettle, or *paiolo*, which is placed over an open fire and stirred for as long as an hour with a long-handled wooden spoon. Afterwards the porridge is ladled on to a towel with some semolina strewn over it or on to a damp cutting board, formed into a rectangle with a wooden spatula and, once it has cooled, cut into slices with thin twine.

Polenta is highly versatile. It can be cooked fresh and served as a meal in itself with melted butter and cheese, but it can also be combined with fish, poultry or meat. Once cooled, it can be sliced and fried, grilled or baked. The Venetians tend

to cook polenta with milk, and in Abruzzo it is prepared like risotto with vegetables. In northern Lombardy, yellow corn semolina is mixed with buckwheat flour, resulting in a dark, flavourful polenta called *polenta taragna*. Perhaps the most sophisticated variation comes from Piedmont, where polenta slices are fried, topped with a fried egg and crowned with finely shaved white truffles.

Polenta e fontina
Polenta with Fontina

1 tsp salt
250 g/9 oz coarsely ground polenta
60 g/2 oz butter, plus extra for greasing
150 g/5 oz fontina cheese
freshly ground white pepper

Follow the basic recipe on page 173 to make the polenta. Rinse a round baking dish with cold water. Transfer the polenta to the dish, spread it smooth and leave to cool. Then remove it from the dish and slice through the polenta twice, horizontally, to yield three even layers. Clean the baking dish and grease it with butter.

Preheat the oven to 200°C/390°F/gas mark 6. Thinly slice the cheese. Lay a slice of polenta in the baking dish. Top it with a third of the cheese slices, season with white pepper, then cover with the next slice of polenta. Repeat, then spread the rest of the cheese on top. Place little knobs of butter over it. Bake for 20 to 25 minutes.

The first step to successful polenta is to stir polenta into boiling salted water.

Simmer the polenta for 30 minutes. Then pour it into a mould, spread it smooth and leave it to cool.

Once it is cool, remove the polenta from the mould, slice it thin, then grill or pan-fry.

Basic Polenta Recipe

1 tsp salt

250 g/9 oz coarsely ground polenta

In a large saucepan, bring 1 litre/1¾ pints of water to the boil with the salt. Add the polenta while stirring constantly and cook for 5 minutes. Reduce the heat and simmer the polenta for about 30 minutes, stirring constantly, until it no longer sticks to the pot.

When the polenta is done, either transfer it to a bowl and serve, or pour it into a mould that has been rinsed with cold water, spread it smooth and leave it to cool. Then slice and grill or pan-fry.

VENETO

The cuisine of the Veneto region rests solidly on four pillars: polenta, rice, beans and dried salt cod, products that were imported from far-away lands by this merchant power from the sixteenth century onwards. In addition to these basic elements, shellfish, anchovies, prawns, squid and spider crabs from the fish-laden lagoons, as well as products from regional livestock breeding and agriculture, were added. The fertile fields of Veneto provide rice for risotto, maize for polenta, as well as a variety of vegetables and fruit.

All of these products were further enhanced with herbs and oriental spices, which make the cuisine of the Veneto region one of the most interesting and refined in all of Italy. Veneto's substantial wealth was based on a longstanding trade monopoly in sugar, salt, coffee and spices. The people of Veneto, called Venetians, not only supplied all of Europe with these items; they also used salt, pepper, cinnamon, coriander, cloves, nutmeg, almonds and raisins in their own cuisine with great imagination. Whereas in other European countries spices were mainly used to preserve food, rather than to enhance flavour, the Venetians created a cuisine from them that perfectly balanced sweet, salty and sour elements. Traditional *polenta fasoa* is a typical Venetian recipe. White polenta is cooked with beans, cooled in a form, then sliced and roasted under a grill. It is served with grilled sardines or cutlets of meat.

Polenta

After wheat and rice, maize is the grain most frequently cultivated on earth. It originally came from Central America and has been grown in Italy since the seventeenth century. There are approximately 50,000 kinds of maize, with yellow, white, red, blue and black kernels. Yellow corn kernels, ground into fine or coarse meal, are most often used for polenta. The finer the polenta, the shorter the cooking time. White polenta is a speciality of Veneto; it has a slightly sweet flavour that is particularly good with fish and poultry. Finely ground polenta is usually served *all'onda* (literally, 'with wave'), meaning it has a consistency similar to mashed potatoes, while coarsely ground polenta is usually served firm.

Rivoli Veronese is an historic village in the 'moraine amphitheatre', natural terraces formed by glacial debris that descend into the Adige Valley.

Polenta con le quaglie
Polenta with Quail

60 ml/2 fl oz olive oil

a few sage leaves, finely chopped

8 quails, ready to cook

4 thick slices Lardo or pork fat

16 bay leaves

250 ml/9 fl oz game stock

500 ml/18 fl oz milk

*250 g/9 oz coarsely ground
white polenta*

salt

freshly ground pepper

Stir salt and pepper into the olive oil. Add the sage. Wash the quails and pat them dry. Cut each slice of pork fat in three pieces. Thread the following on four long wooden skewers: 1 piece of pork fat, 1 bay leaf, a quail, another bay leaf, another piece of pork fat, another bay leaf, a second quail, 1 bay leaf and 1 piece of pork fat. Brush on all sides with the seasoned oil and marinate briefly.

Heat the remaining oil in a deep frying pan and roast the skewers of quail on all sides, then pour in some of the game stock. Leave them to stew on low heat for 15 minutes more, gradually adding the rest of the stock to the pan. Halfway into the cooking time, turn the skewers over and continue to simmer.

Meanwhile, in a large saucepan, bring to the boil the milk and 500 ml/18 fl oz salted water. Stir in the polenta and cook for 5 minutes. Reduce the heat and cook for about 30 minutes, stirring constantly. If necessary, add a little more water. The polenta should be soft but not runny. Serve the skewers of quail on heated plates with the polenta and some of the stewing juices.

Polenta con le sardine
Polenta with Sardines

250 g/9 oz coarsely ground polenta

*8 sardines, ca. 150 g/5 oz,
ready to cook*

75 ml/2½ fl oz olive oil

salt

freshly ground pepper

Prepare the polenta according to the basic recipe on page 173 and place it on a bread board or moistened baking tray. Use a palette knife to spread it to a thickness of about 5 cm/2 inches. Leave the polenta to cool completely and become firm, then cut it into slices about 1 cm/½ inch thick.

Rub salt and pepper into the sardines, both inside and out. Drizzle the olive oil over the fish and polenta slices and roast both on or under a hot grill.

Polenta smalzada trentina
Trentino-style Polenta
with Anchovies and Capers

250 g/9 oz coarsely ground polenta

*125 g/4½ oz butter,
plus extra for greasing*

100 g/3½ oz grated Parmesan

1 tbsp capers in brine

*8 canned anchovies in oil,
finely chopped*

Make the polenta according to the basic recipe on page 173. Preheat the oven to 225°C/435°F/gas mark 7. Grease a baking dish with butter, spread the polenta in it, smooth the surface and sprinkle with the Parmesan.

Melt the butter in a small frying pan. Blend in the capers and finely chopped anchovies, then pour this over the polenta. Bake the dish for 10 minutes and serve.

RICE

Rice was already known in antiquity, but it was not especially prized and was only used as a nutritious meal for gladiators and the sick. The Spaniards first brought rice to wealthy Naples during the Renaissance. From there, it wound its way into the Po River plain via Tuscany, and that is where ideal conditions for growing rice prevailed: a stable climate and a secure supply of clear, pure spring water for the rice fields. Today, rice is cultivated in Piedmont, Lombardy, and on a smaller scale in Tuscany. Italy is Europe's largest producer and exporter of rice.

After harvesting, the rice is first threshed and dried. The kernels are still enclosed in hard husks, which are removed in rice mills. The kernels are shelled, whitened and polished. However, these steps remove the small, protein-rich, silver skin and nutritious rice germ. The rice becomes white, but has lost part of its nutritive value. On the other hand, white rice expands better and has a longer shelf life.

Italy is Europe's largest rice producer. Arborio, Vialone Nano and Carnaroli rice, the types used for risotto, are cultivated first and foremost.

In the springtime, the rice fields on the Po River are flooded by means of a complex canal system. The moisture-loving plants grow quickly in the man-made lagoons.

Before the harvest in autumn, when the rice is fully ripe, the fields are drained.

The harvest used to require arduous manual labour, but is now done largely by machines.

Huge combines instantly separate the unshelled kernels from the straw.

Risotto Rice

Risotto rice contains two different starches. There is a layer of starch on the surface of the rice kernel that partially disintegrates during cooking, whereas the starch on the inside of the kernel remains firm and gives the rice bite. If you hold up a kernel of risotto rice to a light, these two kinds of starch can even be seen with the naked eye. The core is white and firm, while the outer layer looks translucent.

There are three types of risotto rice: Arborio, Vialone Nano and Carnaroli. They differ from one another in their starch content and the size of the rice kernels, and as a result, they cook up differently. Arborio, the type most often found in British supermarkets, is popular in Piedmont, Lombardy and Emilia-Romagna. It has large kernels, and most of its starch disintegrates during cooking. As a result, this kind of risotto is soft and can become sticky if the cook is not attentive.

The starch in Vialone Nano, a small-grain rice, does not disintegrate as easily and is especially favoured in the Veneto region. People here like their rice a little firmer. Canaroli is the highest grade of rice and the most expensive. It was first developed around fifty years ago by a Milanese producer who crossed Vialone with a kind of Japanese rice. The narrow, delicate kernels are enclosed in much softer starch that easily disintegrates during cooking, yet the kernel contains more firm starch than either of the other two types of risotto rice. The critical period of time between 'cooked' and 'overcooked' is longer with Carnaroli than with the other two kinds of risotto rice, which makes it considerably easier to prepare a smooth risotto.

Cooking Risotto

A good risotto is creamy and a little moist, but not runny. The high-quality varieties of rice used in its preparation are grown only in Italy. The method for cooking risotto is based on instructions that date back to the fifteenth century. In those days, the rice was still mixed with soaked barley kernels.

Every risotto starts with a *soffritto*: onions or shallots and often garlic are gently sautéed in olive oil or butter. Additional ingredients such as meat, vegetables, pancetta or ham are then mixed in. Before the unwashed rice is added and lightly browned, while stirring, the ingedients' flavours are allowed to develop in the cooking fat. As soon as the rice kernels are evenly coated with the aromatic fat, the pan is deglazed with wine. The acidity of the wine prevents the starch in the outer layer of the rice kernels dissolving too quickly. At the same time, it stabilizes the kernels so that they do not split open and release the starch all at once.

Hot liquid is then added in portions. Ideally, this should be a home-made meat stock – which is the rule in Italy – except in the case of fish or seafood risotto. By adding the hot liquid in stages and stirring continuously, the soft starch that encloses the rice kernels disintegrates slowly and is reduced to small fragments, which disperse evenly among all the ingredients. When the rice is done, the final step is to stir in butter or cream to give the risotto its characteristic soft, creamy texture. Likewise, some freshly grated Parmesan is mixed in to absorb any remaining liquid.

Basic Risotto Recipe

60 g/2 oz butter
1 small onion, finely chopped
300 g/11 oz risotto rice
1 bay leaf
250 ml/9 fl oz white wine
1 litre/1¾ pints meat stock
60 g/2 oz grated Parmesan
salt
freshly ground pepper

Melt half of the butter in a saucepan and sauté the onion in it until translucent. Add the rice and bay leaf and stir to coat the rice thoroughly.

Deglaze the pan with the wine, stirring continuously, then reduce on medium heat. In a second saucepan, heat the meat stock.

As soon as the wine boils down, pour in one third of the hot stock and stir continuously. When the liquid has thickened, pour in another third of the stock and leave it to reduce as well.

Add the remaining stock, still stirring continuously, and cook the risotto on low heat until the rice is cooked but still chewy. Season to taste with salt and pepper. Remove the bay leaf. Fold in the remaining butter and the Parmesan. Cover and leave it to stand briefly before serving.

The starting point for a genuine Milanese risotto is finely chopped onions that are gently sautéed in butter.

Unwashed risotto rice is then added and browned lightly in the oil, while stirring continuously, on medium heat.

The pan is then deglazed with white wine. Its acidity prevents the starch in the rice kernels disintegrating too quickly.

Risotto con gamberi
Prawn Risotto

500 g/1 lb 2 oz raw prawns
1 onion, spiked with 2 cloves
1 bay leaf
3 tbsp olive oil
2 shallots, diced
2 celery sticks, diced
300 g/11 oz risotto rice
125 ml/4 fl oz white wine
1 tbsp lemon juice
1 tbsp finely chopped parsley
salt
freshly ground pepper

Bring 1 litre /1¾ pints of lightly salted water to the boil and cook the prawns for 3 minutes. Remove them with a slotted spoon and leave to cool a little. Shell and de-vein the prawns. Put the heads and shells back into the cooking water, add the spiked onion and bay leaf, cover the saucepan and simmer for 30 minutes. Then strain the cooking stock through a sieve.

Heat 2 tablespoons of the olive oil in a saucepan and sauté the shallots and celery in it. Add the rice and stir to coat it in the oil. Pour in the wine and reduce it on medium heat. Then pour in one third of the hot prawn stock, stirring continuously. When the stock has been absorbed, pour in another third. Finally, pour in the remaining stock, stir continuously, and cook the risotto on low heat until done but still chewy. Season to taste with salt and pepper.

Stir in the remaining olive oil, lemon juice and parsley. Mix in the prawns and heat the risotto again, stirring occasionally, and serve.

Then hot meat stock is gradually stirred into the rice. Saffron strands can be added to the rice with the last ladle of stock.

As soon as most of the saffron strands have dissolved, a piece of butter and some grated Parmesan are stirred in.

The risotto is then removed from the stove, stirred energetically and seasoned with a little salt prior to serving.

LOMBARDY

Lombardy, today the wealthiest and most densely populated region of Italy, is the birthplace of risotto. But the cuisine of Lombardy has so much more to offer. The region repeatedly came under foreign rule: the Spanish, French and Austrians all left their mark on Lombardian cuisine as well. *Cassoeula*, a hearty stew of Spanish origin, is prepared from the less esteemed parts of the pig, as well as from little sausages and Savoy cabbage. At one time, Lombardians acquired their fondness for breading from the Austrians. And the French contributed a certain refinement to the cuisine. Nonetheless, the cuisine of Lombardy has remained rustic and indigenous.

Cattle are the livestock of choice in Lombardy, and thus many meat dishes and a diverse cheese tradition are found alongside rice dishes. Mozzarella, Gorgonzola and Taleggio are just a few of the most familiar specialities. An unusual gastronomic folk festival, *La Manifestazione Sagra dell'Oca* (The Goose Festival), takes place annually in Mortara on the last Sunday in September. All along the streets of this little town, special sausage made from goose meat, goose-liver pâté and other delicious foods are offered at numerous stands.

Milanese Risotto

The famous golden Milanese risotto was 'invented' in the second half of the sixteenth century while the Milan Cathedral was being built. A group of Belgian artisans were working on the cathedral, which had already been under construction for two centuries. They were supposed to construct several windows. In order to achieve surprising colour effects, a young artisan was in the habit of always mixing a trace of saffron into the batch. His foreman derided this inclination and mockingly opined that one of these days he would even mix saffron into his food. When the foreman's daughter married, the artisan convinced the chef to sprinkle saffron over the rice served at the wedding feast – thus making culinary history.

Lake Mezzola in the Lombardian province of Sondrio features both a Mediterranean climate and spectacular, steeply towering mountain ranges.

Lombardy

Risotto al radicchio

Risotto al radicchio
Risotto with Radicchio

400 g/14 oz radicchio
1 litre/1¾ pints vegetable stock
2 tbsp butter
1 onion, finely chopped
1 tsp tomato purée
300 g/11 oz risotto rice
100 ml/3½ fl oz red wine
1 tbsp icing sugar
1 tbsp balsamic vinegar
3 tbsp grated Parmesan
salt
freshly ground pepper

Cut off the tender upper third of the radicchio heads and set aside. Remove the stalks and cut the radicchio into fine strips. Heat the vegetable stock.

Melt half the butter in a saucepan and gently sauté the onion in it. Add the tomato purée and rice and stir well. Add the radicchio strips, then deglaze the pan with the wine. When the wine has nearly evaporated, pour in one third of the hot stock, stirring continuously. Repeat this process twice more.

Shortly before the rice is done, caramelize the icing sugar in a frying pan until it is light brown. Add the radicchio tops set aside earlier and cook for 1 minute, stirring. Deglaze with the vinegar, then add to the risotto. Stir the remaining butter and the Parmesan into the risotto and season with salt and pepper.

Risotto nero con seppie
Black Risotto with Squid

500 g/1 lb 2 oz squid
1 bunch smooth parsley
4 tbsp olive oil
1 shallot, finely chopped
1 garlic clove, finely chopped
300 g/11 oz risotto rice
250 ml/9 fl oz white wine
1 litre/1¾ pints fish stock
salt
freshly ground pepper

Clean the squid (see page 288) and carefully remove the ink sack from each one. Cut the squid into narrow strips. Wash the parsley, cut off the stalks and finely chop the leaves. Bring a small quantity of water to the boil and cook the ink sacks with the parsley stalks and a pinch of salt for several minutes. Strain through a sieve and save the liquid.

Heat the olive oil in a frying pan and sauté the shallots and garlic. Add the strips of squid and sauté briefly. Stir in the rice and coat with the oil. Deglaze with the white wine.

Heat the fish stock in a saucepan. As soon as the wine has evaporated, pour in one third of the hot fish stock, stirring continuously until the liquid is absorbed. Repeat this process twice more. After about 15 minutes, stir in the ink sauce and simmer for another few minutes. Season the risotto to taste with salt and pepper, and serve sprinkled with the chopped parsley.

Risotto nero con seppie

Risotto con gli asparagi
Risotto with Asparagus

500 g/1 lb 2 oz green asparagus
1 pinch sugar
3 tbsp butter
1 small onion, finely chopped
300 g/11 oz risotto rice
125 ml/4 fl oz white wine
salt
freshly ground pepper

Remove the woody ends of the asparagus. Cut off the tips and set them aside. Cut the rest of the asparagus into pieces.

Bring 1 litre/1¾ pints of water to the boil with the sugar, 1 teaspoon of the butter and a little salt. Blanch the asparagus tips briefly. Remove them with a slotted spoon, refresh in ice water and set aside. Put the asparagus pieces in the cooking liquid and cook them for 15 minutes. Then pour the liquid through a sieve, saving the asparagus stock. Purée the asparagus with an electric hand-held mixer and keep it hot.

Heat 1 tablespoon of butter and sauté the onion. Add the rice, stirring to coat with butter, then deglaze with the white wine. As soon as the wine has evaporated, pour in one third of the hot asparagus stock, stirring continuously until it is absorbed. Repeat this process twice more.

After a cooking time of about 15 minutes, add the remaining butter and the asparagus purée and blend the asparagus tips into the rice. Season to taste with salt and pepper. Remove from the stove, cover the pan, and leave the risotto to rest for 2 to 3 minutes before serving.

Arancini di riso
Stuffed Rice Balls

3 tbsp olive oil
1 onion, finely chopped
150 g/5 oz minced beef
1 tbsp tomato purée
150 g/5 oz frozen peas (petits pois)
200 g/7 oz risotto rice
3 eggs
4 tbsp grated Pecorino Romano
100 g/3½ oz breadcrumbs
salt
freshly ground pepper
oil for frying

Heat the olive oil in a frying pan and sauté the onion until translucent. Add the mince to the pan and brown, stirring frequently. Mix in the tomato purée and frozen peas. Season with salt and pepper. Cook on low heat until the peas are thawed. Remove the pan from the stove and leave it to cool.

Bring a saucepan of salted water to the boil and cook the rice for about 20 minutes or until done. Pour off the water and drain well. Mix in 1 egg and the Pecorino Romano. Leave to cool.

Form the rice into eight balls. Make a hollow in the centre of each, fill the hollow with some of the mince filling, close the opening and reshape into a ball. Whisk the remaining 2 eggs. Dip the rice balls first in the egg, then in the breadcrumbs. Heat the oil in a deep-fryer to 175°C/350°F. Fry the rice balls for about 10 minutes, drain on paper towels and serve hot.

Risi e bisi
Venetian Rice with Peas

2 tbsp olive oil
100 g/3½ oz cooked ham, diced
1 white onion, finely chopped
2 garlic cloves, finely chopped
500 g/1 lb 2 oz fresh-shelled young peas
250 g/9 oz risotto rice
125 ml/4 fl oz white wine
750 ml/1⅓ pints chicken stock
60 g/2 oz grated Parmesan
1 tbsp butter
2 tbsp finely chopped parsley
salt
freshly ground pepper

Heat the oil in a saucepan and sauté the ham, onion and garlic in it. Stir in the peas. Add the rice and stir to coat the rice in oil. Deglaze with the white wine and leave the wine to reduce. In a second saucepan, heat the stock.

Add one third of the hot stock to the rice, stirring continuously. When the stock has been absorbed, pour in another third.

Pour the remaining stock into the rice, stirring continuously, and cook the risotto on low heat until the rice is done but still chewy. Stir in the Parmesan, butter and parsley, and season to taste with salt and pepper. Cover the pan and leave the risotto to rest briefly before serving.

Risi e bisi

Saint Mark is the patron saint of Venice; his symbol, the winged lion, is the emblem of the lagoon city. The annual Doge's Festival held on St Mark's Day (25 April) has always opened with *risi e bisi* (rice with young peas) and the first fresh onions of the season. The peas come from the fields of the lagoon. A tender pea is supposed to accompany each kernel of rice.

Mushrooms, The Finest of Companions

Italians love the flavourful wild mushrooms that grow in the cool, moist forests of northern and central Italy. They accompany almost every course on the menu. Fresh ceps are served as finely sliced carpaccio for appetizers, as are mixed mushrooms marinated with herbs in oil and vinegar. In Tuscany, aromatic mushroom butter is a favourite to spread on white toast. Risotto, pasta and polenta taste especially fine with a flavourful mushroom sauce. For a second course, mushrooms can demonstrably stand alone or as equals with meat and poultry.

Gathering mushrooms is an ancient practice in the history of mankind. Mushrooms were an important component of seasonal nutrition, and not only in Italy. They are rich in high-quality vegetable protein, contain important minerals and are low in calories, although the latter hardly played a role in times gone by.

Unlike in many northern European countries, mushroom hunting is strictly regulated in Italy by regional laws. Anyone who wants to gather mushrooms needs to have an official permit, which is issued by municipalities for a fee.

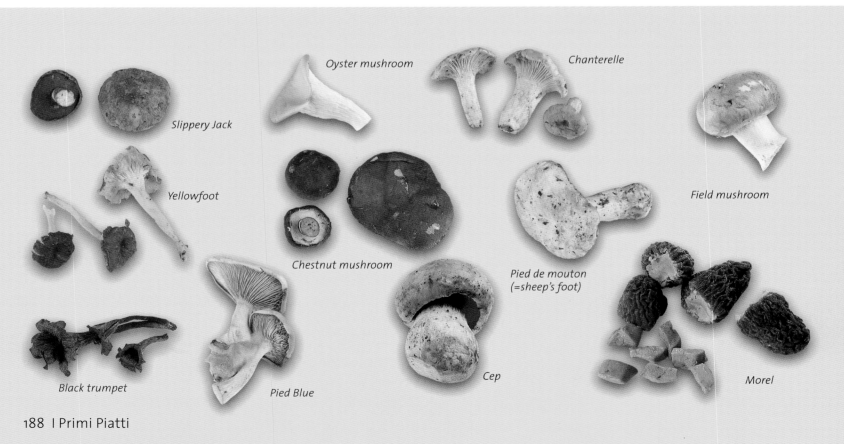

Oyster mushroom

Chanterelle

Slippery Jack

Field mushroom

Yellowfoot

Chestnut mushroom

Pied de mouton
(=sheep's foot)

Black trumpet

Pied Blue

Cep

Morel

Risotto ai funghi porcini
Risotto with Ceps

300 g/11 oz ceps

75 g/2½ oz prosciutto

3 tbsp butter

2 shallots, finely chopped

300 g/11 oz risotto rice

250 ml/9 fl oz Prosecco

1 litre/1¾ pints meat stock

1 tbsp finely chopped parsley

75 g/2½ oz grated Parmesan

salt

freshly ground pepper

Clean and finely slice the ceps. Finely dice the prosciutto.

Melt half of the butter in a saucepan. Fry the shallots and diced prosciutto in the butter. Sprinkle the rice in the pan and continue to cook. Deglaze the pan with the Prosecco. Heat the meat stock in a separate saucepan. When the wine has nearly evaporated, pour in one third of the hot stock, stirring continuously until the liquid is absorbed. Repeat this process twice more.

Meanwhile, melt the rest of the butter and sauté the mushrooms, then add them to the risotto. Season to taste with salt and pepper. Sprinkle each serving with parsley and serve the Parmesan on the side.

Secondi Piatti

The Second Course

The apex of an Italian meal is usually the second or main course, *secondo piatto* in Italian. On holidays and for big family celebrations, every cook tries her (or his) hand at traditional roasts and other time-consuming entrees. In everyday life and at smaller gatherings of friends and relatives, however, simpler dishes take their place. The quality and diversity of the antipasto, soup and pasta have already piqued everyone's curiosity about what will follow. However, the satisfying flavours and refinement stem almost entirely from the products themselves.

In contrast to the French menu sequence, Italians serve either fish or meat as the main course, probably a relic from the days when the Catholic Church issued fasting decrees for the whole year. The strict observance of *vigilie*, periods during which the Church imposed *mangiare di magro* (fasting) upon the faithful, had a profound influence on everyday cuisine. Back then, the culinary year was divided into 210 to 220 meat days and 150 fish days. This presented a real challenge for many cooks and housewives.

Neither complex cooking methods nor elaborate preparation account for the allure of most Italian entrees. Rather, the first-class quality of the basic ingredients and the skilful way in which they are combined is the key. Luigi Barzini, author of *The Italians*, a book on cultural history, gives this advice to anyone who wants to uncover the secrets of *vera cucina italiana*, genuine Italian cuisine: 'Take the best ingredients, the freshest available, and preserve their unique character to the greatest extent possible during preparation.'

Italy's culinary wealth, the diversity of offerings within each province and the care that producers take with the ingredients upfront enable locals to do what lovers of Italian cuisine elsewhere struggle to achieve. At its heart are both the quality of the ingredients and the culinary art that originated thousands of years ago in country kitchens. Even in the most famous restaurants, the peasant and rural roots of Italian cuisine are evident. Thus, there is hardly a region that tires of emphasizing how indebted it is to *cucina casalinga* (home cooking), which goes far beyond the commonly accepted meaning of the term.

A discerning eye and an educated sense of taste, as well as the desire of food growers and cooks to deliver the very best to well-informed consumers, are prerequisites for high-quality fare. Eating and drinking have become a cherished part of everyday life, and are certainly much more than just an obligation to be fulfilled. In the poorest areas, however, for a long time people were concerned with simply getting enough to eat to sustain themselves, as basic ingredients such as rice, polenta and pasta testify. In addition to meat and fish, vegetables frequently play a leading role in Italian meals, while in other European countries they are more often relegated to mere side dishes, which seldom inspire cooks to strive for something more inventive.

Platina's Order of Courses

Following the fall of the Roman Empire, several centuries passed before Italians recalled and revived a culinary practice from antiquity: namely that of serving a meal in several courses. The first printed cookbook, *De honesta voluptate et valetudine* (*On Right Pleasure and Good Health*), appeared in Rome in 1475. The author was Bartholomeo Sacchi, also known as Platina because of the town where he was born. He was a humanist and director of the library at the Vatican. *De honesta voluptate et valetudine* contains approximately 240 recipes and additional information about grains, fish and vegetables, as well as the author's advice concerning a healthy lifestyle and good food.

Platina wanted to rekindle the culinary culture of Rome and Lazio, yet he simultaneously condemned the culinary excesses of ancient Rome. Furthermore, he gave advice that entirely concurs with that of modern nutritionists: divide a meal into several courses and begin with a variety of fruits. Any excess of cold juices in the raw fruit should then be counteracted by means of cooked food in the second course. We know today that the body can actually absorb vitamins better if fresh fruit is eaten as an appetizer. In addition, fruits with the most pectin and highest fibre content also provide an initial sense of warm satisfaction. The popular Italian appetizer of ham with melon or figs is not only delicious, but healthy as well.

Pliny the Elder's cognizance, *qui physicen non ignorat, haec testicatur* ('If the body is at rest, I [the cheese] close the stomach') is still relevant. It remains a tradition in some cultures to round off a fine meal with a selection of cheeses.

High-quality, seasonal fresh ingredients and products form the basis of Italian cuisine (left).

Italian families enjoy eating in cosy trattorias and osterias that offer regional specialities (opposite page).

The Development of Table Culture in Italy

Italy was not only a leader in food, but also set the tone in the refinement of table manners. Even during the time of the Roman Empire, contact with many different peoples led to changes in a culture that was originally agrarian and rustic. When the Romans began to conquer and subjugate other peoples, especially in the Near East and on the Arabian Peninsula, and through encounters with Hellenistic culture, other customs and ways of behaving were introduced. Trade flourished, urban living became the dominant lifestyle, and anyone who could afford it maintained a large kitchen in their home.

The Romans adopted from the Greeks the habit of reclining while eating. Ritualized hospitality required a greater number of utensils and increasingly refined ones, both in the kitchen and at the table. As a rule, flatware was not necessary, because people usually ate with their hands. Only spoons were in vogue, and there were several styles that corresponded with different dishes: special types of spoons were used for eggs, snails and shellfish, as well as others for soups and sauces. Food was served on trays, and for special guests there were also ceramic or metal plates, bowls and drinking vessels. Glass goblets were an exceptional luxury.

Spoons were the only flatware known to the ancient Romans, and there were different styles to go with various dishes. The spoons and bowl pictured here came from Pompeii.

With the break-up of the Roman Empire, the art of table culture also suffered an initial decline, but it came to life again at the close of the Middle Ages and in the Renaissance beginning with the centres of power and commerce, which included Rome, Bologna, Florence, Genoa and Venice. The banquet that the Genoan Admiral Andrea Doria hosted in honour of Emperor Charles V, for example, is legendary. The party ate on a specially built wharf that was directly on the sea, then simply threw their dirty gold and silver plates into the water. Fish nets had been stretched beneath the water, however, enabling them to bring the dishes back on land afterwards.

The guests were provided with more than gold and silver dishes. Inspired by Platina, Catherine de Medici, a great-granddaughter of Lorenzo the Magnificent, was in the habit of eating with a fork. After she married the crown prince and future King Henry II of France, and after she ascended the throne as Queen Regent, she also introduced this utensil in her new homeland, an unheard-of innovation for the French, who were accustomed to using no other implements at the table than knives and, at best, spoons. Even the more refined customs that Piatina had already brought to people's attention – to use a napkin, to wash one's hands before a meal or to refrain from blowing one's nose into the tablecloth – were lastingly implemented by Catherine.

In his *Diary of the Journey to Italy*, Michel de Montaigne, who was a contemporary of the queen, often reported on the Italians' superior table manners as compared with those of his French countrymen. And he was not sparing in his narratives about the cuisine that was served to him, whether as an invited guest of nobles or electors, or at guesthouses and inns.

Elaborate carving at the table also became customary during the Renaissance. Whereas in previous times roasts had merely been cut, attention was now paid to the texture of the meat during carving, resulting in particularly beautiful presentations. Learning to carve was part of a princely education and was later taught at the universities, along with riding, dancing and fencing.

The table culture cherished by the ancient Romans came to life again in the Renaissance. Shown here is a detail from the painting Wedding at Cana, *by Paolo Veronese.*

FISH

In many regions of Italy, fish is a frequent part of the local gastronomy. This is no wonder, given Italy's impressively long coastline. The rival cities and early maritime powers of Venice and Genoa contributed fundamentally to the development of cuisine centred around fish. Isolabona in Liguria is mainly known for its dried cod (stockfish) dishes. Venice also has a large number of recipes for it in its repertoire, even though the Adriatic Sea offers plenty of freshly caught fish.

Then there are the two large islands, Sicily and Sardinia, that are part of Italy. Oddly enough, it is not fish but lamb that predominates in the main courses of the latter, and with good reason. The original inhabitants of Sardinia were shepherds, and they were not interested in seafaring or fishing. These early Sardinians did not believe the sea was safe. An old Sardinian shepherd saying holds that 'what comes from the sea is evil'. The island always existed on the edge of Italian history, and still 'speaks' its own culinary 'language'.

Rich schools of fish on the Sicilian coast make the hearts of divers and gourmets beat faster.

The situation is different in Sicily, where fish and seafood have dominated the menu for ages. Syracuse, in particular, could be considered the centre of Sicilian fish cuisine. Mussels and shellfish are prepared in a refined, yet simple, manner. Both sea creatures and freshwater fish are prized here. The spring of Arethusa, known since antiquity, is named after a nymph who, according to mythology, was pursued by the river god Alpheus, who nevertheless was careful not to mix his fresh water with salt water from the sea. In any case, the proximity of the spring to the sea explains why a massive wall separates the salt water from the fresh.

What may be the best fish in Italy are found on the other side of the boot of southern Italy, along the Adriatic Coast in the Marche, or so say the residents of that region. The most famous fish dish here is *brodetto*. Nearly every coastal town has a traditional, well-guarded recipe for this fish stew, which is based on two different methods of preparation.

In the vicinity of Ancona, many different kinds of fish are cooked in a thick, hearty stock with tomatoes, then seasoned with vinegar. Farther to the south, the fish are often dipped in flour and briefly fried before they are cooked to perfection in a saffron stock.

Fishermen bring their catches to market in the early morning hours.

Not only the sea, but also the lakes and rivers of Italy add rich flavours to the menu. Perch clearly occupies the number one spot around Lake Maggiore. This fish, originally from Mesopotamia, was prized by the ancient Egyptians for its tender, soft meat and is prepared as a delicious fillet or in conjunction with risotto. Numerous restaurants right on the lake or nearby offer this tasty fish. Silverfish, trout, char, tench, carp, pike and whitefish are permanent features of every menu.

Freshwater fish, in particular trout, is also found on the menus in Umbria and Tuscany. Another kind of carp, the coveted roach, comes from Lake Trasimeno. *Tegamaccio*, a traditional Umbrian dish made from freshwater fish, is a rich, hearty soup that is practically a meal in itself. Eel is a traditional speciality in Rome, especially right before Christmas. Families go on shopping expeditions to the central market hall on the night before Christmas Eve, because that is when they can buy it directly from wholesalers.

Nowhere does fish taste so fresh and flavourful as in the small restaurants that are found all along the Italian coastline (above).

Freshly caught anchovies are often for sale at Italian markets, and most are fried and eaten whole (below).

Fresh Fish

Italian home cooks know that even right along the coast, one does not always get freshly caught fish, because there are no laws that regulate how 'fresh' fish really have to be. For this reason, they pay attention to several unmistakable characteristics of freshly caught fish.

If the fishmonger offers whole fish for sale, the first step is a discerning glance at its eyes. The eyes should be clear and shiny, slightly transparent and somewhat prominent. The scales should be shiny and firm; the entire fish should glisten like metal. The skin must be firm and cling tightly to the light, springy flesh and the gills must be red and glisten with moisture. When freshwater fish is fresh, it is covered by a layer of clear mucous.

If the fish has already been filleted, it is harder to determine how fresh it is. In such cases, you have to rely on the trust you place in the fishmonger and your own nose. Fresh fish does not smell fishy and should have only a faint, almost imperceptible scent of seaweed and salt water. The characteristic strong odour of fish develops only after the fifth day after it has been caught.

If the fish will not be prepared right away, it is best to store it in the refrigerator at approximately 0°C (32°F). Unpack the fish and wrap it loosely in clingfilm, then cover it with a little ice. Fatty fish – for example, eel, salmon and mackerel – spoil more quickly than lean fish such as trout, pike and perch.

The quality of frozen fish depends largely on whether it was processed immediately after being caught and frozen, and whether it was kept cold without interruption from the boat to the sales counter. The temperature should always remain at –18°C (0°F). Frozen fish should thaw slowly in the refrigerator, then be prepared quickly.

Whether oysters, prawns or fish, the essential criterion for quality is freshness (right).

Fresh fish can be recognized by their shiny, clear eyes that are somewhat prominent, and by their firm, shiny skin. They should smell only faintly and pleasantly of the sea.

Slow Fish in Genoa

The high status that fish and seafood enjoy in the Italian diet becomes clear when the biennial Slow Fish Exhibition takes place. This event is sponsored jointly by the Slow Food movement and the region of Liguria. Seafood enthusiasts are not the only ones in attendance; the congress is also dedicated to the sustainability and social aspects of fishing, and indeed all aspects of the seas.

The exhibition's purpose is to focus the attention of the wider public on the increasingly urgent problems surrounding the world's oceans, while also promoting the awareness of informed consumption. To protect fish stocks and preserve the culinary culture of the ocean habitat, Slow Fish advocates a gastronomy that makes a lasting contribution to the future of maritime culture. At the same time, fishermen and others employed by the fishing industry also have a say in how the resources are managed and protected.

In 207, an estimated 46,000 visitors attended the Slow Fish event. The programme of events included not only merchants and fishermen, but scientific lectures, discussions and symposia as well. The 'Culinary Theatre of Flavours', in which renowned chefs demonstrated their abilities and tricks of their trade, was an integral part of the offerings, as were the *laboratori del gusto*, characteristic Slow Food seminars that fine-tune guests' sense of taste. The next Slow Fish is scheduled for April 2009.

Preparing Fish

The proper way to handle fresh fish can be learnt quickly and is easier than many beginning cooks first imagine. As a rule, people buy their fish freshly cleaned and scaled from the fishmonger. If not, then the fish must normally first lose its scaly garb. For this purpose, kitchen scissors are used to cut off the fins in the direction of the head. Remove the scales with a fish scaler in the kitchen sink, moving from the tail towards the head, and scale the fish under running water for best results. Reasonably priced scrapers with a vertically serrated blade or punch holes are available in speciality fish markets.

The fish is then gutted and cleaned. If, despite proper precautions, the gall bladder is damaged during removal, the fish must be immediately and thoroughly washed under running water so any bile that escapes does not contaminate the entire fish. If the fish is not fried or poached whole, then cut it into portions. To remove the head, use a heavy, sharp knife to cut into the fish at an angle from both sides, directly behind the gills, down to the backbone. Finally, cut through the backbone. Then cut the fish into slices of equal size, working perpendicular to the backbone. Flatfish, in particular, are well-suited for filleting, which is done by separating the fillets from the backbone and breastbones.

Filleting Fish

1 rainbow trout

Cut off the ventral fins. Cut into the back of the fish along the backbone from head to tail. With a fillet knife, separate the fish fillets from the bones right and left of the backbone.

Detach both fillets down to the ventral side, but do not puncture the stomach or damage the intestines.

Cut through the exposed backbone directly behind the head with kitchen scissors, then sever it from the tail. Pull the bones out of the fish from the tail to the head. Carefully remove the intestines in the same direction.

Remove the tiny bones from the fish fillets with tweezers, then wash the fish thoroughly under running water.

Preparing Eel

Before skinning the eel, remove the fins and cut into the skin at a right angle behind the head.

Either hang the eel up by the head or anchor it by another means and pull back a small section of the skin with a knife.

Cleaning Roundfish from the Dorsal Side

First cut off the ventral fins.

Cut into the back of the fish with a sharp knife from head to tail.

Skinning and Filleting Flatfish

Cut into the skin at the tail and peel back a small section with a knife.

Grasp the skin with one hand and strip it towards the head in one movement.

Separate the fillets by cutting along the backbone and lift the first one off the bones.

Then detach the other fillet by making little cuts parallel to the bones.

Firmly grasp the eel and, using your hands, pull the skin down or back forcefully in one motion.

After washing, pat the eel dry. Cut into the meat at an angle behind the head and down to the backbone.

Cut off the first fillet directly at the backbone in the direction of the tail. Turn the eel over and detach the second fillet.

With a fillet knife, separate the fish fillets from the bones to the right and left of the backbone.

Cut through the exposed backbone behind the gills and at the tail with kitchen scissors.

Remove the backbone and intestines, lifting from the tail to the head, then wash the fish thoroughly.

Cleaning Fish

Hold the fish firmly by the tail and, if necessary, strip off the scales towards the head with a fish scaler.

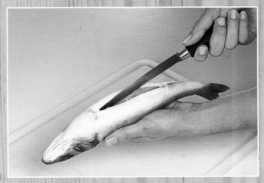

Carefully cut open the stomach cavity from the anal opening towards the head with a very sharp knife.

Lift up the gill covers, then cut off the gills at the contact point and remove.

Loosen the intestines at the tail end and pull them out. Clean out the abdominal cavity with a spoon.

Fish Utensils

In better restaurants, fish dishes are served with special utensils. The tradition goes back to a time when knives still had iron blades that adversely affected the delicate flavour of the fish. For this reason, fish utensils were made entirely of silver. They were used exclusively for fish fillets or whole fish. Fish knives do not have sharpened blades, and are thus intended only to break the fish into pieces or to manipulate it. The blade is symmetrically formed and is clearly distinguishable from the handle.

Fish forks have a special feature as well: an indentation where the prongs meet the body of the fork. However, they are used like regular forks and are practically identical to appetizer or dessert forks. In many restaurants, an additional fork or a gourmet spoon, rather than a fish knife, is provided.

Cooking Fish

Fish can be prepared in a myriad of ways, and the truth is that except for cooking them at a rolling boil, nearly every method of preparation is suitable.

The gentlest cooking method for whole fish is to steam them. Because of the size of saucepan required, when cooking at home this is generally only feasible for smaller fish. The fish – for example, trout – are cooked in a steamer insert over boiling liquid, usually a seasoned stock, at approximately 100°C (212°F). While cooking, the fish should not come into contact with the liquid.

Poaching is the most common way to cook whole fish. It is cooked just below the boiling point in seasoned fish stock that can readily be enhanced with white wine.

When fish is stewed, it is usually cooked in a tightly sealed saucepan on a bed of vegetables with a little liquid. This method is very well suited to delicate fillets and to fish whose meat tends to dry out easily.

Pan-frying works just as well for flatfish (for example, sole) as for roundfish (such as perch) and for fish that is cut into portions. Whole fish are first fried briefly on each side on high heat, then finish cooking on lower heat. Fish fillets are fried on the skin side to begin with, then turned over and cooked at a lower temperature to avoid drying out the meat. When fish is fried, compounds are formed that alter the flavour of the fish, giving it a unique taste.

Whether stewing, baking or roasting, fish always turns out well when prepared in the oven, even for beginning cooks. The fish can be baked in a fish brick, wrapped in baking paper, given a coat of batter or encrusted in sea salt. Another decisive advantage to the oven is that the fish gives off fewer cooking odours.

In Italy, small fish are often cooked whole and fried in a protective coating of batter or flour – head, tail and all. The frying fat is heated to approximately 175°C/350°F. Higher temperatures than that should be avoided, because fish meat has a delicate texture.

Filleting Fish

Using a fish slice, place the cooked fish carefully on a heated serving platter.

First gently separate the fillet from the head with a sharp knife.

Pan-frying Fish

Wash the fish fillets without removing the skin, pat them dry, and season with salt and pepper.

Then coat the fillets in flour and tap off the excess.

Place the fish fillets skin-side down in hot fat and fry.

Deep-frying Fish

Wash the whole fish, pat them dry, and season inside and out with salt and pepper.

Drizzle a little lemon juice over the fish, coat them in flour and tap off the excess.

Heat the oil in a deep-fryer to 175°C/350°F and fry the fish in it.

Remove the entire back fin with a fork and fish knife.

Detach the skin from behind the head and along the back with a fish knife.

Then roll up the skin on a fork and peel it off towards the tail.

Detach the fillet from the backbone with the fish knife, beginning at the head and moving towards the tail.

Then lift the backbone from the fillet lying beneath it. Cut the head and tail off the fillet.

Place the fillet on a plate with the skin side up and remove the skin.

Cooking Fish in Aluminium Foil

Trout

Trout is a member of the salmon family and is also one of the most popular freshwater fish in Italy. At one time, it occupied many of the cold, oxygen-rich lakes, mountain streams and rivers in northern and central Italy. However, due to water pollution, their populations have decreased significantly in the last century.

Most of the trout we eat, mainly rainbow trout, now come from aquaculture. Rainbow trout are fairly robust. They originated in North America, and were not brought to Europe until the nineteenth century. Brown trout are a special delicacy, easily recognized by the bright red dots on their sides. Their delicate white meat is the tastiest of all trout.

The majority of traditional Italian trout recipes come from the northern part of the country. And it is no wonder, because the fish are most at home there in the clear mountain streams and lakes. The delicate flavour of this noble fish is often combined with fresh wild mushroom and herbs, and gently braised in white wine.

Involtini di trotelle
Trout Roulades

8 fresh trout fillets
1 tbsp lemon juice
200 g/7 oz fresh spinach
150 g/5 oz raw prawns, shelled
1 egg white
⅛ tsp cayenne pepper
2 tbsp butter, plus extra for greasing
125 ml/4 fl oz fish stock
125 ml/4 fl oz white wine
salt
freshly ground pepper

Fresh trout, including those raised organically, are often found on Italian menus.

Wash the trout fillets, pat them dry, and season with salt and pepper. Drizzle the lemon juice over them and marinate briefly. Preheat the oven to 175°C/350°F/gas mark 4 and grease a baking dish with butter.

Wash the spinach, removing any wilted leaves and coarse stalks. Place it in a saucepan while still dripping wet. Cover the pan and wilt the spinach on medium heat, then pour off the liquid and drain well.

Purée the prawns in a blender with the egg white, cayenne pepper and a little salt.

Place spinach on the skin side of the trout fillets and spread with the prawn purée. Roll up the fillets and secure the ends with cocktail sticks. Place the trout roulades in the baking dish. Cut the butter in small pieces and scatter over the fish. Pour in the fish stock and wine. Bake for approximately 15 minutes.

Trotelle ai funghi porcini

Trotelle ai funghi porcini
Trout Fillets with Ceps

8 trout fillets
1 tbsp chopped tarragon
500 ml/18 fl oz white wine
500 g/1 lb 2 oz ceps
100 g/3½ oz butter
1 small onion, finely chopped
1 tbsp chopped thyme
salt
freshly ground pepper

Wash the trout fillets, pat them dry, and rub with salt and pepper. Place the fish in a bowl, sprinkle with the tarragon and pour 125 ml/ 4 fl oz wine over them. Cover the bowl and marinate for 30 minutes.

Meanwhile, wipe the ceps with a damp cloth, trim the stalks and cut them into 1-cm/ ⅓-inch thick slices. Heat half of the butter and sauté the onion until translucent. Add the mushrooms and sauté while stirring until the liquid has evaporated. Pour in the rest of the wine and season with salt, pepper and the thyme. Simmer on low heat for 10 minutes.

Melt the rest of the butter in a large, non-stick frying pan. Remove the trout fillets from the marinade, pat them dry and sauté in hot butter for 3 minutes on each side. Then pour in the marinade and bring it to the boil. Serve the mushrooms with the fish.

Trote affogate
Trout in White Wine

4 fresh brook trout, ready to cook
75 ml/2½ fl oz olive oil
1 white onion, finely chopped
2 garlic cloves, finely chopped
1 tbsp finely chopped parsley
125 ml/4 fl oz white wine
salt
freshly ground pepper
flour

Wash the trout, pat them dry, and season with salt and pepper. Coat in flour and tap off the excess.

Heat the oil in a large frying pan and place the trout in the pan. Add the onion, garlic and parsley. Fry the trout for 4 minutes on each side on medium heat.

Pour in the wine and cook the trout on low heat for an additional 10 minutes. Pour the cooking juices over the fish before serving.

Carpa con finocchio
Carp with Fennel

2 large fennel bulbs
1 carp, ca. 1.2 kg/2 lb 10 oz,
ready to cook
100 g/3½ oz smoked ham or bacon
4 garlic cloves, chopped
1 tbsp fennel seeds
2 rosemary sprigs
100 ml/3½ fl oz olive oil,
plus extra for greasing
juice of 1 lemon
salt
freshly ground pepper
lemon wedges to garnish

Preheat the oven to 200°C/390°F/gas mark 6 and grease a baking dish with olive oil.

Wash the fennel and cut it lengthways into thick slices. Bring a saucepan of salted water to the boil and blanch the fennel for 3 minutes, then drain well.

Wash the carp and pat it dry. Put the ham, garlic, fennel seeds and rosemary through the fine blade of a meat mincer. Stuff the fish with the ham mixture.

Place the fennel slices in the baking dish, lay the carp on top and bake for 30 minutes.

Whisk together the olive oil and lemon juice, season with salt and pepper, and brush the carp with this mixture occasionally as it bakes. Garnish with lemon slices and serve.

Carpa con finocchio

Carp and Eel

Carp are thought to be the oldest cultivated fish and originally came from Asia. In the ancient world, they first arrived via the Roman Empire, from whence they spread to the rest of Europe. During the Middle Ages, carp were a favourite food for fast days in cloisters. A Church regulation stipulated that the fish could not extend beyond the edge of the plate, and plump carp had much more meat and were far more filling than slender trout. Wild carp seldom land on plates today, because most of the ones we eat are raised on fish farms.

Even eel, extremely popular in Italy, now come primarily from aquaculture. These snake-like fish migrate with the Gulf Stream from their birthplace in the Sargasso Sea across the Atlantic Ocean to the coasts of Europe. The young creatures are approximately 7 cm (2¾ inches) long and arrive as *cieche,* or diaphanous 'glass eels', before heading upstream into rivers and lakes. *Cieche*, which means 'blind' in Italian, have never spawned and are an increasingly rare culinary speciality that is ecologically quite controversial.

Anguille ripiene
Stuffed Eel

1 kg/2 lb 4 oz fresh eel,
ready to cook (see page 200)
juice of 1 lemon
3 anchovies in oil
60 g/2 oz stoned black olives
2 leeks
3 tbsp olive oil
2 white onions, thinly sliced
2 sprigs sage
500 ml/18 fl oz white wine
salt and pepper

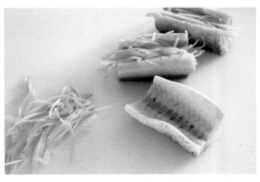

Stuff the marinated eel with the lightly sautéed leek strips.

Sauté the eel, add the remaining ingredients and pour in the wine.

Wash the eel, pat it dry and cut into pieces about 6 cm/2½ inches long. Drizzle with the lemon juice and season with salt and pepper. Marinate for 10 minutes.

Finely chop the anchovies and olives. Cut the leeks into fine strips 6 cm/2½ inches long. Heat the olive oil in a saucepan and sauté the leeks briefly. Remove from the pan and stuff the pieces of eel with the leeks. Sauté the eel in the same pan on both sides. Add the onions and sauté briefly, then add the anchovies, olives and sage. Pour in the white wine and bring to the boil. Cover and simmer on medium heat for 25 minutes. Serve the eel with the cooking juices poured over it.

Eel as the Pope Likes It

Pope Martin IV, head of the Catholic Church from 1281–1285, is said to have had a weakness for eel from Lake Bolsena, a passion that literally proved to be fatal, because he died of digestive trouble after eating a very large eel dinner. Dante, in his *Divine Comedy*, merely exiled the pope to purgatory with the gluttons, suggesting that the Italian 'prince of poets' was able to muster a little sympathy for this particular vice.

In the area around Lake Bolsena, there is still a speciality called *anguille del Papa*, or 'Eel à la Pope'. Celery, carrots, onions and ceps are finely diced, sautéed in olive oil, seasoned and basted repeatedly with Vernaccia. Skinless eel that has been cut into pieces is added at the end, turned once or twice and served from the pot 10 to 15 minutes later. Naturally, a glass of Vernaccia accompanies it.

A sarcastic Latin verse in the form of an epitaph circulated shortly after the death of Martin IV. Roughly translated it says, 'Here below the eels cheer/for one rests in peace here/who slit open his belly/and splashed them with Vernaccia.' (from Josef Imbach, *Was Päpsten und Prälaten schmeckte*, or 'What Popes and Prelates Liked to Eat').

Pike and Perch

Pike, a delicate fish that is unfortunately rich in bones, has appeared on the tables of the aristocracy since the late Middle Ages. During the Renaissance, it was most often sautéed and seasoned with oranges, cinnamon and sugar in sweet-and-sour style, or preserved in a seasoned vinegar marinade. Pike meat is lean and tender, but dries out easily during cooking. The fish is well suited to stuffing with buttery forcemeat or to braising in cream sauce.

Like pike, perch is also a predatory fish with low fat white meat. Perch are indigenous to numerous European rivers and lakes. In Lombardy, river perch are a favourite catch of amateur anglers. Eating perch, however, requires a little effort, because its skin is covered in many serrated scales that are difficult to remove. Small perch are often available from fishmongers in the form of fillets or prepared as fish roulades. Large fish are steamed or stewed on a flavourful bed of vegetables, or sautéed whole.

Pesce persico alla salvia
Perch with Sage

1 kg/2 lb 4 oz perch fillets
juice of 1 lemon
flour
breadcrumbs
2 eggs, whisked
3 tbsp butter
3 tbsp olive oil
20 sage leaves
salt
freshly ground pepper

Wash the fish fillets and pat dry. Sprinkle them with the lemon juice and season with salt and pepper. Place flour, breadcrumbs and the eggs in separate bowls. Coat the fish fillets in flour and tap off the excess. Dip each piece in the egg, and then coat with breadcrumbs. Lightly press the coating on to the fish.

Heat the butter and olive oil in a large frying pan. Over medium heat, fry the fish in portions for 3 minutes per side until golden brown. Remove it from the pan, leave to drain briefly on paper towels, and keep it warm until all the fish has been fried. Fry the sage leaves in the cooking fat until crisp and sprinkle over the fillets before serving.

Brodetto friulano
Friulian Fish Stew

1 kg/2 lb 4 oz mixed freshwater fish
(for example, perch, eel, tench or perch),
ready to cook

1 white onion

2 garlic cloves

2 carrots

2 celery sticks

250 g/9 oz tomatoes

2 tbsp olive oil

500 ml/18 fl oz fish stock

2 bay leaves

1 tbsp balsamic vinegar

4 slices white bread

salt

freshly ground pepper

Wash the fish, pat it dry and cut into bite-sized pieces. Season with salt and pepper. Finely dice the onion and garlic. Cut the carrots and celery into fine dice. Peel and quarter the tomatoes, remove the core, and cut into fine dice.

Heat the olive oil in a saucepan and sauté the onions and garlic. Add the carrots and celery, browning lightly. Mix in the tomatoes, pour in the fish stock and add the bay leaves. Simmer together for 10 minutes.

Add the fish to the soup and cook on low heat for about 10 minutes. Remove the bay leaves and season the soup with salt, pepper and the balsamic vinegar. Toast the white bread and place each slice in a deep bowl. Ladle the fish soup over the toast and serve immediately.

Favourite Freshwater Fish

Carp mainly live in standing pools of water. Their tasty meat is suited to stewing, poaching, frying and baking.

Perch is a predatory fish. It has lean, firm white meat with lots of bones.

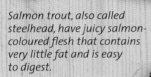

Salmon trout, also called steelhead, have juicy salmon-coloured flesh that contains very little fat and is easy to digest.

Wels catfish have tender white meat and hardly any bones. This large fish is often sold sliced.

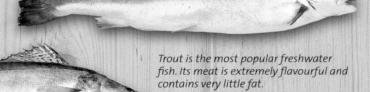

Trout is the most popular freshwater fish. Its meat is extremely flavourful and contains very little fat.

Delicate zander is a kind of perch. This predator has very juicy white meat that can be prepared in many different ways.

You can recognize a brook trout (also called speckled trout) by its yellow spots. Its delicate, pink-to-salmon-coloured flesh is soft and juicy.

The eel is a migrating fish that is equally at home in rivers or in the ocean. It has firm, bone-less, oily flesh.

Fresh fish caught in clear waters – on the right, a magnificent rainbow trout – enjoy great popularity.

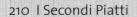

Italy's Blue Fish

Pesce azzurro (literally, 'blue fish') is the name Italians use for sardines, anchovies, mackerel, swordfish and tuna. From a scientific point of view, however, these fish do not belong in the same biological classification. They have only one thing in common: their backs are a shimmering dark blue and their stomachs are silver.

At one time, classic blue fish were primarily small sardines and anchovies. For centuries, they were a staple for fishermen and their families, an economical food that was available in large quantities in Italian coastal areas. Nowadays, even chefs appreciate the fine flavour of these fish, and nutritionists value their health benefits. The oily meat of sardines, anchovies and mackerel contains omega-3 fatty acids, which are reputed to prevent heart disease and lower harmful cholesterol.

Like all saltwater fish, blue fish contain high-quality protein, essential fatty acids, vitamins and many minerals, among them iodine, an important trace mineral. That is why nutrition experts advise us to eat saltwater fish twice per week. Fish is also easier to digest than meat and places less of a burden on the body.

One 200-gram serving of fish is sufficient to meet the daily adult requirement for animal protein.

The smallest of the blue fish – that is, anchovies and sardines – in particular must be prepared as freshly as possible. They are often simply coated in flour, whole, and then fried until crisp. In the area around Venice, they are also served with slices of grilled polenta and, of course, a glass of nicely chilled white wine, making a simple and delicious meal that even landlubbers can appreciate.

Because of their colour, mackerel are considered 'blue fish', pesce azzurro, which bring the taste of the sea to the table like no other fish.

Aquaculture

Aquaculture designates the controlled breeding and raising of aquatic organisms through the use of technologies that are geared towards increased production and result in yields that exceed those that are feasible under the conditions normally found in nature.

There are two kinds of aquaculture: raising freshwater fish on fish farms, and marine aquaculture, which takes place in salt water. There are presently more than 200 species are produced in aquaculture worldwide.

Within the European Union, Italy currently ranks third in aquaculture production. Trout, eel and shellfish, in particular, are intensively raised, and commercial farming of fish, crabs and molluscs is also booming. The aquaculture sector occupies an increasingly important segment of the fishing industry in the European Union.

At the Market

Fish markets are not for late sleepers. Anyone who wants to see the colourful, tumultuous market activity in all its bustle and glory will have to get up early. Things get really lively in the early morning starting at 5 am, which is when the fishermen return to the harbours with their catch. The fishmongers outdo one another with their deafening cries, advertising their freshly caught perch and bream, sardines and sole, shellfish and seafood. Housewives and chefs haggle with each other, keeping an expert eye open in their search for Neptune's finest treasures. The variety of fish and shellfish represented here may be confusing to non-natives, but for those in the know it is a promising fairyland of pleasures to come. Famous fish markets that are especially worth visiting are the Pescheria in Catania, Sicily and the market on the Rialto Bridge in Venice. The best inland fish markets are found in Milan and Bergamo.

Even in Italy, a whole tuna hanging in front of a fish shop prior to being cut up is an unusual sight.

Anyone who wants the best selection at fish markets has to get up early (left).

Tuna (above) and swordfish (below) are wonderful sights at any fish market and are cut into ready-to-cook slices before being sold.

Edible Fish from the Sea

The dragonhead is a favourite ingredient for fish soups and stews. Its firm, white meat is very flavourful.

The grunting sounds made by the gurnard have led to the alternative name 'crooner'. They have delicious, firm meat.

Like the gilthead sea bream, the common pandora is a premium fish. It has delicate, lean meat.

White sea bream tastes almost as good as premium gilthead sea bream. It is perfect for baking in a salt crust.

Because of its juicy, delicious meat, gilthead sea bream is indispensable to Italian fish cuisine.

Mackerel is rich in oil and has juicy, reddish brown meat that is suited chiefly for frying, grilling and smoking.

Anchovies are a maximum of 15 cm (6 inches) long. In Italy, they are often fried and eaten whole.

Sardines are 10–20 cm (4–8 inches) long and have oily, very tasty meat that is well suited to grilling.

Slender hake is a lean fish. Its flavourful meat is delicious in fish stews and is suitable for steaming in foil or grilling.

Because of its appearance, monkfish is often sold without the head. It has almost no bones and the meat is delicate.

Delicious sole is not exactly a traditional Mediterranean fish, but it is a favourite of Italian gourmets.

Codfish is not a 'native' Italian, either. South of the Alps it is mainly sold dried, as stockfish or clipfish.

The odd-looking John Dory has tender, moist meat, and fish lovers consider it one of the finest fish in the Mediterranean.

Only pieces from the large, sail-like wings of the skate are eaten. These have coarsely textured, flavourful meat.

Turbot, a member of the flatfish family, is one of the most delicious and expensive edible fishes. Its firm white meat keeps well.

Bluefin tuna, also called red tuna, has a very intense flavour and makes excellent raw fish.

Firm, flavourful grouper tastes especially good grilled or fried.

Albacore tuna has more delicate meat than red tuna. Many fish lovers know it mainly as a canned good.

Because of its delicious meat, gourmets consider sea bass a premium fish.

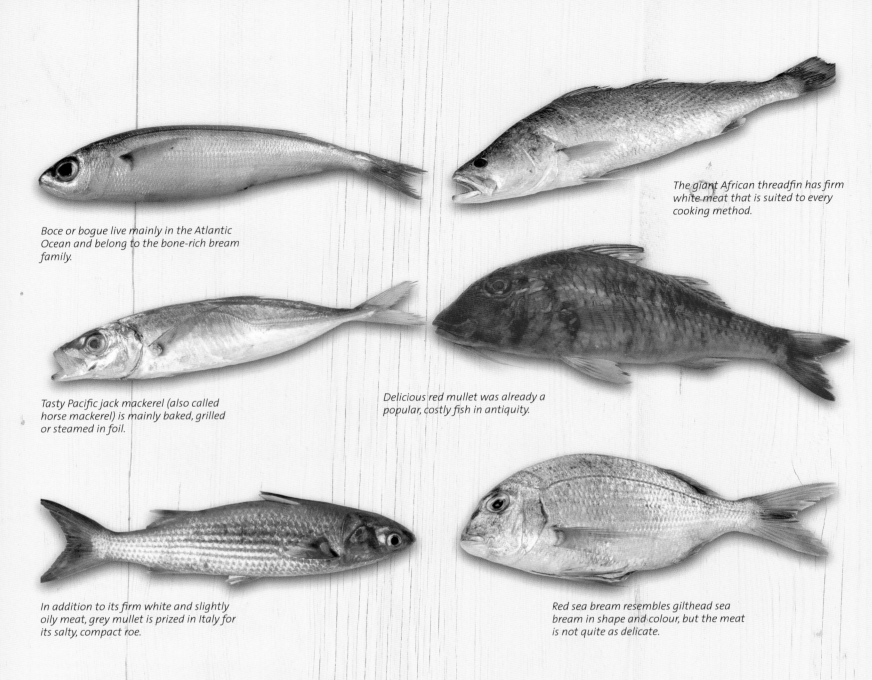

Boce or bogue live mainly in the Atlantic Ocean and belong to the bone-rich bream family.

The giant African threadfin has firm white meat that is suited to every cooking method.

Tasty Pacific jack mackerel (also called horse mackerel) is mainly baked, grilled or steamed in foil.

Delicious red mullet was already a popular, costly fish in antiquity.

In addition to its firm white and slightly oily meat, grey mullet is prized in Italy for its salty, compact roe.

Red sea bream resembles gilthead sea bream in shape and colour, but the meat is not quite as delicate.

The harmless little soupfin shark is sold sliced and prepared like swordfish.

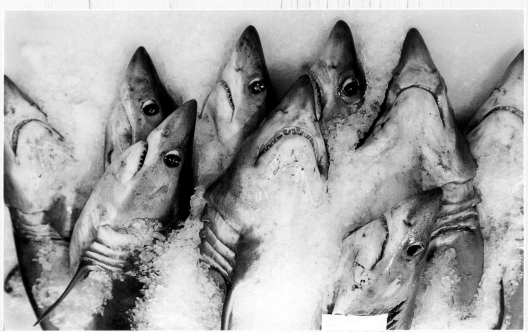

Fish in Mythology and Religion

The sea and its inhabitants were always the subject of numerous myths, sagas and religious interpretations. The idea that all life came from the sea was already proposed by the philosopher Thales of Miletus, who lived in the sixth century BCE. The astrological sign Pisces can be traced back to the Greek saga of Aphrodite, the goddess of love, and her son, Eros. While fleeing from the behemoth Typhon, they sprang into the Euphrates River and escaped by turning into fish. And the Chinese ideograph for fish is synonymous with that of wealth.

In early Christendom, the fish symbol was the means by which Christians confessed their faith. The Greek word *ichthys* ('fish') became an apronym (a kind of acronym in which the first letter of each word in a series form another existing word) for Jesus Christ. It stands for Jesus Christ (*Iesous Christos*), God's (*Theou*) son (*Yio*), the saviour (*Soter*). In 7 BCE, an event known as the great planetary conjunction of Jupiter and Saturn occurred three times within the horoscope sign of Pisces, fuelling conjectures that this heavenly phenomenon could be the source of the Star of Bethlehem.

The fish has towering significance in Christian symbolism. In the Gospels, Jesus performed a miracle when he fed five thousand people with just five loaves of bread and two small fishes. After his resurrection, Jesus appeared to his disciples on the Sea of Galilee and ate fish with them. He made the Apostle Paul a 'fisher of men'. Paul, like some of the other Apostles, was a fisherman by trade. To this day, the signet ring that the pope, Paul's successor, receives following his election is called the 'Ring of the Fisherman'. And the John Dory, or Saint Pierre, a fish named after Saint Peter, has a dark spot on each side. According to legend, those spots represents the apostle's fingerprint, which supposedly came about when he pulled a gold coin from the fish's mouth.

Detail from the fresco The Feeding of the Five Thousand *by Francesco Figini Pagani.*

Fish Soup

Zuppa di pesce, or fish soup, originated on board cutter ships, and the recipe was simply conceived. Traditional ingredients that would keep for a long time and were available in every ship's galley formed the basis for it: tomato purée, salt, pepper, olive oil, dried pasta, rice and hardtack (or sea biscuit). Fresh fish was added to the soup and, when prepared on home hearths, vegetables were also included. The once simple dish has long since taken over every menu on the Italian coasts, and this poor people's food has metamorphosed into a high-priced delicacy that is often served as a stand-alone main course. And nowadays not only odds and ends of the fish end up in the pot or on the plate, but whole fish as well.

Brodetto is cooked along the Adriatic coast and absolutely must include thirteen kinds of fish and seafood: red mullet, mackerel, flounder, small turbot, prawns, grey mullet, Dungeness crab, dragonfish, small sea bass, codfish, cuttlefish, tope and gurnard. The high art of making *brodetto* lies not only in procuring the many ingredients, but also in knowing precisely the right cooking time for each one.

In Tuscany – in Livorno, to be precise – *cacciucco* is their homegrown version. As one Tuscan journalist proudly put it, this is no ordinary soup, but rather 'a dish born out of the tradition of seafarers who came to found a free, open, impulsive city, just as impulsive as their well-loved ocean'. Thirteen kinds of fish are also required for *cacciucco*, although some cooks are satisfied with just five, representing the five 'c's in the name of the recipe.

Cassola, a substantial fish soup of Spanish origin, comes from the Sardinian capital of Cagliari. There it is made with various kinds of fish, squid, shellfish and snails, and enriched with little noodles. In contrast to other soups, the bones are removed from *cassola* before it is served, a special service that is nice for the guest.

Brodetto alla vastese
Spicy Vasto-style Fish Stew

1 kg/2 lb 4 oz mixed fresh fish, ready to cook
100 ml/3½ fl oz olive oil
1 white onion, finely chopped
2 garlic cloves, finely chopped
4 fresh red chillies
2 tbsp red wine vinegar
500 ml/18 fl oz fish stock
2 tbsp finely chopped parsley
salt
freshly ground pepper

Wash the fish, pat it dry and cut it into bite-sized pieces. In a large saucepan, heat the olive oil and sauté the onion and garlic until the onions are translucent. Add the chillies and roast lightly. Remove the chillies and crush them, with the vinegar, to a paste with a mortar and pestle. Put them back in the pan and pour in the fish stock. Bring to the boil and simmer for 5 minutes.

Put the pieces of fish in the stock and season with salt and pepper. Cover the pan and cook 15 to 20 minutes on low heat. Add the parsley to the pan about halfway through the cooking time.

Zuppa di pesce
Fish Soup

750 g/1 lb 10 oz mixed fresh fish,
ready to cook
2 tbsp olive oil
1 onion, finely chopped
2 garlic cloves, finely chopped
1 leek, cut into thin rings
1 tbsp tomato purée
1 tsp fennel seeds
4 tomatoes, peeled and diced
1 tbsp finely chopped parsley
salt, freshly ground pepper

Bring 1 litre/1¾ pints of salted water to the boil and add the fish. Cook for 10 minutes, but do not boil. Remove the fish from the stock, drain and leave to cool slightly. Heat the olive oil in a pan and fry the onion, garlic and leek on medium heat. Stir in the tomato purée, then pour in the fish stock and bring to the boil. Crush the fennel seeds with a mortar and pestle. Add the tomatoes and fennel seeds to the soup and simmer for 10 minutes.

Skin the fish and remove the bones. Cut the fish into bite-sized pieces and poach in the soup. Season to taste with salt and pepper. Sprinkle the soup with chopped parsley before serving.

Wash the fish and pat them dry.

Crush the roasted chillies into a paste with the vinegar.

Remove the fins, head and tail from the fish.

Cut the fish into bite-sized pieces, leaving the skin on.

Poach the fish in the seasoned stock until done.

Brodetto alla vastese

Salt

Human beings need salt to live, not because it is an essential seasoning, but because it regulates the body's water supply and Ph balance. The sodium contained in salt ensures that nerves and muscles respond properly. Chloride contributes to the formation of stomach acid, among other things, and is thus of critical importance in the absorption of nutrients.

About 30 per cent of table salt is derived from ocean water, and the remainder from subterranean salt deposits and saltworks. Gourmets swear by the intense flavour of sea salt, which, moreover, is considered better for our health. However, most sea salts contain less than 2 per cent of important minerals such as calcium and magnesium and have negligible health benefits. Natural sea salt does not contain enough iodine to meet human needs and, like other salt, should be iodized. The iodine contained in sea water, in fact, evaporates along with the water during the crystallization process.

In antiquity, salt, or *sale*, was considered a gift from and a food of the gods. This 'white gold' was expensive, and Roman legionnaires and officials received part of their 'salaries' in salt. The oldest salt road in Italy, the Via Salaria, led over the Apennine Mountains from the salt evaporation ponds in Ostia and ended near San Benedetto del Tronto on the Adriatic Sea. Venice was extremely prominent as a salt-trading city during the Middle Ages.

The Trapani and Pacaco Saltworks

An old Sicilian proverb says 'Stranger, you are not truly at home in Sicily until you have consumed seven handfuls of salt with your meals.' Over the course of centuries, the island has been a centre of salt production. The Arabs built more than thirty salt evaporation ponds between Trapani and Marsala in the fifteenth century, and they were among the largest in Europe at that time. Today the landscape is still dominated by the salt evaporation ponds, which give the landscape the appearance of an irregular chessboard from a distance, and the windmills that were used to pump the water and grind the salt.

The Trapani and Pacaco Saltworks has since become a nature preserve and a World Wildlife Fund (WWF) reserve. About 170 species of birds live there, including flamingos, storks, spoonbills and herons. In the middle of the last century, one salt-work after another was forced to close for financial reasons, finally giving way to oil refineries in 1984. These developments drew environmentalists to the scene, who became involved in the preservation of this unique landscape and in the reopening of at least some of the saltworks and windmills. Today about half the previous surface area is in operation again. Unlike other Italian saltworks, here much of the work is still done by hand.

A salt museum is housed in the three-hundred-year-old Salina di Nubia salt house. The museum displays tools that were used for mining salt in centuries past and features an exhibit that illustrates the salt-mining process. Alberto Calcusi, the owner of the saltwork, proudly shows visitors his extensive collection and occasionally offers guests a simple saltworker's meal: bread with sardines, tomatoes, cheese, olives, wine and – naturally – salt.

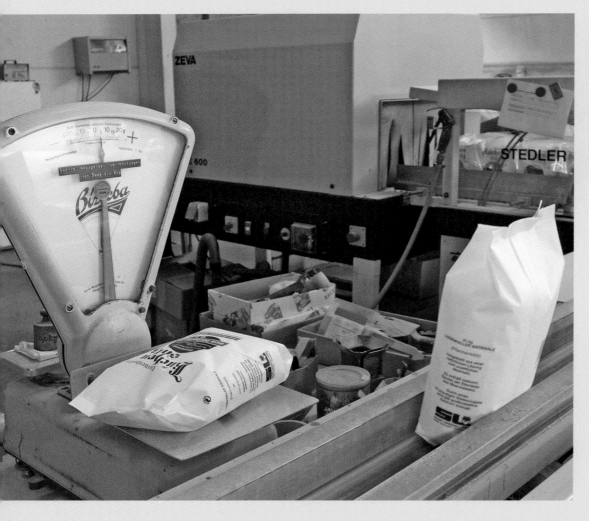

Salt Mining

Sea salt is obtained the same way today as it was in antiquity. When exposed to sun and wind, sea water evaporates and crystalline salt remains. This traditionally occurs in shallow pools called salt evaporation ponds or saltworks. First, clean sea water is conveyed into a large pool. After the initial evaporation, it is drained into a shallower neighbouring pool, and from there it is pumped into even smaller pools from which it further evaporates. In about three months' time, moist, coarse salt crystals remain. They are stripped off the floor of the salt evaporation ponds with a special tool, piled up into a conical shape and dried in the sun.

Sea salt it still obtained today the same way it was in antiquity. The first step is to convey sea water into shallow pools.

With the help of sun and wind, the water gradually evaporates, leaving behind moist, coarse salt crystals.

The crystals are mounded into cones and dried over the course of months. The salt hills are held in place with terracotta bricks.

In the old salt mills, dried salt crystals are ground into table salt.

Acchiughe fritte
Fried Anchovies

500 g/1 lb 2 oz anchovies,
as small as possible

flour for coating

olive oil for frying

1 lemon

coarse sea salt

Wash and salt the anchovies. If the fish are larger than 9 cm/3½ inches cut off and discard the heads. If they are smaller, you can use the entire fish. Coat the anchovies with flour and tap off the excess. Heat some olive oil in a frying pan, add the fish and fry. Cut the lemon into quarters. Place the anchovies on a plate, sprinkle with coarse sea salt and serve with the lemon quarters.

Orata al sale
Salt-encrusted Gilthead Bream

1 gilthead sea bream,
ca. 1.2 kg/2 lb 10 oz, ready to cook

1 lemon

3 sprigs dill

3 egg whites

2 kg/4 lb 8 oz coarse sea salt

freshly ground pepper

oil for greasing

Preheat the oven to 200°C/390°F/gas mark 6 and grease a baking tray with oil. Wash the fish thoroughly and pat it dry. Rub it with pepper inside and out. Cut the lemon into thick slices. Stuff the fish with the lemon slices and dill.

Beat the egg whites until semi-firm. Gradually stir in the sea salt, adding a little water if necessary. Layer 3 thick sheets of aluminium foil and fold them into a strip approximately 5 cm/2 inches wide. Bend the strip into the shape of a fish, slightly bigger than the bream, and interlock the ends to close off the fish mould. Set the mould on the baking tray and fill it with one third of the salt paste. Lay the bream on top and spread the rest of the salt paste evenly over the fish. Bake for about 40 minutes. Serve the fish in the salt crust, breaking open the crust at the table.

Branzino al forno
Baked Sea Bass

1 sea bass, ca. 1.2 kg/2 lb 10 oz,
ready to cook

1 bunch parsley

2 fennel bulbs

1 white onion, cut into thin rings

4 tbsp olive oil,
plus extra for greasing

150 ml/5 fl oz vegetable stock

salt

freshly ground pepper

Preheat the oven to 200°C/390°F/gas mark 6 and grease a baking dish with olive oil. Wash the fish and pat it dry. Make several diagonal slits in the skin on both sides with a sharp knife. Rub salt and pepper into the fish and stuff it with 3 sprigs of parsley. Trim and slice the fennel.

Place the fennel slices and onion rings in the baking dish. Season with salt and pepper, and lay the fish on top.

Place the remaining parsley sprigs on the fish, sprinkle with the olive oil, and pour on the vegetable stock. Cover the dish with aluminium foil and bake for 25 to 30 minutes.

Sardine alla griglia
Chargrilled Sardines

800 g/1 lb 12 oz fresh sardines,
ready to cook

1 sprig rosemary

125 ml/4 fl oz olive oil,
plus extra for greasing

1 small fresh red chilli, finely chopped

1 small garlic clove, finely chopped

1 tbsp lemon juice

salt, freshly ground pepper

Wash the sardines and pat them dry. Season the inside of each fish with salt and pepper and a little rosemary. Brush them with a little olive oil and barbecue or grill at medium heat for approximately 4 minutes per side.

Whisk together the olive oil, chilli, garlic and lemon juice. Serve with the sardines.

Baking in Salt Crust

Baking with a protective salt crust is especially suitable for whole fish that are large and have firm meat such as gilthead sea bream, sea bass, grouper and turbot. This cooking method keeps the fish juicy and tender. Because the salt crust evenly distributes the heat, overcooking can also be avoided. While steaming in the protective coating, herbs and spices that are included in the salt paste, as well as minerals contained in the sea salt, add optimal flavour to the fish.

Sardine alla griglia

Triglie di fango al pesto
Red Mullet with Parsley Pesto

4 red mullet or red snapper,
300 g/11 oz each, ready to cook
juice of 1 lemon
60 g/2 oz pine kernels
2 garlic cloves, chopped
1 tsp salt, plus extra to season
2 bunches parsley, finely chopped
150 ml/5 fl oz olive oil
2 tbsp grated Parmesan
freshly ground pepper
flour for coating
lemon wedges to garnish

Wash the fish, pat it dry and sprinkle with the lemon juice. Season the fish inside and out with salt and pepper.

Dry-roast the pine kernels in an ungreased frying pan until golden brown. Remove from the heat and leave to cool.

Crush the garlic and salt with a mortar and pestle. Add the pine kernels and parsley, and crush into a paste. Gradually work in 7 tablespoons of the olive oil. Mix in the Parmesan last, adding a little water if needed.

Heat the remaining oil in a large frying pan. Coat the fish in flour and shake off the excess, then fry the fish in the hot oil for 4 to 5 minutes per side. Remove them from the pan and place on four heated plates. Serve topped with the parsley pesto and garnished with lemon wedges.

Sogliola ai carciofi
Sole with Artichokes

8 small purple artichokes
juice of 1 lemon
125 ml/4 fl oz olive oil
4 garlic cloves, finely sliced
250 ml/9 fl oz dry white wine
400 ml/14 fl oz stock
800 g/1 lb 12 oz fillet of sole
salt
freshly ground pepper
flour for coating
1 tbsp finely chopped parsley

Clean the artichokes, then shorten the stalks to about 4 cm/1½ inches and peel them. Remove the tough outer leaves and trim the hard thorns from the remaining leaves. Mix the lemon juice and some water in a bowl. Slice the artichokes lengthways and immediately put them in the lemon water. Marinate for a short time, then pour off the liquid and pat the artichokes dry.

Heat 6 tablespoons of the olive oil in a large frying pan and sauté the artichokes. Add the garlic and sauté until golden brown. Deglaze with the wine, pour in the stock, and add salt and pepper. Simmer for 20 to 25 minutes, then remove from the stovetop.

Season the fish fillets with salt and pepper, coat in flour and shake off the excess. Heat the remaining oil and fry the fish on both sides. Serve the fish over the artichokes, sprinkled with the chopped parsley.

Branzino ripieno
Stuffed Sea Bass

10 g/⅓ oz dried ceps
100 g/3½ oz cooked prawns, shelled
1 tbsp chopped thyme
1 egg
1–2 tbsp breadcrumbs
1 sea bass, ca. 1.4 kg/3 lb, ready to cook
1 onion, cut into thin rings
2 tbsp butter
250 ml/9 fl oz white wine
oil for greasing
freshly grated nutmeg
salt
freshly ground pepper

Soak the ceps in 150 ml/5 fl oz hot water for 15 minutes, then pour the liquid through a fine sieve and reserve it for later. Drain and finely chop the ceps.

Preheat the oven to 175°C/350°F/gas mark 4 and grease a baking dish with oil. Finely chop the prawns and mix with the mushrooms, thyme, egg and breadcrumbs. Season with nutmeg. Wash the fish, pat it dry, and rub inside and out with salt.

Stuff the fish with the mushroom-prawn mixture and close the opening with wooden skewers. Place the onion rings in the base of the baking dish, then lay the fish on them. Put little pats of butter on top of the fish. Pour in the reserved soaking water and half the wine. Bake the fish for about 45 minutes, gradually adding the rest of the wine during that time.

Transfer the fish to a heated platter. Pour off the cooking juices, season with salt and pepper, and serve with the fish.

Branzino alla pugliese
Braised Sea Bass with Courgette

1 sea bass, ca. 1 kg/2 lb 4 oz, ready to cook
2 firm potatoes
2 large courgettes
2 garlic cloves, finely chopped
½ tsp salt, plus extra to season
150 ml/5 fl oz olive oil
2 tbsp finely chopped parsley
250 ml/9 fl oz white wine
freshly ground pepper

Preheat the oven to 180°C/355°F/gas mark 4. Wash the fish, pat it dry, and season inside and out with salt and pepper. Peel and thinly slice the potatoes. Wash the courgettes and finely slice them lengthways.

Crush the garlic and salt with a mortar and pestle, then stir them into the oil and mix with the parsley. Pour half of the oil mixture into a baking dish and place the courgette slices in it. Season with pepper. Lay the fish on the courgette. Arrange the potato slices so they fan out around the fish and drizzle the rest of the oil mixture over them.

Bake the fish for 15 minutes. Then pour in the white wine and braise for an additional 30 minutes. Serve in the baking dish.

Coda di rospo al rosmarino
Monkfish with Rosemary

800 g/1 lb 12 oz monkfish
(without the head)
150 ml/5 fl oz olive oil
3 sprigs rosemary
3 garlic cloves, peeled
salt
freshly ground pepper

Detach the monkfish fillets from the backbone, wash them, pat dry, and season with salt and pepper.

Heat the olive oil slightly in a deep frying pan. Add the rosemary and garlic and sauté for several minutes. Then remove the garlic and put the fish in the pan. Fry on medium heat for 3 minutes on each side. Serve the monkfish over a vegetable risotto.

Involtini di pesce spada
Swordfish Roulades

4 long, thin swordfish slices,
ca. 200 g/7 oz each
5 tbsp olive oil
1 small onion, finely chopped
1 garlic clove, finely chopped
2 tbsp finely chopped parsley
2 tbsp grated Pecorino Romano
2 tbsp breadcrumbs
125 ml/4 fl oz white wine
1 tbsp chopped thyme
lemon juice for sprinkling
salt
freshly ground pepper
cayenne pepper
flour for coating

Wash the fish, pat it dry and sprinkle with lemon juice. Heat 2 tablespoons of olive oil in a frying pan and sauté the onion and garlic. Mix in the parsley, then remove from the stove and leave to cool.

Stir the Pecorino Romano and breadcrumbs into the onion mixture. Season with salt and cayenne pepper. Spread the mixture on the fish slices, roll them up and secure with wooden skewers.

Heat the remaining olive oil in a separate pan. Coat the fish roulades in flour and fry on all sides for 10 to 12 minutes on low heat. Then remove from the pan and keep warm. Deglaze the pan drippings with wine and season the sauce with thyme, salt and pepper. Serve the roulades with the sauce.

Involtini di mullo alle erbe
Red Mullet with Herb Stuffing

20 red mullet or
red snapper fillets (with skin)
juice of 1 lemon
2 garlic cloves
1 small onion
3 tbsp olive oil, plus extra for greasing
2 tbsp finely chopped parsley
8 sage leaves, finely chopped
10 thin slices raw ham, halved
125 ml/4 fl oz white wine
4 tbsp breadcrumbs
salt
freshly ground pepper

Preheat the oven to 200°C/390°F/gas mark 6 and grease a baking dish with olive oil. Wash the fish fillets, pat them dry, and season with salt and pepper. Lay them on a platter and sprinkle with the lemon juice.

Mince the garlic and onion. Heat 1 tablespoon of the olive oil in a frying pan and sauté the garlic, onion and herbs. Remove from the stove and leave to cool slightly.

Place the fillets skin-side down on a work surface. Spread some of the herb and onion mixture over each one, then lay a half slice of ham on top. Roll up the fillets and secure with wooden skewers.

Place the roulades in the baking dish side by side. Bring the wine to the boil, then pour it over the fish. Sprinkle breadcrumbs over the top and drizzle on the remaining oil. Bake for 15 minutes.

Coda di rospo al rosmarino

Involtini di mullo alle erbe

Scilla and Swordfish

The little Sicilian town of Scilla on the Strait of Messina was described ages ago by Homer in the *Odyssey*. Skylla, as it was called then, was named after a sea monster that was embroiled in many legends. Dangerous currents, whirlpools and frequent heavy winds in this strait threatened maritime journeys, and those who escaped the whirlpools often ended up shipwrecked on the Skylla coast.

Scilla, which was once laid out in the shape of an amphitheatre, encompasses the bays of Chianalea and Marina Grande and is a modern-day centre for swordfish angling.

Actually, the sport is closer to a hunt. Traditionally, swordfish have been hunted from motor boats with masts that tower as much as 20 metres (65 ft) above the deck, including the crow's nest. From these lofty heights, when the sea is smooth and calm, swordfish up to 5 metres (16 ft) long can be sighted as they plough through the water. Once a fish is spotted, it is tracked and slain with harpoons thrown from the crow's nest, which juts out several metres from the bow of the ship. The harpoon is called a *draffinera* or *ferru* in Sicilian dialect, and the artisans who make them are called *ferrara*, also one of the most common surnames on the coast of Sicily. *Impanata*, a sweet dough filled with swordfish and baked, is a very special gastronomic delight.

Pesce spada ai ferri
Barbecued Swordfish

2 swordfish steaks, 300 g/11 oz each
2 bay leaves, crushed
1 sprig rosemary
1 small onion, cut into thin rings
250 ml/9 fl oz olive oil
2 garlic cloves
1 tbsp capers
2 tbsp lemon juice
1 tbsp finely chopped parsley
salt
freshly ground pepper

Wash the swordfish, pat it dry, rub with salt and pepper, and place it in a bowl. Add the bay leaves, rosemary and onion rings to the fish. Pour about 200 ml/7 fl oz of the olive oil over it, cover and marinate the swordfish in the refrigerator for 3 hours, turning several times in the marinade.

Remove the fish from the marinade and barbecue on a hot rack over medium heat for 8 to 10 minutes on each side. Brush it with the marinade several times while cooking. Finely chop the garlic and capers. Whisk with the remaining olive oil, lemon juice, parsley, salt and pepper. Halve the fillets and serve the sauce over the barbecued fish.

The little town of Scilla, once laid out in the form of an amphitheatre, is on the Strait of Messina.

Swordfish, the culinary symbol of Sicily, have firm, flavourful meat.

Boneless swordfish is cut into thick steaks. It is particularly well suited to barbecuing.

Swordfish meat tastes best when it is cooked to perfection on the barbecue over medium heat.

Perfectly barbecued swordfish is still slightly pink in the centre. When barbecued for too long, it tastes somewhat dry.

Pesce spada ai ferri

SICILY

The largest island in the Mediterranean and Italy's southernmost region has the oldest, most diverse regional cuisine in the country. The Mediterranean was the centre of the Western world for nearly three thousand years, and Sicily lay at the intersection of east and west, north and south. A colourful, richly varied cuisine evolved here that was deeply marked by numerous influences of non-native peoples. The Greeks got things started: they founded Syracuse, Catania and Gela, and introduced olives and salty ricotta cheese. For the Romans, Sicily was an important producer of winter wheat, earning the island the title of 'Granary of the Empire'. The Arabs came after the Romans, bringing with them sugar, spices, almonds and rice. The Normans contributed dried cod; and the Spanish chocolate, tomatoes and aubergine.

Native citrus fruits, tomatoes, olives, peppers and, of course, aubergine form the basis for modern Sicilian cuisine. To these are added fresh pasta, fish, herbs and wild vegetables such as fennel, asparagus and chard. The most popular kinds of seafood are sardines, anchovies, swordfish, tuna and crustaceans.

Milazzo on the northern coast of Sicily has existed since antiquity. From the picturesque bay, you can see Mount Etna, Europe's highest active volcano.

Salumi di Pesce

The Ligurian seaport of Alassio is the centre of production for *salumi di pesce*, which are protein-rich by-products made from fish. Among these are pressed and dried fish roe as well as *busecca* (sliced tripe), which is air-dried in the sun just like stockfish.

These specialities are the result of the long-standing fishermen's tradition of gathering the leftovers from the fish after they were cut up and sold, and using them to make something else rather than just throwing them away. Tripe, for example, is the main ingredient for an old dish from Alassio that is only seldom available in restaurants today. To prepare it, strips of tripe are stewed together with tomatoes, potatoes, peperoncini, garlic, parsley and pine kernels until a light crust develops.

Triglie alla siciliana
Red Mullet with Oranges

4 red mullet or red snapper,
200 g/7 oz each, ready to cook

5 tbsp olive oil

2 oranges

125 ml/4 fl oz white wine

juice of 1 lemon

1 tbsp finely chopped parsley

salt

freshly ground pepper

flour for coating

Wash the fish, pat them dry, and rub with salt and pepper. Place the fish in a bowl, drizzle with 3 tablespoons of the olive oil and marinate for 10 minutes.

Wash the oranges in hot water, rub dry and use a zester to finely zest the peel. Juice the oranges.

Heat the remaining olive oil in a large, non-stick frying pan. Coat the fish in flour and pan-fry in the oil for 5 to 6 minutes per side on medium heat. Remove from the pan and keep them warm.

Deglaze the pan juices with the wine. When the wine has nearly evaporated, pour in the orange juice and lemon juice, and season the sauce with salt and pepper. Transfer the red mullet to a heated platter and pour the sauce over them. Garnish with the parsley and orange zest.

Fishermen build a system of nets for traditional mattanza.

This ancient form of catching tuna is not for the faint of heart.

Using the nets, the fish are rounded up in an ever-decreasing space.

The fishermen wait until the tuna gradually become exhausted.

Then they harpoon them and haul them on board with the help of the nets.

It requires strength and skill to heave the heavy fish on board.

Tuna Fish

Tuna are unusual inhabitants of the sea. These powerful, torpedo-shaped fish are untiring swimmers and travel thousands of kilometres during their migrations. Since they do not have an air bladder, they must be in constant motion to take in enough oxygen.

Tuna fish is boneless and, like swordfish, has a firm consistency that is more typical of meat than of fish. When fried, grilled or barbecued tuna retains its delicate structure, but when cooked for a longer period it can become dry. Bluefin tuna is the largest variety and, due to its dark-red meat, is also sometimes called red tuna. A bluefin tuna can measure up to 4.5 metres (15 ft) long and achieve a weight of 800 kg (1,700 lb).

In Italian cuisine, *tonno*, Italian for tuna, is unquestionably one of the most popular fish. Large slices of fresh tuna, which also taste wonderful raw, are for sale at every fish market.

Sicilians have a special relationship with tuna fish. These fish pass through the Strait of Sicily every year on their way to their breeding grounds in the Aegean Sea. They have been hunted according to the ancient method of *mattanza* in Sicily since the ninth century. *Mattanza* involves driving a swarm of tuna into a central chamber, *la cammera della morte* ('chamber of death'), via a system of weirs and nets. From there, the fish can be hauled on board the waiting fishing boats with grappling hooks.

Tuna is quite perishable, so it is important that the fish be sold and processed quickly after being caught.

Tonno fresco al forno
Baked Tuna

700 g/1 lb 9 oz tuna steak
2 tbsp lemon juice
2 bay leaves
several sprigs fennel greens
4 shallots, diced
100 ml/3½ fl oz olive oil
250 ml/9 fl oz dry white wine
salt
freshly ground pepper
flour for coating

Preheat the oven to 175°C/350°F/gas mark 4. Wash the tuna, pat it dry, and season with salt and pepper. Sprinkle it with the lemon juice, then coat in flour and tap off the excess.

Place the fish in a baking dish and lay the bay leaves and fennel greens on top of it. Scatter the diced shallots around the fish. Drizzle with the olive oil and pour in the white wine.

Cover the dish with aluminium foil. Bake the tuna for 40 minutes, removing the aluminium foil for the last 10 minutes. Cut the fish into four pieces of equal size and serve with the shallots.

Tonno all'alloro
Tuna with Bay Leaves

4 fresh tuna steaks, 250 g/9 oz each
120 ml olive oil
juice of 1 lemon
12 bay leaves
salt
freshly ground pepper

Wash the tuna and pat it dry with paper towels. Whisk together 5 tablespoons of the olive oil, the lemon juice, and salt and pepper. Brush the tuna steaks with the dressing.

Crush the bay leaves several times to release their essential oils. Stack the tuna steaks on top of one another with the bay leaves in between them. Wrap the fish in clingfilm and chill in the refrigerator for about 3 hours.

Heat the remaining olive oil in a large frying pan. Remove the clingfilm and bay leaves from the fish, then fry the fish steaks in oil for about 5 minutes per side.

Coda di rospo al vino bianco
Monkfish in White Wine Sauce

8 small monkfish fillets
5 tbsp olive oil
1 onion, finely chopped
2 garlic cloves, finely chopped
2 celery sticks, diced
2 tbsp finely chopped parsley
250 ml/9 fl oz white wine
salt
freshly ground pepper
flour for dusting

Wash the fish fillets and pat dry. Preheat the oven to 200°C/390°F/gas mark 6.

Heat 2 tablespoons of the olive oil in a frying pan and sauté the onions, garlic and celery. Stir in the parsley and then transfer the vegetables to a baking dish.

Season the fish fillets with salt and pepper, then dust lightly with flour. Heat the remaining oil in a frying pan and fry the fish briefly on both sides. Then remove the fish from pan and place it on the vegetables. Pour the pan juices over it and add the wine. Bake for 10 to 15 minutes until done.

Tonno fresco al forno

Filetti di sogliola al cartoccio
Fillet of Sole in Baking Paper

4 large sole fillets
50 g/1¾ oz stoned black olives
1 tbsp finely chopped oregano
2 tbsp finely chopped parsley
3 tbsp olive oil, plus extra for greasing
2 tbsp lemon juice
salt
freshly ground pepper

Preheat the oven to 180°C/355°F/gas mark 4. Wash the fish fillets and pat them dry. Finely chop the olives and combine them with the oregano, parsley and olive oil.

Grease four sheets of baking paper with olive oil and lay one sole fillet on each. Season with salt, pepper and lemon juice, then spread the olive-herb mixture over the fish. Enclose the fish fillets in baking paper, being sure to seal the packets tightly. Bake the fish for 6 to 7 minutes. Serve in the baking paper.

Cooking in Baking Paper

From very early in history, our ancestors began to wrap vegetables, meat, fish and poultry in a protective covering of leaves or clay and then cook them gently and slowly.

Wrapping food in something serves two functions. First, it protects the flavouring on the inside and prevents the food drying out. The meal stews in its own juices and retains valuable nutrients, its unique flavour and original shape. Also, unhealthy by-products of roasting are prevented from developing by this method. This gentle means of cooking is especially well suited to fish.

Baking paper has two qualities that are ideal for cooking: it does not get too hot, and it 'breathes', which promotes the unfolding of flavours during the cooking process. Baking paper was developed specially for this gentle cooking method, but simple greaseproof paper can also be used, in layers of three sheets and well oiled, because it must not become saturated. Caution is advised: the oven temperature must not exceed 190°C (375°F) or the paper can catch fire.

Pesce spada al cartoccio
Swordfish in Foil

1 swordfish steak, ca. 700 g/1 lb 9 oz
juice of ½ lemon
4 tbsp olive oil
1 onion, sliced
2 garlic cloves, sliced
12 fresh mint leaves
125 ml/4 fl oz white wine
salt
freshly ground pepper
polenta for coating

Preheat the oven to 180°C/355°F/gas mark 4. Wash the fish, pat it dry, sprinkle with the lemon juice, and season with salt and pepper. Coat in polenta and tap off the excess.

Heat the olive oil in a frying pan and fry the fish briefly on both sides. Remove from the pan and place in a covered baking dish. Sauté the onion and garlic in the same oil, then pour over the fish. Place the mint leaves on top and pour the wine into the dish.

Cover the dish with aluminium foil and cover with a lid. Braise the fish in the oven for approximately 25 minutes.

Slice the fish and serve it on a heated platter with the onion-mint sauce.

Wash the fish fillet, dry it with paper towels and season.

Peel the tomatoes, then slice them evenly.

Place the fish, onions, garlic, tomatoes and herbs in greased aluminium foil.

Fold the aluminium foil over the fish, being careful to fold the ends down.

Basic Recipe for
Fish in Foil

4 fish fillets, 200 g/7 oz each
juice of 1 lemon
4 tomatoes
1 onion
1 garlic clove
4 tbsp olive oil, plus extra for greasing
8 sprigs thyme
salt
freshly ground pepper

Preheat the oven to 175°C/350°F/gas mark 4 and brush four pieces of aluminium foil with olive oil.

Wash the fish fillets, pat them dry, and season with the lemon juice and salt and pepper. Peel and slice the tomatoes, onion and garlic. Place 3 tomato slices on each piece of foil, sprinkle with onion and garlic, and season with salt and pepper. Place a fish fillet on top, cover with the remaining tomato slices, top with 2 sprigs of thyme and drizzle with oil.

Fold the aluminium foil over the fish and fold the ends down. Bake for 15 minutes. Serve in the foil.

Burrida, Bagnun and Ciuppin

Along the Italian coasts, recipes for fish soups and stews are as numerous as the little trattorias in the fishing villages. Every restaurateur, every family and every fishmonger has their own family recipe that differs just slightly from what the neighbours make. The really big differences are from region to region.

Liguria, known for its diversity of soups, serves up three typical fish soups: *burrida* (recipe page 241), *bagnun* and *ciuppin*. *Bagnun de anciue* is a speciality of the little fishing village of Riva Trigoso. The dish was invented about two hundred years ago on board a fishing boat, made from ingredients that were inexpensive and readily available to fishermen: oil, tomatoes, fresh anchovies and ship biscuit. Sestri Levante is not far from Riva Trigoso and is the birthplace of *ciuppin*, originally a fish stock made from leftover fish and toast or ship biscuit and passed through a sieve. Over time it was 'souped up' with more premium fish and slightly thickened. Today *ciuppin* is often served as a complete meal.

Couscous

Couscous originally came from Middle Eastern cuisine – from North Africa, to be precise – and is a food made from finely shredded wheat or millet. But while couscous is prepared with meat, fish, seafood and vegetables in its place of origin, Sicilian cuisine uses only fish for *cuscusu*. Of course, its name comes directly from that of the grain product. To make that, wheat is first ground, then steamed and finally formed into tiny balls by means of a rather time-consuming process.

Burrida
Fish Stew

1 kg/2 lb 4 oz mixed fish (for example, monkfish, eel, dragonhead), ready to cook
2 beef tomatoes
5 tbsp olive oil
2 garlic cloves, chopped
1 onion, chopped
1 anchovy in oil, finely chopped
5 shelled walnuts
250 ml/9 fl oz white wine
1 bay leaf
100 ml/3½ fl oz fish stock
salt, freshly ground pepper

Wash the fish and cut into bite-sized pieces. Blanch, peel and finely dice the tomatoes. Heat the olive oil in a saucepan and sauté the onion and garlic. Add the anchovy and tomatoes to the pan and sauté. Crush the walnuts with a mortar and pestle, and stir them into the wine. Then mix the wine into the tomatoes, season with salt, pepper and the bay leaf and reduce slightly. Add the fish pieces and stock and bring to the boil. Cover the pan and simmer for 10 minutes on low heat. Season with pepper before serving.

Zuppa di acciughe
Anchovy Soup

600 g/1 lb 5 oz fresh anchovies, ready to cook
4 tbsp olive oil
1 onion, cut into thin rings
2 garlic cloves, finely chopped
1 carrot, finely diced
1 small Hamburg parsley root, finely diced
1 celery stick, finely diced
125 ml/4 fl oz white wine
250 g/9 oz canned crushed tomatoes
salt and pepper

Wash the anchovies and pat dry. Heat the olive oil in a saucepan and sauté the onion. Add the garlic and vegetables and sauté, stirring often. Add the wine to deglaze, then reduce. Stir in the tomatoes and bring everything to the boil. Add the anchovies, season with salt and pepper, then simmer for 30 minutes, gradually adding 1 litre/1¾ pints of hot water. Gently shake the pan occasionally while cooking, but do not stir the soup to avoid breaking apart the anchovies.

Burrida is made in countless variations, but the most important ingredient is always freshly caught fish.

Cuscusu
Sicilian Fish Couscous

1 kg/2 lb 4 oz small Mediterranean fish (for example, red mullet or red snapper, gurnard)
100 ml/3½ fl oz olive oil
3 tomatoes
1 onion, finely chopped
2 garlic cloves, finely chopped
1 carrot, diced
1 bay leaf
⅛ tsp cayenne pepper
½ cinnamon stick
4 squid, ready to cook
300 g/11 oz couscous
1 tbsp finely chopped parsley
salt
freshly ground pepper

Wash the fish, remove the bones, and set aside the heads and bones. Cut the fish into bite-sized pieces. Place them in a bowl, add salt and pepper, and drizzle with 5 tablespoons of the olive oil. Cover the bowl with clingfilm and chill.

Blanch and peel the tomatoes. Quarter them, remove the seeds, and cut into small dice. Heat the remaining oil in a saucepan and sauté the onions. Add the garlic, carrots, and fish heads and bones. Season with the bay leaf, cayenne pepper, cinnamon stick, and salt and pepper. Sauté briefly. Stir in the tomatoes and 500 ml/18 fl oz water. Simmer for 30 minutes on low heat.

Cut the squid into rings. Pour the fish stock through a fine sieve into a separate saucepan. Add the squid rings to the pan. Pour in 250 ml/9 fl oz water, bring it to the boil and cook the squid rings for 30 to 35 minutes until soft. Remove the squid and keep warm.

Put the couscous in a bowl, pour 250 ml/9 fl oz hot fish stock over it and set aside for 10 minutes. Fluff the couscous several times with a fork.

Bring the rest of the fish stock to the boil, add the fish and simmer on low heat for 3 to 4 minutes until done, but do not boil. Add the squid, heating it in the stock.

Place the couscous on a heated platter, remove the fish and squid from the stock and place on the bed of couscous. Sprinkle with the parsley and serve.

Clipfish and Stockfish

Even if it seems incredible at first glance, Italians have a special penchant for dried codfish from the far northern reaches of Europe. Depending on how it is processed, it is sold as *baccalà* (dried cod or clipfish) or *stoccafisso* (salt cod or 'stockfish'). The Normans were the first to bring this foodstuff to Italy, but today it comes mainly from Norway. Long before the invention of the deep freezer, dried fish was the only way for people who lived inland to partake of high-quality saltwater fish year-round. It was a favourite food during periods of fasting for many centuries and, thanks to its long shelf life, served as a protein-rich provision for sailors on voyages because it lasts for months.

Clipfish and stockfish differ from each other significantly in both flavour and

Salt cod has been popular in Italy since Norman times. Dried, salted codfish gives fish dishes a very special flavour.

texture, despite the fact that both are made from fresh, cleaned and gutted codfish. To make clipfish, the cod is first cut into two halves lengthways and the backbone is removed. Then the fish is salted and set out

to air-dry. This originally took place on the cliffs of Norway. The Norwegian word for cliff is *klippe*, hence the name. For stockfish, the whole cod, unsalted, is dried in the wind on wooden racks.

Before it can be prepared as clipfish or stockfish, the cod must be thoroughly soaked and rinsed, as every good fishmonger in Italy does before selling it. This is done by placing the fish in a container through which fresh water flows continually. While stockfish can be processed after just one day of rinsing, clipfish must be rinsed for two or three days to remove most of the salt used in the drying process. Even though the fish is quite sturdy when dried, it becomes delicate again when rehydrated. Clipfish should not be cooked too long, or it will become stringy.

Dried stockfish are a common sight in the displays of many shops devoted to fish.

Baccalà in ziminio
Clipfish with Chard

750 g/1 lb 10 oz clipfish
flour for coating
500 g/1 lb 2 oz chard
4 tbsp olive oil
1 small onion, chopped
1 garlic clove, chopped
125 ml/4 fl oz stock
1 tsp grated orange rind
1 tbsp finely chopped parsley
salt
freshly ground pepper

Soak the clipfish in cold water for at least 48 hours, changing the water frequently. Then remove the fish from the water, drain well and pat dry. Remove the skin and bones from the fish. Cut it into pieces about 5 cm/ 2 inches long and coat them in flour, shaking off the excess.

Wash and drain the chard and cut it into strips. Heat the olive oil in a frying pan and fry the fish on both sides. Remove it from the pan and keep warm. Sauté the onion and garlic in the same pan, then add the chard and sauté briefly. Pour in the stock, then season with the orange rind, parsley, and salt and pepper. Cover the pan and cook for 10 minutes.

Place the fish on top of the vegetables and simmer on low heat for another 10 minutes before serving.

Baccalà alla bolognese
Bologna-style Clipfish

750 g/1 lb 10 oz clipfish, rinsed
100 ml/3½ fl oz olive oil
2 tbsp butter
2 garlic cloves, chopped
2 tbsp finely chopped parsley
1 tsp grated lemon rind
juice of 1 lemon
salt
freshly ground pepper

Soak the clipfish in cold water for at least 48 hours, changing the water frequently. Then remove the fish from the water, drain well and pat dry. Remove the skin and bones from the fish. Cut it into large chunks. Preheat the oven to 175°C/350°F/gas mark 4.

Heat the olive oil and 1 tablespoon of the butter in an ovenproof pan. Place the fish side by side in the pan and brown lightly on the stovetop. Carefully turn over the fish and season with salt and pepper. Sprinkle the garlic, parsley and lemon rind over it and top with the remaining butter cut into small pieces.

Bake the fish for 10 minutes, then remove from the oven and sprinkle lemon juice over the fish. Serve in the pan.

Stoccafisso alla fiorentina
Florentine-style Stockfish

750 g/1 lb 10 oz stockfish
flour for coating
6 tbsp olive oil
1 white onion, finely chopped
500 g/1 lb 2 oz canned crushed tomatoes
2 bay leaves
600 g/1 lb 5 oz fresh spinach
salt
freshly ground pepper
freshly grated nutmeg

Soak the stockfish in cold water for at least 24 hours. Then pat the fish dry, remove the skin and bones, and cut into bite-sized pieces. Coat the pieces of fish in flour, shaking off the excess.

Heat 4 tablespoons of the olive oil in a frying pan and fry the fish on all sides. Remove the fish and sauté the onions in the same pan. Stir in the crushed tomatoes, add the bay leaves, and season the sauce with salt and pepper. Place the fish in the sauce and simmer for 15 minutes.

Meanwhile, thoroughly wash the spinach. Heat the remaining oil in a saucepan and add the dripping wet spinach. Cover and steam on low heat for several minutes. Season with salt and nutmeg and serve with the fish.

Stoccafisso alla fiorentina

Cappon Magro

Cappon magro, perhaps the most famous Ligurian fish dish, is a social climber. Over the course of centuries, it has made the big leap from Genoese poor people's food to the top of the charts as gourmet fare. On its long way up, this simple dish has become a luscious delicacy. *Cappon magro* was originally prepared using leftovers and fresh ingredients that sailors could obtain in the harbour: a little fish and vegetables were placed on sea biscuits, which had been rubbed with garlic and sprinkled with olive oil.

Nowadays, *cappon magro* appears as a lavish, almost baroque, fish-and-vegetable salad with rich herbed mayonnaise. The collage of many different vegetables, fish and kinds of seafood depends entirely on personal taste. The key, however, is that it should be an amalgam of as many different flavours and textures as possible.

The classic *cappon magro* is a highly artistic creation. As always, it starts with sea biscuit that has been rubbed with garlic and sprinkled with salt water. Many layers of fresh vegetables and fish are built up in the form of a pyramid on the ship biscuit and enriched with a herbal mayonnaise. This culinary masterpiece is then crowned with cooked crustaceans, and the base is wreathed with fresh oysters and mussels. Even a strip of dolphin meat, once food for Genoese sailors on board a ship, is among the traditional ingredients that are part of a 'genuine' *cappon magro*.

By the way, this former sailor's dish got its name on land. The enjoyment of capons – fattened, castrated roosters that were especially favoured in Liguria – was forbidden during strict fasting periods, for example, Lent. Church politics properly permitted their replacement with a fish dish that, admittedly, carries the inappropriate adjective 'lean'. *Capponada*, a 'poor cousin' of *cappon magro*, is still prepared today on the Riviera di Ponente. It is made from dried tuna and sea biscuit.

Cappon magro
Ligurian Seafood Caponata

This dish contains so many ingredients that it is worth making only when serving a larger group. This version will satisfy about twelve hungry guests. All the ingredients used to be arranged on sea biscuit, but today the biscuit or toast is more typically served on the side.

4 celery sticks
500 g/1 lb 2 oz carrots, cut into thin sticks
1 cauliflower, broken into florets
750 g/1 lb 10 oz broccoli, broken into florets
4 fennel bulbs, quartered
6 courgettes
ca. 500 ml/18 fl oz olive oil
300 ml/11 fl oz white wine vinegar
1 kg/2 lb 4 oz cod fillet
2 tbsp lemon juice
12 eggs, hard boiled
2 slices day-old white country bread
3 garlic cloves, chopped
100 g/3½ oz pine kernels
7 anchovies in oil
3 tbsp finely chopped parsley
3 tbsp finely chopped basil
12 artichoke hearts in oil
1 cooked lobster
2 lemons
12 cooked scampi tails
salt
freshly ground pepper
black and green olives to garnish

Bring a saucepan of lightly salted water to the boil. Cut the celery into 6-cm/2½-inch pieces. Blanch the celery, carrots, cauliflower, broccoli and fennel separately, and drain well.

Wash the courgettes and cut lengthways into quarters. Heat 4 tablespoons olive oil and sauté the courgettes lightly. Turn them into a bowl with the pan juices, add 4 tablespoons vinegar, and season with salt and pepper.

Whisk 250 ml/9 fl oz olive oil, 200 ml/ 7 fl oz vinegar, salt and pepper together into a marinade. Place the vegetables in separate bowls and drizzle with the marinade. Cover the bowls and marinate overnight.

The next day, bring a saucepan of water to the boil with the lemon juice and poach the cod fillets. Remove from the heat, cover the pan and set the cod aside to cool in the stock. Then break the fish into bite-sized pieces.

For the sauce, shell 6 of the hard-boiled eggs. The egg whites are not needed in this recipe. Cut the crusts from the bread and dice the bread. Purée the egg yolks, bread cubes, garlic, pine kernels, anchovies and herbs in a food processor until smooth. Pour in the remaining olive oil in a thin stream to make the mayonnaise. Season with salt, pepper and vinegar, and pour into a bowl.

Halve the remaining eggs and the artichoke hearts. Cut the lobster in half lengthways, remove the tail meat from the shell, and slice it. Arrange all the ingredients decoratively on two large serving platters. Cut each lemon into 8 wedges. Garnish the dish with the scampi tails, lemon wedges and olives. Serve the mayonnaise on the side.

Cut the courgettes, fennel, celery and carrots into pieces.

Season the sautéed courgettes with salt and pepper, then marinate in wine vinegar.

Bring lightly salted water and lemon juice to the boil and poach the fish.

Together with the remaining ingredients, whisk the olive oil into a mayonnaise.

SEAFOOD

Italians purportedly eat just about anything that swims. And this certainly applies to many representatives of *frutti di mare* – seafood, that is. Whether it be tiny shrimp, mussels or oysters, squid or octopus, spider crabs, sea urchins or Dungeness crabs, crayfish or lobsters, the same fate awaits all residents of the oceans, large or small. Into the cooking pot they go, assuming they are not eaten right on the beach with a little lemon juice.

Nearly all regions of Italy border on the sea, so it is no wonder that ocean creatures awakened culinary interest among coastal residents early in history. They knew how to take advantage of the nearly inexhaustible, nutritious and tasty ocean reservoir. For centuries, the sea has borne more fruit, metaphorically speaking, than any orchard or vegetable garden. Mussels have always been special favourites. They are easy to harvest and do not have to be hunted.

The delicate meat of lobsters, prawns and oysters was prized in antiquity. Classical writers including Ovid and Pliny the Elder busied themselves with these creatures, and described the devices and methods used to capture them in their writings. Mosaics and wall paintings in Pompeii and other ancient cities are proof that *frutti di mare* were already welcome guests on the tables of cheerful epicures many centuries ago.

Fresh seafood is not just pleasing to the eye on the dinner table; it has also delighted gourmets for millennia (right).

Fishing is the main occupation on the tiny Sardinian island of Sant'Antioco, which was already settled in prehistoric times (below).

Neptune

The bearded Roman god Neptune is a familiar figure in Italy who not only decorates the magnificent fountains of many Italian cities, but also comes on board ships in the flesh during a Christian equator-crossing ritual. He splits rocks with his trident, and wellsprings issue from it. Whenever he rides across the sea in his golden horse-drawn chariot, he whips up the waves into storm surges, or he can calm raging waters.

In antiquity, Neptune was the master of the sea, and it was not only mariners who revered him. After he and his brothers had removed their father, Saturn, from his divine throne, they divided up his kingdom among themselves. Jupiter took the heavens, Pluto the underworld and Neptune the seas and all running water. The Romans celebrated him on 23 July, holding an annual Neptunalia Festival to combat drought. The date was chosen to coincide with the time when the Tiber River was at it lowest ebb.

Neptune was rediscovered during the Renaissance and became a favourite motif for magnificent fountains, which still figure prominently in the look of many Italian cities, for example the Piazza della Signoria in Florence and the Piazza del Duomo in Trent.

Italian Coastlines

According to its residents, Cinque Terre has the most beautiful coastline in Italy. Residents of the Amalfi Coast claim that their shores are the loveliest, while residents of Vieste are convinced that the coastline between Vieste and Mattinata dwarfs all others in Italy. Which section of the approximately 8,500 km (5,300 miles) of coastline wins the prize will always be in the eye of the beholder. Italy's special attraction lies precisely in the extraordinary diversity of its highly diverse and contrasting coastal landscapes, which extend from the craggy cliffs of the Riviera to the wide, sandy beaches of the Adriatic.

Many seas swirl around this long, drawn-out peninsula: the Ligurian Sea in the north-west, the Tyrrhenian Sea along the western coast of Sicily, the Ionian Sea at the southern tip of the boot and the Adriatic Sea, which stretches along the east coast to the Gulf of Trieste. They give the stretches of land that border them their unique characteristics.

Constantly changing views and colours, the scent of wild herbs mixed with salty sea air, and gentle breezes that blow over the sea and far inland are what have attracted travellers to Italy for centuries. From the second half of the eighteenth century onwards, artists as well as nobles and sons of the great dynastic families have come to Italy in order to cultivate a more refined sense of beauty.

For those who live along the coasts, however, the sea is not only aesthetically pleasing, but also a stern taskmaster. Long before the tourist industry discovered the Italian coasts, life here was rather humble and modest. Many foods that were cooked and eaten simply as a matter of necessity in times past, for example *frutti di mare*, are today sought-after delicacies that can sometimes be expensive. Seafood is usually still prepared in a traditional way – with care, fantasy and a dash of love for the sea and its culinary treasures.

Cinque Terre is among Italy's most beautiful coastal regions. Together with nearby Portovenere, the Ligurian coastline was declared a Unesco World Heritage Site in 1997.

Preparing Seafood

Frutti di mare always taste best freshly caught along the coast. Yet few aficionados live in close proximity to a habour, and must depend instead on the availability of good products farther inland. Of course, it is important to remember that quality comes at a price, and crustaceans, in particular, are not an inexpensive culinary delight.

Shellfish and crustaceans also spoil rapidly, which means that lobster, spiny lobster and crayfish should be bought fresh from a fish vendor and prepared as soon as possible, ideally on the day they are purchased. Transporting them over long distances or storing them for several days is not conducive to quality. One way to test for freshness is to touch the creatures; they should bend their tails immediately.

A prerequisite for the enjoyment of spiny lobster and lobster is that they must be cooked while still alive. If you flinch at throwing living creatures into boiling water, you may want to order such delicacies in a restaurant and leave the preparation to professional chefs. Now that good-quality crustaceans are available frozen, they can be used in pre-cooked form for many dishes. However, you do have to lower your sights a little with respect to flavour.

Mussels filter sea water to nourish themselves on the plankton it contains. Unfortunately, they also collect contaminants in the process. Almost all the mussels that are available in markets today come from fish farms, where there are strict regulations and controls in place, which ensure that contaminants are kept to a minimum. Mussels are another kind of seafood that needs to be alive until it is cooked. You will know they are alive if the shells are tightly closed or shut when gently tapped. Any open mussels, as well as those that do not open after being cooked, must be discarded.

Oysters, which are often eaten raw, must also be alive prior to consumption or preparation. This is easy to determine by dribbling one or two drops of lemon juice on the edge of the opened shell. If the oyster shrivels visibly, due to its great sensitivity to acidity, then it can be eaten without hesitation.

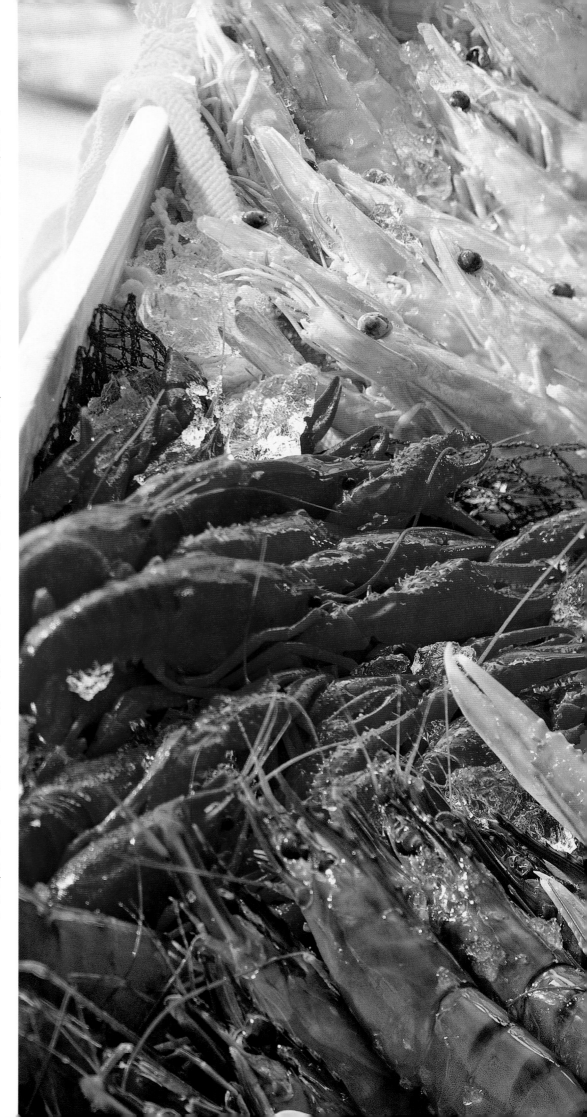

Fish Stock

Rich fish stock, which is the basis for many fish and seafood dishes, is made from fish carcasses, that is, the bones and heads of lean fish. The gills have to be removed, because they would otherwise make the stock bitter. To prepare fish stock, first root vegetables and onions are sautéed in butter, then cold water and either white or red wine are poured in. Then the finely chopped carcasses are added and the stock is seasoned with bay leaves, salt and pepper. The stock is then simmered, uncovered, for about thirty minutes, after which it is strained. If the strained stock is reduced to one quarter of the original amount, the resulting concentrate is called *giace de poisson*. This can be conveniently frozen in ice cube trays and is ideal as a seasoning. An aromatic stock can also be made from roasted crustacean shells.

Frozen Seafood

Although raw, unshelled prawns on ice at the fish counter may look like they are freshly caught, they are almost always flash frozen on the spot after being caught, and are sold thawed at fish markets. There are numerous advantages to flash freezing: the sensitive creatures die instantly, they cannot spoil, and they retain their full flavour and nutrients.

The highest-quality frozen shellfish are those that have been frozen according to what is known as the IQF process, or 'Individually Quick Frozen'. This process takes place immediately after the shellfish are frozen, and involves giving them an additional protective 'frosting', either by plunging them in water several times or by spraying them with water, then freezing again. The ice shield provides a further protective layer for the delicate meat and helps prevent freezer burn.

In addition to frozen prawns, Italian fish markets are more and more frequently carrying pre-cooked frozen seafood mixtures, scallops or squid. Thanks to modern freezing methods, these frozen products are now of excellent quality, and preferable to many 'fresh products' that are no longer completely fresh. In order for frozen seafood to retain its unique characteristics, it should be allowed to thaw slowly in the refrigerator.

Prawns of all kinds are also favourite seafood in Italy. Today the majority of them are raised in aquaculture.

Mussels and Squid

Scungilli (whelks) are the largest European sea snails. They are cooked in liquid like mussels, and the meat is then removed from the shells with little skewers.

The common periwinkle is one of the most plentiful sea snails in Europe. It is often added to fish soups.

Ancient Romans especially prized the purple dye of the murex for its powerful pigment. They used the lubricant produced by the hypobranchial gland to make royal purple dye.

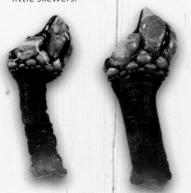

Cockles have thick domed shells with ribs in the form of a fan.

Thumb-sized goose barnacles are not mussels, but an absolutely delicious Mediterranean delicacy.

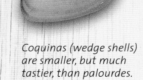

Coquinas (wedge shells) are smaller, but much tastier, than palourdes.

There are more than 500 kinds of clams. All of them have hard ribbed shells and are found in sandy coastal areas.

Blue mussels are the type most frequently eaten, also in Italy. They are usually cooked in a wine stock with vegetables.

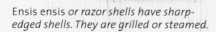

Ensis ensis or razor shells have sharp-edged shells. They are grilled or steamed.

Striped palourdes are members of the clam family. They are the finest representatives of this type of shellfish.

In Italy as elsewhere, oysters are often eaten raw. They are slurped right from the oyster shell, along with the juices.

European oysters are round and flat. They have a more delicate flavour than the oval, more elongated types of oysters, and are named after their place of origin or method of cultivation.

Rock oysters have an elongated shape and taste slightly nutty.

Scallops are found in the coastal shelf areas of nearly all seas. They are very popular in Italy and are among the most delicately flavoured of all shellfish.

The octopus is considerably larger than its relatives, the calamari and squid. The long tentacles are usually cut into pieces and either grilled or fried.

Squid and the larger cuttlefish have firm, white, delicious meat. The ink from its sack, sepia, is used to colour noodles and risotto.

Calamari have longer, narrower bodies than squid. They are often cut into rings, then breaded and fried.

Crustaceans

Shrimps do not have pincers and their tails taper at the end.

Prawns can approach lengths of 30 cm (12 inches).

Crayfish have wide breastplates that are about as long as their tails.

Mantis shrimp have long, thin shells.

Portunidae (swimming crabs) have trapezoidal shells and short pincers.

The Mediterranean slipper lobster is a relative of the crayfish and has a very flat body.

Scampi, called by the same name in Italian, range in colour from orange to salmon and look very much like lobsters, though smaller.

Spider crabs, a kind of salt-water crab, get their name from their spiderlike legs.

Spiny lobster, also called rock lobster, are edible crustaceans that can be up to 30 cm (12 inches) in size. They do not have pincers.

When it comes to crustaceans, lobsters are king. Their shells turn deep red during cooking.

The shell of the ten-footed Cancer pagurus (edible crab) can be up to 30 cm (12 inches) wide.

Lobsters are caught in special baskets called lobster traps, which are filled with bait and placed on the sea floor (opposite).

APULIA

Residents of Apulia, or Puglia, as it is known in Italy, have two treasures at their disposal: fertile soil and a climate in which vegetables and grains thrive. Even now, many Apulians live mainly from agriculture. Their simple, rustic gastronomy is based on products that the land and sea have to offer, including vegetables, grains, fish, seafood, olive oil and wine. The recipes are uncomplicated and, above all, emphasize the unique tastes of individual ingredients.

Apulia is currently Italy's bread basket. The majority of durum wheat, from which pasta secca is made throughout Italy, is cultivated in the plains of the Tavogliere di Puglia. Thus, it is no wonder that noodles and bread are the pillars of Apulian cooking. Furthermore, the region is Italy's second-largest producer of olive oil.

But Apulia also enjoys an outstanding reputation among fish lovers. The picturesque fish markets in towns such as Porto Cesareo, Galipoli, Bari, Ostuni, Monopoli and Otranto have a wide variety of fish and seafood for sale. The catch of the day can be enjoyed in any of the little eateries surrounding the markets. Sea urchins can be savoured here in the spring, just as oysters can elsewhere. Apulians swear there is nothing finer.

Sea urchins are eaten fresh along the coast. To open one, hold it in your hand so that the mouth faces upwards.

Using a very sharp knife, pierce the skin around the mouth opening, which is spineless, and cut out the urchin.

The glistening turquoise waters of Baia dei Turchi (left), located on Italy's boot, are an an ideal destination for a seaside holiday.

The orange-coloured parts of the sea urchin (below) are delicious and a real delicacy. The juice is used in sauces.

Carciofi ripieni Seafood-stuffed Artichokes

4 large, round artichokes (globe)
3 tbsp lemon juice
4 tbsp olive oil
1 small onion, finely chopped
2 garlic cloves, finely chopped
250 g/9 oz frozen, pre-cooked mixed seafood
2 tbsp finely chopped parsley
2 tbsp breadcrumbs
salt
freshly ground pepper

Remove the stalks and leaves from the artichokes. Carefully remove the fuzzy choke from the inside with a spoon and wash the artichoke bases.

Combine 300 ml/11 fl oz water with the lemon juice and a little salt in a saucepan and bring to the boil. Add the artichoke bases and simmer for 30 minutes, then set them upside down in a sieve to drain.

Heat 2 tablespoons of the olive oil in a frying pan and sauté the onion and garlic. Add the frozen seafood and cook until the thawing liquid has evaporated. Then remove from the stovetop, stir in the parsley, and season with salt and pepper. Stuff the artichoke bases with the seafood mixture. Preheat the grill.

Place the stuffed artichokes side by side in a baking dish, sprinkle with the breadcrumbs and drizzle with the remaining olive oil. Grill until golden brown.

Fritto misto
Fried Seafood

300 g/11 oz fresh anchovies
400 g/14 oz seppioline (small squid),
ready to cook
300 g/11 oz small raw prawns
150 g/5 oz flour
½ tsp salt
2 tbsp olive oil
2 egg whites
freshly ground white pepper
oil for frying
lemon wedges to garnish

Wash the anchovies, squid and prawns and drain well. Cut the squid in half. Mix the flour, salt, olive oil, 200 ml/7 fl oz lukewarm water and some pepper into a smooth dough. Beat the egg whites until they are semi-firm and fold them into the dough. Leave it to rest for 10 minutes.

Heat frying oil to 180°C/355°F. Dip the anchovies, squid and prawns into the batter, one at a time, and fry in portions until golden brown. Drain briefly on paper towels and serve with lemon wedges.

Sorrento Lemons

In the seventeenth century, Jesuits on the Sorrento Peninsula and in the Massa Lubrense municipality on the Amalfi Coast began to cultivate a lemon with especially superb qualities, the *limone di massa* or Sorrento lemon, which differs from other lemons in both shape and flavour.

These shiny, bright yellow, oval lemons are characterized by very juicy fruit that has considerable acidity as well as a touch of sweetness.

Sorrento lemons now carry the IGP stamp of quality (Protected Geographical Indication). Their pleasant tartness harmoniously rounds out the flavour of fish and seafood.

Oysters

Oysters were already in demand as a delicacy in Greek and Roman times, and no good table could be without them. They were so popular that, in the second century BCE, officials tried in vain to decrease consumption by legal decree. Shortly thereafter, the Romans constructed the first oyster beds so that they could cultivate these fine shellfish.

Sergius Orata was the reputed inventor of the first oyster bed. As the writer Pliny the Elder described it, Sergius laid out the first oyster breeding grounds at his country estate on Lucrine Lake. Even so, native oysters could no longer satisfy the steadily increasing demand, and oysters began to be imported from distant colonies such as Brittany and Britannia. The Romans developed astounding skill in packing the delicate oysters so that they survived transport without being harmed. The Roman gastronome and cookbook author Marcus Gavius Apicius, for example, supposedly sent fresh oysters to Emperor Trajan in the heartland of Persia. They allegedly arrived alive and were greatly enjoyed.

The story of Emperor Vitellius, who boasted of having devoured a thousand oysters at a single banquet, is somewhat less credible. That Julius Caesar conquered Britannia primarily because he wanted to have a steady supply of the delicious oysters is also probably of little substance. What is true is that oysters have not been enjoyed simply for their taste: their supposed aphrodisiac effects have also been a factor.

Oyster Merchants in Naples

In the old days, the words *ostricano fisico* ('powerful oyster merchant') were posted on colourful signs at Neapolitan oyster stands. Ferdinand II, King of Sicily, was supposedly responsible for this. Upon visiting the fishing village of Santa Lucia and seeing a well-built oyster merchant, he is said to have called out, '*Tu si nu fisico!*' ('My, you have a powerful body!'). The person the king had praised was flattered and wrote the royal compliment on his shop sign. His colleagues, not wanting to be outdone, gave themselves the title of *ostricano fisico*, as well.

Oysters are easiest to open with a special oyster knife that has a sharp, powerful blade.

Place the oyster in your hand with the flat side up and slip the knife into the opening at the hinge.

Ostriche ai ferri
Baked Oysters

2 tomatoes
1 shallot
2 tbsp breadcrumbs
1 tbsp finely chopped parsley
1 tbsp Parmesan
1 kg/2 lb 4 oz coarse sea salt
16 fresh oysters
50 g/1¾ oz butter
freshly ground pepper

Preheat the oven to 225°C/435°F/gas mark 7. Blanch, peel and quarter the tomatoes, remove the seeds, and cut into dice. Finely grate the shallot with a vegetable grater. Mix them with the diced tomatoes, breadcrumbs, parsley and Parmesan, then season with pepper.

Spread the sea salt on a baking tray. Carefully open the oysters with an oyster knife, pour off the salt water inside and break off half of the oyster shell. Brush the oyster meat in the other half of the shell with some of the breadcrumb mixture and place pats of butter on top. Place the oysters in the bed of salt and bake for 10 minutes.

Move the knife along the inside of the oyster shell and sever the muscle that holds the shell together.

Then lift the upper half of the shell, being careful the liquid does not run out of the lower shell.

Oysters are sold fresh and live. Packed in boxes, they can last for up to three weeks by repeatedly replenishing the salt water that remains inside their shells (large photo).
To make sure the oysters are still alive, just splash on a little lemon juice. If they contract, they are fresh enough to eat without concern.

Blue Mussels

Blue mussels, or *cozze* in Italian, grow in clusters and cling to rocks, sea moles or ships' hulls by means of threads that they produce themselves. Humans soon took advantage of this trait and learned to cultivate mussels in what are called mussel gardens. While northern Europeans often cultivate mussels in the unique mudflats of the Wadden Sea in floor culture, in Italy they mainly grow in suspended culture. In suspended culture, the mussel seeds, which are young mussels approximately 1 cm (½ inch) long, are hung in the water on long narrow nets or placed in long tubing made of a net-like material that is wrapped around poles in the water. After a few months, new mussels form along the ropes or tubing. They grow to full size and can be harvested after fourteen months. The advantage to this method is that the mussels remain relatively free of sand, because they do not come into contact with the sea floor.

Small, young mussels are hung in the sea on ropes, in long narrow nets or net-like tubing.

Surrounded by water, they grow to full size in 12 to 14 months and can be harvested.

Cozze al vino bianco
Mussels in White Wine Sauce

2 kg/4 lb 8 oz blue mussels, ready to cook
3 tbsp butter
2 white onions, finely chopped
2 garlic cloves, finely chopped
2 carrots, finely diced
100 g/3½ oz Hamburg parsley root, diced
2 celery sticks, diced
1 litre/1¾ pints white wine
1 small bouquet garni of thyme, parsley and bay leaves
½ tsp black peppercorns
salt
a few chillies

Wash the mussels under cold running water. Discard any mussels that are already open, as well as any with damaged shells.

Heat the butter in a large saucepan. Lightly sauté the onions, garlic and vegetables in it. Add the mussels, cover the pan and cook on high heat for 4 minutes, shaking the pan several times as they cook. Pour in the wine, add the bouquet garni, peppercorns and some salt and chillies, then cover the pan and cook the mussels for another 5 minutes on medium heat.

Remove and discard any mussels that still have closed shells. Serve in heated bowls with the cooking stock.

The stands of mussels are first hung up, then separated and pre-cleaned (above).

Mussels are sorted for selling (opposite); smaller ones are again laid out in nets (left).

Cozze alla napoletana
Neapolitan-style Mussels

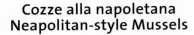

2.5 kg/5 lb 8 oz blue mussels, ready to cook
3 tbsp olive oil
2 onions, finely chopped
1 garlic clove, finely chopped
1 leek, cut into rings
500 g/1 lb 2 oz tomatoes, roughly chopped
1 litre/1¾ pints white wine
3 tbsp finely chopped parsley
salt
freshly ground pepper

Wash the mussels under cold running water, discarding any that are already open, as well as any with damaged shells.

Heat the olive oil in a large saucepan and sauté the onions, garlic and leek. Stir in the tomatoes, season with salt and pepper, and cook briefly. Add the mussels, cover the pan and cook for 4 minutes, shaking the pan several times as they cook. Pour in the wine, then blend in the parsley. Cover the pan and cook the mussels for an additional 10 minutes on medium heat.

Discard any shells that have not opened. Serve the mussels in heated bowls with the stock.

Zuppa di vongole
Spicy Shellfish Ragout
with Fennel

1 kg/2 lb 4 oz mixed shellfish such as clams, cockles and blue mussels, ready to cook
1 fennel bulb
60 ml/2 fl oz olive oil
2 onions, finely chopped
2 garlic cloves, finely chopped
2 fresh red chillies, finely chopped
2 potatoes, cubed
2 carrots, diced
1 bay leaf
3 tomatoes, diced
500 ml/18 fl oz vegetable stock
125 ml/4 fl oz white wine
1 tbsp finely chopped parsley
salt

Wash the shellfish and drain it. Cut off the fennel greens and set them aside; remove the stalk and cut the bulb into fine strips. Bring a saucepan of salted water to the boil and blanch the fennel strips, then drain. Heat 2 tablespoons of the olive oil in a pot and lightly sauté 1 onion, 1 garlic clove and 1 chilli. Add the potatoes, carrots and bay leaf, then season with salt and continue to cook. After about 10 minutes, add the tomatoes and fennel strips. Pour in the vegetable stock and simmer on low heat.

Meanwhile, heat the remaining olive oil, onions, garlic and chilli in a large saucepan with a lid. Deglaze with the white wine and reduce slightly. Add the shellfish, cover the pan and stew for 4 minutes, shaking the pan several times as they cook.

Remove the shellfish from the pan. Pour the liquid through a fine sieve and save the stock. Discard any shellfish that have not opened. Set aside a few of the prettiest shellfish and remove the meat from the rest. Mix the meat into the vegetables and pour in the shellfish stock. Simmer gently for a few minutes, but do not allow it boil.

Finely chop the fennel greens. Fill heated bowls with the shellfish ragout, sprinkle with the parsley and fennel greens, and garnish with the reserved shellfish.

Vongole veraci al vino bianco
Clams in White Wine

500 g/1 lb 2 oz clams
4 garlic cloves
½ bunch flat-leaf parsley
olive oil
250 ml/9 fl oz dry white wine

Wash the clams and discard any with open shells. Peel the garlic and cut each clove in half. Wash and dry the parsley and roughly chop it.

Heat some olive oil in a saucepan and sauté the garlic. Add the clams and parsley, pour in the white wine, cover the pan and cook on high heat for about 10 minutes until the shells open, shaking the pan several times as they cook. When finished, discard any unopened shells. Serve the clams in small bowls with the cooking juices.

Scallops

In Italy, delicate scallops are offered under four different names: *capesante, canestrelli, ventagli* and *pellegrini*. The final name, meaning 'pilgrims', references a story about the scallop shell. Scallop shells were once carried as drinking vessels by pilgrims along the pilgrimage route to Santiago de Compostela in northern Spain, the Way of Saint James. At the same time, they were a means of identifying fellow pilgrims.

Art lovers are familiar with the shell from the famous painting *The Birth of Venus* by Renaissance painter Sandro Boticelli, in which Venus stands gracefully in a scallop shell. According to myth, the goddess of love was born from sea foam and reached the Island of Cythera on a scallop shell that was pulled by six seahorses. In the last century, the shell took on an entirely secular meaning as the company logo of an international oil concern.

In terms of cuisine, scallops are among the most coveted and expensive shellfish. They consist of three parts: the firm white muscle meat, the yellow or orange roe and the darker innards, which are not eaten. In Italy, the delicious meat is most often poached in white wine or grilled right in the shell.

Place the scallop in your hand with the flat side up and insert the knife between the shell halves.

Run the knife along the inside of the shell and flush with it, severing the muscle. Then fold back the upper half of the shell.

Take out the meat, separating the dark organs as a piece from the white meat and orange roe.

Capesante di Chioggia
Chioggia-style Scallops

8 scallops, ready to cook
60 ml/2 fl oz olive oil
1 garlic clove, finely chopped
125 ml/4 fl oz white wine
1 tbsp finely chopped parsley
salt and pepper

Wash the scallops and roe and pat dry. Heat the olive oil in a saucepan and sauté the garlic in it. Pour in the wine, add the parsley and simmer for 2 minutes.

Add the scallops to the pan and cover it. Reduce the heat and poach for 5 minutes. Season with salt and pepper. Serve in 4 shells with some of the cooking liquid.

On the coasts, scallops are offered live in the shell. The shells are opened with a short, sturdy knife.

Trieste and Dungeness Crabs

Trieste, located in north-eastern Italy on the gulf of the same name, has been one of the country's most important habours for centuries, a trans-shipment centre that has always been open to the most varied influences, including culinary ones. Fish and seafood are prepared around this 'seaside city', as Trieste is also called, in a refined manner that incorporates many flavours. *Canocie in busara*, stewed Dungeness crabs, are a particular speciality. A *busara* was originally a cooking pot made of iron or clay and used by fishermen in a ship's galley. Today the word also signifies a method of preparation: Dungeness crabs are layered in a pot with a mixture of peeled tomatoes, breadcrumbs, salt and pepper between each layer. White wine is poured over them, then the pot is covered and placed in a hot oven for about 10 minutes.

FRIULI-VENEZIA GIULIA

The cuisine of this region is as diverse as the landscape. The Carnic Alps on the border with Austria, the green Friulian hills and the karst (limestone) landscape around the Gulf of Trieste are barely an hour's drive by car from one another. In the tumultuous history of the land, many cultures have left their mark over the course of several millennia.

Nevertheless, extremely varied cuisines, including Venetian, Austrian, Greek, Hungarian, Jewish and Slavic, have not been superimposed on one another in the past, but have come together without losing their individuality. Beans and polenta are as much a part of the basic diet as fresh vegetables. In the north, meat dishes including goulash and Wiener Schnitzel reflect the culinary proximity of the former Austro-Hungarian Empire, while fish specialities such as *brodetto*, a nutritious fish soup made of prawns, and in the area around Trieste, Dungeness crab *in busara*, dominate in the south.

The Canale Grande with the Church of Sant'Antonio Nuovo is at the heart of the Borgo Teresiano district of Trieste. In the 18th century, Queen Maria Theresa of Austria ordered the district to be built.

Shrimps, Prawns and Scampi

Whether it is tiny bay shrimp, prawns or scampi, these delicious creatures taste best when they are freshly caught and boiled, grilled or baked right in their shells. Diners encountering prawns for the first time may wonder how best to handle these armoured delicacies. The easiest way is to use one's fingers. Even in the best restaurants, this method is entirely customary.

Since the head is simply unpalatable, start by removing it and setting it aside. Then bend the armored shell outwards along the stomach and detach the meat from the shell. If the dark vein along the back of the prawn is still visible, it can be removed with the point of a knife. If no extra plates have been provided, just slide the discarded parts to the edge of the plate.

Now nothing stands in the way of delicious eating. The shelled prawns are taken in the hand, dipped into a sauce or dip and eaten. The little bowl of lemon water that is served with them in many Italian restaurants is intended for washing your hands after the meal.

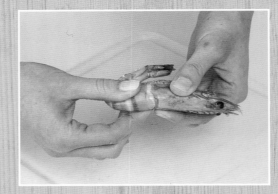

Pick up the prawn with your hand, remove the head and set it aside. It is not edible.

With your fingers, remove the shell from the stomach outwards.

Cut along the back of the prawn with a sharp knife to de-vein.

Dip the shelled prawn in the sauce with your fingers. Enjoy!

Gamberoni arrabbiati
Prawns Arrabbiata

500 g/1 lb 2 oz raw prawns
145 ml/5 fl oz olive oil
1 fresh red chilli, finely chopped
2 tbsp lemon juice
2½ tbsp Italian brandy
2 garlic cloves
500 g/1 lb 2 oz tomatoes, diced
125 ml/4 fl oz white wine
salt
freshly ground pepper
several small basil leaves

Prepare the prawns as described above. Stir 6 tablespoons of the olive oil together with the chilli, lemon juice and brandy. Peel the garlic and press it into the seasoned oil. Marinate the prawns in it for 1 hour.

Heat the remaining olive oil in a frying pan and sauté the prawns for about 3 minutes per side. Remove them from the pan and keep warm. Cook the tomatoes in the pan oil and deglaze with the wine. Put the prawns back in the pan, then season the sauce with salt and pepper. Serve garnished with basil leaves.

Gamberoni alla griglia
Chargrilled Prawns

20 raw prawns
3 large garlic cloves
100 ml/3½ fl oz olive oil
⅛ teaspoon cayenne pepper
1 tsp dried oregano
1 lemon

Soak four wooden skewers in water. Wash the prawns and pat them dry. Peel the garlic and press it into the olive oil. Stir in the cayenne pepper and oregano. Place the prawns in a bowl and pour the garlic oil over them. Cover the bowl and marinate the prawns in the refrigerator for 4 hours, turning once. Place five prawns on each of the wooden skewers, and barbecue or grill for 5 minutes per side. Cut the lemon into wedges and serve with the prawns.

Crayfish

Italian rivers and brooks were once filled with crayfish, which were popular, everyday fare. However, their populations decreased drastically as water pollution became increasingly prevalent. Today these freshwater relatives of lobster are mainly imported from China, Scandinavia, Poland and Turkey. They taste best from May through August, and may be sold only live or canned. In the case of cooked crayfish, if the tail is rolled inwards, that signals that the crayfish was fresh when cooked. The edible portions are the meat from the tail and claw.

Gamberoni arrabbiati

Scampi ai pomodori
Scampi in Tomato Sauce

2 tbsp butter
2 shallots, finely chopped
1 garlic clove, finely chopped
450 g/1 lb tomatoes, diced
100 ml/3½ fl oz double cream
2½ tbsp sambuca
600 g/1 lb 5 oz raw scampi, shelled
1 tbsp finely chopped parsley
salt
freshly ground pepper

Melt the butter in a deep frying pan and sauté the shallots and garlic in it. Add the tomatoes and simmer on medium heat for 15 minutes. Stir in the cream and simmer for an additional 5 minutes.

Season the tomato sauce with salt, pepper and the sambuca. Add the scampi to the pan and simmer in the sauce for 3 to 4 minutes. Serve sprinkled with the parsley.

Not everything caught in the shrimp net can be sold later at market (below).

Put the soaked beans, garlic and rosemary in a deep kettle and add water.

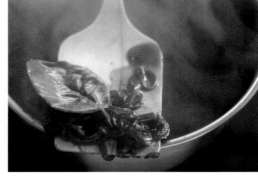

Simmer the onion rings in red wine with bay leaf, cinnamon stick and vinegar until the liquid has evaporated.

Pour the water off the beans, purée with olive oil and season generously with salt and pepper.

Wash the unshelled scampi and steam them in a double boiler over hot water.

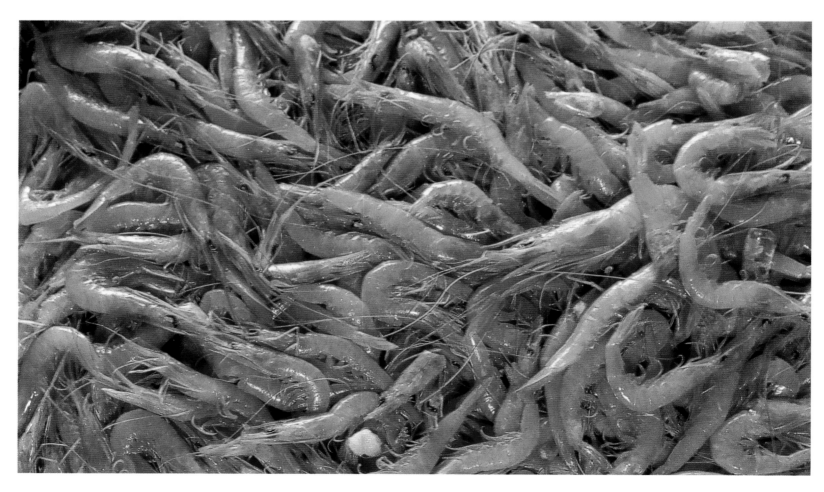

Scampi con fagioli e cipolle
Steamed Scampi
with Puréed Beans
and Red Onion Compote

200 g/7 oz dried white beans
1 garlic clove, finely chopped
1 sprig rosemary
3 red onions
400 ml/14 fl oz sweet red wine
3 tbsp balsamic vinegar
1 bay leaf
1 small cinnamon stick
1 tsp honey
3–4 tbsp olive oil
600 g/1 lb 5 oz raw scampi, shelled
1 bay leaf
½ tsp grated lemon rind
salt
freshly ground pepper

Cover the beans with cold water and soak them overnight. The next day, pour off the soaking water, cover with fresh water and bring to the boil. Add the garlic and rosemary and cook together with the beans for 1 hour.

Meanwhile, finely slice the onions. In a second saucepan, combine the red wine, vinegar, onions, bay leaf and cinnamon. Bring to the boil and simmer on low heat until the liquid reduces. Add the honey and season with salt and pepper.

When the beans are cooked, drain them, reserving the cooking liquid. Purée the beans with a little of the cooking liquid and 2 tablespoons of olive oil. Season with salt and pepper and keep warm.

Wash and drain the scampi in a sieve. In a large saucepan with a lid, bring 1 litre/ 1¾ pints of water to the boil with the bay leaf and lemon rind. Place the scampi, still in the sieve, in the pan above the steaming water and close the lid. Steam the scampi for 8 to 10 minutes.

Mound the bean purée in the middle of a serving platter and drizzle the remaining olive oil over it. Place the scampi on the purée and top with the onions.

The Rich Cuisine of Capri and Ischia

Shortly after the birth of Christ, the Roman emperor Tiberius commissioned the construction of a summer house, the *Villa Jovis* (Villa Jupiter), on the steeply sloping eastern tip of Capri. Covering an area of more than 7,000 square metres (75,000 ft²) and standing eight stories and 40 metres (130 ft) high, it was certainly luxurious. Here, in his self-imposed 'gilded exile', he enjoyed a superb view of one of the most beautiful bays on the Mediterranean. And many prominent people would follow him here.

However, it is not only the beauty of the unique landscape and the mild climate that have attracted visitors for two millennia. To this day, the healing effects of the hot thermal springs draw hundreds of thousands of visitors annually to these islands off the Amalfi Coast. No wonder that a 'rich' cuisine, characterized by the great variety of fish from the surrounding sea, has developed in this opulent, chic setting. Typical of the cuisine are a wide variety of crustaceans of highest quality, whose appeal lies in their unique tastes.

But there is also a truly outstanding folk cuisine that does not rely on expensive foods. Its luxury lies mainly in the time it takes to carefully prepare the meal. Salads with fresh wild herbs and thousands of nuanced flavours are just as much a part of this tradition as *sartu' di riso in bianco*, a lavish rice dish with fresh mushrooms, and *torta caprese*, a sweet chocolate cake with almonds and liqueur.

Berths in Capri's main habour, the Marina Grande, are desirable spots to drop anchor.

Shelling Lobsters

Lay the cooked lobster on its stomach and pierce it behind the head with a large knife.

In a single motion, cut the lobster in half lengthways and separate the two halves.

Lay the two halves side by side on a clean chopping board.

Cut into each of the large lobster claws with the knife.

Gently extract the tail meat from the shell with your fingers.

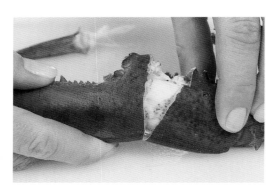

Open the claws and remove the lobster meat in one piece.

Astice lesso
Boiled Lobster

1 onion, spiked with 1 bay leaf and 2 cloves
1 celery stick, diced
1 carrot, diced
1 Hamburg parsley root, diced
2 lemon slices
1 tbsp sea salt
2 lobsters

Put all ingredients except the lobsters in a deep kettle of water. Bring to the boil and simmer for 25 minutes.

Put the lobsters headfirst into the boiling stock. Cook for 5 minutes at a rolling boil, then reduce the heat and simmer for an additional 25 minutes. Leave them to cool in the cooking liquid.

Astice arrosto

Astice arrosto
Grilled Lobster

2 large lobsters,
800 g/1 lb 12 oz each, cooked

5 tbsp olive oil

2 tbsp breadcrumbs

2 tbsp finely chopped parsley

salt

pepper

Grease a baking dish with a little olive oil. Cut both lobsters in half lengthways. Remove the stomach and intestines from both halves.

Place the lobster halves in the baking dish and season the meat with salt and pepper. Combine the breadcrumbs and parsley, then spread over the lobster meat. Drizzle on the remaining olive oil and set under the grill until golden brown.

Lobsters are mainly sold live. Until they are sold, they are kept in vivaria, or lobster tanks.

Alghero and Spiny Lobster

Alghero is located on the west coast of Sardinia. Often called *Barcelonetta de Sardegna*, it is Sardinia's 'little Barcelona'. For nearly 150 years, until the end of the fifteenth century, the city was firmly in the hands of the Catalonians. This can be seen even now in the architecture of the old city and in many dishes that incorporate Spanish influences. Along with local specialities – including artichokes, tomatoes and suckling pig – seafood, in particular spiny lobster, play an important role in the local cuisine.

The waters around Sardinia provide ideal living conditions for spiny lobsters. The sea there has an ideal saline content, and there is a rich supply of mussels, squid and octopus, plus a special type of algae, *erba riccia*. All these nutrients help the spiny lobsters develop their unmistakable flavour, which is prized by gourmets throughout Europe. In 1947, lobsters from Alghero were even served at the wedding feast of the future queen of England, Elizabeth II. They have also lent their name to a light Sardinian white wine, *Aragosta*.

An event called *L'Aragosta nella cucina algherese* ('Spiny Lobsters in Alghero Cuisine'), takes place each year in May and June. Many restaurants offer special menus and prices during that time. The lobsters are either boiled and served with olive oil and lemon, or charcoal grilled with a combination of aromatic herbs. *Alla catalana*, a method of preparation that includes green pepper, tomatoes, cayenne pepper, saffron, parsley and a splash of brandy, is reminiscent of the Spanish past.

The picturesque little town of Alghero on the west coast of Sardinia is a well-known centre for catching spiny lobsters (right).

Spiny lobsters are caught in special traps or with nets, as shown in the photo.

The fisherman carefully frees the spiny lobster from the net without injuring it in the process.

Freshly caught spiny lobster is a coveted delicacy for locals and visitors alike.

Aragosta alla sarde
Sardinian-style Spiny Lobster

2 tbsp salt

5 tbsp mild white wine vinegar

2 spiny lobsters, ca. 800 g/1 lb 12 oz each

2 celery sticks

4 plum tomatoes

1 onion

1 garlic clove

juice of 1 lemon

6 tbsp olive oil

1 tbsp finely chopped parsley

freshly ground pepper

In a deep kettle, bring 5 litres/9 pints of water to the boil with the salt and 4 tablespoons of the vinegar. Put the spiny lobsters into the boiling water headfirst, one at a time. Cook for 5 minutes at a rolling boil, then reduce the heat and simmer for an additional 20 to 25 minutes until done.

Chop the celery on the diagonal and slice the tomatoes. Cut the onion into thin rings. Lightly salt the garlic and crush it with the back of a knife. Whisk the remaining vinegar together with the garlic, lemon juice, olive oil, parsley, salt and pepper to make a dressing.

Remove the spiny lobsters from the kettle and leave them to cool slightly. Then cut them lengthways, removing the intestines in the centre of the tail in the process. Remove the lobster meat and cut it into 4-cm cubes. Lay the tomato slices on a platter. Arrange the celery, onion rings and lobster meat on it decoratively and drizzle the dressing over everything.

Barbecuing over charcoal accentuates the natural flavour of spiny lobsters (below).

Aragosta alla griglia
Barbecued Spiny Lobster

2 tbsp sea salt

2 spiny lobsters, ca. 800 g/1 lb 12 oz each

4 stalks wild fennel

2 tbsp olive oil

freshly ground pepper

In a deep kettle, bring 5 litres/9 pints of water to the boil with the salt. Put the spiny lobsters into the boiling water headfirst, one at a time, and cook for 5 minutes at a rolling boil.

Remove the spiny lobsters from the kettle and cut them in half lengthways. Season each half with a little salt and pepper. Place the lobsters on a hot barbecue with the cut surface up. Place the fennel on the lobsters and drizzle with the olive oil. Barbecue on medium heat for 25 minutes, turning them over just before the end of the cooking time.

The Treasures of the Lagoon

The sea still affects life in the Venetian lagoon today. A narrow strip of land separates the Adriatic Sea from the nearly still waters of the lagoon, which is about 50 km (30 miles) long and 14 km (9 miles) wide. About 8 per cent of the lagoon consists of islands, including Murano, Burano, Torcello and the world-famous lagoon city itself. Eleven per cent of the area is always covered by water, and the rest consists of marshes and wetlands.

The lagoon still provides habitat for a multitude of fish and seafood. Visitors to Venice can best witness the abundance on a stroll through the busy fish market on the Rialto Bridge or – assuming they are out and about very early in the morning – in Chioggia, a fishing port about 45 km (28 miles) away.

The names by which fish and seafood are sold here can be confusing at first. For example, clams are called *peoci* in Venetian dialect, rather than *cozze*. Along with the more familiar seafoods, the lagoon offers particular specialities, including *gra'ncevole* (spider crabs) and *mo'leche* (softshell crabs). In addition to *seppioline* (little squid), prawns and refined pleasures such as oysters, they reveal a whole symphony of subtle flavours to seafood epicures.

Granceola mimosa
Mimosa-style Spider Crab

4 spider crabs, cooked
3 eggs, hard boiled
3 tbsp olive oil
juice of 1 lemon
1 tbsp finely chopped parsley
salt
freshly ground white pepper

Open the spider crab shell, then remove the meat and dice it. Shell the eggs and make a dressing of the egg yolks, olive oil, lemon juice, and salt and pepper. Chop the egg whites and combine them in a bowl with the crabmeat and parsley. Pour on the dressing and blend carefully. Serve the mixture in clean spider crab shells.

In gratitude for being saved from the plague, the 17th-century baroque church of Santa Maria della Salute was built between the canal and the Bacino di San Marco at the entrance to the Canale Grande in Venice (right).

Cicheti

Anyone who avoids the crowded tourist paths and sets out to find authentic Venetian cuisine will eventually land at one of the little *bacaros*, which are mainly family run. These Venetian wine taverns have a bistro atmosphere and are divided into two dining areas. The bar, where one can drink a glass of wine or an aperitif and enjoy a bite to eat, is located in the front. The connecting dining room is usually wood paneled and luxuriously furnished, but windowless. This is where gourmets settle in to enjoy all the delicious local fish specialities. Many bacaros offer guests a local delicacy, *cicheti* ('little hors d'oeuvres'), which are all the rage again. For Venetians, that signifies a medley of all sorts of very special treats from the lagoon: warm squid, spider crabs, mussels and other delicacies on small appetizer plates.

Granciporro con marinata
Edible Crabs
with Spicy Marinade

4 crabs, cooked
100 g/3½ oz cherry tomatoes, diced
5 spring onions, chopped
2 celery sticks, diced
juice of 1 lemon
juice of 1 orange
⅛ teaspoon cayenne pepper
1 tbsp white balsamic vinegar
4 tbsp olive oil
1 tbsp finely chopped parsley
salt
freshly ground pepper
curly endive to garnish

Remove the pincers and legs from the crab shells, as well as the tail plate from the underside of each shell. Insert a sharp knife between the underside and shell, and separate them at the edge. Extract the body and cut it in half. Wash the shell thoroughly and break off the inner pieces. Remove the meat from the body, pincers and legs, and cut it all into small pieces.

Combine the tomatoes, spring onions and celery with the crabmeat. Whisk together the lemon and orange juices, cayenne pepper, vinegar and olive oil to make a marinade. Salt and pepper to taste, then stir in the parsley.

Pour the marinade over the crab salad, stir well and marinate the salad in the refrigerator for 30 minutes.

Fill the crab shells with the salad mixture and serve them on a bed of curly endive.

Edible crabs have tender, juicy and delicate meat. Their livers are also considered an exceptional delicacy.

To extract the meat from an edible crab, first break off the pincers and legs, then remove the tail plate.

Remove the meat from the body and pincers, and clean the shell.

Combine tomatoes, spring onions and celery with the crabmeat. Pour on the marinade.

Season the salad, marinate it for 30 minutes, then fill the shells and serve.

Octopus

For thousands of years, legends have included accounts of sea monsters with many tentacles that would threaten sailors' lives. The Roman writer Pliny the Elder told of a huge octopus with arms 10 metres (33 ft) long, which supposedly plundered seaside fish ponds in Carteia and was then killed by sentinels. Octopuses were described in *The Natural History of Norway*, a book that appeared in 1755, as 'indisputably the most ungainly sea monsters in the world' at more than 2.5 km (1.5 miles) long.

Today scientists do believe it is possible that giant octopuses live in the deep sea and could be more than 25 metres (80 ft) in length, with suckers as big as soup bowls. Octopuses that end up on dinner plates in Italy are up to 3 metres (10 ft) long and live near the coasts. Their meat is chewy, and therefore must be cooked for a long time or tenderized before cooking. At the fish markets in the early morning, one can observe fishermen beating the octopuses fifty to sixty times heftily against the stone floor. The octopuses are then laid in wicker baskets and shaken firmly so that they drape into a shape that resembles a flower.

Octopuses are traditionally cooked in a mixture of salt and fresh water. For the most part, only the thick tentacles are used in cooking. They are either boiled and then sliced, or grilled whole and seasoned with lots of garlic and lemon.

The octopus has certainly not lost its formidable reputation, at least not entirely. Particularly in southern Italy, octopuses are synonymous with the Mafia, whose long arms reach into many areas of public life.

Traditionally, octopuses are first cooked whole in a mixture of salt water and fresh water.

Octopuses are first stewed on low heat in a covered kettle for an hour.

Then the tentacles are removed and cut into bite-sized pieces.

The pieces are simmered in spicy tomato sauce on low heat for an additional 30 minutes.

Polpo con le patate

Polpo con le patate
Octopus and Potatoes

1 octopus, ca. 1 kg/2 lb 4 oz, ready to cook
5 tbsp olive oil
1 large onion, finely chopped
2 garlic cloves, finely chopped
4 tomatoes, diced
1 bay leaf
500 g/1 lb 2 oz potatoes, chopped into cubes
200 g/7 oz frozen peas, thawed
sea salt
freshly ground pepper

Place the octopus in a deep kettle without any water. Add salt, cover the pot and stew it in its own juices for about 1 hour. Three times during the hour, remove the octopus from the pot with a meat fork, immerse it in a pot of boiling water, rinse it in cold water and then put it back in the stewing stock.

Heat the olive oil in a large saucepan and sauté the onion and garlic. Add the tomatoes and cook briefly. Season with salt and pepper, then add the bay leaf and potatoes. Remove the octopus from its pot, cut it into small pieces, and add to the rest of the ingredients in the soup kettle. Pour in enough of the stewing liquid to cover everything generously. Cover the soup kettle with a lid and simmer for 30 minutes on medium heat. Mix in the peas and cook 5 minutes longer before serving.

Polpo alla luciana
Octopus in Garlic Sauce

1 octopus, ca. 1 kg/2 lb 4 oz, ready to cook
100 ml/3½ fl oz olive oil
4 garlic cloves, finely chopped
1 fresh red chilli, finely chopped
juice of 2 lemons
3 tbsp finely chopped parsley
sea salt
freshly ground pepper

Place the octopus in a deep kettle, cover it and stew on low heat for about 1 hour. Then remove it from the pot and slice the tentacles. Heat the olive oil in a large saucepan and sauté the garlic and chilli. Add the sliced octopus and as much stewing liquid as needed to completely cover everything. Cover the pan and simmer for another 30 minutes.

Season with the lemon juice, sea salt and pepper. Mix in the parsley. Transfer the octopus to a serving bowl and allow to stand for a moment before serving.

Squid

Squid are popular all over Italy and are prepared in many different ways along the coasts. *Moscardini* – tiny squid – often appear in seafood medleys and sauces. In Liguria, *moscardini* are braised with tomatoes, garlic and rosemary and served as an antipasto.

Calameretti – slightly larger squid with especially succulent meat – are typically grilled whole or cooked with vegetables. A speciality from the area around Naples is *calameretti* in tomato sauce with sultanas, pine kernels and olives.

Seppie – medium-sized squid – are superb for stuffing and can also be barbecued whole or fried. In the Veneto region, they are stewed in their own ink, often in a risotto. The dish does look strangely black, but it tastes fantastic.

Calamari have firm meat. They are usually cut into rings, breaded and fried. Fried calamari are an especially popular dish with tourists.

First, cut off the tentacles just below the eyes.

Cut into the back of the head and pull out the colourless beak.

Remove the head and attached innards from the body.

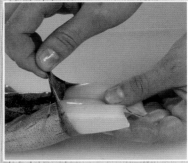

Strip off the dark skin and wash the body cavity thoroughly.

Seppie con il nero alla veneziana
Venetian-style Squid

750 g/1 lb 10 oz whole squid
1 bunch flat-leaf parsley
4 tbsp olive oil
1 small onion, finely chopped
1 garlic clove, finely chopped
250 ml/9 fl oz white wine
1 tbsp lemon juice
salt
freshly ground pepper

Clean the squid and carefully remove the ink sack from each. Then cut the squid into thin strips. Wash the parsley, cut off the stalks (do not discard them) and finely chop the leaves. Cook the ink sacks with the parsley stalks, a pinch of salt and a little water for several minutes. Then strain and save the liquid.

Heat the olive oil in a saucepan and sauté the onion and garlic until the onion is translucent. Add the sliced squid and sauté briefly. Pour in the wine and the squid stock. Stir in half of the chopped parsley. Cover and simmer for 30 minutes on low heat. Before serving, add the lemon juice and adjust the seasoning with salt and pepper. Sprinkle with the remaining parsley and serve.

Seppie ripiene

Wash the squid tubes and pat dry with paper towels.

Stuff each squid with an equal portion of the rice mixture.

Close the tube openings with cocktail sticks.

Fry the stuffed squid in olive oil.

Add diced tomatoes and white wine.

Seppie ripiene
Stuffed Squid

4 squid
2 shallots
1 garlic clove
100 g/3½ oz cooked ham
3 tbsp cooked rice
1 egg
1 tbsp finely chopped parsley
1 tsp grated lemon rind
500 g/1 lb 2 oz tomatoes
2 tbsp olive oil
200 ml/7 fl oz white wine
salt
freshly ground pepper

Trim, wash and pat dry the squid. Finely chop the tentacles. Finely dice the shallots, garlic and ham. Thoroughly combine the tentacles, shallots, garlic, ham, rice, egg, parsley and lemon rind. Season with salt and pepper. Stuff the squid tubes with the mixture, then close the openings with cocktail sticks.

Blanch, peel and quarter the tomatoes, remove the seeds, and cut into small dice. Heat the olive oil in a deep frying pan and sauté the stuffed squid on all sides. Add the diced tomatoes to the pan, pour in the white wine and bring to the boil. Cover the pan and simmer on low heat for around 45 minutes, then season the sauce with salt and pepper. Serve the squid in the sauce.

Calamari fritti
Fried Calamari Rings

800 g/1 lb 12 oz whole calamari, ready to cook
juice of 2 lemons
2 eggs
salt
freshly ground pepper
oil for frying, flour for coating

Cut the whole calamari into rings. Drizzle the lemon juice over them and marinate for about 15 minutes.

Heat the oil in a deep-fryer to 175°C/350°F. Whisk the eggs with salt and pepper. Coat the calamari rings with flour, then dip them in the whisked egg. Fry the calamari in the hot oil until golden brown. Drain briefly on paper towels before serving.

Calamari fritti

MEAT, GAME AND FOWL

Although Italians seldom do entirely without meat, the portions are usually small because the *primi piatti* have already assuaged the initial hunger. Meat is cut into very thin slices and prepared with very little fat, which still leaves room for dessert, even after a multi-course meal. One of the best examples of Italian meat cuisine is Roman *saltimbocca* (literally, 'spring in the mouth'), consisting of wafer-thin slices of veal, raw ham that is sliced equally thin, and a sage leaf.

Different kinds of meat are divided into three basic categories:

- *Animali da macello*: animals that are butchered, including cattle, calves, pigs, horses, lambs, sheep and goats.
- *Animali da cortile*: barnyard animals, including chickens, turkeys, ducks, geese, guinea fowl, pigeons and rabbits.
- *Selvaggina e cacciagione*: game, including deer, wild boar, hare and game birds such as pheasant, quail and partridge.

The wealth of meat products that are created in the various Italian regions and provinces is further evidence that there is no *single* Italian cuisine.

In the north, Alto Adige and Friuli-Venezia Giulia, the influences of Alpine, Austro-Hungarian and Slavic traditions can still be felt. Accordingly, pork dominates in typical northern dishes. During the Council of Trent (1545–1563), the region

experienced a culinary golden age, as rich gastronomic traditions arrived along with the delegates from all over the Christian realm. It goes without saying that the bishops and cardinals would never have travelled to Trent without their chefs.

Although there is no longer a strict division between the rich and the poor, it is still pork that plays a large role in everyday cooking alongside grain products, fruits and vegetables. Many varieties of sausage have became famous; ham and bacon even more so. Salted meat, made mainly from beef or sheep, was and remains typical of simpler cuisine. The meat is cured for twenty days in wooden barrels with brine, pepper, garlic, bay leaf, rosemary, juniper and white wine.

In the Veneto, on the other hand, one finds much more of the Italian cuisine that we are accustomed to. During the Middle Ages and especially in the seventeenth century, *La Serenissima* ('the most serene'), as Venice was respectfully called, held the region's key position of gateway to the world. The golden age of the city and the clearly oriental influence that accompanied it live on still in the generous use of spices in the cuisine. Instead of sheep and goats, there are plenty of cows in Veneto. Beef and veal are fixtures on Venetian menus, along with pork, game and poultry. Famous ham and sausage varieties – for example, *sanguinacci* (black puddings) – are made according to traditional recipes. Cattle farming has also led to a series of delicate and aromatic cheeses, among them Grana Padano, asiago and Monte Veronese.

The provinces of Piedmont, Emilia-Romagna, and Lombardy form a kind of Italian 'bacon belt'. Whether beef, veal, pork, poultry, rabbit or game, meat is the main attraction in kitchens here. Milan and Bologna, which also goes by the nickname of *La Grassa* ('rich, fatty'), are famous for their culinary products. Butter and bacon take precedence over olive oil; meat products including mortadella and cheeses such as Parmigiano-Reggiano are world famous. The great richness of this cuisine is manifested in *bollito misto*, a sumptuous dish that includes chicken, beef and veal.

Cooked ham, zampone, bollito misto: these and many other meat specialities are found in great abundance in Piedmont, Emilia-Romagna and Lombardy, Italy's 'bacon belt'.

To make the stock, first roughly chop the onions and root vegetables.

Place the chicken, beef and vegetables in a large saucepan, then add water.

After the tongue has cooked, leave it to cool, then remove the skin.

Slice the tongue, boned chicken breast and brisket.

Bollito misto piemontese
Piedmont-style
Mixed Boiled Meats

Serves eight

soup vegetables such as carrots, celery or other root vegetables
2 onions
1 fresh stewing chicken, ca. 2 kg/4 lb 8 oz, ready to cook
1 kg/2 lb 4 oz beef brisket
2 tsp salt
1 tsp black peppercorns
1 calf's tongue
2 bay leaves
1 kg/2 lb 4 oz firm potatoes
4 carrots
2 Hamburg parsley roots
2 leeks
3 tbsp finely chopped parsley
butter for frying

Coarsely chop the soup vegetables and onions. Place the chicken and beef in a large saucepan. Add the onions and soup vegetables, 1 teaspoon of salt, ½ teaspoon of the peppercorns and enough water to cover everything well. Cover the pan and simmer for 2 hours.

Wash the calf's tongue, remove any fat and cartilage, and place the meat in a second saucepan. Cover with water, add the bay leaves and remaining salt and peppercorns, and bring to the boil. Skim off the foam that rises to the top, cover the pan and cook for about 1 hour on medium heat.

Remove the calf's tongue, chicken and brisket from their respective stocks and leave them to cool slightly. Pour the chicken-beef stock through a sieve into a bowl.

Dice the potatoes, carrots and parsley root. Wash the leeks and cut them into thick rings. Heat some butter in a saucepan and briefly sauté the vegetables. Then pour in the strained chicken-beef stock and simmer for 25 to 30 minutes. Preheat the oven to 200°C/390°F/gas mark 6.

In the meantime, skin the calf's tongue and chicken. Remove the chicken breast and bone it, then slice the tongue, chicken breast and brisket. Arrange these meats and the chicken legs in a baking dish. Add the potatoes, other vegetables and stock. Heat everything in the oven for about 10 minutes. Sprinkle with the parsley before serving.

Bagnetto verde, a spicy green sauce (see recipe on page 358), is always served with *bollito misto*.

Meat in Central and Southern Italy

In contrast to northern regions such as Piedmont or Lombardy, meat is not usually braised in Tuscany, but is served barbecued or fried instead. This is particularly true in the case of *bistecca fiorentina*, which is dished up with a little salt, pepper and a few drops of the very best olive oil. Chianina cattle, which are also popular with their neighbors to the north in Emilia, provide the choicest meat here. Pork and wild boar nonetheless have their place in Tuscan cuisine, as well.

Meat consumption is quite high in the Marche in comparison to other regions of Italy. One speciality is *porchetta*, grilled suckling pig stuffed with herbs. Even if *porchetta* is also well known in Tuscany, Umbria and Lazio, Marchigians clearly believe that the original recipe comes from their part of the country. Regional differences are mainly expressed in the seasoning. For example, rosemary and fennel are used in Tuscany, while a spicier version comes from Perugia, the capital of Umbria. Pork

has an important place in Umbrian cuisine. In addition to hearty meat dishes, sausage specialities are popular across the entire region. The cuisine of Basilicata also relies mainly on pork. There it is seasoned with *peperoncini*, or chillies, which adds bold pungency to every dish.

In Lazio, which is located in the centre of the Italian peninsula and includes the capital, Rome, livestock constitute an important part of agricultural life. Here it is mainly sheep that are raised in the pastures of this scenically diverse region. The plentiful grass in the mountainous areas makes their meat particularly flavourful, so it is not surprising that lamb dishes such as *abbacchio alla cacciatora* (milk-fed lamb cacciatora) rank among Lazio's acclaimed delicacies. Since ancient times, Romans have held *testicciuola di abbacchio* (lamb's head) in high esteem. It is stuffed with bread, garlic and parsley, drenched with plenty of olive oil and then baked in the oven. But the region of Lazio is also known for its poultry dishes as well as bacon and sausage specialities. Lard is used more frequently in cooking here than in most of the rest of the country.

The southern provinces of Italy, in contrast to the wealthier northern areas, have always been marked by a culture of country fare. And this does not mean that Apulia, Campania and Calabria, for example, have impoverished cuisines. On the contrary: what has been called *cucina povera* (peasant cuisine) has undergone a development here, the ingenuity of which is the envy of other countries, whose humble cuisine pales by comparison. In addition, the gastronomy of southern Italy contrasts strongly with those of northern and central Italy due to greater Arab and Greek influence in the south.

The Umbrian city of Norcia is renowned for its sausages, which are proudly presented both inside and in front of butcher shops (above).

In eastern Sardinia, shepherds have grazed their sheep in the green hollows of the Codula di Luna Gorge for centuries (large photo on right).

SARDINIA'S MEAT DISHES

Especially in the interior, Sardinian cuisine continues to be an 'earthy cuisine', centred around roasted and grilled meat from wild animals and *porceddi* ('young pigs'). *Carne a carraxiu* ('buried meat'), which has nearly faded into obscurity today, is among the traditional dishes. A deep hole is dug in the ground and a whole, freshly slaughtered lamb or calf is placed in it. The animal is covered with various wild herbs, then the hole is covered over again and a brimstone fire is ignited on top of it. In the hours that follow, the meat slowly cooks in the hot earth.

Su malloru de su sabatteri is another culinary speciality of the island. A cow is stuffed with a pig that is in turn stuffed with a lamb that contains a rabbit that, last but not least, can be stuffed with a quail. The whole ensemble is cooked slowly over a wood fire on a constantly turning spit.

Sardinian Juniper

The evergreen juniper shrub, a symbol of Sardinia, is a member of the cypress family. It is an important element of Sardinia's characteristic macchia landscape, which consists of low trees, shrubs and a variety of aromatic plants including myrtle, rosemary, thyme, bay, sage, lavender, fennel, peppermint and lemon balm. While in many countries only the dried, dark violet fruit of the juniper bush is used as a seasoning for game, hearty meat dishes, pies and marinades, the Sardinians also make use of the wood. They lay it in the embers when barbecuing, and it gives the meat a special taste that is spicy, sweet and slightly resinous.

Sardinia

Meat in the Kitchen

Boning Veal Loin

Lay the veal loin on a board with the flesh side down and cut the long ribs free.

Now lay the veal loin on the rib side and detach the loin from the bones in a single piece.

Then separate the fillet from the backbone, cutting out the meat from between the bones as you go.

Finally, trim the meat and carefully remove the fat layer, skin and tendons from the veal loin.

For generations, the Martini family has run their butcher shop in Sansepolcro, Tuscany, in the traditional way (right). Here they proudly present pieces of Chianina beef.

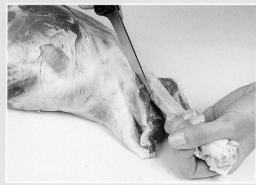

Boning Leg of Lamb

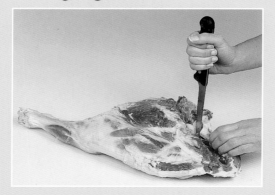

Lay the leg of lamb on a board with the pelvic bone facing up and cut the bones free.

Open the pelvic bone at the joint, sever the tendons and remove the bone.

Expose the lower leg (shank) bone at the end of the leg, severing all the tendons.

Cuts of Meat

Once again, great emphasis is placed on exceptional quality when purchasing meat in Italy. Italian home cooks are well informed and know exactly which cuts are best suited for particular cooking methods. Admittedly, there is a bewildering variety of expressions for certain pieces of meat, some of them also in dialect. Although a government directive specifies the correct terms, many butchers do not adhere to them.

Raise the lower leg bone slightly and separate it from the thigh bone at the knee joint.

With the boning knife, cut away the meat around the thigh bone and expose the bone.

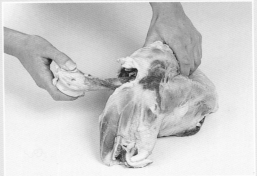

Hold the bone firmly at the joint and pull it out with a rotating motion, then sever the tendons.

Veal

Lean, juicy veal is easy to digest and especially rich in high-quality protein. Veal is finely marbled, free of tendons and delicately textured. It has a certain firmness to the touch. Due to its higher price, veal was once prepared mainly on feast days.

Both male and female calves are butchered, most often between the ages of five and six months. The animal's age and the type of feed it ate determine the colour of the meat. Calves that were raised organically and were already let out to pasture have light to dark red meat. Milk-fed calves that were nourished only with milk or milk substitutes have whitish pink meat.

Many Italian veal recipes typically involve wrapping or layering the meat with ham, pancetta or strips of bacon so that the veal does not become too dry during cooking. Among the most famous dishes are *vitello tonnato*, cooked veal served cold with tuna mayonnaise; *ossobuco*, veal shank that is sliced and braised with bones and marrow; delicious *involtini*, delicate, gently braised roulades; and many different kinds of cutlets.

Scaloppine al limone
Lemon Cutlets

4 thin veal cutlets, 50 g/1¾ oz each
2 tbsp olive oil
4 tbsp lemon juice
2 tbsp butter
2½ tbsp dry white vermouth
salt
freshly ground pepper
sugar

Wash the cutlets, pat them dry, then press them as flat as possible with the ball of your hand. Lay the cutlets in a shallow bowl. Whisk together the oil and lemon juice and drizzle it over the veal. Cover the bowl and marinate for 30 minutes.

Remove the meat from the marinade, drain and pat dry with paper towels. Melt the butter in a deep frying pan and brown the cutlets on both sides. Remove from the pan, season with salt and pepper, and keep them hot. Deglaze the pan with the marinade, stirring to loosen the pan drippings, and add the vermouth. Reduce the sauce slightly, then season it to taste with salt, pepper and sugar. Serve the cutlets in the sauce.

Saltimbocca alla romana
Roman Sage Cutlets

8 small, thin veal cutlets, 75 g/2½ oz each
8 slices coppa di Parma, or substitute prosciutto di Parma
16 sage leaves
200 ml/7 fl oz dry white wine
flour for coating
butter for frying
salt
freshly ground pepper

Pound the veal cutlets flat. Place a slice of ham and 2 sage leaves on each cutlet, fold them over and secure with cocktail sticks. Then coat each piece with a little flour and shake off any excess.

Melt butter in a large frying pan and fry the cutlets on high heat for about 2 minutes per side. Season with salt and pepper, and drizzle with a little of the wine. As soon as the wine reduces, transfer the cutlets from the pan to a heated platter.

Deglaze with the rest of the wine and stir to loosen the pan drippings. Pour through a sieve and pour over the cutlets.

Scaloppine al limone

Lay the veal cutlets between two layers of clingfilm and gently pound them flat.

Top each cutlet with 2 sage leaves and a slice of ham.

Fold the veal cutlets together and fasten them with cocktail sticks.

Saltimbocca alla romana

Involtini in umido

Involtini in umido
Veal Roulades with Ham

8 thin veal cutlets, 100 g/3½ oz each
50 g/1¾ oz grated pecorino cheese
8 thin slices prosciutto di San Daniele
2 tbsp butter
2 tbsp olive oil
1 onion, finely chopped
1 garlic clove, finely chopped
1 tbsp tomato purée
125 ml/4 fl oz Marsala
125 ml/4 fl oz veal stock
2 tomatoes, diced
1 small sprig sage
flour for coating
salt and pepper

Pound the cutlets thin between two layers of clingfilm and place them side by side on a work surface. Season with salt and pepper. Sprinkle the pecorino over them and top each with a slice of prosciutto. Roll up the cutlets and secure with cocktail sticks, then salt and pepper the roulades and coat with flour.

Heat the butter and oil in a pan and brown the roulades on all sides. Remove from the pan and set aside. Sauté the onion, garlic and tomato purée in the same pan. Deglaze with the wine, stirring to loosen the pan drippings, and pour in the stock. Add the veal roulades, tomatoes and sage to the pan and bring to the boil. Cover and cook on low heat for 20 minutes. Then remove the veal from the pan and keep hot on a serving platter. Remove the sage from the sauce, bring it to the boil, and season with salt and pepper. Pour the sauce over the veal roulades.

Costolette alla milanese
Milanese Veal Chops

4 veal chops, 200 g/7 oz each
2 eggs
100 g/3½ oz breadcrumbs
60 g/2 oz clarified butter
flour for coating
salt and pepper
1 lemon, cut into wedges

Wash the chops, pat them dry, and rub with salt and pepper. Whisk the eggs. Coat the chops first in flour, then in whisked egg and finally in breadcrumbs. Press the breading firmly in place.

Heat the clarified butter in a large frying pan, add the chops and fry on medium heat for 5 to 6 minutes per side until golden brown. Serve the lemon wedges with the veal chops.

Cotolette alla milanese

Golden Dishes

For about fifty years, the rumour stubbornly persisted that the appetizingly golden Milanese cutlet was virtually the fore-runner of the Wiener Schnitzel that Field Marshal Radetzky brought to Vienna from Lombardy in 1848. The fact is, however, that thin pieces of meat had been breaded and fried to a golden brown for hundreds of years in Italy and France, as well as in Austria. This method of preparation was born of necessity, invented by chefs who could not afford gold leaf and sought a reasonably priced substitute for the seductive gold wrapping.

In the days of the ancient Byzantines, foods were not only gold-plated for aes-thetic reasons, but also because gold was believed to be good for the heart. This exclusive ingredient found its way to the wealthy trading cities of Venice and Milan by way of Constantinople. From that point on, wafer-thin leaves and flakes of fine, pure gold shimmered on the foie gras, risotto and confections enjoyed by rich nobles and patricians.

The delicate gold leaf was produced by goldsmiths. They used a very elaborate procedure in which high-carat gold went through many stages of rolling, hammering and beating until it was transformed into gossamer sheets only a few hundredths of a millimetre thick. Incidentally, consumption of this treasure is harmless from a medical point of view; unfortunately, it offers no health benefits.

Medaglioni di vitello alla pizzaiola
Veal Medallions
with Olives and Tomatoes

8 tomatoes	
100 g/3½ oz stoned black olives	
8 veal medallions, 75 g/2½ oz each	
2 tbsp olive oil	
1 garlic clove, finely chopped	
½ tsp dried oregano	
50 ml/1½ fl oz dry white wine	
sugar to taste	
salt	
freshly ground pepper	

Peel and quarter the tomatoes, remove the seeds, and dice. Quarter the olives. Wash the veal medallions and pat dry.

Heat the olive oil in a large frying pan and brown the medallions on both sides. Remove them from the pan, season with salt and pepper, and keep hot.

Add the garlic, tomatoes and olives to the pan. Season with sugar, salt, pepper and the oregano. Pour in the wine, stir to loosen the pan drippings and reduce on high heat, but the tomatoes should not fall apart. Return the medallions to the pan and simmer on low heat for a few more minutes before serving.

Cotolette con peperonata
Stuffed Veal Cutlets
with Peperonata

2 pickled anchovy fillets	
1 tbsp capers	
1 garlic clove	
1 small sprig each: rosemary and sage	
3 tbsp olive oil	
4 veal cutlets, 200 g/7 oz each	
salt	
1 onion, finely chopped	
freshly ground pepper	
300 g/11 oz prepared peperonata	
(see page 64)	

Preheat the oven to 160°C/320°F/gas mark 3. Rinse and drain the anchovies and capers in a colander. Peel the garlic clove. Strip the rosemary leaves from the branch and pluck the sage leaves. Place these ingredients in a mortar or blender, add pepper and 1 tablespoon of the olive oil, and work into a paste.

Wash the meat and pat it dry. Using a sharp knife, cut a pocket horizontally into each cutlet. Stuff the pockets with the herbal paste and secure with cocktail sticks. Season with salt and pepper.

Heat the remaining olive oil in a frying pan and brown the cutlets on both sides, then place in a baking dish.

Sauté the onion in the pan drippings. Add the peperonata, heat and spread over the meat. Bake for 20 minutes.

Cotolette con peperonata

Purée or mince the anchovies, capers, garlic, rosemary and sage with olive oil.

Using a sharp knife, cut a horizontal pocket in each cutlet.

Stuff the pockets with the herbal paste and secure them with cocktail sticks.

Brown the stuffed cutlets on both sides in olive oil on medium heat.

Secondi Piatti I 303

The Art of Gentle Cooking

'Good things take time', as the saying goes, and even modern kitchens with their high-tech, multi-functional ovens have not changed that. Granted that these days something cold can be transformed into a hot meal in about a minute in the microwave, or several dishes can be prepared at the same time in a convection oven. But a fine, juicy roast still requires the discipline of a patient, attentive cook.

In the past, when people used wood to both heat and cook, the optimal use of fire was the foremost concern. The tenderness of the meat was more of a coincidental, though much appreciated, side effect, the result of slow cooking for several hours in clay or cast iron pots in the heat remaining in the oven where bread had previously been baked.

Today we know that it takes time for the collagen contained in meat to disintegrate and for the meat to become tender. Top European chefs were the first to return to the old, low-temperature methods of cooking at 70°C (160°F) over a period of several hours. But in Italy, these traditional methods never went out of fashion.

Brasato alla milanese
Milanese-style Roast Beef

Serves six

1 kg/2 lb 4 oz beef roast
2 garlic cloves
1 carrot
2 celery sticks
1 kohlrabi
2 onions
2 tbsp olive oil
2 tbsp butter
1 bay leaf
1 small sprig thyme
1 clove
300 ml/11 fl oz Barolo or other strong red wine
500 g/1 lb 2 oz tomatoes
300 ml/11 fl oz meat stock
3 tbsp finely chopped parsley
salt
freshly ground pepper

Wash the meat and pat it dry. Peel and slice the garlic. Cut into the meat with a sharp knife and insert the garlic slices into the openings. Season the meat with salt and pepper. Wash or peel and finely dice the carrot, celery, kohlrabi and onions.

Heat the olive oil and butter in an iron casserole and brown the meat on all sides on medium heat.

Add the bay leaf, thyme and clove to the casserole. Deglaze with the red wine and reduce slightly.

Peel and quarter the tomatoes, remove the seeds and roughly chop the flesh. Add the tomatoes to the meat, pour in some of the stock and bring to the boil. Cover the casserole and stew for at least 2 hours over low heat. Baste the meat from time to time with the stewing liquid, and gradually add the remaining stock.

When the roast has finished cooking, remove it from the casserole. Pour the stewing liquid through a fine sieve into a small saucepan, bring to the boil again, and season the sauce to taste with salt and pepper. Slice the roast and place it on a heated serving platter. Pour the hot sauce over it and sprinkle with the chopped parsley.

Barding

Beef rump steak, bacon and aromatic herbs are needed for a brasato.

Wash the meat, pat it dry and rub it with salt, pepper and chopped herbs.

Then cover the meat on all sides with thin slices of pork fat or bacon.

To secure the pork fat, tie up the meat lengthways with kitchen twine.

Then wrap the kitchen twine around your hand, loop it around the meat and pull tight.

Repeat this step until the meat is fully wrapped. Fasten the twine with a knot.

Slowly stew the roast in stock or wine. Leave it to rest a few minutes before carving.

Remove the twine and cut the meat into uniform slices with a sharp carving knife.

Rub the veal shank with salt and pepper, then coat with flour.

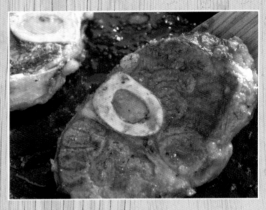

Over medium heat, brown the meat on both sides in melted butter.

Brasato al Barolo
Pot Roast in Red Wine

Serves six

1 kg/2 lb 4 oz loin of beef
2 tbsp olive oil
1 large carrot, diced
2 garlic cloves, sliced
2 celery sticks, diced
2 sprigs rosemary
2 bay leaves
750 ml/1⅓ pints Barolo
or other red wine
salt
freshly ground pepper

Wash the meat, pat it dry, and rub with salt and pepper. Heat the olive oil in an iron casserole and brown the meat on all sides. Add the carrot, garlic, celery, rosemary and bay leaves and fry briefly. Pour in the red wine, cover the casserole, and stew the meat on low heat for about 2 hours. Turn the meat several times in the stock as it cooks.

Remove the roast from the casserole and leave it to rest for 5 minutes. Pour the stewing liquid through a sieve and season it with salt and pepper. Slice the meat, place it on a heated serving plate and pour over the sauce.

Coda alla vaccinara
Braised Oxtail

1.5 kg/3 lb 5 oz oxtail, sliced
3 tbsp olive oil
250 ml/9 fl oz red wine
1 litre/1¾ pints meat stock
2 tbsp chopped herbs
(rosemary, thyme, oregano)
2 tbsp raisins
2 tbsp pine kernels
50 g/1¾ oz plain chocolate, grated
5 celery sticks
salt
freshly ground pepper

Preheat the oven to 175°C/350°F/gas mark 4. Wash the oxtail, pat it dry, and rub vigorously all over with salt and pepper. Heat the olive oil in a roasting tin and brown the pieces of meat on both sides. Deglaze the pan with the red wine.

When the wine has nearly evaporated, pour in the stock. Add the herbs, raisins, pine kernels and chocolate. Cover the roasting tin with a lid and braise the oxtail in the oven for 1½ hours.

Cut the celery into finger-length pieces. After the oxtail has cooked for 90 minutes, add the celery to the roasting tin, cover and braise for an additional 30 minutes, adding a little wine as needed.

Deglaze the pan with white wine and reduce the wine slightly.

Add the tomato purée, cover the pot and stew the meat for at least 1½ hours.

Ossobuco alla milanese
Milanese-style Ossobuco

4 slices veal shank,
each ca. 4 cm/1½ inches thick

50 g/1¾ oz butter

125 ml/4 fl oz white wine

400 g/14 oz canned tomato purée

1 garlic clove

1 tbsp grated lemon peel

2 tbsp finely chopped parsley

flour for coating

salt

freshly ground pepper

Wash the meat slices and pat dry with paper towels. Then rub with salt and pepper and coat with flour, shaking off any excess.

Melt the butter in a deep frying pan and brown the veal slices on both sides. Deglaze the pan with the wine, then reduce slightly. Stir in the tomato purée and season with salt and pepper. Cover the pan and stew the meat on low heat for at least 1½ hours, turning the slices over several times in the tomato sauce as they cook. When the meat begins to separate from the bone, it is done. Finely chop the garlic and combine it with the lemon peel and parsley. Sprinkle over the sliced meat just before serving.

Arrosto di vitello al latte
Roast Veal in Milk

800 g/1 lb 12 oz veal roast

5 tbsp olive oil

1 carrot, diced

1 large onion, diced

2 celery sticks, diced

600 ml/1 pint milk

400 g/14 oz shallots

50 ml/1½ fl oz white wine vinegar

50 ml/1½ fl oz white wine

3 bay leaves

10 peppercorns

salt

freshly ground pepper

Wash the meat, pat it dry, and season with salt and pepper. Heat 3 tablespoons of the olive oil in an iron casserole and brown the roast on all sides. Add the carrot, onion and celery to the pot and sauté. Pour in half of the milk, bring it to the boil, cover the casserole and simmer for about 1 hour on low heat. Baste the roast frequently as it cooks, gradually adding the rest of the milk.

Meanwhile, peel the shallots and cut them into rings. Heat the remaining olive oil in a saucepan and sauté the shallots until golden brown. Deglaze with the vinegar and wine, then add the bay leaves and peppercorns. Simmer over low heat for 30 minutes until the liquid thickens. Remove and discard the bay leaves and peppercorns.

Remove the roast from the casserole and keep it warm. Strain the sauce through a fine sieve and add it to the shallots. Bring the sauce briefly to the boil again, and season to taste with salt and pepper.

Thinly slice the roast, transfer the meat to a serving platter and pour a little sauce over it. Serve the remaining sauce on the side.

Involtini alla barese
Beef Roulades with Pecorino

8 thin slices of beef, 100 g/3½ oz each
80 g/3 oz chopped stoned green olives
8 slices coppa ham
80 g/3 oz medium-aged
pecorino cheese, shaved
2 tbsp olive oil
1 onion, finely chopped
1 garlic clove, finely chopped
1 tbsp tomato purée
100 ml/3½ fl oz dry red wine
250 ml/9 fl oz beef stock
salt
freshly ground pepper
1 sprig sage

Wash the sliced beef, pat it dry and pound flat. Finely dice the olives. Lightly season the meat with salt and pepper on both sides and cover each slice with a slice of ham. Sprinkle olives and pecorino on the ham. Roll up the roulades and tie them with kitchen twine.

Heat the olive oil in a large frying pan and brown the roulades on medium heat. Add the onion, garlic and tomato purée. Then deglaze the pan with the wine, stirring to loosen the pan drippings, and reduce the liquid.

Pour in the stock, add the sage sprig, place the lid so that it half covers the pan and braise for 30 to 40 minutes on low heat. Then take the roulades out of the pan, remove the twine, and keep the meat warm. Bring the sauce to the boil and season to taste with salt and pepper. Serve the roulades on heated plates with sauce poured over them.

Bistecca

This dish is the quintessence of Florentine cooking, well-loved by its devotees. Called simply *fiorentina*, it resists all attempts to 'enhance' it with extravagant ingredients or cooking techniques. The delicious secret of *bistecca fiorentina* is based on four very simple principles:

• The meat must come from Chianina cattle and be well aged.
• Just the right cut of meat is crucial, and only Tuscan butchers seem to have mastered it: *bistecca* is a high-cut tenderloin with fillet and lumbar vertebrae bone that looks like the letter T. Sirloin steak is a good approximation.
• The meat should be about 2.5 cm (1 inch) thick and weigh between 600 and 900 grams (1 lb 5 oz–2 lb).
• The meat is neither marinated nor coated with oil prior to char-grilling. It is placed on a very hot grate and turned as soon as the surface turns dark brown.

   A perfect *bistecca* is crisp and very dark outside, yet still raw inside, *al sangue* (literally, 'bloody'). Known as *carbonate* in antiquity, it was already very popular back then. Its present-day name comes from a corruption of the English term 'beefsteak'.

When an entire ox was spit-roasted on the Piazza San Lorenzo in Florence in 1565, among the merrymakers there were some English travellers who, delighted at the sight of the juicy meat, called out, 'Beefsteak!' The word *bistecca* was soon reserved for the best part of the steer. The *Sagra della Bistecca* (Bistecca Festival) takes place each year on 14 and 15 August in Cortona, in the heart of the Chiana Valley.

Bistecca alla fiorentina
Steak Florentine

2 well-aged steaks,
ca. 2.5 cm/1 inch thick,
600 g/1 lb 5 oz each

3–4 tbsp olive oil

salt, freshly ground pepper

lemon wedges to garnish

Place the unseasoned steaks directly on the hot grate of a charcoal grill. Grill one side for 3 minutes, then turn. Season the grilled side with salt and pepper. Grill the other side for 3 minutes as well. Turn the steaks again, season with salt and pepper, and grill for an additional minute. Remove from the grill, place on a heated platter, and drizzle the olive oil over the steaks. Serve immediately garnished with lemon wedges.

Just the right cut of meat, which only Tuscan butchers seem to have mastered, is a prerequisite for genuine bistecca fiorentina.

Chianina Cattle

No other animals in Italy enjoy such classical, nearly mythical, status as Chianina cattle, which have been bred in the area between Arezzo and Lake Trasimeno for more than two millenia and are among the oldest and largest breeds of cattle in the world. Treasured as work animals by the Etruscans and Romans, Chianina oxen pulled the chariots in Roman triumphal parades. Today the animals are bred purely for their meat, which is especially tender and juicy, and contains a lot of valuable protein but very little cholesterol.

Although Chianina cattle are very large and sturdy, the animals have an elegant, dignified appearance. Breeders praise their penetrating black eyes, long eyelashes and expressive face; broad shoulders, athletic physique and shiny white coat – in short, the beauty of these cattle – in glowing terms. The animals are impervious to cold and heat, but are very demanding in terms of food. A single Chianina cow eats between 22 and 26 kg (48–57 lb) of hay each day and needs large pastures on which it can constantly wander in search of the best food. And the calves, born with reddish brown coats that turn white after four to five months, have an intense attachment to their mothers, from whom they can be separated only quite late in comparison to other cattle. All of these requirements make breeding Chianina a time-consuming and expensive enterprise.

Cooking à la Rossini

Gioacchino Antonio Rossini was born in 1792 in Pesaro, and is considered the most important representative of Italian *opera buffa* (a style of lively, comic opera). His greatest operatic successes include *The Barber of Seville*, *La Cenerentola* (Cinderella) and *William Tell*. However, fewer people are aware that he was also a master 'composer' in the kitchen. As one biographer described it, Rossini attempted 'to produce the same harmonies at the kitchen stove as on the piano'. His meals were 'a series of chords, whose choruses came on stage as half of Europe's agriculture and handicrafts'.

Rossini's macaroni, for example, stuffed with truffle forcemeat and cooked in a fragrant steam, were legendary. The same was true of the gala dinners that he hosted with his wife, the famous soprano Isabella Colbran, during his years as head of the Italian Opera in Paris. Antonin Careme, the most famous chef of that era, let it be known that no one understood food better than the Italian composer.

Tournedos alla Rossini are still famous today and unite three extravagant products on a single plate: fillet of beef, foie gras and truffles. There are two versions of the story explaining the genesis of the recipe. According to the first, the chef at La Maison Dorée Restaurant invented the dish and dedicated it to Rossini. The second version goes like this: when Rossini's chef wanted to try out the new recipe, the maestro required him to prepare it in the dining room so that he and his guests could watch. But the chef explained that it would embarrass him to cook in front of all those people, to which Rossini responded, 'Very well then – just turn your back to me'.

Opera buffa still enjoys great popularity today. The photo shows a performance of Rossini's opera La Cenerentola, *with Raquela Sheeran (as Clorinda), Lucia Cirillo (as Tisbe) and Luciano Di Pasquale (as Don Magnifico).*

Tournedos alla Rossini
Tournedos à la Rossini

4 thick beef fillet steaks
2 tbsp olive oil
2 tbsp butter
4 slices white bread, toasted
4 slices pâté de foie gras
4 tbsp Madeira
1 small truffle
salt
freshly ground pepper

Tie the fillet steaks into rounds with kitchen twine. Heat the oil and butter and brown the meat on medium heat for about 3 minutes per side. Season with salt and pepper. Cut each slice of toast into the shape of a tournedo, place the meat on it and set on a heated platter. Top with pâté de foie gras. Deglaze the pan with the Madeira and pour over the meat. Finely grate the truffle over the tournedos.

Opera Buffa

'Apart from doing nothing at all, for me there is no occupation lovelier than food, good food, if you know what I mean. Appetite is to the stomach what love is to the heart. An empty stomach sounds like an unhappy, snarling bassoon or a piccolo squeaking jealously.

'A full stomach, on the other hand, sounds like a cheerful triangle or a merry tambourine. As far as love is concerned, she is the prima donna par excellence, a diva, who sings the main cavatinas and delights the ear, stealing your heart.

'Eating and loving, singing and digesting are truly the four acts of this opera buffa called life, which passes away like the bubbles in a bottle of champagne. Anyone who forsakes these pleasures must be mad.'

Gioacchino Antonio Rossini

Filletto all'alloro
Fillet of Beef in Laurel Wreath

4 beef fillet steaks, 250 g/9 oz each
4 tsp spicy mustard
12 fresh bay leaves
3 tbsp olive oil
1 tbsp peppercorns, coarsely crushed
60 ml/2 fl oz Italian brandy
salt

Preheat the oven to 130°C/265°F/gas mark ½. Brush the edges of the steaks with the mustard. Place 3 bay leaves around each steak and secure with kitchen twine. Season with salt.

Heat the olive oil in an ovenproof pan and thoroughly brown the steaks on both sides, then cook in the oven for 15 to 20 minutes.

Place the steaks on heated plates. Pour off the frying fat and sprinkle the peppercorns in the pan. Pour in the brandy, heat slightly, then flambé. Drizzle the brandy sauce over the fillets and serve immediately.

Pork

For centuries, Italians have eaten literally every part of the pig. Every scrap – even the trotters, fat with rind, cheeks and tail – is utilized to make delicious dishes and pork products. In the Marche region, many families used to make a type of spreadable sausage from 'second-hand' pork. The meat was finely cut, seasoned with garlic and fennel, and used as a spread. In the area around Ancona, salted pork casings are stuffed with giblets, hot pepper, fennel seeds and rosemary. *Ciarimboli*, a kind of salami that is rarely produced nowadays, was dried or smoked, then charcoal grilled or pan fried with garlic.

In Italy today, most pigs are bred for processing into ham, bacon and sausage products, rather than for their fresh meat. These products, some of which require a long maturation period, require heavy pigs with an average butchering weight of approximately 160 kg (350 lb), and ripe meat with a firm consistency. That is why the animals are not fattened too quickly, and they must also be at least ten months old. In northern Europe, in contrast, where most pig meat is destined for immediate consumption, pigs are butchered when they reach a weight of around 100 kg (220 lb).

In rural regions of Italy, pigs are still allowed to enjoy their lives in the open air.

UMBRIAN PIGS

The pig must be acknowledged as the uncrowned king of Umbrian cuisine. The small black pigs raised there, which are fed primarily a diet of acorns and chestnuts, are neither too fat nor too thin, and have an intense yet mild flavour. Their firm meat is ideally suited for producing ham and sausages. In the kitchen, the meat is seasoned chiefly with wild marjoram or fennel seeds, then charcoal grilled or oven roasted with herbs, including rosemary and bay leaf.

The area around Norcia is the centre of pig breeding and sausage production. Typical products include *mazzafegato* (liver sausage), *mortadella*, *capocollo* (pork neck sausage) and the renowned raw ham with protected designation of origin. The artisanal, air-dried, finely spiced, hard-cured sausages have long been highly prized by gourmets. One testament to their status, among others, is the fact that *norcino*, the term that designates the residents of the city, has become a synonym for 'butcher' in many parts of Italy.

Arista

As with many Italian dishes, there is an anecdote regarding the origin of the term *arista* ('roast'). On the occasion of a banquet given during the Council of Florence in 1439, the Byzantine patriarch caught sight of a magnificent roast pork and is reported to enthusiastically have called out '*aristos*', which means 'excellent' in Greek. The other guests believed this was the name of the dish, and henceforth called it *arista*. It is more likely, however, that the term comes from Latin. The general Latin meaning of *arista* is 'something that stands up', which refers to pork loin cooked on the bone, as is the practice in Tuscany.

Arista di maiale all'umbra
Pork Fillet with Herb Sauce

800 g/1 lb 12 oz pork fillet
2 sprigs rosemary
4 garlic cloves
1 large pork caul
3 tbsp olive oil
250 ml/9 fl oz white wine
125 ml/4 fl oz stock
salt
freshly ground pepper

Wash the meat and pat it dry. Chop the rosemary and garlic and combine both with some salt and pepper. Rub the pork fillet with the garlic-herb mixture and set it aside for 20 minutes.

Preheat the oven to 200°C/390°F/gas mark 6. Rinse the pork caul, drain well, then place it on a board and pat dry with paper towels. Wrap the fillet in the caul. Heat the olive oil in a roasting tin and brown the meat on all sides. Deglaze the pan with the white wine, then place the pan in the oven and roast for 45 to 50 minutes, gradually adding the stock as the meat cooks.

Remove the pork fillet from the roasting tin and leave it to rest for 10 minutes. Pour off the roasting juices and season with salt and pepper. Cut the meat into thin slices and serve with the seasoned roasting juices.

On the hills of the Umbrian provincial capital, Perugia, there are many churches and monasteries worth seeing. Perhaps the most famous is the Monteridido Monastery (opposite).

Rub the pork fillet with the garlic-herb mixture.

Wrap the seasoned fillet in a rinsed pork caul.

Brown the pork fillet on all sides in hot olive oil.

As soon as the meat is browned, pour on the white wine and stock.

Umbria

Suckling Pig

A whole barbecued or roast suckling pig with an apple in its mouth was once the centrepiece of any great Italian banquet table. Before cooking, the young pig is seasoned inside and out with a mixture of garlic, wild fennel seeds, pancetta and white wine, then barbecued over charcoal or roasted in a large oven. Even today, *porchetta* ('suckling pig') is a must at any village festival or fair. It is also often sold from mobile roadside stands, sliced and accompanied with bread.

In Sardinia, a small suckling pig is traditionally seasoned with myrtle leaves, placed on a hand-cut wooden spit and then slowly roasted over a fire made with aromatic macchia wood. They eat the entire piglet, called *porceddu*, including the ears and crisp rind.

In Abruzzo, Tuscany and Lazio, suckling pig is boned prior to cooking. Then the meat is rubbed with aromatic herbs, salted, peppered, rolled up and tied up like a rolled roast. Afterwards, the meat is roasted in the oven at a high temperature until crisp, then cut into thick slices for serving.

Porchetta is also the term for a very special method of preparation found in the Marche, where chicken, rabbit, dried cod or snails are wrapped in fresh wild fennel and garlic, then cooked in this herbal blanket. This cooking method lets foods retain their unique flavours, which are accentuated by the seasoned mixture.

Cosciotto suino alla Maremma
Leg of Suckling Pig, Maremma Style

Serves eight

4 garlic cloves
1 sprig rosemary
1 tsp fennel seeds
60 ml/2 fl oz olive oil
1 leg of suckling pig, ca. 2.5 kg/5 lb 8 oz, boned
500 ml/18 fl oz white wine
salt
freshly ground pepper

Preheat the oven to 180°C/355°F/gas mark 4. Finely chop the garlic and rosemary leaves. Make a paste of the fennel seeds, salt, pepper and 1 tablespoon of olive oil.

Rub the leg inside and out with the paste. Form it into the desired shape and secure with kitchen twine.

Heat the remaining olive oil in an iron casserole and brown the meat all over. Pour on a little of the wine, then roast in the oven for 2 hours. Baste the leg occasionally with the cooking juices, and gradually add the rest of the wine.

When the meat is cooked, remove the leg from the casserole, cut off the kitchen twine, and slice the roast. Serve on a heated serving platter with the pan juices poured over it.

Bone the leg of the suckling pig to the lower leg bone and make a paste of olive oil and seasonings.

Wash the meat and rub it inside and out with the seasoned paste.

Tie the meat with twine in the shape of a rolled roast down to the lower leg.

Brown the leg on all sides in olive oil over medium heat, then deglaze the pan with white wine.

On the most important feast days, Italian tables are still richly decked. A whole roast suckling pig is part of that tradition.

Cosciotto suino alla Maremma

Favourite Pork Dishes

Pork is prepared and seasoned differently from region to region in Italy. In Abruzzo they make a hearty stew called *'ndocca 'ndocca* – meaning something like 'in large pieces' – from the feet, shoulders, snout, ears and ribs. The pieces of meat are cooked slowly, over low heat, with garlic, bay leaves, rosemary, chillies, vinegar, salt and pepper for as long as it takes for the stock to begin to thicken. The finished dish is usually eaten cold.

Typical of Piedmont is *rôstida*, a hearty ragout made from pork loin, heart and lung with tomatoes. And in Calabria, pork liver, lungs and heart are cooked with tomatoes and chilli for *morseddu* (morceau, or 'tiny morsels').

An Umbrian speciality is *fettine di maiale*, thinly sliced pork that is roasted in red wine sauce and served with capers. Pork roulades stuffed with chicken liver, parsley, sage, Parmesan cheese and bacon come from Milan, and in Sicily one can enjoy roast pork with caramelized lemons and fresh rosemary.

Sanguinaccio

In Tuscany, *sanguinaccio* was long the term used for a confection made from pig's blood and chocolate, or for little pancakes made from crushed almond biscuits and pig's blood, then fried in olive oil. Nowadays, the confection is made without blood.

Sanguinaccio also refers to a type of sweet black pudding made in Liguria. It consists of equal parts of pig's blood and fresh milk, to which pine kernels, salt and pepper are added. Originally, raisins were mixed in, as well. The mixture is then stuffed into pork casings and tied with thread to make thick sausages.

Zampone con lenticche
Stuffed Pig's Trotter with Lentils

1 onion
1 carrot
150 g/5 oz celeriac
1 Hamburg parsley root
50 g/1¾ oz smoked bacon
2 tbsp olive oil
300 g/11 oz lentils
700 g/1 lb 9 oz zampone
(stuffed pig's trotter sausage, see right)
salt

Finely dice the onion, carrot, celeriac and parsley root. Finely dice the bacon as well. Heat the olive oil in a saucepan and lightly brown these ingredients. Then add the lentils and 1 litre/1¾ pints of water. Cover the pan and simmer for about 1 hour.

Meanwhile, thoroughly wash the zampone and prick it with a fork several times. Place it in a second saucepan and cover with cold water. Add salt and slowly bring to the boil. Simmer for about 40 minutes.

Add several ladles of the cooking stock to the lentils and continue to cook them until the liquid is absorbed. Remove the zampone from its pan and cut it into slices 2 to 3 cm/ ¾–1 inch thick. Serve on top of the lentils.

Zampone

Allegedly, there are more pigs than people living in Emilia-Romagna. In the small town of Castelnuovo Rangone, near Modena, the residents have even erected a monument to the succulent animal. Pig breeding and sausage production have existed in the region since ancient times.

The characteristic sausage of the region is *zampone*, which is stuffed into a pig's trotter rather than a more typical casing, thus demonstrating that almost every part of a pig can be utilized. *Zampone* is made from the rind, shoulder, cheek and hock. The ingredients are very finely minced and seasoned with salt, pepper, ground cloves and nutmeg. The mixture is then stuffed into an unprocessed, natural, boned pig's trotter, including the still-attached claws and hooves. Then the *zampone* is dried in special ovens.

It used to be the case that someone wanting to prepare *zampone* had to soak it in cold water for twelve hours, then slowly cook it for at least three hours. Today you can buy pre-cooked *zampone*, which only needs to be reheated. In Emilia, *zampone* with lentils is a classic dish served on New Year's Eve. It is said to bring good luck in the coming year.

Spezzatino con piselli
Pork Goulash with Peas

3 tbsp olive oil
600 g/1 lb 5 oz pork, cubed
2 white onions, roughly chopped
2 garlic cloves, minced
1 fresh red chilli, minced
200 ml/7 fl oz red wine
4 tomatoes, diced
500 g/1 lb 2 oz fresh peas, shelled
1 tbsp finely chopped parsley
salt and pepper

Heat the olive oil in an iron casserole and brown the meat all over. Season it with salt and pepper. Add the onions, garlic and chilli and sauté. Deglaze with the red wine and stir in the tomatoes. Cover the pot and stew on medium heat for 30 minutes, then add the peas and cook for another 30 minutes. Before serving, season to taste with salt and pepper and sprinkle with the parsley.

Polpette dei preti
Priests' Meatloaf

1 pork caul
100 g/3½ oz prosciutto
100 g/3½ oz mortadella
soup vegetables such as carrots, celery
or other root vegetables
1 onion
400 g/14 oz mixed minced meat
1 egg
3 tbsp breadcrumbs
75 g/2½ oz grated Parmesan
1 tbsp clarified butter
1 litre/1¾ pints hot milk
1 garlic clove
1 bay leaf
salt
freshly ground pepper

Rinse the pork caul for 30 minutes, then drain. Finely dice the prosciutto and mortadella. Wash and roughly chop the soup vegetables. Peel and finely dice the onion.

Combine the minced meat with the prosciutto, mortadella, egg, breadcrumbs and Parmesan. Season with salt and pepper. Form the meat into a loaf. Spread out the drained pork caul, place the meatloaf on it and wrap with the caul.

Heat the clarified butter in an iron casserole and briefly brown the meatloaf on all sides. Remove it from the pot, then lightly brown the soup vegetables and onion in the pan drippings. Return the meatloaf to the pot and pour on 250 ml/9 fl oz of the hot milk. Mash the garlic clove with a knife and add it to the milk along with the bay leaf. Bring to a boil and simmer, covered, on low heat for about 1 hour. Gradually add the remaining hot milk during that time.

Place the finished meatloaf on a heated platter. Season the sauce with salt and pepper. Serve the meatloaf with the sauce on the side.

Cassoeula
Lombardian Stew

1 pig's trotter, chopped
600 g/1 lb 5 oz spare ribs
150 g/5 oz pork fat with rind
3 tbsp butter
3 tbsp olive oil
1 large onion, finely chopped
1 litre/1¾ pints meat stock
4 carrots, sliced
2 celery sticks, diced
1 small cabbage
4 Lombardian mini salamis
salt
freshly ground pepper

Wash the meat and pat it dry. Cut the pork fat into strips. Heat the butter and oil in an iron casserole and lightly brown the onion. Add the pork fat and chopped pig's trotter, brown them all over, and season with salt and pepper. Add the pork ribs, then deglaze the pot with two thirds of the stock. Cover the casserole and simmer on low heat for 30 minutes. Then add the carrots and celery to the meat, stir and simmer for an additional 20 minutes.

Bring a saucepan of salted water to the boil. Quarter the cabbage and remove the stalk. Blanch the leaves for 3 minutes, then refresh in ice water. Remove the thick ribs and cut the leaves into wide strips.

Add the cabbage strips and salami to the casserole, pour on the rest of the stock and simmer another 20 minutes. When the stew is finished, the cooking liquid should have a syrupy consistency.

Spezzatino di maiale
Pork Goulash

600 g/1 lb 5 oz lean pork
2–3 tbsp olive oil
1 tsp fennel seeds
5 garlic cloves, finely chopped
1 fresh red chilli, finely chopped
300 g/11 oz tomatoes, peeled and diced
salt
freshly ground pepper

Wash the meat, pat it dry and cut into bite-sized pieces. Heat the olive oil in an iron casserole, then add the fennel seeds and garlic to it. Season the meat with salt and pepper.

Brown the meat on all sides in the hot olive oil. As soon as the meat browns, add the chilli and tomatoes. Cover the pot and stew over low heat for about 1 hour, adding a little warm water as needed.

Lamb, Sheep and Mutton

In many parts of Italy and for a long time, sheep guaranteed people's survival, particularly during the cold season. They provided wool for warmth, daily milk and cheese and, not least of all, meat. Sheep used to be a poor man's food, but nowadays it is a treasured delicacy among gourmets.

Many shepherds still rear their flocks of sheep in the tradition pasture. The animals wander freely in nature and eat natural food, resulting in exceptionally lean meat with a wonderfully aromatic flavour. The main areas for sheep farming are Molise, Abruzzo and Sardinia. Sardinian sheep are among the best dairy breeds in the world.

Lamb and mutton are offered under the following names:

Agnello da latte is the term for three-to-four-week-old lamb that has been nourished solely on its mother's milk. The meat is mild in taste and incredibly tender. At twelve weeks the lamb is called *agnello*, and is ideal for barbecuing and pan-frying.

Agnellone are butchered at around six months of age and have the classic lamb flavour. Their meat is especially well suited for stews and casseroles.

Pecora are adult sheep. Their aromatic meat is chiefly prized in southern Italy.

Montone and *castrato* are castrated rams, but these play a minor role in cuisine.

Spiedini al rosmarino
Rosemary and Lamb Kebabs with Lemon-garlic Sauce

1 shallot
2 garlic cloves
1 fresh red chilli
juice of 1 lemon
80 ml/3 fl oz olive oil
800 g/1 lb 12 oz lamb, back or leg
4 large sprigs rosemary
1 tsp dried oregano
salt
freshly ground pepper

Peel the shallot and garlic. Remove the seeds from the chilli. In a food processor, blend the chilli, lemon juice, a pinch of salt and 4 tablespoons of olive oil to make a creamy sauce.

Cut the meat into evenly sized cubes. Thread the cubed meat first on to one of four metal skewers, then pierce with a sprig of rosemary. Season with salt and pepper, then brush with the remaining olive oil.

Grill the kebabs on both sides on a barbecue or under the grill until crisp. Place on a heated serving plate and sprinkle with the oregano. Serve with the lemon-garlic sauce on the side.

Sheep are still reared mainly in herds in the open, wandering from one pasture to another. Fresh grass and herbs lend additional flavour to the delicate lamb.

Cut the lamb into bite-sized chunks and place on metal skewers.

Strip the leaves off the sturdy rosemary sprigs to the top. Sharpen the ends of the branches to a point.

Stick the pieces of meat on to the rosemary branches, then season with salt and pepper.

Favourite Lamb Dishes

Agnello all'uovo e limone
Lamb Goulash with Egg and Lemon

800 g/1 lb 12 oz lamb shoulder
2 tbsp flour
1 onion
60 g/2 oz pork fat
2 tbsp oil
300 ml/11 fl oz white wine
125 ml/4 fl oz stock
juice of 1 lemon
2 egg yolks
1 garlic clove
salt
freshly ground pepper
grated lemon peel for seasoning

Rinse the lamb, pat it dry and cut into 3-cm/1-inch cubes. Salt and pepper the lamb, then sprinkle with the flour. Peel the onion. Finely dice it and the pork fat.

Heat the oil in an iron casserole and fry the pork fat. Add the lamb in portions and brown it, stirring frequently. Add the onion and fry until translucent. Deglaze with half of the wine, scraping the pan to loosen the drippings. Once the wine has reduced, add the stock, cover the casserole and simmer for about 1 hour on low heat. Gradually add the rest of the wine.

Remove the pieces of cooked lamb with a slotted spoon and keep warm on a serving plate. Whisk together the lemon juice and egg yolk. Put the garlic through a press and add it to the egg yolk mixture. Bring the pan juices to the boil again and add the egg-lemon mixture, stirring continuously, but do not allow the sauce to boil. Season it to taste with salt, pepper and lemon peel. Pour over the lamb and serve hot.

Filletto alle verdure
Fillet of Lamb on Vegetable Pasta

2 carrots
2 small courgettes
100 g/3½ oz mushrooms
4 lamb fillets, 130 g/4½ oz each
2 tbsp clarified butter
400 ml/14 fl oz lamb stock
200 ml/7 fl oz double cream
250 g/9 oz tagliatelle
4 tbsp butter
salt
freshly ground pepper

Peel the carrots and slice into long strips with a vegetable peeler. Wash the courgettes and cut them lengthways into thin strips. Bring a saucepan of lightly salted water to the boil and blanch the vegetable strips for 2 minutes. Refresh them in cold water, then drain.

Preheat the oven to 100°C/210°F/gas mark 6. Clean and finely slice the mushrooms. Rinse the lamb fillets and pat dry. Salt and pepper the meat. Heat the clarified butter in a frying pan and brown the fillets on both sides. Place on an ovenproof plate and roast for 20 minutes.

Pour the fat from the pan. Pour in the lamb stock and stir to dissolve the pan drippings in the stock. Add the cream and simmer until the sauce is reduced by half. Bring a large saucepan of salted water to the boil and cook the tagliatelle until al dente.

Melt the butter in a second pan and gently sauté the mushrooms. Add the vegetable strips to heat them up. Drain the pasta, then combine it with the vegetable strips and mushrooms. Season with salt and pepper.

Remove the meat from the oven and slice it diagonally. Stir the meat juice into the sauce and heat it up. Serve the pasta on heated plates topped with the meat, with a liberal serving of sauce over it.

Spezzatino di castrato
Mutton Ragout

1 kg/2 lb 4 oz mutton, shoulder cut
100 ml/3½ fl oz white wine vinegar
2 sprigs rosemary
2–3 garlic cloves
5 tbsp olive oil
400 g/14 oz canned peeled tomatoes
2 bay leaves
200 ml/7 fl oz white wine
salt
freshly ground pepper
sugar

Rinse the mutton, pat dry, then remove any skin, tendons and fat. Cut the meat into bite-sized chunks. In a large saucepan, bring to the boil 1 litre/1¾ pints of water, the vinegar and 1 rosemary sprig. Add the meat cubes to the pot and cook for about 10 minutes, then remove them and drain well.

Chop the garlic and the leaves from the second rosemary sprig. Heat the olive oil in an iron casserole, add the meat cubes and brown on all sides. Add the garlic and rosemary and sauté briefly. Season liberally with salt and pepper. Drain the tomatoes and add them to the meat with the bay leaves. Pour on the white wine, then bring everything to the boil. Cover the ragout and stew on low heat for around 1½ hours, stirring occasionally. Remove the lid 15 minutes before the end of cooking time so the sauce can thicken. Adjust the seasoning with salt, pepper and sugar before serving.

Agnello con olive
Lamb with Black Olives

800 g/1 lb 12 oz lamb
2 sprigs rosemary
1 bay leaf
½ tsp black peppercorns
2 garlic cloves
100 ml/3½ fl oz olive oil
200 g/7 oz chickpeas
1 onion
1 leek
2 carrots
150 g/5 oz black olives
2 tomatoes
flour for coating
1 litre/1¾ pints vegetable stock
1 tsp grated orange rind
freshly ground pepper
1 tbsp finely chopped sage

Cut the meat into bite-sized chunks and place it in a bowl. Add the rosemary leaves, bay leaf, peppercorns and garlic, then pour on the olive oil. Cover with clingfilm and marinate in the refrigerator overnight. Turn the meat several times in the seasoned oil. Soak the chickpeas overnight in plenty of water.

The next day, chop the onion, leek and carrots into small pieces. Set aside a few olives for garnish; stone and roughly chop the rest. Peel and quarter the tomatoes, remove the seeds, and cut into fine dice.

Remove the meat from the herbed oil and drain. Coat it with a little flour, shaking off any excess. Strain the herbed oil through a sieve into a bowl. Pour the water off the chickpeas and also drain thoroughly.

Heat 3 tablespoons of the herbed oil in an iron casserole and lightly brown the meat in it. Add the onion and tomato and cook for a few minutes, then stir in the chickpeas. Pour in the stock and bring to the boil. Cover the casserole and simmer for 30 minutes over low heat, then add the olives, leeks, carrots and orange peel. Stew for another 30 minutes.

Season the lamb ragout with salt and pepper. Serve on heated plates, sprinkled with sage and garnished with whole olives.

Easter Lamb

An old proverb from Molise says, 'Marz' e aprile, agnell' e caprette gendile' ('March and April, lambs and kids are most tender of all'). Since sheep only bring their young into the world in the springtime, milk-fed lambs are only available around Easter, which is how the term 'Easter lamb' came about.

Even in ancient times, lambs were among the most important sacrificial animals and symbolized reconciliation with the divine. For thousands of years, the lamb has represented life, security, celebration, sacrifice and reconciliation. The slaughter of lambs on the occasion of the Passover Feast is an ancient Jewish ritual.

In the Jewish faith, the lamb refers to the coming Messiah. In Christianity, it symbolizes Jesus, as well as the Church itself, the four Gospels and the virtues of innocence and purity. The early Christians placed lamb meat beneath the altar. Since the Middle Ages, lamb has been baked in fine dough at Easter in remembrance of Jesus Christ, the Lamb of God, who sacrificed himself for the sins of the world.

Arrosto pasquale
Roast Easter Lamb

1 pork caul
1 boneless leg of lamb, ca. 1 kg/2 lb 4 oz
3 garlic cloves
1 tsp salt
5 sprigs thyme
2 sprigs rosemary
400 ml/14 fl oz white wine
freshly ground pepper

Rinse the caul. Wash the leg of lamb and pat it dry with paper towels. Preheat the oven to 175°C/350°F/gas mark 4.

Crush the garlic and salt in a mortar. Rinse the herbs, pat dry and strip the thyme leaves from the stalks. Mix the garlic paste, thyme and pepper, then spread the paste on the leg of lamb. Wrap it in the pork caul and place in a roasting tin. Add the rosemary sprigs. Roast the meat for about 1 hour, basting several times with white wine, about 250 ml/9 fl oz altogether.

Remove the lamb from the roasting tin and turn off the oven. Leave the meat to rest in the oven for 10 minutes. Meanwhile, deglaze the roasting tin with the remaining wine. Pour the sauce through a sieve and season with salt and pepper. Cut the meat into thin slices, place them on a heated platter and top with the sauce. Serve very hot.

Molise

Molise

Gently rolling hills and wide green pastures characterize the landscape of Molise. Encompassing a mere 140 villages, it is the second smallest region in Italy, after Valle d'Aosta. Many of these villages lie on picturesque outcroppings or green mountain slopes. For thousands of years, shepherds have driven their flocks to summer and winter pastures at various altitudes along the horse paths, which stretch like a net across the landscape.

The cuisine of Molise is simple and rustic. The goats and sheep raised here not only supply milk for some of Italy's most well-known cheeses; they also provide the meat for the highly seasoned regional dishes such as lamb with egg and lemon or stewed goat. The meat is often roast on a spit. Another speciality is *salsiccia ferrazzanese*, sausage flavoured with chillies and wild fennel seeds, which is made from the meat of pigs fattened on acorns.

Capra alla molisana
Molise-style Goat

700 g/1 lb 9 oz goat meat from the leg
1 fresh red chilli
2 bay leaves
2 sprigs rosemary
750 ml/1⅓ pints red wine
1 white onion
500 g/1 lb 2 oz plum tomatoes
4 tbsp olive oil
salt
freshly ground pepper

Abbacchio alla romana
Roast Suckling Lamb

750 g/1 lb 10 oz boned suckling lamb
3 tbsp olive oil
4 tbsp wine vinegar
200 ml/7 fl oz red wine
500 g/1 lb 2 oz small potatoes, sliced
4 shallots, sliced
2 sprigs rosemary
2 salt-cured anchovy fillets, finely chopped
salt
freshly ground pepper

Wash the meat, pat it dry and cut it into cubes. Preheat the oven to 175°C/350°F/gas mark 4.

Heat the olive oil in a roasting tin and brown the meat on all sides. Season with salt and pepper, and deglaze with the vinegar. As soon as the vinegar has thickened, pour in the red wine and 125 ml/4 fl oz hot water. Add the potatoes, shallots and rosemary.

Roast the lamb for 30 minutes, adding a little more water if necessary, then remove from the oven. As soon as the meat is cooked, purée the anchovies in a food processor and add 3 tablespoons of the pan juices from the roasting tin. Stir this into the rest of the pan juices and simmer for a few more minutes before serving.

Italian gourmets are not the only ones who treasure the delicate, lean meat of young goats.

Cut the meat into small pieces and place in a ceramic bowl. Cut the chilli in half lengthways, remove the seeds, and finely chop. Add the bay leaves and rosemary to the meat, then pour on the red wine. Cover the bowl with clingfilm and marinate overnight in the refrigerator, turning the meat several times in the marinade.

Remove the meat from the marinade and pat it dry. Strain the marinade through a sieve into a bowl. Finely dice the onion. Peel and quarter the tomatoes, remove the seeds and chop the flesh.

Heat the olive oil in a large saucepan and brown the meat in it on medium heat. Add the onion and fry until golden. Add the tomatoes, season with salt and pepper, and pour in half of the red wine marinade. Bring to the boil, then cover the pot and stew the meat on low heat for about 45 minutes or until done.

Pietrabbondante, an idyllic mountain village in the province of Molise, is surrounded by green meadows (above). One of the most important archaeological sites from the time of the Samnites is located here.

Offal

While offal – which includes heart, lung, kidney, brain, liver and tripe – has almost disappeared from the range of everyday fare in many countries, in Italy it continues to be held in high regard. The tradition of these meats dates back to antiquity, when a well-known gourmet named Apicius recommended that fresh figs be fed to pigs so that their livers would acquire an especially fine flavour. His rearing and fattening method, called *ficatum*, gave liver its Italian name, *fegato*.

Frattaglie (Italian for offal) is nutritious because it contains many vitamins and minerals but very little fat. Whereas the lungs, tripe and heart can be enjoyed without any concern, the kidneys, liver and sweetbreads are 'detoxification organs' that sometimes accumulate heavy metals, among other things. This is one reason to choose organic products when eating offal, and these should ideally come from young animals. The organs of young animals contain fewer harmful ingredients and are more tender. Some speciality shops offer offal that is ready to cook. It should always be as fresh as possible when cooked.

Favourite Types of Offal

Ever since the mad cow crisis of the 1990s, only lamb, pork and veal brains are permitted to be sold. Before cooking, they are cleaned, rinsed for several hours, briefly poached, then breaded or simply fried in butter.

Tripe, the edible part of the stomach of a cow, calf or lamb, has a permanent place in rustic Italian cuisine. It can readily be purchased already cleaned and pre-cooked.

Tongue is often sold cured; more tender calf, lamb or pig tongues are sold raw. Italians boil tongue with root vegetables and spices, after which it is skinned, then the gullet and fat at the base of the tongue are removed. The meat is cut into thin slices and served in an aromatic sauce or pickled in vinegar.

Liver is most often fried, grilled or stewed, but it also features nicely in pies, fillings and various terrine dishes. The most expensive, calf's liver, is also the most tender, followed by lamb's liver. Because of their intense flavour, beef and pork liver are often soaked in milk for a time before cooking.

The heart consists of firm muscle meat. Calf's heart can be stuffed and braised whole, while beef heart is sliced prior to cooking. It is steamed, fried or grilled with herbs.

Kidneys are most often sold ready to cook. Before preparing them, they simply need to be cut in half and washed thoroughly once the fatty core has been removed. They are often soaked in milk or vinegar water for a while before cooking. Lamb's and calf's kidneys are used in gourmet cooking, whereas beef and pork kidneys are part of everyday cuisine.

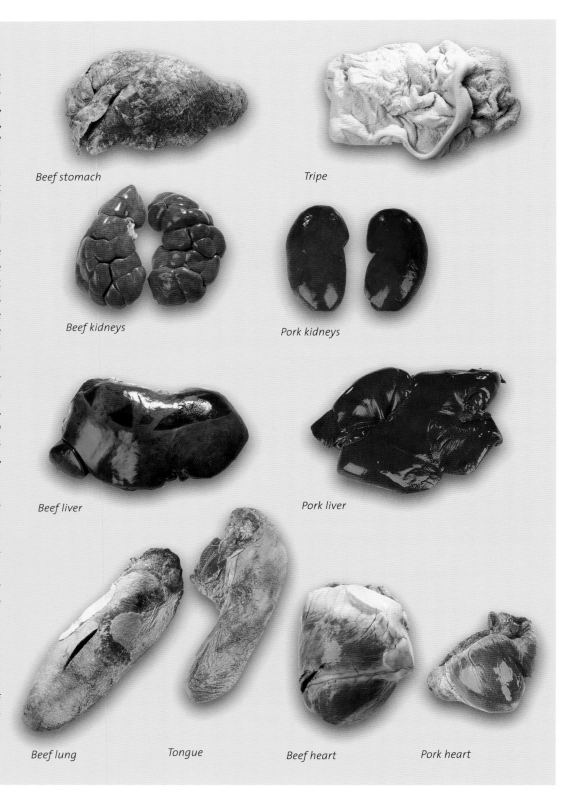

Beef stomach

Tripe

Beef kidneys

Pork kidneys

Beef liver

Pork liver

Beef lung

Tongue

Beef heart

Pork heart

Lingua alla piemontese
Piedmont-style Tongue

1 onion
1 carrot
1 celery stick
1 calf's tongue
5 peppercorns
2 bay leaves
1 fresh red chilli
2 tbsp olive oil
1 tbsp tomato purée
1 tbsp flour
350 ml/12 fl oz meat stock
1 tbsp capers
1–2 tbsp balsamic vinegar
salt
freshly ground pepper
1 tbsp finely chopped parsley

Peel or trim and halve the onion, carrot and celery stick. Place half of each of these vegetables in a saucepan of water with the calf's tongue. Add the peppercorns, bay leaves and 1 teaspoon of salt. Bring to the boil and simmer for 1 hour on low heat. Then rinse the tongue with cold water and set aside to cool.

Finely dice the remaining onion, carrot and celery. Cut the chilli in half lengthways, remove the seeds, and finely chop. Heat the olive oil in a frying pan and sauté the vegetables. Stir in the tomato purée and heat, then sprinkle on the flour and pour in the stock, stirring constantly. Simmer the sauce on low heat for about 20 minutes. Season with the capers, vinegar, and salt and pepper.

Skin the tongue and cut into slices. Add the meat to the sauce and heat it briefly in the sauce. Sprinkle with the chopped parsley before serving.

Sguazzetto
Offal Ragout

600 g/1 lb 5 oz chicken gizzards
(liver, stomach, heart and neck)
2 tbsp olive oil
4 garlic cloves, roughly chopped
10 almonds, roasted and ground
125 ml/4 fl oz wine
2 tbsp finely chopped parsley
salt
freshly ground pepper

Wash the gizzards, pat them dry, trim as needed and chop them finely. Heat the olive oil in a frying pan and brown everything except the liver on all sides. Add the garlic and fry gently. Mix in the almonds and liver, pour in the wine, and season with salt and pepper.

Stew the ragout on low heat until the sauce thickens. Sprinkle the chopped parsley over it before serving.

Fegato alla veneziana
Venetian-style Calf's Liver

500 g/1 lb 2 oz calf's liver
3 onions
4 tomatoes
4 tbsp olive oil
1 tbsp flour
100 ml/3½ fl oz red wine
5–6 sage leaves
salt
freshly ground pepper

Slice the calf's liver and remove any tendons, veins and skin. Then cut the slices into narrow strips. Finely slice the onions. Peel and quarter the tomatoes, remove the seeds, and cut into small dice.

Heat the olive oil in a deep frying pan, add the onion rings, cover the pan and steam for 15 minutes. Then stir the calf's liver into the onions and cook, stirring frequently. Dust the meat with the flour, then pour in the red wine and add the tomatoes and sage leaves. Cook everything on low heat for 5 minutes. Season to taste with salt and pepper and serve on heated plates.

Rognone alla parmigana
Parma-style Calf's Kidneys

600 g/1 lb 5 oz calf's kidneys
500 ml/18 fl oz milk
1 tbsp butter
2 tbsp olive oil
1 garlic clove, finely chopped
2 tbsp finely chopped parsley
125 ml/4 fl oz veal stock
juice of 1 lemon
salt
freshly ground pepper

Cut the kidneys in half lengthways and remove the fatty core. Thoroughly wash the kidneys, place them in a bowl and pour the milk over them. Marinate for 30 minutes, then remove the kidneys, pat dry and cut into thin slices.

Heat the butter and oil in a frying pan and sauté the garlic and 1 tablespoon of parsley. Add the kidneys to the pan and brown, stirring constantly. Pour in the veal stock. Cook the kidneys in it for 3 to 4 minutes. Season with lemon juice, salt and pepper. Serve sprinkled with the remaining parsley.

Spiedini alla toscana
Tuscan Liver Kebabs

600 g/1 lb 5 oz turkey livers
100 g/3½ oz lardo di Colonnata,
thinly sliced
12–15 fresh bay leaves
2 tbsp olive oil
freshly ground pepper

Halve each turkey liver, season with pepper and wrap in a slice of bacon. On four metal skewers, alternately thread a piece of liver followed by a bay leaf, then another piece of liver. Continue filling the skewers in this way until all the ingredients have been used.

Heat the olive oil in a large frying pan and fry the liver kebabs on all sides until crisp.

Chicken and Turkey

Tender, lean chicken and turkey meat are highly favoured by nutrition-conscious Italian epicures. Poultry is not only versatile, but also a delicious and economical alternative to ever-popular veal. Poultry is raised in rural regions throughout the country. The fact is that most chickens and turkeys that arrive on tables around Italy are still cage raised, but the demand for organic, free-range poultry is growing here as well.

The classic Italian chicken is white, has a yellow beak, yellow legs and to this day still resembles the chickens raised by the ancient Romans in the countryside. The second most widespread type, Sicilian chickens, are also an ancient breed and are especially prized for their ability to mature quickly. A male Sicilian chick can already crow at the age of four to five weeks, and the hens begin to lay astoundingly early. Both breeds were frequently taken aboard ships during Atlantic crossings, more as a source of fresh eggs than as a provision. Once arrived in the New World, some of the Italian chickens were bred and crossed with other birds, resuting in the Sicilian Buttercup. The new breeds were then brought back to Europe around the end of the nineteenth century.

The *tacchino* (turkey) is a 'genuine' American immigrant. Once a lean wild bird, the turkey has developed over time and through breeding into a rather powerful domestic animal. Today it is almost twice as large as its ancestors. Dishes made from turkey breast or braised turkey legs are popular year round. At Christmas time, turkeys are classically stuffed with chestnuts, plums, little sausages, celery and carrots.

For years, turkeys – here a male in a breeding display strut – have enjoyed increasing popularity in Italy.

Capons

In many regions of Italy, *cappone* (capon) is the traditional Christmas roast. Capons are young roosters that are castrated before reaching sexual maturity, and they were highly valued in ancient times. So that their meat becomes as tender and white as possible, they are given milk to drink and fattened for at least five months on a diet of millet flour and butter. Capons grow quickly and plump out nicely. With an average weight of 3 kg (6–7 lb), they provide an ideal holiday meal for a family.

Cutting Up Chicken

In order to cut up poultry properly, you need a sharp knife and poultry scissors.

First remove the legs: using a knife, slice through the skin between the thigh and breast.

Then separate the meat at the backbone so that it is still attached to the thigh joint.

Bend the joint in a rotating motion until the bone pops out of the socket.

Then cut off the wing tips, including the middle section, and set aside for the sauce.

Lay the chicken on its back and cut through the breast meat to the bone.

Cut through the body lengthways with a knife or poultry scissors.

Divide the chicken into eight pieces: halve each breast and separate the legs between the thigh and lower leg.

Carving a Turkey

Large poultry is best carved in the kitchen (rather than at the table). Begin by cutting off the wing tips with a knife.

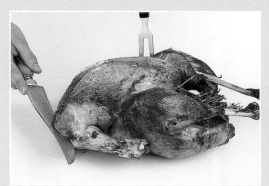

Put a meat fork in the back of one thigh in order to hold the turkey firmly in place. Cut into the bird horizontally at the wing joint.

Then detach one drumstick with a meat knife, bend it away from the body and remove.

Hold the leg with a napkin and cut through the joint between the thigh and lower leg.

Slice the meat off the thigh and leg, working parallel to the bone, and keep the meat warm in the oven.

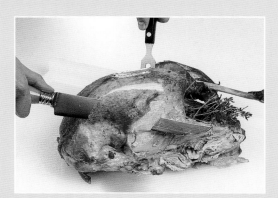

Finally, slice the breast meat diagonally into slices of equal size and keep warm until the entire turkey has been carved.

Favourite Chicken and Turkey Dishes

Pollo alla salvia
Sage Chicken

4 boneless chicken breasts with skin
2 slices prosciutto
8 sage leaves
1 garlic clove
1 tbsp fennel seeds, ground in a mortar
4 tbsp olive oil
½ lime, sliced
salt
freshly ground pepper

Preheat the oven to 170°C/340°F/gas mark 3. Gently loosen the skin on each chicken breast and place half a slice of prosciutto and 1 sage leaf underneath it. Cut the remaining sage leaves into strips. Peel and finely chop the garlic. Season the meat with salt and pepper, then rub the fennel seeds and garlic into it.

Heat the olive oil in a frying pan. Fry the meat on the skin side first, then on the other side. Remove from the pan and lay in a baking dish. Pour the pan drippings over the chicken, then place the lime slices and remaining sage leaves on top. Cook in the oven for about 30 minutes, then serve on a heated platter.

Pollo alla Marengo
Marengo Chicken

1 chicken, ready to cook
3 tbsp olive oil
125 ml/4 fl oz white wine
50 g/1¾ oz pearl onions
2 garlic cloves
2 tbsp flour
500 ml/18 fl oz poultry stock
4 small vine tomatoes
200 g/7 oz small mushrooms
4 crayfish tails, cooked
1 tbsp finely chopped parsley
salt
freshly ground pepper

Wash the chicken, pat it dry and cut it into 4 portions. Rub generous amounts of salt and pepper into the skin. Heat the olive oil in an iron casserole and brown the chicken quarters on all sides. Deglaze with the wine, then cover the pot and simmer for 10 minutes.

Peel the pearl onions and garlic. Cut the pearl onions in half and finely chop the garlic. Add both to the chicken, dust with the flour and cook briefly. Then pour in the poultry stock. Cover the pot and simmer for 20 minutes on medium heat.

Meanwhile, peel the tomatoes and cut into quarters. Cut the mushrooms in half. Add the vegetables to the chicken and season with salt and pepper. If necessary, add a little more wine. Simmer on low heat for another 25 to 30 minutes.

Add the crayfish tails and warm them in the sauce. Sprinkle the parsley over the chicken and serve on heated plates.

Pollo alla diavola
Spicy Chicken

2 dried red chillies, chopped
2 tbsp lemon juice
3 tbsp orange juice
500 ml/18 fl oz white wine
1 bay leaf
1 chicken, ready to cook
salt
freshly ground pepper

In a bowl, stir the chillies, citrus juices and wine together, then crumble the bay leaf into the mixture.

Cut the neck and wing tips off the chicken. Cut through the chicken along the breastbone and pull it open. Then carefully pound it as flat as possible without damaging the bones in the process. Lay the chicken in a bowl and pour the wine marinade over it. Cover and marinate in the refrigerator for a day, turning it over once.

Remove the chicken from the marinade, pat it dry and rub salt and pepper into it. Set under the grill or barbecue over charcoal for about 40 minutes until crisp and brown, turning periodically.

The Battle of Marengo

Marengo, a little village in the Italian province of Alessandria, set the stage for the historic battle of 14 June 1800, in which Napoleon scored a decisive victory over the Austrians. When the glorious commander then clamoured for something to eat, Dunant, his chef and a native of Switzerland, had to improvise, because he had lost his all of his provisions and baggage in the heat of battle. So he sent soldiers off in search of food.

They returned, bringing him chicken, tomatoes, mushrooms and crayfish that Dunant ingeniously combined into a very delicious dish, Polla alla Marengo. This fortuitous meal is said to have met with the French emperor's enthusiastic approval, and it has not lost any of its freshness or spontaneity in the past two centuries. Today gourmets in France, Italy and elsewhere love this uncommon recipe (left).

Pollo alla diavola

Pollo alla cacciatora
Chicken Cacciatore

1 chicken, ready to cook
2 tbsp olive oil
50 g/1¾ oz pancetta, diced
1 white onion, finely chopped
125 ml/4 fl oz white wine
4 tomatoes
250 ml/9 fl oz meat stock
salt
freshly ground pepper

Wash the chicken, pat it dry and cut it into 8 pieces. Rub generous amounts of salt and pepper into the skin. Heat the olive oil in an iron casserole and fry the pancetta and onion until the onions are translucent. Add the chicken pieces and brown on all sides. Deglaze the pan with the white wine and simmer for 5 minutes.

Peel and quarter the tomatoes, remove the seeds, and cut into small dice. Add to the chicken, then pour in the meat stock. Cover the pot and stew for 30 to 40 minutes. Season to taste with salt and pepper before serving.

Pollo alla griglia
Barbecued Chicken

1 maize-fed chicken,
ca. 1.2 kg/2 lb 10 oz, ready to cook

2 tsp grated lemon rind

3 garlic cloves, finely sliced

juice of 3 lemons

6 tbsp olive oil

salt

coarsely ground pepper

Wash the chicken, pat it dry and cut it in half lengthways. Lay the chicken halves in a bowl and season them with pepper. Spread the lemon rind and garlic over the chicken. Pour on the lemon juice and olive oil, then cover and marinate overnight in the refrigerator.

The next day, take the chicken halves out of the marinade and drain. Season the meat with salt and barbecue slowly over charcoal or set under a medium grill until crisp on both sides. Brush the chicken occasionally with the marinade while grilling.

Pollo al vino bianco
Chicken in White Wine

1 chicken, ca. 1.3 kg/3 lb,
ready to cook

2 tbsp olive oil

150 g/5 oz pancetta, diced

5 shallots, diced

1 tbsp flour

750 ml/1⅓ pints white wine

1 sprig rosemary

salt

freshly ground pepper

Wash the chicken, pat it dry and cut it into portions. Rub each piece with salt and pepper. Preheat the oven to 175°C/350°F/gas mark 4.

Heat the olive oil in a roasting tin and brown the meat on all sides. Add the pancetta and shallots and fry. Dust with the flour and pour in the wine. Add the rosemary sprig. Cover the roasting tin and put it in the oven for 30 minutes.

After that time, remove the lid from the roasting tin and return the chicken to the oven to continue cooking until the wine has nearly evaporated. Remove the rosemary sprig before serving.

Tacchino ripieno
Turkey with Stuffing

Serves six

1 young turkey, ca. 3.5 kg/7–8 lb,
ready to cook

100 g/3½ oz pancetta, diced

2 onions, finely chopped

2 tsp dried thyme

2 celery sticks, diced

3 apples, diced

50 g/1¾ oz sultanas

50 g/1¾ oz currants

100 g/3½ oz dried fruits
(apricots, cherries, prunes), diced

2 eggs

75 g/2½ oz breadcrumbs

2 tbsp olive oil, plus extra for greasing

500 ml/18 fl oz poultry stock

125 ml/4 fl oz red wine

salt

freshly ground pepper

Wash the turkey and pat dry. Generously rub it with salt and pepper, inside and out. Preheat the oven to 175°C/350°F/gas mark 4 and grease a roasting tin with olive oil.

Render the pancetta in a frying pan. Add the onions and sauté until translucent. Stir in the thyme and celery and sauté a few minutes. Remove the pan from the stove. Combine the onion mixture with the apples, sultanas, currants and dried fruits. Cool slightly, then stir in the eggs and breadcrumbs. Season the stuffing with salt and pepper.

Fill the turkey with the stuffing and close the cavity with wooden skewers. Place the turkey in the roasting tin. Brush the turkey with olive oil. Roast for 3½ to 4 hours, basting from time to time with the poultry stock.

When the turkey is done, remove it from the roasting tin and keep it warm. Pour the cooking juices into a saucepan and skim off the fat. Add the red wine, then boil for several minutes. Season the sauce with salt and pepper and serve with the turkey.

Pigeon and Guinea Fowl

When many non-Italians hear the word pigeon, the idea of those unpopular birds on Saint Mark's Square in Venice or some other major tourist location comes to mind. Perhaps others think of that delicious dove-shaped Easter cake, *colomba pasquale*, made from sweet leavened dough. But Italians immediately think of culinary pleasures. Pigeons have aromatic meat and an intense flavour. Their lean meat is easily digested. Young farm-raised pigeons, sold at a weight of 300 to 400 grams (11–14 oz), taste best of all. They are roast, barbecued or stewed, and their aromatic meat is also very popular as a pasta filling.

Faraona is the Italian word for guinea fowl. Although they have long since been domesticated, they have to some extent retained the flavour of wild game. This fine fowl with a distinctive flavour is a favourite holiday food. Strict quality standards for breeding and fattening have been imposed in Italy. Guinea fowl are kept on straw or wood shavings in special stalls and only the adults are killed. The comparatively long breeding process and high-quality feed make guinea fowl a rather expensive treat. Guinea fowl with a mark of quality are raised free-range. Greenstuff and the fresh air of the cage-free environment make their meat even more delicious. By the way, these fowl are especially cantankerous. Guinea fowl are much maligned for being in constant conflict with domestic chickens, turkeys and geese.

Faraona in porchetta
Guinea Fowl
with Fennel and Olives

3 tbsp olive oil
1 guinea fowl, ca. 1.3 kg/3 lb, ready to cook
1 fennel bulb, diced
1 white onion, finely chopped
125 ml/4 fl oz white wine
500 ml/18 fl oz chicken stock
50 g/1¾ oz pine kernels
100 g/3½ oz large, stoned green olives
salt and pepper

Heat the oil in an iron casserole. Cut the guinea fowl into 4 sections and brown it on both sides. Season with salt and pepper. Add the fennel and onion to the pan and fry until the onions are soft. Deglaze with the wine and reduce slightly, then add half the stock. Cover and stew on low heat for 30 minutes.

Dry-roast the pine kernels in an ungreased frying pan until golden. Finely dice the olives. Add both to the guinea fowl, pour in the remaining stock, cover and cook 30 minutes longer. Transfer the meat to a serving platter. Season the sauce with salt and pepper, and pour over the meat.

Faraona con miele e rosmarino
Guinea Fowl with
Honey and Rosemary

1 guinea fowl, ready to cook
150 g/5 oz fresh pearl onions
2 tbsp olive oil
2 sprigs rosemary
200 ml/7 fl oz white wine
2 tbsp pine kernels
2 tbsp Sardinian citrus honey (or orange blossom honey)
125 ml/4 fl oz poultry stock
salt
freshly ground pepper

Cut the guinea fowl into 4 sections, then rub them with salt and pepper. Peel the pearl onions. Heat the olive oil in a large, deep pan and fry the meat on medium heat until both sides are golden brown. Then remove the meat from the pan and sauté the pearl onions briefly in the same oil. Return the meat to the pan with the skin-side up. Add the rosemary and white wine. Bring to the boil and reduce slightly, then cover the pan and stew the guinea fowl on low heat for 30 minutes.

Dry-roast the pine kernels in an ungreased frying pan until golden brown, then add to the guinea fowl. Glaze the guinea fowl skin with honey. Pour in the poultry stock and bring to the boil. Cover and stew for another 30 minutes.

Remove the meat from the pan and place on a heated serving platter. Remove and discard the rosemary. Season the pan juices with salt and pepper and serve the meat surrounded by the sauce and pearl onions.

Remove the pigeon legs and breasts. Chop the remaining bones into small pieces.

Lightly brown the bones. Add finely diced root vegetables and cook them, as well.

Add the blanched strips of Savoy cabbage, season and cook on low heat.

Brown the drumsticks and breasts on all sides in a pan, then cover and cook until done.

Piccione alla fiorentina
Florentine-style Pigeon

2 pigeons, ready to cook
1 onion
1 garlic clove
1 carrot
1 celery stick
60 ml/2 fl oz olive oil
100 ml/3½ fl oz white wine
1 bay leaf
400 ml/14 fl oz vegetable stock
½ Savoy cabbage
100 g/3½ oz pancetta
salt
freshly ground pepper
freshly grated nutmeg

Wash the pigeons and pat dry. With a sharp knife, cut off the drumsticks and breasts (as separate pieces). Cover the meat and place in the refrigerator. Chop the remaining bones into small pieces.

Finely dice the onion, garlic, carrot and celery. Heat 2 tablespoons of the olive oil in a saucepan and lightly brown the bones in it. Add the vegetables and cook everything to a golden brown. Deglaze with the white wine, then add the bay leaf and pour in the stock. Simmer on low heat for 1 hour. Pour the stock through a fine sieve into a bowl.

Wash the Savoy cabbage and remove the core. Bring a saucepan of salted water to the boil and blanch the cabbage leaves for 2 minutes, then refresh in cold water. Press the liquid out of the leaves and cut them into fine strips.

Dice the pancetta. Heat 1 tablespoon of olive oil in a frying pan and fry the diced bacon in it. Add the cabbage and season with salt, pepper and nutmeg. Add 200 ml/7 fl oz water, partially cover the pan and steam the cabbage on low heat for 15 minutes.

Season the drumsticks and breasts with salt and pepper. Heat the remaining oil in a large pan. First fry the drumsticks on all sides, then add the breasts and brown lightly on both sides. Put a lid on the pan and cook the pigeons on low heat for 10 minutes.

Transfer the drumsticks, breasts and cabbage to a heated serving platter. Bring the stock to the boil again and season with salt and pepper. Pour some of the sauce over the meat and serve the rest on the side.

Goose

The goose is a highly versatile creature. As is true with pigs, every part of the goose can be utilized: their feathers make soft, warm filling for pillows, quilts and coats; the fat is a delicate seasoning; the liver can be made into exquisite pâtés; and the meat is nutritious and savoury. Geese are about as easy to raise as pigs and are also very alert. In 374 BCE, their loud honking awakened the sentinels at the statehouse, thus preventing the conquest of Rome by the Gauls. The writer Pliny (23–75 BCE) thought geese were clever and devoted to people. Pliny reported that the Greek philosopher Lacydes had had a goose that was always by his side, day and night. This led him to conclude that these birds must have a certain intellectual capacity.

According to an old tradition, roast goose is eaten in Tuscany on All Saint's Day, the first of November. On the day beforehand, a large goose market took place on the Piazza

San Giovanni. Those who did not have an oven in their homes had their goose – or at least some portion thereof – cooked in the public ovens. And to this day, the street where the bakehouse was located is called *Via dell'Oche* (Goose Street).

Oca in onto, goose meat in its own fat, was prepared in the homes of wealthy Venetian and Paduan families so that there would be enough nutritious meat and fat available for the winter. Goose were cooked slowly in a sauce consisting of olive oil, rosemary, garlic, salt and pepper. The skin and bones were then removed, and the breast and shank sliced. The slices were then layered with goose fat and bay leaves in large, clay storage vessels and covered in olive oil. This way the meat stayed fresh for several months.

A crisp roast goose is the traditional meal for many Tuscans on All Saint's Day (above).

Lots of running around in fresh air is important for the optimal quality of the meat (below).

Petto d'oca al nasturzio
Breast of Goose with Watercress

2 goose breasts with bones,
ca. 500 g/1 lb 2 oz each

50 g/1¾ oz raisins

100 ml/3½ fl oz dessert wine

2 tbsp goose fat

300 ml/11 fl oz vegetable stock

3 handfuls watercress

1 pomegranate

60 ml/2 fl oz olive oil

2 tbsp red wine vinegar

2 tbsp pine kernels

salt

freshly ground pepper

Preheat the oven to 180°C/355°F/gas mark 4. Wash and pat dry the goose breasts, then salt and pepper them. Marinate the raisins in the dessert wine. Heat the goose fat in an iron casserole. Brown the meat in it on the skin side first, then turn it over. Pour in the vegetable stock and bring to the boil. Cover the casserole with a lid and place it in the oven for about 25 minutes.

In the meantime, wash the watercress, pat it dry, and pluck the leaves from the stalks. Cut the pomegranate into quarters and remove the kernels. Whisk together the olive oil, vinegar and a pinch of salt. Take the raisins out of the wine and stir them into the dressing along with the pomegranate seeds. Dry-roast the pine kernels in an ungreased frying pan until golden brown.

Take the meat out of its stewing liquid. Remove the breast meat from the bones and slice it on the diagonal.

Divide the watercress between 4 plates. Top with the pomegranate-raisin dressing and sprinkle with the pine kernels. Arrange the sliced goose breast on the watercress in the shape of a fan and drizzle sauce over it.

Remove the wings and, holding the duck firmly in place with a meat fork, cut off the legs.

Duck à la Verdi

Giuseppe Verdi (1813–1901), one of Italy's most famous composers, counts among those who reformed Italian opera. *Nabucco*, *Rigoletto*, *La Traviata* and *Aïda* are among his most well-known operatic works. The composer's 'second life' as a farmer, however, is less familiar to most people. Several years after his first worldwide success in the musical arena, he bought the run-down county estate *Sant'Agata di Villanova* in Bassa Padana, a plain between Parma and Piacenza, and brought it back to life. He built dairies and cheese-making facilities and, along with over 200 farm hands, managed to successfully cultivate the land and breed livestock for over fifty years.

Verdi was not only a farmer, as he himself repeatedly and proudly emphasized; he was also a generous host, an avowed gourmet and a talented amateur chef. Following a celebrated opera premiere, his wife Giuseppina wrote, 'If people only knew what a great *risotto alla milanese* he composes, God only knows what kind of ovations would then rain down on him.'

To this day there is a duck recipe that recalls Verdi the farmer and chef, *Anatra alla Verdi*, named in his honour. A fresh farm-raised duck is salted and peppered all over, then coated in olive oil. It is placed on a bed of onions and carrots, covered with diced fatty prosciutto and rosemary, and baked in the oven to a crisp brown.

Ducks are still raised in free-range conditions on many Italian farmsteads. Gourmets value not only their meat, but their livers as well.

Petto d'anatra farcito con radicchio
Breast of Duck with Radicchio Stuffing

4 small duck breasts, 200 g/7 oz each	
2 radicchio trevigiano	
4 tbsp olive oil	
50 g/1¾ oz pancetta, diced	
1 red onion, finely chopped	
2 garlic cloves, finely chopped	
1 tsp sugar	
1 tbsp balsamic vinegar	
50 ml/1½ fl oz red wine	
1 tsp chopped rosemary leaves	
salt	
freshly ground pepper	

Wash the duck breasts and pat dry. Cut a pocket in the meat lengthways with a sharp knife. Cut the radicchio into narrow strips.

Heat half of the olive oil in a pan and fry the pancetta, onion and garlic in it. Add the radicchio, salt and pepper. As soon as the radicchio wilts, sprinkle the sugar over it and leave it to caramelize. Deglaze the pan with the vinegar, then pour on the wine. Continue cooking until all the liquid has thickened. Remove from the stove and set aside to cool.

Preheat the oven to 150°C/300°F/gas mark 2. Fill the pocket in the duck breast with the radicchio mixture and rosemary, then close the opening with wooden skewers. Salt and pepper the duck breasts.

Heat the remaining olive oil in a frying pan and brown the duck breasts on medium heat, skin side down, for 10 minutes. Then turn and cook for another 3 minutes. Place the duck breasts in a flat baking dish or on a platter and roast for 15 minutes.

Remove the duck breasts from the oven and remove the wooden skewers. Cut the meat into slices on the diagonal, then serve.

Then cut horizontally into the breast at the wing joint.

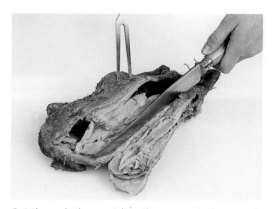

Cut through the meat lengthways to the bone and remove it parallel to the rib cage.

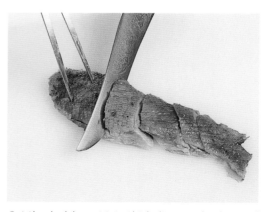

Cut the duck breast into thick slices on the diagonal without removing the skin.

Anatra con verdure
Duck with Vegetables

1 young duck, ca. 1.4 kg/3 lb,
ready to cook
1 onion
1 bay leaf
3 cloves
1 bouquet garni
5 peppercorns
5 allspice berries
500 g/1 lb 2 oz carrots
500 g/1 lb 2 oz Hamburg parsley root
2 tbsp olive oil
250 ml/9 fl oz veal stock
2 tbsp finely chopped parsley
salt, freshly ground pepper

Wash the duck and place it in a large saucepan. Spike the onion with the bay leaf and cloves, then add it and the bouquet garni to the pot. Add enough water to cover the duck entirely. Add salt, pepper and the allspice berries. Bring to the boil, skimming off the foam that forms on the surface, and simmer on low heat for about 1¼ hours.

Cut the carrots and parsley roots into equal-sized pieces. Heat the olive oil in a frying pan and sauté the vegetables, then pour on the veal stock, cover and simmer for 10 minutes. Season with salt and pepper and mix in the parsley. Keep the vegetables warm.

Remove the duck from the stock and drain it well. Remove the skin. Bone the breast meat and legs, then slice the meat. Serve the duck meat and vegetables on a heated serving platter.

The Versatile Rabbit

Coniglio, or rabbit, is a very popular element of country cuisine throughout Italy. Lean, white, tender rabbit meat is versatile enough to be suitable for simple dishes as well as more festive fare. It is served primarily in the colder months of the year.

In Valle d'Aosta, people have a preference for spicy *coniglio*. The rabbit is cut up into serving-sized pieces, pan-fried with pancetta and onions, then stewed in meat stock with rosemary, garlic, anchovies and fresh peppers. In Liguria they make *coniglio in umido*, a rabbit stew that includes tomatoes, fresh herbs, pine kernels and garlic in white wine. From the island of Ischia comes a similar recipe, called *coniglio all'ischitana*, but their version is also seasoned with fresh chillies.

Coniglio con patate (rabbit with potatoes) originated in Sardinia. In that version, the entire rabbit is roasted in the oven with fresh wild herbs, garlic and, of course, lots of potatoes.

A Sicilian speciality is sweet-and-sour rabbit, for which a whole rabbit is cut into pieces, briefly browned in olive oil, then stewed in an aromatic tomato sauce that includes olives, capers, almonds, cinnamon and red wine vinegar. Umbrian cuisine favours rabbit stuffed with fennel root, salami and pancetta that is gently braised in fennel stock.

Prepare all the ingredients for stuffed rabbit and have them within arm's length.

Render diced pancetta, then add onion, garlic and offal.

Wrap the stuffed rabbit in bacon slices and cook in an iron casserole.

Coniglio ripieno
Stuffed Rabbit

1 rabbit (including heart and liver), ready to cook
2 day-old rolls
100 g/3½ oz pancetta, diced
1 small onion, finely chopped
1 garlic clove, finely chopped
2 tbsp finely chopped parsley
2 eggs
2 tbsp grated Parmesan
6 rashers fatty bacon
200 ml/7 fl oz poultry stock
1 tsp chopped thyme
oil for greasing
sugar
salt
freshly ground pepper

Wash the rabbit and pat it dry with paper towels. Vigorously rub with salt and pepper, inside and out. Trim and finely chop the heart and liver. Soak the day-old rolls in hot water. Preheat the oven to 200°C/390°F/gas mark 6 and grease an iron casserole with oil.

Heat a frying pan and render the pancetta. Add the onion, garlic and offal and fry briefly. Remove from the heat, mix in the parsley and set aside to cool. Squeeze excess water from the rolls. Combine the bacon-onion mixture with the bread, eggs and Parmesan. Season with salt and pepper.

Stuff the rabbit with the mixture, then sew the cavity shut with kitchen twine. Wrap the rabbit in the bacon rashers, lay it in the casserole, cover and roast for 45 minutes.

Remove the lid from the casserole and return the rabbit to the oven for an additional 20 to 25 minutes. Then lift it out of the casserole and carve, removing the kitchen twine in the process. Deglaze the casserole with the poultry stock, stirring to loosen the drippings, and reduce slightly on medium heat. Season this sauce with the thyme, sugar, salt and pepper. Serve with the meat.

Coniglio al vino rosso
Rabbit in Red Wine

1 rabbit, ready to cook
1 rabbit liver
4 garlic cloves, roughly chopped
5 peppercorns
grated peel of ½ lemon
5 tbsp olive oil
250 ml/9 fl oz red wine
1 cinnamon stick
4 cloves
2 sprigs rosemary
2 small onions, finely chopped
100 g/3½ oz bacon, finely diced
1 tsp Spanish (hot) paprika
2 beef tomatoes, peeled, cored and quartered
⅛ teaspoon cumin
coarse salt

Cut the rabbit into pieces. Trim the liver, wash it and pat dry, and place it in a bowl. Crush the garlic, peppercorns, lemon peel and some salt in a mortar. Whisk together 3 tablespoons of olive oil, the wine and the contents of the mortar to make the marinade. Add the cinnamon stick, cloves and rosemary. Pour the marinade over the rabbit pieces and liver and place in the refrigerator overnight.

Remove the meat and pour the marinade through a sieve into a bowl. Chop the liver and set aside. Heat the remaining oil in a large saucepan, fry the onions and bacon, add the rabbit pieces and fry to a golden brown. Add the liver to the pot, then deglaze with the marinade. Add the paprika and tomatoes and stew on low heat. Adjust the seasoning with salt, pepper and cumin before serving.

Coniglio con le olive
Rabbit with Olives

1 kg/2 lb 4 oz rabbit pieces
2 carrots
4 tomatoes
1 garlic clove, finely chopped
3 tbsp olive oil
40 ml/2½ tbsp brandy
100 g/3½ oz large, stoned green olives
1–2 tbsp white wine vinegar
salt
freshly ground pepper

Wash the rabbit, pat dry and cut it into portions. Rub vigorously with salt and pepper, then place in an unheated iron casserole.

Peel and slice the carrots. Peel and quarter the tomatoes, remove the seeds, and cut into fine dice. Add the carrots, tomatoes and garlic to the rabbit. Drizzle the olive oil over everything, then place the pot on the stove and heat.

Stir the meat and vegetables, pour in the brandy and allow it to nearly evaporate. Pour in 125 ml/4 fl oz warm water, cover the pot and simmer on medium heat for about 40 minutes.

Coarsely chop the olives and mix them into the rabbit. Simmer for another 10 to 15 minutes, then season with the vinegar, salt and pepper, and serve.

Coniglio con patate
Rabbit with Potatoes

1 rabbit, ca. 1.2 kg/2 lb 10 oz, ready to cook
6 tbsp olive oil
4 garlic cloves, finely chopped
1 sprig rosemary
500 ml/18 fl oz white wine
1 kg/2 lb 4 oz potatoes
salt
freshly ground pepper

Wash the rabbit, pat dry and cut it into portions. Heat half of the olive oil in a large iron casserole and lightly brown the rabbit on all sides. Season with salt and pepper and add the garlic and rosemary. Fry briefly, then deglaze the pot with half of the white wine.

Stew the rabbit on low heat for 40 minutes with the lid just slightly open. Gradually add the rest of the wine.

In the meantime, peel the potatoes and cut them into large chunks. Heat the rest of the olive oil in a frying pan and fry the diced potatoes until golden brown. Add the potatoes to the rabbit and simmer for 20 minutes more, adding a little more water as needed. Season to taste with salt and pepper. Serve the rabbit and potatoes in the casserole.

Wild Boar

In October, the wild boar hunting season begins in Tuscany and Lazio. For three months, hunters from all over Italy comb through the woods with their dogs and foreign guests in search of these savoury four-legged roasts. Tumultuous wild boar festivals take place in many locations. Hunting wild boar was already a very popular pastime in ancient times, as one sculpture of a hunting scene that was found during excavations at Pompeii reveals.

Wild boar are large, heavy animals that prefer to live in damp, boggy forests. Their populations have been decimated to such an extent over the course of the past several centuries, especially due to increased use of land for agriculture, that there were almost no wild boar left in Tuscany by 1900. Since then, however, wild boar have migrated to the forests of Tuscany from other regions. Nevertheless, the vast majority of wild boar meat for sale in shops comes from animals that were raised in large parks.

Wild boar live mainly in the forests of Tuscany, Lazio, Umbria and the Marche.

Cinghiale agrodolce
Sweet-and-sour Wild Boar Ragout

800 g/1 lb 12 oz wild boar shank
3 tbsp olive oil
50 g/1¾ oz coppa ham, diced
1 white onion, finely chopped
2 carrots, sliced
2 celery sticks, diced
1 Hamburg parsley root, diced
1 tbsp flour
500 ml/18 fl oz game stock
2 bay leaves
50 g/1¾ oz raisins
100 ml/3½ fl oz dessert wine
30 g/1 oz plain chocolate, grated
1 tbsp crystallized fruit, finely chopped
2 tbsp sugar
2 tbsp balsamic vinegar
2 tbsp pine kernels
salt
freshly ground pepper

Wash the meat, pat it dry and cut into bite-sized chunks. Heat the oil in an iron casserole and brown the meat on all sides. Season with salt and pepper. Add the ham, onion, carrots, celery and parsley root and sauté briefly. Dust with the flour, then pour in the game stock and bring to the boil. Add the bay leaves. Cover the pot and stew on low heat for about 2 hours, stirring periodically.

Marinate the raisins in the dessert wine for 10 minutes, then remove the raisins and add them to the meat along with the chocolate and crystallized fruit. Simmer for 10 minutes. Season the ragout with the sugar, vinegar, and salt and pepper to taste.

Dry-roast the pine kernels in an ungreased frying pan until golden brown. Add them to the wild boar ragout just before serving.

Delicious cured meat products made from wild boar are a wonderful Tuscan speciality and include salami and ham (right).

Cosciotto di cinghiale alla cacciatora
Wild Boar Shank Hunter's Style

1 kg/2 lb 4 oz wild boar shank, boned
4 tbsp olive oil
2 onions, finely chopped
100 g/3½ oz pancetta, diced
1 tbsp tomato purée
250 ml/9 fl oz red wine
2 tomatoes
25 g/1 oz dried ceps
salt
freshly ground pepper

Wash the meat and pat it dry with paper towels. Tie the roast together with kitchen twine and vigorously rub in salt and pepper. Preheat the oven to 175°C/350°F/gas mark 4.

Heat the olive oil in an iron casserole, brown the meat on all sides, then remove it from the pot. Brown the onions and pancetta in the same pan. Stir in the tomato purée and heat through, then deglaze with the red wine, stirring to loosen the drippings. Put the meat back in the casserole.

Peel and quarter the tomatoes, remove the seeds, and dice. Add the tomatoes and ceps to the sauce, pour in 300 ml/11 fl oz water, and bring to the boil. Cover the casserole and braise in the oven for about 2 hours.

Then remove the meat from the sauce and discard the kitchen twine. Leave the roast to stand for 5 minutes, then slice it. Season the sauce to taste with salt and pepper and serve on the side.

Favourite Wild Game Dishes

Fagiano in carpione
Marinated Pheasant

2 pheasants, ready to cook
7 black peppercorns
5 juniper berries
soup vegetables such as carrots, celery or other root vegetables, diced
2 bay leaves
250 ml/9 fl oz dry white wine
5 tbsp olive oil
1 tbsp flour
salt
freshly ground pepper
sugar

Cut each pheasant into 4 pieces, then wash and pat dry. Crush the peppercorns and juniper berries in a mortar. Place the meat and diced soup vegetables in a ceramic bowl. Add the bay leaves and crushed spices, then pour the wine over everything. Cover with clingfilm and marinate in the refrigerator for 8 hours. During this time, turn the meat in the marinade repeatedly.

Preheat the oven to 150°C/300°F/gas mark 2. Take the pheasant out of the marinade, thoroughly pat it dry, then rub salt and pepper into it. Heat the olive oil in a roasting tin, add the meat to the pan and brown on all sides. Dust with the flour, then add the marinade and vegetables and bring to the boil. Cover the roasting tin and braise in the oven for 2 hours.

Remove the meat and bay leaves from the cooking juices. Purée the sauce, then season to taste with salt, pepper and sugar. Return the meat to the sauce for a few minutes to heat through before serving.

Quaglie al mandarino
Quails with Tangerines

4 quails, ready to cook
4 slices prosciutto
8 bay leaves
2 tbsp olive oil
200 ml/7 fl oz white wine
4 tangerines
100 ml/3½ fl oz Marsala
salt
freshly ground pepper

Wash the quails, pat them dry and season with salt and pepper. Wrap each quail in a slice of prosciutto, cover with 2 bay leaves and tie together with kitchen twine.

Heat the olive oil in an iron casserole and fry the quails, turning frequently. Deglaze the pan with the wine, cover the pot and simmer for 10 minutes.

Leaving the rind on the tangerines, cut them into wedges and add to the quails. Pour in the Marsala. Cover the casserole and cook for another 10 minutes, then adjust the seasoning and serve.

Pernici con lenticchie
Partridge with Lentils

4 partridges, ready to cook
75 g/2½ oz pancetta
2 shallots
2 celery sticks
1 tbsp lard
250 ml/9 fl oz chicken stock
200 g/7 oz Castellucio lentils
2 garlic cloves, finely chopped
1 fresh red chilli
100 g/3½ oz sun-dried tomatoes in oil
3 tbsp olive oil
salt
freshly ground pepper

Wash the partridges and pat dry. Rub salt and pepper into them, inside and out. Cut the pancetta into strips. Dice the shallots and celery. Chop the celery greens and set aside.

Heat the lard in a roasting tin and brown the partridges on all sides. Add and lightly brown the bacon, shallots and diced celery. Pour in the poultry stock and bring to the boil. Cover and stew on low heat for about 40 minutes.

Meanwhile, put the lentils in a saucepan and add enough water to cover them completely. Bring to the boil, add the celery leaves and garlic, and simmer for 20 minutes. Pour off the liquid and drain well. Cut the chilli in half lengthways, remove the seeds, and finely chop. Cut the tomatoes into narrow strips. Heat the olive oil in a frying pan and sauté the chilli and tomatoes. Add the lentils and combine thoroughly.

Remove the partridges from their stewing juices and cut them in half. Serve on heated plates with the lentils and vegetables.

Quaglie risotto
Quail Risotto

4 quails, ready to cook
1 handful fresh thyme
100 g/3½ oz butter
8 rashers fatty bacon
1 white onion, finely chopped
300 g/11 oz Arborio rice
500 ml/18 fl oz chicken stock
500 ml/18 fl oz milk
100 ml/3½ fl oz white wine
4 tbsp grated Parmesan
salt
freshly ground pepper
oil for greasing

Preheat the oven to 220°C/430°F/gas mark 7 and grease a baking dish. Wash the quails and pat dry. Season them inside and out with salt and pepper. Place 1 small sprig of thyme and 1 teaspoon of butter inside each quail. Wrap each bird in 2 rashers of bacon and tie together with kitchen twine.

Place the quails in the baking dish and roast for 15 minutes. Melt 3 tablespoons of butter in a saucepan and sauté the onion until translucent. Add the rice and toast it lightly. Add the stock and cook on low heat as the rice absorbs the liquid.

Heat the milk and add it to the risotto in portions, stirring constantly.

Add the white wine to the baking dish with the quails. Reduce the oven temperature to 180°C/355°F/gas mark 4 and return the quails to the oven for another 10 to 15 minutes. As soon as the rice is cooked al dente, stir in the rest of the butter and the Parmesan. Serve the risotto on heated plates and place a quail on each serving.

Capriolo alla griglia
Grilled Medallions of Venison

8 venison medallions, ca. 60 g/2 oz each
8 rashers lean bacon
3 tbsp olive oil
2 sprigs rosemary
400 g/14 oz small potatoes, boiled
salt
freshly ground pepper

Wrap each medallion in 1 rasher of bacon and hold in place with a wooden skewer.

Heat the olive oil in a griddle pan, add the rosemary sprigs and fry the potatoes in the oil. Add the venison medallions to the pan and season with salt and pepper. Cook the meat for 2 to 3 minutes per side. Serve with the potatoes.

Sella di capriolo all'Amarone
Saddle of Venison in Amarone

1 saddle of venison,
ca. 1.2 kg/2 lb 10 oz
4 tbsp olive oil
1 onion, finely chopped
1 carrot, diced
1 celery stick, diced
1 tsp flour, plus extra for coating
750 ml/1⅓ pints Amarone
salt
freshly ground pepper

Wash the saddle of venison and pat it dry. Cut along the spine on both sides between the spine and the meat. Then remove the meat from the bones. Trim off the skin and tendons and discard them. Finely chop the bones.

Heat half of the olive oil in an iron casserole and thoroughly brown the chopped bones and meat. Add the onion, carrot and celery and continue cooking. Dust with the flour and stir briefly, then deglaze the pot with half of the wine. Pour in 500 ml/18 fl oz water and simmer on low heat for 1 hour, stirring periodically.

Preheat the oven to 160°C/320°F/gas mark 3. Pour the stock through a fine sieve into a bowl and set aside for later. Season the meat with salt and pepper, then coat it with flour. Heat the remaining oil in an ovenproof casserole and brown the meat on all sides. Deglaze with half the remaining wine and put it in the oven for 15 minutes.

Then remove the meat from the casserole and keep it warm. Pour the remaining wine into the casserole and scrape to loosen the drippings. Stir in the stock and heat until slightly reduced. Season the sauce to taste with salt and pepper. Slice the meat on the diagonal, arrange on plates and pour the sauce over it.

Capriolo in salmì
Venison Shank in Chocolate

1 kg/2 lb 4 oz venison shank
2 cloves
1 bay leaf
4 allspice berries
½ tsp black peppercorns
soup vegetables such as carrots, celery or other root vegetables, diced
750 ml/1⅓ pints red wine
125 ml/4 fl oz red wine vinegar
2 tbsp olive oil
2 tbsp butter
100 g/3½ oz pancetta, diced
1 white onion, finely chopped
1 tbsp flour
50 g/1¾ oz plain chocolate, grated
salt
freshly ground pepper

Wash the meat, pat dry and cut it into bite-sized chunks. Coarsely crush the cloves, bay leaf, allspice berries and peppercorns with a pestle and mortar.

Place the meat, diced soup vegetables and crushed spices in a ceramic bowl. Pour the red wine and vinegar over them, making sure the meat is completely covered in liquid. Cover the bowl with clingfilm and marinate the meat in the refrigerator overnight.

The next day, remove the meat from the marinade and pat dry. Pour the marinade through a fine sieve into a bowl.

Heat the olive oil and butter in an iron casserole and brown the meat on all sides. Add the pancetta and onion and fry in the oil and cooking juices. Season with salt and pepper and dust with the flour. Pour on half of the marinade and stir in the chocolate. Cover the pot and braise on low heat for about 50 minutes.

Lepre con cantarelli
Hare with Chanterelles

4 hare legs
2 onions, finely chopped
250 ml/9 fl oz red wine
250 ml/9 fl oz game stock
300 g/11 oz small chanterelles
1 tbsp butter
2 shallots, finely diced
1 tbsp finely chopped parsley
salt
freshly ground pepper
flour for coating
oil for browning

Skin the hare and cut each leg in two at the joint. Season the meat with salt and pepper, then coat with flour.

Heat some oil in a frying pan and brown the meat. Add the onions and fry lightly. Pour in the red wine and game stock. Cover the pan and simmer for 50 minutes.

Clean the chanterelles. Heat the butter in a second pan and sauté the chanterelles and shallots until the liquid evaporates. Season with salt and pepper.

Remove the meat from the cooking liquid and pour it through a sieve into a bowl. Serve the hare legs and chanterelles in portions with cooking juices poured over them, and sprinkled with chopped parsley.

Hunting Rabbits

During a rabbit hunt, the dogs are tasked with tracking down the prey.

Field hares like to hide in the brush or ground cover.

Once the prey has been startled and tries to flee, it is brought down with a shotgun.

Trim the saddle of venison, cutting away fat, skin and tendons with a sharp knife.

Cut the meat along the spine, close to the bone, then remove it from the bones.

Remove the other fillet in the same manner. Use the bones to make the sauce.

Verdure e Contorni

Vegetables
and
Side Dishes

VEGETABLES

Italian cuisine would be unimaginable without vegetables! Many foods we still enjoy today such as asparagus, for example, have their roots in antiquity, or can be traced as far back as the Middle Ages, as is the case with the recipe for Jewish-style Artichokes on page 365. In Italy, vegetables are enjoyed raw in salads, cooked in hearty soups and sauces, or roughly chopped and lightly sautéd in olive oil with a little water or white wine so that they are still crunchy. They are seasoned simply with sea salt and freshly ground pepper, and enhanced with the typical Mediterranean herbs: basil, sage, thyme and rosemary.

Vegetables play a large part throughout the courses of an Italian meal, beginning with briefly cooked and cold or warm marinated vegetables served as antipasti. Minestrone, certainly the peninsula's most famous soup, is prepared with seasonally varying vegetables. Many vegetables appear during the *secondi piatti*, at the latest, as *contorni* (side dishes). And of course, one should not forget that numerous pasta dishes are based on combination with vegetables. Finally, raw vegetables are often served as an accompaniment to cheese.

On average, Italians eat about four times as many vegetables as northern Europeans.

The Big C

To this day in Italy, the taste of not only salad and raw vegetables, but also of steamed and grilled vegetables, are enhanced with a little olive oil. Just the right amount of oil – not too much and not too little – is very important. *Fare una C* ('to write a C') is how the ideal quantity is described in Tuscany. A trail of oil in the shape of a large C on plain vegetables is enough to turn them into a true delicacy.

Dishes based solely on vegetables have a long tradition, especially in the south. Popular produce includes artichokes, courgettes, aubergines, peas and broad beans, fennel, pumpkin, chard, asparagus, celery and, of course, tomatoes of all kinds. Depending on the region, there may also be mushrooms, wild herbs and *maroni* (chestnuts). Even in the eighteenth century, Johann Wolfgang von Goethe was astonished by the 'unbelievable amount of vegetable consumption' he witnessed on his travels through Italy. At about this time, the first recipes with tomatoes began to appear in Neapolitan cookbooks, although not in connection with pizza or pasta; this combination, which would become emblematic of Italy for the rest of the world, first arrived in the nineteenth century.

Vegetable Cultivation

In Italy, vegetables and fruits including tropical fruits are sold in tremendous variety and in every season. Everywhere, whether in private gardens or in professional agriculture, vegetables are grown and used fresh in the kitchen, where they are transformed into true delectations. Produce is cultivated throughout the peninsula, and a large part is exported.

Each type of vegetable and fruit has found an area with the ideal climactic conditions for its cultivation, from the apples of South Tyrol to the citrus fruits of Sicily. Veneto is home to radicchio and asparagus. Lumignano is famous for its delicate peas, Lamon for its broad beans and Chioggia for its pumpkins. Lazio boasts a multitude of vegetables, from artichokes to onions, and Abruzzo is known for its red garlic. A staggering variety of tomatoes is grown in Campania and Basilicata, while Calabria specializes in aubergines and peppers, and Apulia in new potatoes and fennel.

Italians do not like vegetables grown in greenhouses, nor do they like them bottled – the only exception being tomatoes – instead placing great value on fresh, flavourful produce of high quality. They have long been enthusiastic gardeners, and even in the smallest gardens there is a corner reserved for vegetables. Home-made bottled tomatoes and pickled vegetables are also widely made as preserves for the winter months.

Ripe seasonal vegetables and fruits from the region complete a street scene in many Italian cities.

Favourite Dips for Vegetables

### Bagnetto verde ### Savoury Green Sauce	### Salsa al cren ### Bolzano Sauce with Horseradish	### Salsa alla tartara ### Tartare Sauce
2 tbsp breadcrumbs	*1 slice day-old white bread*	*1 egg, hard-boiled*
2 tbsp white wine vinegar	*2 tbsp milk*	*1 tbsp salted capers*
1 small white onion	*150 g/5 oz fresh horseradish*	*¼ red pepper*
1 garlic clove	*100 ml/3½ fl oz double cream*	*200 g/7 oz home-made mayonnaise*
½ tsp salt	*salt*	*1 tbsp finely chopped parsley*
2 eggs, hard-boiled	*sugar*	*salt*
1–2 bunches flat-leaf parsley	*1–2 tsp lemon juice*	*freshly ground pepper*
175 ml/6 fl oz olive oil		
freshly ground pepper		

Place the breadcrumbs in a small bowl and sprinkle with the vinegar. Leave it to soak briefly. Peel and finely chop the onion. Peel the garlic and crush it with a fork along with the salt. Combine with the onion and breadcrumbs.

Remove the yolks from the hard-boiled eggs (the whites are not needed for this recipe). Rinse the parsley, dry it thoroughly and chop the leaves. Crush the yolks and mix with the parsley into the breadcrumb mixture. Gradually stir in the olive oil until a thick sauce develops. Season to taste with salt and pepper.

Remove the crusts from the bread and soak the bread in the milk. Peel and finely grate the horseradish. Thoroughly press any excess milk from the bread and mix with the horseradish. In a separate bowl, whip the cream and blend it with the horseradish. Season to taste with salt, sugar and lemon juice.

Peel the egg, cut it in half and remove the yolk. Finely chop the egg white, capers and pepper. Crush the yolk with a fork and stir it into the mayonnaise. Blend the egg white, capers, pepper and parsley into the mayonnaise. Season to taste with salt and ground pepper.

Salsa alle olive
Olive Dip

200 g/7 oz black olives
1 shallot
175 ml/6 fl oz olive oil
3 tbsp tomato purée
1 tsp finely chopped rosemary
salt
freshly ground pepper

Stone and chop the olives. Finely dice the shallot. Heat the olive oil in a frying pan and sauté the shallot. Add the olives, tomato purée and rosemary. Simmer on low heat for 10 minutes, then season to taste with salt and pepper.

Salsa di pomodoro
Raw Tomato Dip

4 tomatoes
2 shallots
2 garlic cloves
150 ml/5 fl oz olive oil
1 bunch basil
salt
freshly ground pepper

Peel and quarter the tomatoes, remove the seeds, and cut into dice. Finely dice the shallots and garlic. Mix all three with the olive oil, adding salt and pepper. Wash and pat dry the basil and pluck the leaves. Cut the leaves into thin strips and stir into the tomato sauce. Refrigerate for 1 to 2 hours before serving.

Tomatoes

Certainly no other vegetable is so closely associated with Italian cuisine in the minds of gourmets as the tomato – and this despite the fact that the fruits of this nightshade plant did not appear in Italian kitchens until the middle of the eighteenth century! Introduced to southern Italy (which at the time belonged to the Spanish crown) by the Spaniards at the beginning of the sixteenth century, due to the luminous red colour of its fruit, the tomato was first cultivated as an ornamental plant in aristocratic gardens. Because their leaves contain toxins that cause abdominal pain, the fruit was also reputed to be poisonous.

The other names by which the tomato is known – Eve's apple, love apple, apple of paradise – result from its seductive appearance, which one is apparently supposed to resist. The fruit's original yellow colour, the source of the moniker *pomo d'oro* ('golden apple'), changed through cultivation into a magnificent red, which visually harmonized best of all with the light yellow of pasta. In the meantime, highly aromatic, robust, older varieties of tomatoes in colours ranging from luminescent yellow to almost black are being grown once again.

Tiella di pomodori e patate
Baked Tomato-potato Casserole

1 kg/2 lb 4 oz tomatoes
750 g/1 lb 10 oz potatoes
1 bunch spring onions
125 ml/4 fl oz olive oil,
plus extra for greasing
2 garlic cloves, finely chopped
1 tsp dried oregano
50 g/1¾ oz breadcrumbs
75 g/2½ oz grated Parmesan
salt
freshly ground pepper

Preheat the oven to 175°C/350°F/gas mark 4. Grease a baking dish with olive oil.

Wash and trim the tomatoes and potatoes and slice both. Cut the spring onions, including some of the green, into thin rings. Place a layer of tomato slices on the base of the dish. Cover them with a layer of potato slices and spring onions. Season with some of the chopped garlic, oregano, and salt and pepper. Repeat the process until all the vegetables have been used. The top layer should be potatoes.

Combine the breadcrumbs and Parmesan and scatter them over the top. Sprinkle with olive oil and bake for 1 hour or until golden brown. Serve hot or warm in the baking dish.

In Italy, older varieties such as the Sicilian beef tomato are being revived.

Small, sweet cherry tomatoes are well-loved not only in Italy, but have also been a hit on the export market.

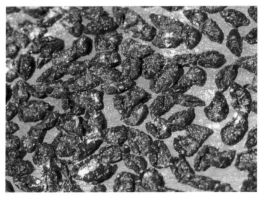

Sun-dried tomatoes are halved and dried in the sun. Added salt speeds up the drying process.

Drying is the oldest method of tomato preservation. When dried, their aroma increases dramatically.

Tomato Preserves

In many Italian kitchens, tomatoes are the only fruit or vegetable that are tolerated in canned form. Freshly picked tomatoes are only available during a brief season, but they are an indispensable ingredient year-round. Before settling for unripe tomatoes, or ones grown in a greenhouse that have no flavour, Italians will rely on finished products made from ripe-harvested fruits, including peeled or diced tomatoes or tomato purée.

In the Campania and Puglia regions, which are the centres of cultivation and industrial processing of tomatoes in Italy, plum tomatoes are widely grown. This variety is fleshy, thick-skinned and flavourful, all qualities that make it especially well-suited to processing. The best canned fruits are San Marzano tomatoes. They are peeled and sold whole or diced, for example, as pizza tomatoes.

Tomato purée is used primarily as a seasoning for sauces, or to give certain dishes a more intense red colour. To make tomato purée, ripe fruits are chopped, strained, juiced and then concentrated through heat and vacuum drying. In Italy, tomato purée is available in five different concentrations. Most popular for everyday use in the kitchen is the double concentrate, which consists of at least 28 per cent dry matter.

The first tomatoes in Italy, which came from South America, were round and yellow. Hence the Italian pomodoro, or 'golden apple'.

Due to its crisp, sweet flavour, the egg-shaped Roma tomato is also called the 'praline of tomatoes'.

These small, sweet vine fruits are sold as cherry tomatoes.

Pine Kernels

Pine kernels, which are the seeds of large pine cones, are a popular ingredient in salads, pastas and meat dishes. They have a sweet, nutty flavour that is somewhat reminiscent of almonds, and a delicate bite. When pine kernels are roasted, their taste intensifies. With their high fat content (over 50 per cent), they can spoil quickly. Due to their short shelf life and complicated harvesting process – the kernels must be removed from hard, black shells – pine kernels are relatively expensive.

For connoisseurs, this is the tomato: the San Marzano, from the foot of Vesuvius, an old variety with protected designation of origin.

The ribbed, green-red Costoluto tomato of Sardinia has firm flesh and an intensely aromatic flavour.

The large, ribbed beef tomatoes have a lower acidity than their round cousins.

Vine-ripened tomatoes have a mildly sweet taste. They are harvested with stalk and calyx intact.

Pomodori ai pinoli
Tomatoes with Pine Kernels

750 g/1 lb 10 oz ripe tomatoes
30 g/1 oz pine kernels
1 white onion
1 garlic clove
2–3 Savoy cabbage leaves
3 tbsp olive oil
salt
freshly ground pepper

Peel and quarter the tomatoes, remove the seeds, and cut into small dice. Tip them into a strainer, salt generously and leave to drain for about half an hour.

Heat a non-stick frying pan and dry-roast the pine kernels until golden brown. Cut the onions into quarters and then into thin strips. Finely chop the garlic.

Bring a saucepan of lightly salted water to the boil and briefly blanch the cabbage leaves, then refresh in cold water and dry thoroughly.

Heat 2 tablespoons of the olive oil in a frying pan and sauté the onions and garlic until translucent. Add the tomatoes and briefly heat, then remove from the stove. Stir in the remaining olive oil, season with pepper and arrange on the cabbage leaves.

In Campania, this aromatic summer dish is often served with meat dishes, for example beef stew.

Aubergines

In the middle of the thirteenth century, Arabs cultivated the first aubergines on Sicily and in southern Italy, but several centuries passed before this fruit spread to all parts of the country. For a long time, consumption of this nightshade was thought to result in licentiousness and insanity.

Aubergines come in many shapes and colours: small, white and egg-shaped; round and yellow; or large, crooked and purple. This last variety is the most commonly grown. According to one saying, 'an aubergine without garlic is an aubergine without a soul'. Since the aubergine, in Italian *melanzane*, has relatively little flavour of its own, it needs herbs and spices – and lots of olive oil – for its taste to develop.

Due to the toxin solanine, found in many nightshade plants, aubergines cannot be eaten raw – they must be cooked, roasted, grilled or barbecued. Aubergines may also contain bitter compounds, and are therefore often cut into slices and salted before further preparation. The fluid that is drawn from the aubergine through this process carries away most of the bitterness.

Cut the aubergine lengthways into slices of equal thickness.

Fry the aubergine in hot olive oil on both sides until golden brown.

Melanzane alla parmigiana
Aubergine Parmesan

4 aubergines
1 large onion
125 ml/4 fl oz olive oil, plus extra for greasing
800 g/1 lb 12 oz canned peeled tomatoes
2 mozzarella balls, each 150 g/5 oz
1 handful basil
flour for coating
50 g/1¾ oz grated Parmesan
salt
freshly ground pepper

Cut the aubergines lengthways into thin slices, salt the slices and place in a strainer for 30 minutes to draw off water. Finely chop the onion. Heat 2 tablespoons of the olive oil and fry the onion until translucent. Add the tomatoes, including their juice. Season with salt and pepper and cook until thickened.

Preheat the oven to 200°C/390°F/gas mark 6 and grease a baking dish. Slice the mozzarella and cut the basil leaves into thin strips. Rinse the aubergine slices and pat dry with paper towels. Coat them in flour and fry on both sides in the remaining olive oil until golden brown. Then drain on paper towels.

In the dish, layer aubergine slices, tomato sauce, basil and mozzarella, with tomato sauce as the topmost layer. Sprinkle the Parmesan on top and bake 30 to 40 minutes. Serve hot or cold.

Then leave the fried aubergine to drain on paper towels.

Melanzane ripiene
Stuffed Aubergine

4 aubergines
1 onion, finely chopped
3 garlic cloves, finely chopped
2 tbsp finely chopped parsley
75 g/2½ oz stoned olives, finely chopped
250 g/9 oz minced beef
1 egg
2 beef tomatoes
125 ml/4 fl oz olive oil
salt
freshly ground pepper

Preheat the oven to 175°C/350°F/gas mark 4. Wash the aubergines and halve them lengthways. Use a spoon to remove the flesh, leaving a shell about 1 cm/½ inch thick.

Mix the scooped-out aubergine, onion, garlic, parsley and olives into the minced beef. Knead the egg thoroughly into the beef mixture, season with salt and pepper, and fill the aubergine shells. Place the filled aubergines side by side in a baking dish.

Peel and halve the tomatoes, cut them into strips and lay them on top of the aubergines. Pour the olive oil over the aubergines slowly, so that it is absorbed right away. Bake for about 30 minutes.

Place all the ingredients for the aubergine rolls within arm's length in the work area.

Involtini di melanzane
Aubergine Roulades

2 large aubergines
125 ml/4 fl oz olive oil
2 garlic cloves, finely chopped
400 g/14 oz canned crushed tomatoes
1 small handful basil, cut into thin strips
300 g/11 oz buffalo mozzarella, sliced
1 tbsp dried oregano
1–2 tbsp red wine vinegar
salt
freshly ground pepper

Cut the aubergines lengthways into slices about 1 cm/½ thick, salt the slices and leave them in a strainer for 30 minutes to draw off water.

Heat 3 tablespoons of the olive oil and sauté the garlic. Add the crushed tomatoes, season with the basil, salt and pepper, and simmer on low heat for 15 minutes.

Rinse the aubergine slices, pat them dry with paper towels and fry on both sides in the remaining olive oil until golden brown. Remove and drain on paper towels.

Spread out the aubergine slices on a work surface. Top each with mozzarella and sprinkle with oregano. Roll the slices into roulades and secure with cocktail sticks. Place them in a flat baking dish and sprinkle with the vinegar. Spread the tomato sauce on top. Leave it to stand for several hours before serving.

This dish is often served hot, as well. For this version, cook the roulades in the tomato sauce in an oven preheated to 175°C/350°F/gas mark 4 for 20 to 25 minutes.

Aubergines come in many shapes and colours. The most common variety is long and purple.

When cut, the white aubergine quickly turns brown. To prevent this, sprinkle slices with lemon juice.

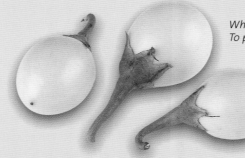

The skin of the small, white, round aubergine contains no pigment, so the white flesh shimmers through.

Small, slender purple aubergines have more flavour than the thicker varieties because they contain less water.

In southern Italy, long and thin aubergines with a firmer flesh are preferred.

The large and delicious fruit of the heavy-bearing Italian variety 'Listada de Gandia' has white and purple stripes.

Lazio

LAZIO

The good domestic cooking traditions of Lazio (*Latium* in Italian), of which Rome is the capital, reach back into antiquity. Even today, the gastronomy of this region is still hearty and well seasoned. The guiding principle of using as much as possible of every product has also remained intact into our time. Vegetables and meats are prepared according to simple recipes. Chicken giblets, oxtail ragout, beef tripe and pig's cheeks are typical specialities of this region's kitchens. The predilection of Rome's inhabitants – actually, of people throughout Lazio – for heavy pasta dishes such as *bucatini all'amatriciana* and *spaghetti alla carbonara* is legendary.

The variety of local crops is immense, and vegetables play a special role in regional cooking. A short stroll through the Roman market *Campo dei fiori* reveals the colourful multitude of local produce: myriad types of cabbage, tomatoes, broad beans, onions and garlic are cultivated on a grand scale. Not to be forgotten is the popular artichoke 'carciofo romanesco,' the only Italian artichoke variety protected by European Union statute, and the 'puntarelle' chicory, which grows only in Lazio. In no other region of Italy is the influence of Jewish culinary tradition so apparent, evidenced by the many vegetable dishes prepared *alla giudia* ('Jewish style').

Carciofi alla giudia
Jewish-style Artichokes

8 young globe artichokes
oil for deep-frying
2 lemons

Remove the hard outer leaves from the artichokes. Trim the upper halves of the tender inner leaves so they taper to a point, giving the artichokes a shape like that of a lemon. Shorten the stalks to 2 cm/³/₄ inch and peel them.

Heat oil to 175°C/350°F and deep-fry the artichokes for 8 to 10 minutes, then remove from the oil and drain on paper towels. Cut the lemons into eighths and serve with the artichokes.

Many traditional villas and lovely villages dot the magnificent landscape of Lazio.

Onions

The onion has been a popular seasoning and healing agent for four millennia. Originating in the Middle East, this robust plant was first introduced to Europe through Italy. Although it was already prized in antiquity for its medicinal qualities, its culinary breakthrough did not occur until the Middle Ages. Ever since then, this pungent, seven-skinned vegetable has been a firm part of almost all of the world's cuisines, whether raw, steamed or fried.

The most popular kind is the common, garden-variety, brown-skinned yellow onion, which has a pleasantly sharp flavour. Its larger relative, the Bermuda onion, can weigh as much as a pound and is ideal for stuffing. Pearl onions, small and white, are usually pickled, although they are also suitable for cooking. The shallot is the finest and mildest variety of onion. Spring onions, also called salad onions or scallions, are usually sold in a bunch, and together with their long green leaves are often used in salads and light vegetable dishes.

The most famous Italian variety is the red onion from Tropea, which grows along the Calabrian coast between Capo Vaticano and Vibo Valentina. The area in which it is cultivated includes a total of twenty-one communities. The protected geographical indication (PGI) *Cipolla Rossa di Tropea Calabria* applies to three forms of this mild onion:

- *Tonda piatta*, the large, sweet, delicate, white early crop.
- *Mezza campana*, harvested later in the season but just as delicate; sweet violet-red onions.
- *Allungata*, the mild, crunchy late crop, which can be stored and is also sold in beautiful plaits.

Artichokes

Since antiquity, artichokes of all shapes and shades have been a key food item around the Mediterranean Sea. In ancient Rome, they were a highly sought-after and expensive commodity, and along with asparagus were considered one of the most elegant vegetables. The Etruscans were supposedly the first to cultivate artichokes on a large scale, as the tomb murals in Etruria testify. After the collapse of the Roman Empire, this edible thistle with its delectable blossoms was almost forgotten. Rediscovered during the Renaissance, it triumphantly made its way into France, as well.

But artichokes are not only popular because of their refined, delicately bitter taste, which is somewhat reminiscent of celery and hazelnuts. Their leaves also contain the active ingredient cynarin, which both stimulates and protects the liver and gall bladder. 'He who takes to bed after bad food cures himself with the artichoke', reported a visitor to Naples in the sixteenth century, long before the medicinal properties of this vegetable were scientifically proven.

One can see the relationship between the artichoke and the thistle in the hard leaf tips and the hairy choke covering the heart in its centre.

Carciofi in fricassea
Artichoke Fricassee

8 young globe artichokes
juice of 1 lemon
1 garlic clove
75 ml/2½ fl oz olive oil
1 tbsp finely chopped parsley
125 ml/4 fl oz white wine
2 egg yolks
60 ml/2 fl oz grated Parmesan
salt
freshly ground pepper

Trim the artichokes, shorten the stalks to about 6 cm/2½ inches and peel them. Remove the tough outer leaves and the hard thorns on the remaining leaves. Combine the lemon juice and some water in a bowl. Slice the artichokes lengthways and immediately place them in the bowl of lemon water.

Peel and finely slice the garlic. Drain the artichokes and pat them dry.

Heat the olive oil in a frying pan and briefly cook the artichokes. Add the garlic and parsley. Season with salt and pepper and add the white wine. Cover the pan and steam on low heat for 15 to 20 minutes.

Whisk the egg yolks with 1 tablespoon of water and the Parmesan. Remove the artichokes from the stove, stir in the egg mixture and serve immediately.

Carciofi ripieni
Stuffed Artichokes

4 globe artichokes
juice of 1 lemon
salt

For the filling:
2 avocados
100 ml/3½ fl oz double cream
50 g/1¾ oz mascarpone
150 g/5 oz Milan salami, cubed
1 tbsp lemon juice
2 tbsp grated Parmesan
1 tsp ground green pepper
salt
freshly ground black pepper

Cut off the top 1.5 cm/½ inch of each artichoke. Carefully break off the stalks and sprinkle the exposed areas with lemon juice to prevent them browning. Use scissors to cut the tips off the remaining leaves.

Bring a saucepan of lightly salted water to the boil. Add the remaining lemon juice and artichokes and cook for 20 minutes. Then transfer the artichokes to a strainer and leave to drain. When they are cool, pluck the inner, brighter leaves and scrape out the choke with a spoon.

To make the filling, halve the avocados, remove the stones and place the flesh in a bowl. Mash the avocado flesh with the cream and mascarpone, then stir in all the remaining ingredients except the ground green pepper.

Stuff the hollowed-out artichokes with the filling and sprinkle with green pepper before serving.

Insalata di carciofi
Artichoke Salad

8 small, young globe artichokes
6 tbsp olive oil
1 garlic clove
2 tbsp white wine vinegar
juice of 1 lemon
salt
coarsely ground pepper

Remove the hard, outer leaves of the artichokes to expose the hearts. Shorten and peel the stalks and quarter the hearts lengthways.

Heat half of the olive oil and the garlic in a frying pan. On medium heat, fry the artichoke hearts on all sides. Pour off the oil, remove the garlic from the pan and deglaze with the vinegar. Transfer the artichoke hearts to a bowl and toss them with the lemon juice, some salt and the remaining olive oil. Sprinkle with pepper and serve.

Cardoon

On the outside, cardoon (also called cardoni) resembles overgrown celery, while its prickly flowers are reminiscent of thistles. But in terms of taste, this vegetable has a flavour that is a mix of artichokes and asparagus. The only parts of the plant that are eaten are the blanched, fleshy petioles, or leafstalks. Apart from the original barbed variety, new varieties without thorns are now cultivated; these are easier to handle, but they are less flavourful. Traditionally, cardoon is dug up after the first frost, roots and all, and is stored in a cellar, where it turns white within two to three weeks. In commercial cultivation, the branches of the mature plants, which can grow to 1.5 metres (5 ft) long, are tied together in the second half of October. They are then wrapped in dark plastic, which causes the leaves to lose their colour. After three weeks, the plastic is removed, the leaves are cut, any thorns are removed and the pale stalks are sold at market.

Cardi alla parmigiana
Cardoon Parmesan

1 kg/2 lb 4 oz cardoon
3 tbsp lemon juice
75 g/2½ oz butter, plus extra for greasing
125 ml/4 fl oz chicken stock
salt, freshly ground pepper
freshly ground nutmeg
100 g/3½ oz grated Parmesan
5 tbsp breadcrumbs

To prepare the cardoon, remove the thickest stalks and leaves. Separate the stalks and cut into 5–6-cm/2–2½-inch pieces. Mix the lemon juice and water in a bowl and immediately place the cut cardoon in the lemon water to prevent them browning.

Preheat the oven to 230°C/450°F/gas mark 8 and grease a baking dish. Bring a saucepan of salted water to the boil and cook the cardoon for 10 minutes, or just al dente. Remove from the water and drain. Melt 4 tablespoons of the butter in a frying pan and add the cardoon. Pour in the chicken stock, season with salt, pepper and nutmeg, and simmer for 5 minutes.

Alternate layers of cardoon with Parmesan and breadcrumbs in the baking dish until all the ingredients have been used, ending with Parmesan and breadcrumbs. Dot the remaining butter on top and bake for about 15 minutes, or until golden brown.

Favourite Vegetable Dishes

Broccoli strascinati
Broccoli with Anchovy Sauce

1 kg/2 lb 4 oz broccoli
4 anchovy fillets in oil
100 ml/3½ fl oz olive oil
salt
freshly ground pepper

Clean the broccoli and separate it into small florets. Peel the stalks, halve or quarter them according to their thickness and slice finely.

Bring a saucepan of salted water to the boil and cook the stalks for about 10 minutes, then add the florets and simmer for another 8 to 10 minutes.

Rinse the anchovies in cold, flowing water, then pat them dry and chop finely.

Heat the olive oil in a deep frying pan. Add the anchovies and mash them into a paste. Drain the broccoli well, then combine with the anchovy sauce. Season with pepper and serve hot.

Carote al Marsala
Carrots with Marsala

500 g/1 lb 2 oz carrots
1 white onion
2 tbsp olive oil
1 tsp soft brown sugar
4 tbsp Marsala
2 tbsp pine kernels
salt
freshly ground pepper

Peel and slice the carrots. Peel the onion and dice it. Heat the olive oil in a saucepan and fry the onion. Add the carrots and cook lightly, then sprinkle with the sugar, turn the heat on high and caramelize the vegetables. Add 100 ml/3½ fl oz water and season with salt and pepper. Over low heat, cook the carrots for an additional 10 minutes until the water has evaporated. Pour the Marsala over the vegetables and reduce once again.

Heat a frying pan and dry-roast the pine kernels until golden brown. Before serving, sprinkle them over the carrots.

Favourite Vegetable Dishes from the Oven

Cavolini di Bruxelles alla panna
Scalloped Brussels Sprouts

1 kg/2 lb 4 oz Brussels sprouts
4 tbsp butter, plus extra for greasing
1 onion, finely chopped
1 garlic clove, finely chopped
250 ml/9 fl oz vegetable stock
2 eggs
250 ml/9 fl oz double cream
60 g/2 oz grated Parmesan
salt
freshly ground pepper
freshly grated nutmeg

Preheat the oven to 175°C/350°F/gas mark 4 and grease a baking dish with butter. Trim the Brussels sprouts. Melt half the butter in a saucepan and sauté the onions and garlic until the onions are translucent. Add the Brussels sprouts, season with salt, pepper and nutmeg, and pour on the stock. Cover the pan and simmer on medium heat for 15 minutes.

Pour the Brussels sprouts and cooking liquid into the baking dish. Whisk the eggs and cream together and pour over the Brussels sprouts. Sprinkle with the Parmesan and dot with the remaining butter. Bake for about 20 minutes.

Finocchi gratinati
Fennel Gratin

4 fennel bulbs
1 tbsp lemon juice
2 tbsp butter, plus extra for greasing
2 tbsp flour
500 ml/18 fl oz warm milk
100 ml/3½ fl oz double cream
2 tbsp white wine
125 g/4½ oz grated fontina cheese
50 g/1¾ oz pine kernels
salt
freshly ground pepper
freshly grated nutmeg

Remove the fennel greens and set aside. Slice the bulbs about 5 mm/¼ inch thick and blanch in boiling salted water, with the lemon juice, for 3 minutes. Remove the fennel with a slotted spoon and refresh in cold water, then drain. Preheat the oven to 175°C/350°F/gas mark 4 and grease a baking dish with butter.

In a heavy saucepan, melt the butter, stir in the flour and cook briefly. While stirring continuously, add the warm milk and cream and leave the sauce to thicken. Blend in the white wine and season to taste with salt, pepper and nutmeg.

Lay the fennel slices in the baking dish. Pour the sauce over the fennel and sprinkle the cheese on top. Bake for about 25 minutes or until golden brown. Heat a frying pan and dry-roast the pine kernels until golden brown. Finely chop the fennel greens. Before serving, sprinkle the greens and roasted pine kernels over the gratin.

Peperoni ripieni
Stuffed Peppers

2 red peppers
2 yellow peppers
7 anchovy fillets in oil
4 tomatoes
75 ml/2½ fl oz olive oil,
plus extra for greasing
1 white onion, finely chopped
2 tbsp finely chopped parsley
2 tbsp grated Parmesan
2 tbsp breadcrumbs
salt
freshly ground pepper

Wash the peppers, halve them lengthways, and remove the cores. Rinse the anchovies under cold water, pat dry, then chop them finely. Peel and quarter the tomatoes, remove the seeds, and cut into dice. Preheat the oven to 230°C/450°F/gas mark 8 and grease a baking dish with olive oil.

Heat 2 tablespoons of the olive oil and fry the anchovies and onion. Tip them into a bowl and mix with the tomatoes, parsley, Parmesan and breadcrumbs. Season the mixture with salt and pepper, then fill the pepper halves with it.

Place the stuffed peppers side by side in the baking dish. Cover it with aluminium foil and bake for 15 minutes. Remove the foil, sprinkle the peppers with the remaining olive oil and bake for another 10 to 15 minutes. Serve hot or cold.

Wash the beetroots, pat dry and wrap individually in aluminium foil.

After baking, unwrap the beetroots and leave them to cool slightly.

Barbabietole al forno
Baked Red Beetroots
with Balsamic Vinaigrette

500 g/1 lb 2 oz red beetroots
2 tbsp balsamic vinegar
1 tsp mustard
5 tbsp olive oil
salt and pepper
1 small handful fresh mint

Preheat the oven to 200°C/390°F/gas mark 6. Wash and dry the beetroots and wrap each one individually in aluminium foil. Place them on a baking tray and bake 40 to 60 minutes, depending on their size.

When done, remove the beetroots from the foil, cool, then peel. Beetroots stain skin dramatically, so kitchen gloves are recommended. Slice the beetroots and arrange them on a serving platter.

Whisk the vinegar, mustard and olive oil together, season with salt and pepper, and pour over the beetroots. Wash the mint, pat dry and pluck the leaves. Cut them into narrow strips and sprinkle over the beetroots.

Squash and Courgette

With over 800 varieties, the squash exemplifies nature's diversity. Even in antiquity, it was more than simply food: because of the nutrients it contains, it was used in ancient medicine. Dried and hollowed, squash served as containers for water or wine, while smaller ones served to contain salt. Renaissance chefs stuffed large squash with poultry, served them with capon or filled the delicate flowers with forcemeat.

The squash was also a popular motif in the verbal and visual arts. In 1543, Florentine writer Francesco Doni composed his famous satirical work *La zucca* ('The Pumpkin'). In addition to many recipes, it contained numerous anecdotes about pumpkin and squash. And towards the end of the sixteenth century, Italian painter Giuseppe Arcimboldo executed a curious portrait of Emperor Rudolf II as the ancient god Vertumnis, constructing his likeness entirely out of fruits, flowers, grains, vegetables and a gourd. Despite the composition, this 'portrait' bore an eerie resemblance to its subject.

Zucca gialla in agrodolce
Sweet-and-sour Pumpkin

750 g/1 lb 10 oz pumpkin flesh
1 garlic clove
125 ml/4 fl oz olive oil
1 cinnamon stick
2 cloves
1 tbsp brown sugar
200 ml/7 fl oz mild white wine vinegar
10 basil leaves
salt
freshly ground pepper

Cut the pumpkin into bite-sized pieces. Peel and finely chop the garlic.

Heat the olive oil in a deep frying pan. Add the pumpkin and garlic and sauté. Season with salt and pepper, then add the cinnamon stick and cloves. Cook on low heat, stirring occasionally, for 30 minutes; the pumpkin should still be firm to the bite.

When the pumpkin has cooked, remove the cinnamon and cloves from the pan. Season to taste with the sugar and vinegar. Cut the basil into fine strips and blend in. Serve hot or cold.

Zucca gialla in agrodolce

Zucca al forno con patate
Baked Pumpkin with Potatoes

500 g/1 lb 2 oz pumpkin flesh
1 onion
5 potatoes
5 tomatoes
1 tbsp chopped thyme leaves
3 tbsp olive oil, plus extra for greasing
100 g/3½ oz mozzarella
salt
freshly ground pepper

Preheat the oven to 180°C/360°F/gas mark 4 and grease a baking dish. Cut the pumpkin into slices 5 mm/¼ inch thick. Peel the onion and potatoes. Slice the onion into rings and slice the potatoes very finely. Peel and quarter the tomatoes, remove the seeds and cut the flesh into dice.

In the baking dish, alternate layers of pumpkin, onion and potatoes. Season with salt and pepper, sprinkle with the thyme and top off with the tomatoes. Drizzle on the olive oil and bake for about 45 minutes.

Slice the mozzarella and place it on the casserole. Bake another 15 minutes.

The gourd family are among humanity's oldest food plants. The number of different varieties is astonishing, ranging from pumpkins through winter squash to courgette and rondini.

Zucchine fritte
Deep-fried Courgette

4 courgettes
150 g/5 oz flour
200 ml/7 fl oz white wine
1 egg, separated
chilli powder to taste
salt
olive oil for deep-frying
2 lemons

Thinly slice the courgettes lengthways. Combine the flour, wine and egg yolk to make a batter. Season with chilli powder and salt, and set it aside to rest for 20 minutes.

Heat olive oil to 175°C/350°F in a deep-fryer and fry the courgette slices, in portions, until golden yellow. Lay on paper towels to drain and cool.

Beat the egg white until stiff and fold it into the batter. Coat the courgette slices one by one in the batter and deep-fry until golden brown, again draining on paper towels afterwards. Cut the lemons into eight wedges. Serve the courgette garnished with lemons.

Before filling, remove pistils from the courgette blossoms.

Take the blossoms in hand and gently fill them with the veal stuffing.

Close the blossoms and twist the tips of the petals together.

Fiori di zucca ripieni
Stuffed Courgette Blossoms

200 g/7 oz lean veal
100 g/3½ oz ricotta
1 tbsp grated Parmesan
1 egg yolk
1 tbsp finely chopped oregano
12 courgette blossoms
5 tbsp olive oil, plus extra for greasing
2 tbsp lemon juice
salt
freshly ground pepper

Preheat the oven to 200°C/390°F/gas mark 6 and grease a flat baking dish. Cut the veal into cubes and pass it through the fine plate of a meat mincer twice. Combine the meat with the ricotta, Parmesan and egg yolk and season with the oregano and salt and pepper. Transfer the mixture into a piping bag with a large nozzle.

Remove the pistils from the courgette blossoms. Squeeze the veal stuffing into the them, close the blossoms over it and twist the tips of the petals together.

Lay the stuffed courgette blossoms side by side in the baking dish. Drizzle the olive oil and lemon juice over the courgette blossoms, then bake for 15 to 20 minutes.

Chard and Spinach

Erbette, bietole (biete) and *coste* – these three names all describe the same vegetable, one that in northern Italy is preferred to spinach: chard. *Erbette* is young chard, whose small leaves still resemble those of the spinach plant; they are used frequently in soups and stuffings, but they also taste good raw in salads with wild herbs. *Bietole* or *biete* are the older, somewhat larger chard leaves in which the centre rib is already clearly pronounced. *Coste* are the largest leaves with very prominent centre ribs and stalks.

Both the centre ribs and stalks require a longer cooking time than the leaves, so they are finely chopped and added to the cooking pot before the rest. In Liguria, the stalks are also blanched, breaded and then fried in oil.

Another essential vegetable in the Italian kitchen is spinach. In the form of delicate leaf spinach, it is one of the first heralds of springtime, and in the summer it is not only cooked, but also delicious served raw in salads. In autumn and winter spinach has a coarser texture, but its flavour is all the more intense.

Unlike in northern European countries, where the leafy green is more often finely chopped and served as creamed spinach, Italians have a soft spot for leaf spinach that has been cooked just briefly. As spinach is very sensitive, it should only be cooked in its own juices to preserve as much of its valuable nutrients as possible.

Bietole alla genovese
Genoa-style Chard

1 kg/2 lb 4 oz baby chard
2 tbsp olive oil
5 anchovy fillets in oil, finely chopped
1 onion, finely chopped
2 garlic cloves, finely chopped
125 ml/4 fl oz white wine
50 g/1¾ oz pine kernels
salt
freshly ground pepper

Bring a saucepan of salted water to the boil and briefly blanch the chard, then refresh in cold water and drain.

Heat the olive oil in a frying pan and sauté the anchovies, onion and garlic. Deglaze with the white wine and add the chard. Stirring continuously, simmer on low heat for a few minutes, then season with salt and pepper.

Heat a non-stick frying pan and dry-roast the pine kernels until golden brown. Before serving, stir the pine kernels into the chard.

Catherine de' Medici and Spinach

It was Catherine de' Medici who put spinach – her favourite vegetable – on the culinary map. When she left her hometown of Florence in 1533 to marry Henry, Duke of Orléans, who later became the king of France, this healthy, green leafy vegetable suddenly became fashionable at the French court. Ever since then, Italian dishes that contain spinach or are served on a bed of spinach have been called *alla fiorentina*, regardless of whether the other ingredients are fish or *crespelle*, which are delicate filled crepes. The combination of spinach and ricotta, or baked pasta with spinach and cheese (for example, cannelloni or lasagne) are especially popular. In general, *alla fiorentina* simply refers to the typical cooking style of the Tuscan capital, namely straightforward and uncomplicated.

Spinaci al gorgonzola
Spinach in Gorgonzola Sauce

1 kg/2 lb 4 oz leaf spinach
4 tbsp butter
125 ml/4 fl oz milk
125 ml/4 fl oz white wine
125 g/4½ oz mild Gorgonzola
2 egg yolks
salt
freshly ground pepper
freshly grated nutmeg

Thoroughly wash the spinach, removing any wilted leaves and coarse stalks.

Melt half the butter in a large saucepan. Add the spinach while it is still dripping wet and wilt it. Season with salt, pepper and nutmeg and keep warm on low heat.

In a saucepan, simmer the milk and wine to reduce slightly. Crumble the Gorgonzola into the pan and melt it, stirring constantly. Remove from the stovetop. Whisk the egg yolk with a little of the sauce, then add it to the rest of sauce and fold in the spinach. Adjust the seasoning with salt and pepper.

Wash the spinach leaves and remove the coarse stalks.

Wilt the wet spinach in a deep saucepan.

Drain the spinach and press out any remaining water with your hands.

Tuscan Bean Traditions

In addition to their availability fresh, pulses are also sold – in fact, almost preferred – dried in Italy. But in no region are they so well loved as they are in Tuscany, and it is thus no coincidence that Italians from the other regions refer to Tuscans as *mangia fagioli*, or bean eaters. While people in other places used to gather potatoes in autumn to store for the winter, the Tuscans bought a year's supply of beans as soon as the harvest was over.

Pope Clement VII, who was born into the powerful Medici family, is credited with introducing the first beans to Florence in the sixteenth century; they made their way to Italy from the Americas by way of Spain. From their base here, they conquered the rest of Italy – first at magnificent banquets, and later on the tables of the poor as an inexpensive and nutritious meat substitute. Beans owe their success to the fact that they are not only tasty and versatile, but also very filling.

In the Tuscan kitchen, it is primarily the fresh or dried bean seeds that are used, especially those of the mild but delicious haricot bean. The perfect preparation of beans is still considered an art, and is it passed down from one generation of home cooks to the next. The beans must not be hard, but neither should they become too soft or burst. Aiming for this happy medium, they are cooked on low, constant heat, just under boiling point.

Fresh beans are traditionally dressed with nothing more than good olive oil, a little salt and pepper, and chopped onions. Also popular are *fagioli all'uccelletto* (literally, 'bird beans'). This name originated in a time when hunting – including of songbirds – was the privilege of the landed gentry. The poor farmers and peasants thus substituted beans for birds, which they prepared in exactly the same way: with tomatoes and sage, the typical herb used in roasting fowl.

Fagioli all'uccelletto
French Beans with Tomatoes

750 g/1 lb 10 oz green beans
4 shallots
2 garlic cloves
250 g/9 oz plum tomatoes
2 tbsp olive oil
250 ml/9 fl oz vegetable stock
several sprigs savory
salt
freshly ground pepper
2 tbsp finely chopped parsley

Trim the beans and cut them into bite-sized pieces. Peel and finely slice the shallots and garlic. Peel and quarter the tomatoes, remove the seeds, and chop into dice.

Heat the olive oil in a frying pan and fry the shallots and garlic. Add the beans and tomatoes and sauté briefly, stirring constantly. Deglaze with the vegetable stock, then add the savory and season with salt and pepper. Cook the beans for about 20 minutes; the beans should still be firm to the bite. Sprinkle with the chopped parsley before serving.

Piselli alla menta
Peas with Mint

1 kg/2 lb 4 oz fresh peas
1 white onion
2 garlic cloves
4 anchovy fillets in oil
1 handful fresh mint
3 tbsp olive oil
125 ml/4 fl oz vegetable stock
salt
sugar
freshly ground pepper

Remove the peas from their pods. Peel and finely dice the onion and garlic. Finely chop the anchovy fillets. Cut the mint leaves into narrow strips.

Heat the olive oil in a frying pan and fry the onion and garlic. Add the anchovies and continue cooking briefly, then add the peas, stock and a little salt. Cook the peas for 5 minutes until they are cooked but still firm to the bite, then remove from the stovetop.

Stir in the mint and season to taste with sugar and pepper.

Fagioli con peperoncini
Spicy Broad Beans

4 shallots
2 garlic cloves
2 fresh chillies
2 tomatoes
2 tbsp olive oil
250 ml/9 fl oz vegetable stock
400 g/14 oz fresh broad beans, shelled
2 sprigs savory
1 bay leaf
100 g/3½ oz pancetta, diced
1 tbsp finely chopped parsley
salt
freshly ground pepper

Peel, halve and finely slice the shallots and garlic. Halve the chillies lengthways, remove the seeds, and chop finely. Peel and quarter the tomatoes, remove the seeds, and chop into small dice.

Heat the olive oil in a frying pan and fry the shallots, garlic and chillies. Pour in the vegetable stock and bring to the boil. Add the beans, savory and bay leaf, cover the pan and simmer for about 30 minutes.

Remove the herbs, stir in the tomatoes and season to taste with salt and pepper.

In an ungreased frying pan, fry the pancetta until it is crisp. Stir the pancetta and parsley into the vegetables and serve.

Savory

Savory, or *santoreggia*, was known in antiquity for its taste as well as its healing properties. In addition, it was reputed to be an aphrodisiac. When cultivation was attempted, it went wild and spread throughout the eastern Mediterranean. When fresh, the herb has an intense, somewhat peppery flavour that develops fully when heated. It is often combined with garlic and rosemary, and apart from vegetable dishes, its aroma adds character to meat, especially lamb and mutton.

Cook the white beans with seasonings and chillies until soft.

Mix flour and cooled bean stock together into a smooth dough.

Stir the cooked beans and leeks into the dough.

Fry small portions of the dough in hot olive oil until golden brown.

Frittelle
Bean Cakes

100 g/3½ oz dried small haricot beans
1 bay leaf
1 garlic clove
1 dried red chilli
300 g/11 oz flour
1 leek
salt
freshly ground pepper
freshly grated nutmeg
olive oil for frying

Soak the beans overnight in enough water to cover them completely. The next day, pour off the water, put the beans in a large saucepan and add enough fresh water to cover them. Add the bay leaf, garlic and chilli, bring to the boil and cook until the beans are soft. Pour through a strainer, collecting the stock. Cool completely, then remove the spices.

Put the flour in a mixing bowl. Stir in a ladle full of cooled bean stock, then add just enough stock to give the dough a creamy consistency. Season with salt, pepper and nutmeg. Cover the dough and leave it to rest for about 30 minutes.

Wash the leek, halve it lengthways and cut into narrow strips. Stir the beans and leek strips into the dough.

Heat olive oil in a frying pan. Add spoonfuls of dough and fry on both sides into small, crisp patties. Drain the finished bean cakes on paper towels and keep hot until serving.

Chickpeas

The chickpea, also known as the garbanzo bean, or *Cicerum italicum*, was a dietary staple back in antiquity. It is a pea by name alone. The part of the plant that we eat is the hazelnut-sized dried seed. It has a lovely nutty flavour and retains its firm texture during cooking. Due to its high content of fat, protein, minerals and vitamins, it is among the most nutritious members of the numerous pulse family.

Pasta e ceci
Chickpeas and Pasta

200 g/7 oz dried chickpeas
1 tsp Bovril
1 onion, chopped
1 bay leaf
2 sprigs rosemary
200 g/7 oz ziti or macaroni
3 tbsp olive oil
1 fresh red chilli, finely chopped
2 garlic cloves, sliced
2 tbsp tomato purée
salt
freshly ground pepper
1 tbsp finely chopped parsley

Soak the chickpeas overnight in enough water to cover them completely. The next day, pour off the water, put the chickpeas in a large saucepan and add enough fresh water to cover them. Stir in the Bovril. Add the onion, bay leaf and rosemary, bring to the boil and simmer for 1 hour on low heat. Drain the chickpeas, collecting the cooking stock.

Bring a large saucepan of lightly salted water to the boil. Break the ziti into small pieces and cook al dente. Pour off the water and drain the pasta.

Heat the olive oil in a saucepan and sauté the chilli and garlic. Stir in the tomato purée and heat briefly. Pour 500 ml/18 fl oz of chickpea stock into the pan, then add the pasta and half of the chickpeas. Purée the remaining chickpeas and stir into the noodles. Steep a few minutes on low heat, then season to taste with salt and pepper. Before serving, sprinkle with the parsley.

BASILICATA

Between the Ionian and Tyrrhenian seas lies the Basilicata region, previously known as Lucania, which was already settled in prehistoric times. This small region only received its current name following World War II. In many parts of Italy, the *salsiccia* is still called *lucanica*, or Lucanian sausage, as its recipe dates from antiquity. Cicero and Apicius praised the delectable merits of this spicy sausage in no uncertain terms.

The simple, straightforward cuisine of Basilicata has maintained its traditional character into the modern era. Vegetables and pulses form the basis of many dishes, often served as a first course, either alone or in combination with pasta. Cheese, especially sheep's or goat's milk cheese, is a part of every meal, as is bread, which in many places is still baked in old, wood-fired ovens. Fresh herbs and chillies lend the peasant fare aroma and bite, but they are used judiciously. One local speciality is *lampascioni*, a type of wild onion that is served by itself or in combination with other vegetables.

Mountains and hills are typical of the landscape of Basilicata. Artificial lakes such as Lago Pietra del Pertusillo have developed into natural paradises over the years.

Peperoni ripieni con l'abbacchio
Meat-stuffed Peppers

4 green peppers
1 onion, finely chopped
2 garlic cloves, finely chopped
100 g/3½ oz cooked rice
400 g/14 oz minced beef
2 eggs
1 tbsp chopped fresh parsley
1 tsp dried oregano
500 g/1 lb 2 oz canned crushed tomatoes
salt
freshly ground pepper
olive oil for greasing

Preheat the oven to 230°C/450°F/gas mark 8. Grease a deep baking dish with olive oil. Wash the peppers, cut off the tops (complete with stalks) to form lids, and remove the seeds. Thoroughly combine the onion, garlic, rice, minced beef and eggs. Season with the parsley, oregano, salt and pepper. Fill each of the peppers with the meat mixture and top with a lid.

Place the stuffed peppers next to each other in the baking dish. Cover the dish with aluminium foil and bake for 15 minutes. Remove the foil and pour over the crushed tomatoes, then bake for 30 minutes longer. Season the sauce with salt and pepper. Serve hot, in the sauce.

To prepare the peppers, cut them in half and remove the seeds.

Sauté chopped onions and garlic in olive oil, then add parsley.

Thoroughly combine all the ingredients for the filling in a bowl.

Finally, fill the pepper halves with the rice and vegetable mixture.

Peperoni ripieni
Rice-stuffed Peppers

1 each: red, yellow, orange and purple pepper
4 tbsp olive oil, plus extra for greasing
1 onion, finely chopped
2 garlic cloves, finely chopped
2 tbsp finely chopped parsley
3 small tomatoes
100 g/3½ oz stoned black olives
100 g/3½ oz Gorgonzola
150 g/5 oz cooked rice
2 eggs
salt
freshly ground pepper

Preheat the oven to 200°C/390°F/gas mark 6 and grease a baking dish. Halve the peppers, including the stalks, and remove the seeds.

Heat 1 tablespoon of olive oil in a frying pan and sauté the onions and garlic. Remove from the stove, stir in the parsley and leave it to cool.

Peel and quarter the tomatoes, remove the seeds, and cut into dice. Chop the olives. Crumble the Gorgonzola and mix it with the rice, onion mixture, eggs and tomatoes. Season to taste with salt and pepper. Fill the pepper halves with rice mixture.

Place the filled peppers next to each other in the baking dish. Sprinkle with the remaining olive oil and bake for about 30 minutes.

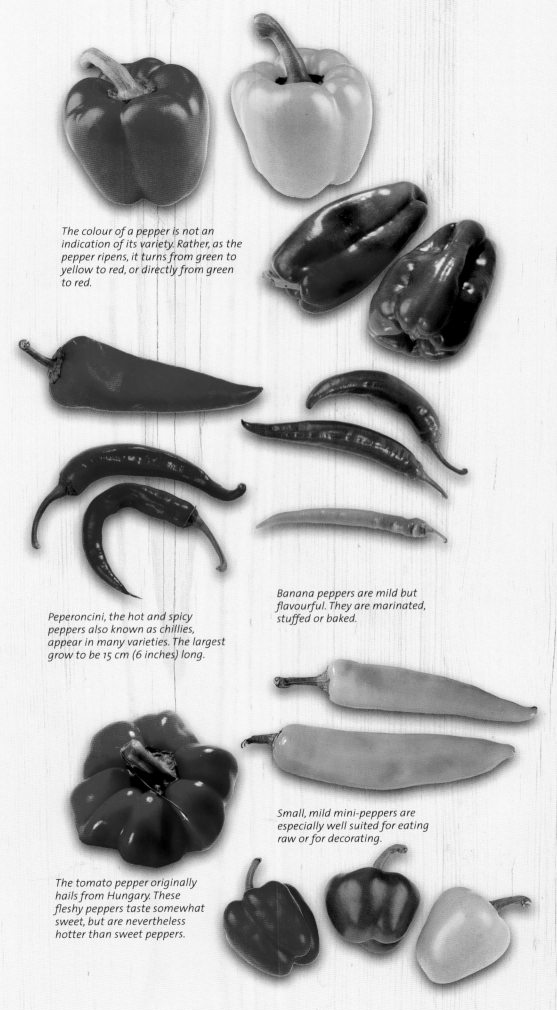

The colour of a pepper is not an indication of its variety. Rather, as the pepper ripens, it turns from green to yellow to red, or directly from green to red.

Peperoncini, the hot and spicy peppers also known as chillies, appear in many varieties. The largest grow to be 15 cm (6 inches) long.

Banana peppers are mild but flavourful. They are marinated, stuffed or baked.

Small, mild mini-peppers are especially well suited for eating raw or for decorating.

The tomato pepper originally hails from Hungary. These fleshy peppers taste somewhat sweet, but are nevertheless hotter than sweet peppers.

Asparagus

While the ancient Greeks used asparagus only for medicinal purposes, to purify the blood, the Romans recognized how tasty the delicate stalks are. Pliny described them as sheer flattery to the palate, and the most salubrious of all foods for the stomach. In ancient Rome, asparagus was a popular accompaniment to fish and other seafood. The first instructions for cultivating and harvesting asparagus were written by Cato the Elder, Roman statesman and general, in the second-century BCE and another Roman general – Lucullus – is reputed to have said, 'Only he who can prepare asparagus with no other ingredients, and bring it to the table in its most delightful perfection, is a true chef.'

In the course of their military campaigns, Roman soldiers brought asparagus with them to Germania, where it was grown in the milder regions along the shores of the rivers Rhine, Main and Danube. In 300 CE, this delicate vegetable was so popular in Rome that Emperor Diocletian considered it necessary to fix a ceiling for the price of asparagus. Demand continued to increase nevertheless, and asparagus soon had to be imported from the distant northern regions of Germania.

The collapse of the Roman Empire brought cultivation to a temporary halt, and it was not until the fifteenth century that courtly chefs rediscovered asparagus. Unfortunately, it remained a prohibitively expensive delicacy for several centuries.

Asparagi alla fiorentina
Asparagus Florentine

1.5 kg/3 lb 5 oz green asparagus
150 g/5 oz butter
4 eggs
salt
freshly ground pepper
60 g/2 oz Parmesan, finely shaved

Wash the asparagus, cut off the woody ends and trim all stalks to same length. Bring a saucepan of salted water to the boil and cook the asparagus on medium heat for about 15 minutes. The asparagus should be tender yet firm. Remove from the water and drain.

Melt 100 g/3½ oz of butter in a large frying pan and sauté the asparagus on low heat for a few minutes, carefully turning it several times.

In a second frying pan, fry the eggs on one side in the remaining butter. Place the eggs on a plate and arrange the asparagus on top. Season with salt and pepper and garnish with Parmesan shavings.

Asparagi al formaggio
Asparagus Gratin

1 kg/2 lb 4 oz green asparagus
1 pinch sugar
100 g/3½ oz fontina cheese, sliced
50 g/1¾ oz grated Parmesan
100 ml/3½ fl oz double cream
salt
freshly ground pepper
butter for greasing

Preheat the oven to 250°C/480°F/gas mark 9 and grease a baking dish with butter. Wash the asparagus and cut off the woody ends. Bring a saucepan of salted water to the boil, add a pinch of sugar and cook the asparagus for about 15 minutes until it is just barely firm to the bite.

Drain the asparagus and lay it in the baking dish. Cover with sliced fontina, sprinkle with the Parmesan and pour the cream over top. Bake for about 8 minutes. Sprinkle with some freshly ground pepper before serving.

Italians prefer green and purple asparagus, which have more flavour than the white variant. A very special delicacy is thin, wild asparagus (picture below left, on the right), which is only rarely found at markets.

Asparagi alla fiorentina

CAMPANIA

Long before the 'Mediterranean diet' became a synonym for healthy eating, its main ingredients – vegetables, olive oil, bread and pasta, fish and cheese – were staples of the Campanian cuisine. This is the birthplace of such simple, healthy and delicious dishes as *caprese* – the classic salad consisting of buffalo mozzarella, ripe tomatoes and fresh basil – the classic tomato sauce (as well as sauces made from other vegetables) and pizza, an inexpensive yet nutritious meal. For centuries, the people of this region were poor and had to subsist on what they could afford, which was primarily vegetables and dairy products. Meat and fish were served only on special occasions.

The opulent kitchens of the royalty, which during the Renaissance period produced lavish and expensive dishes inspired by the royal court of France, were an exception to this general rule. But the culinary inventiveness of people of modest means – resulting not least from a desire to emulate or equal the creations of the court kitchens – produced dishes that were so rich in colour and aroma, that their reputation as the original Mediterranean gastronomy transcended national borders.

Vegetables are still the cornerstone of Campania's cuisine. In the eighteenth century, the tomato joined the ranks of the classic vegetal varieties of the *agro campano* (Campanian fields), quickly becoming one of the most important ingredients in the region. Almost as important are cabbage and lettuce, which are also very popular here. This second predilection is the root of the nickname Italians use to identify the inhabitants of Campania: leaf eaters.

Positano is the pearl of the Amalfi coast. This former sailors' city was built in terraces on the steep cliffs of Monte Sant'Angelo al Tre Pizzi and Monte Commune.

For the sauce, first peel the tomatoes, remove the seeds and chop the flesh into cubes.

Sauté the onion, garlic and tomatoes in olive oil, then add the wine.

Involtini di cavolo verza
Stuffed Cabbage

750 g/1 lb 10 oz plum tomatoes
60 ml/2 fl oz olive oil
1 white onion, finely chopped
2 garlic cloves, finely chopped
125 ml/4 fl oz white wine
1 pinch sugar
8 large Savoy cabbage leaves
200 g/7 oz buffalo mozzarella
200 g/7 oz cooked rice
1 egg
2 tbsp finely chopped parsley
salt
freshly ground pepper

Briefly blanch the Savoy cabbage leaves in lightly salted water.

Remove the thick rib in the centre with a wedge-shaped cut.

Peel and quarter the tomatoes, remove the seeds, and cut into dice. Heat 3 tablespoons of the olive oil in a saucepan and sauté the onion and garlic. Add the tomatoes and wine, then season with the sugar and salt and pepper. Simmer on low heat for 20 minutes.

Bring a large saucepan of salted water to the boil and briefly blanch the cabbage leaves. Remove them with a slotted spoon, refresh in cold water and place in a strainer to drain. For the filling, finely dice the mozzarella and mix it with the rice, egg and parsley. Season to taste with salt and pepper.

Place a portion of the rice-mozzarella filling on the centre of each leaf.

Then fold the top part of the leaf over the filling.

Place the cabbage leaves on a work surface and place a spoonful of filling in the middle of each leaf. Fold over the edges, starting at the top, and roll into a bundle. If necessary, tie with kitchen string.

Next, fold the sides of the cabbage lead over the filling and roll it up.

Fry the roulades in olive oil and lay them in the tomato sauce.

Heat the remaining olive oil in a pan and briefly fry the roulades on both sides. Lay the roulades in the tomato sauce with the seams facing down. Cover the pan and stew about 40 minutes on low heat. If the sauce becomes too thick, add a little water or wine as needed.

Cavolo in umido
Stewed Savoy Cabbage

1 small Savoy cabbage
2 tbsp olive oil
1 tbsp butter
1 small onion, finely chopped
juice of 1 lemon
250 ml/9 fl oz vegetable stock
2 bay leaves
⅛ tsp ground allspice
salt
freshly ground pepper
freshly grated nutmeg

Clean the cabbage, cut it in quarters and remove the stalk with a wedge-shaped cut so that the leaves remain attached.

Heat the olive oil and butter in a large saucepan and sauté the onion. Add the cabbage quarters and briefly fry. Sprinkle with the lemon juice and pour the stock over the cabbage. Add the bay leaves and season with the allspice, salt, pepper and nutmeg. Cover the pot and braise the cabbage on medium heat for 25 to 30 minutes.

Herbs

Many food aficionados associate Italy with sun-drenched, southern landscapes awash in the seductive fragrances of rosemary, thyme and oregano.

And indeed, in addition to garlic, pepper and olive oil, fresh herbs provide the fundamental flavour of Italian cuisine. For almost every main ingredient, there is an appropriate herb, most of which grow wild in Italy. The herbs' glowing reputation and wide popularity are due not only to their beguiling aromas, but also to their qualities as gentle but effective and versatile natural remedies with proven healing properties.

Italians have always been more generous in their use of herbs than northern and central Europeans. In Italian cooking, herbs have a firm place in everyday food and are not reserved for special occasions. Parsley, whose taste harmonizes with many other spices, is the universal herb. Its aroma is powerful but its taste is not overbearing; finely chopped fresh parsley is used to add flavour to sauces, soups, eggs, vegetables, fish and meat.

Typical Mediterranean herbs include basil, oregano, bay leaves, rosemary and thyme. These aromatic plants have finally made their way into cuisine around the world, especially during the last century.

With a sharp knife, cut the radicchio in half from top to base.

Coat the halves in flour, then whisked eggs and finally in breadcrumbs.

Fry the breaded radicchio in olive oil, one portion at a time.

Salad Leaves

Salad leaves have a long tradition in Italian cuisine. They are not only enjoyed raw, however, but also as cooked vegetables. The leafy green *barba di frati* (literally, 'monk's beard'), a relative to chicory, is little known outside of Italy. Also known as buck's horn plantain or minutina in English, it is served raw or cooked. *Lattughe ripiene*, stuffed lettuce, is a popular dish in Liguria. To make it, blanched lettuce hearts are filled with a stuffing made with meat, sweetbreads and calf's brain and then cooked in meat stock. In Calabria, lettuce hearts are layered in a terrine with garlic, chopped chillies and olive oil, then weighted with a board and marinated for two days in the refrigerator. *Pizza di scarola* is a speciality from Campania made with blanched endives, pine kernels, raisins, anchovies and olives. In the Alto Adige, a potato casserole is prepared with strips of endive, raw ham and cheese. Grilled or fried radicchio served as a side dish with meat dishes is enjoyed in its home region of Veneto and further abroad as well.

Radicchio fritto
Fried Radicchio

300 g/11 oz radicchio di Trevisano
flour for coating
2 eggs, whisked
breadcrumbs for coating
oil for frying
salt
freshly ground pepper

Remove and discard the outer leaves of the radicchio. Rinse the heads, pat them dry and cut each in half from the top down.

Place the flour, whisked eggs and breadcrumbs on three separate deep plates. Coat the radicchio halves first in flour, then in egg and finally in breadcrumbs.

In a deep frying pan, heat oil and fry the radicchios until golden brown, one portion at a time. Drain on paper towels, then season with salt and pepper and serve while hot.

Italians prefer to buy their fruits and vegetables at one of the many markets that can be found in every city district. Shopping at the local markets also provides an opportunity to catch up on the neighbourhood gossip.

Indivia a crudo
Endive with Mint

1 large endive
3 tbsp olive oil
2 red onions, finely chopped
150 ml/5 fl oz double cream
1 tbsp finely chopped mint
salt
freshly ground pepper

Wash and trim the endive and drain thoroughly. Cut the leaves into broad strips.

Heat the olive oil in a deep frying pan and fry the onions. Add the endive strips and continue to cook for several minutes. Stir in the cream and leave it to thicken somewhat. Add the mint and season to taste with salt and pepper. Serve hot or cold.

Potatoes

In Italy, potatoes are not merely a filling side dish, but – like all other vegetables – are significant in their own right. The nutritious tubers are fried with aromatic herbs, or used as the main ingredient in casseroles and vegetable timbales. Especially in northern Italy, potatoes also make their way to the table in the form of gnocchi.

Spanish conquistadors 'discovered' the potato in the Andes in the sixteenth century. The Incas prepared dishes out of these tubers that greatly appealed to the Spaniards. Since at first sight the invaders thought that these new vegetables growing underground were truffles, they called the unknown food Incan *taratoufli*.

Timballo verde
Vegetable Timbale

600 g/1 lb 5 oz baking potatoes
500 g/1 lb 2 oz leaf spinach
1 tbsp olive oil
1 white onion, finely chopped
2 bunches parsley
4 eggs
100 ml/3½ fl oz double cream
100 g/3½ oz grated Parmesan
3 tbsp butter, plus extra for greasing
salt
freshly ground pepper
freshly grated nutmeg

Bring a large saucepan of salted water to the boil. Wash the potatoes and cook them, in their skins, for about 20 minutes.

Thoroughly wash the spinach, removing any wilted leaves and coarse stalks. Heat the olive oil in a frying pan and briefly sauté the onion, then add the dripping-wet spinach. Cover the pan and steam for 2 to 3 minutes. Pour off the water and drain the spinach. Peel and mash the potatoes while still hot.

Preheat the oven to 175°C/350°F/gas mark 4 and grease a round baking dish with butter. Wash the parsley, pat it dry and pluck the leaves. Purée the parsley and spinach with a hand-held mixer. Season with salt, pepper and nutmeg.

Whisk the eggs and cream together and stir into the mashed potatoes. Stir in the spinach purée and half of the Parmesan, and season again with salt and pepper.

Fill the baking dish with the potato-spinach mixture. Sprinkle the remaining Parmesan and dot the butter on top. Bake for about 25 minutes or until golden brown.

Peel the cooked potatoes and mash them while they are still hot.

Thoroughly wash the spinach, removing any wilted leaves or coarse stalks.

Purée the parsley and spinach with a hand-held mixer until smooth.

Stir the spinach purée, eggs and cream into the mashed potatoes.

Fill a round baking dish with the potato-spinach mixture and bake.

Patate al rosmarino
Rosemary Potatoes

750 g/1 lb 10 oz potatoes

3 garlic cloves

3 sprigs rosemary

75 ml/2½ fl oz olive oil,
plus extra for greasing

salt

freshly ground pepper

Wash and peel the potatoes and cut them into small cubes. Peel and roughly chop the garlic. Pluck the leaves from the rosemary and roughly chop them as well. Preheat the oven to 200°C/390°F/gas mark 6. Grease a flat baking dish with olive oil.

Place a layer of potatoes on the base of the baking dish. Season with some of the garlic and rosemary, salt and pepper. Repeat this procedure until all the ingredients have been used. Drizzle the olive oil over the top and bake for about 45 minutes, tossing the potatoes several times. Serve in the baking dish while hot.

EGG DISHES

While eggs are considered a breakfast food in many countries, Italians enjoy them in many different forms and at all meals. The basis of these popular dishes nowadays is fresh chicken eggs, but it was not always so. In earlier times, duck and turkey eggs were common ingredients in Italian kitchens.

The best-known egg-based dish is the *frittata*, an Italian take on the omelette. The word *omelette*, by the way, is supposedly derived from a combination of the Latin words *ovum* (egg) and *mellitus* (honey-sweet). And indeed, the Roman epicure Marcus Gavius Apicius wrote down the recipe for a sweet omelette that contains peaches, honey and nuts.

A classic *frittata* contains only eggs, salt and pepper, but there are countless variations made with such ingredients as fresh herbs, vegetables, pulses, salami, ham, fish, cheese and potatoes. Clearly, the *frittata* is very versatile. It can be served as an appetizer, a main course or an uncomplicated, inexpensive dish served between courses.

Picnics

Easter is not only an important religious occasion in Italy. it is also the beginning of a long series of festive, outdoor meals. On Easter Monday – also called *Pasquetta*, or 'little Easter' – families, friends and acquaintances traditionally join together and drive into the countryside for the first picnic of the year. Whether at the seashore, in olive groves or in parks, no choice picnic spot remains free on this day.

Throughout the entire summer and well into the autumn, many Italians spend their Sundays outdoors, usually equipped with folding chairs and tables, and often with a portable stove for cooking fresh pasta. Wherever possible, a barbecue is also set up. In addition to bread, fresh and pickled vegetables, sweet baked treats and a bottle of wine, no well-stocked picnic basket is complete without delicious egg dishes such as a *frittata*.

Anyone who doesn't have the time or inclination to cook on the weekends can visit one of the many delicatessens and *pasticcerie*, which are also open on Sundays. These businesses offer a rich variety of *panini* and *crostini* (breads with different toppings), snacks and cakes. Those who have no home barbecue can find roast chicken, pork or even complete meals at a *rosticceria*. Fresh bread or *grissini* straight from the oven, found at a *panetteria*, complete the perfect meal.

At many of the local markets, farmers from the surrounding countryside sell fresh chicken eggs.

Frittata con prezzemolo
Frittata with Parsley

| 1 bunch flat-leaf parsley |
| 6 eggs |
| 4 tbsp olive oil |
| salt |
| freshly ground pepper |

Rinse and pat dry the parsley, then roughly chop the leaves. Beat the eggs in a bowl with some salt and pepper until foamy, then blend in the parsley.

Heat the olive oil in a heavy frying pan until it starts to smoke. Pour in the eggs and smooth the surface with a wooden spatula. Reduce the heat to low and leave the eggs to thicken.

As soon as the frittata begins to brown on the underside, use a lid or plate to turn over the omelette carefully. Cook the other side until it is golden brown. Cut the frittata into 4 slices and serve while hot or warm.

The classic frittata is prepared with fresh eggs, parsley, salt and pepper.

Beat the eggs with salt and pepper until they are foamy, and then stir in parsley.

Heat olive oil in a frying pan and pour in the eggs.

Fry the omelette on both sides until golden brown.

ABRUZZO

The Gran Sasso Massif, reaching heights of almost 3,000 metres (10,000 ft), separates Abruzzo from its eastern neighbour, Lazio. Mountains have kept this region isolated from the rest of Italy for hundreds of years, helping to preserve traditions, customs and culinary secrets for just as long. For the local population, eating has always served one purpose above all: providing an opportunity for pleasant companionship. One tradition still maintained in some villages here is the *Panarde*, a feast that can have as many as fifty courses. Another ritual is the preparation of *Minestrone delle Virtù*, the soup of virtues. A symbol of the seven cardinal virtues, it is served during the May festivities and contains seven varieties of pulses, seven spring vegetables, seven types of meat and seven different pastas.

During the Roman era, saffron was already being cultivated on the Navelli Plateau – and it was already one of the most expensive spices available. Saffron not only flavoured elegant dishes, it also coloured food an attractive gold, and when ground, was used as pigment in paint. Even though the province of Aquila was a centre of saffron production into the sixteenth century, this spice did not play much of a role in the local peasant's kitchen. It was simply too expensive and was grown primarily for export. Every year in mid-August, Navelli hosts the *Sagra di Ceci e dello Zafferano*, a celebration of the locally grown chickpeas and saffron. For the duration of this festival, restaurants in the medieval town serve regional specialities such as gnocchetti with chickpeas and potato pancakes with saffron.

In the early morning hours, the blossoms of the Crocus sativus *are harvested by hand.*

Almost 2,000 blossoms are needed to make just one gram of saffron, which is extracted from the stigma.

The yellow-gold stigmas of the saffron plant are the source of the most expensive spice on earth.

Abruzzo

Frittata allo zafferano
Saffron Frittata

2 potatoes, cooked

1 tbsp butter

1 white onion, finely chopped

several saffron threads

50 ml/1½ fl oz hot milk

12 large basil leaves

6 eggs

2 tbsp grated Parmesan

4 tbsp olive oil

salt

freshly ground pepper

Peel the potatoes and put them through a potato ricer. Heat the butter in a frying pan and fry the onion. Remove the pan from the stovetop and add the contents to the potatoes. Soak the saffron in the hot milk, then stir into the potatoes as well.

Cut the basil leaves into narrow strips. In a bowl, whisk the eggs with salt and pepper until foamy, then add the Parmesan and basil and combine thoroughly with the potatoes.

Heat the olive oil in a heavy frying pan until it starts to smoke. Pour in the egg-potato mixture and smooth the surface with a wooden spatula. Reduce the heat to low and leave the eggs to thicken.

As soon as the frittata begins to brown on the underside, use a lid or plate to turn over the omelette carefully. Cook the other side until it is golden brown. Cut the frittata into 4 slices and serve while hot or warm.

The old Abruzzan village of Caramanico Terme is picturesquely situated on a rocky promontory between two valleys. Sulphuric springs feed the thermal baths, which have been in use since the Middle Ages.

Torta verde
Spinach Pie

*250 g/9 oz flour,
plus extra for dusting*

5 tbsp olive oil

1.5 kg/3 lb 5 oz leaf spinach

1 onion, finely chopped

1 garlic clove, finely chopped

5 eggs

100 g/3½ oz grated Parmesan

1 egg yolk

salt

freshly ground pepper

oil for greasing

Sift the flour on to a work surface and make a well in the centre. Put 2 tablespoons of olive oil, a pinch of salt and 2–4 tablespoons of water into the well and knead everything into a smooth, supple dough. Form the dough into a ball, cover it in clingfilm and chill for 30 minutes in the refrigerator.

Thoroughly wash the spinach, removing any wilted leaves and coarse stalks. Blanch it for a few minutes in boiling salted water. Pour off the hot water and refresh the spinach in cold water. Drain and finely chop the spinach.

Grease a 26-cm/10-inch springform cake tin and preheat the oven to 200°C/390°F/gas mark 6.

Heat the remaining olive oil and sauté the onion and garlic briefly. Add the spinach, season with salt and pepper, and sauté a few minutes longer, stirring constantly. Remove from the stovetop and leave to cool. Whisk the eggs, stir in the Parmesan and combine with the spinach.

On a floured surface, roll out the dough. Cut out two circles of dough the size of the springform tin. Lay one circle on the base of the tin and use scraps of dough to form a border up the side. Spread the spinach mixture over the base, smoothing the surface, and lay the second dough circle on top. Prick several holes in the top with a fork. Fold over the sides of the dough and press together firmly. Decorate with the remaining dough, if desired, and brush the surface with the egg yolk. Bake for about 1 hour. Serve hot or cold.

Wash the spinach and blanch it for a few minutes in boiling salted water.

Combine the blanched spinach with eggs and grated Parmesan.

Spread the spinach mixture evenly over the lower crust.

Cover with the second circle of dough and press the edges firmly together.

Erbazzone
Chard Pie

250 g/9 oz flour,
plus extra for dusting

50 g/1¾ oz butter, softened

3 tbsp olive oil, plus extra for greasing

750 g/1 lb 10 oz chard

75 g/2½ oz pancetta, diced

2 garlic cloves, finely chopped

2 tbsp finely chopped parsley

75 g/2½ oz grated pecorino

1 egg

salt

freshly ground pepper

Sift the flour on to a work surface and make a well in the centre. Put the butter (in small pieces), a pinch of salt and 1 tablespoon of olive oil into the well and knead everything into a smooth, supple dough, adding a little water if needed. Form the dough into a ball, cover it in clingfilm and chill for 1 hour in the refrigerator.

Trim the chard. Wash it thoroughly and blanch briefly in boiling salted water. Pour off the hot water and refresh the chard in cold water. Drain and finely chop the chard.

Grease a 26-cm/10-inch springform cake tin and preheat the oven to 200°C/390°F/gas mark 6.

Heat the remaining olive oil and fry half the pancetta. Add the garlic, chard and parsley and fry for several minutes, stirring constantly. Remove from the stovetop, season with salt and pepper, and leave to cool. Stir in the pecorino and the egg.

On a floured surface, roll out two thirds of the dough and line the springform tin with it. Spread the chard mixture over the base, smoothing the surface. Roll out the remaining dough to the size of the tin and place it on top. Fold over the sides of the dough and press together firmly. Sprinkle the remaining pancetta on top and bake for about 1 hour. Serve hot or cold.

Frittata di carciofi
Artichoke Frittata

6 artichoke hearts in oil
1 handful rocket
6 eggs
3 tbsp double cream
1 tbsp finely chopped parsley
2 tbsp olive oil
1 tbsp butter
1 onion, finely diced
1 garlic clove, finely diced
salt
freshly ground pepper

Drain and quarter the artichoke hearts. Thoroughly wash the rocket, removing any wilting leaves and coarse stalks, and chop the leaves.

Whisk the eggs and cream together, then season with salt and pepper and stir in the chopped parsley.

Heat the olive oil and butter in a non-stick frying pan. Fry the onion and garlic until the onion is translucent. Add the artichokes and cook briefly. Pour the egg-cream mixture over the artichokes and reduce the heat. As soon as the surface solidifies, use a lid or plate to turn over the frittata gently and cook the other side until golden brown.

Serve the frittata hot, or leave to cool and cut it into bite-sized pieces.

Crespelle Basic Recipe

3 eggs
150 g/5 oz flour
250 ml/9 fl oz milk
1 pinch salt
60 g/2 oz butter

Beat the eggs, then stir in the flour and milk to make a thin batter. Season with a pinch of salt. Leave the batter to rest for 30 minutes.

Melt a little butter in a non-stick frying pan and pour in one small ladle of batter. Swivel the pan to distribute the batter evenly. Fry the *crespelle* on both sides until golden brown, then set aside and keep hot. Repeat this procedure to make 8 *crespelle*.

Crespelle al prosciutto di Parma
Crespelle with Prosciutto

8 crespelle (see basic recipe)
3 tbsp olive oil, plus extra for greasing
1 small onion, finely chopped
1 garlic clove, finely chopped
400 g/14 oz canned chopped tomatoes
1 tbsp chopped basil
100 g/3½ oz prosciutto, finely sliced
50 g/1¾ oz grated Parmesan
salt
freshly ground pepper

Prepare the crespelle according to the basic recipe and cool slightly. Heat 2 tablespoons of the olive oil in a frying pan and sauté the onion and garlic until the onion is translucent, then add the tomatoes. Season with the basil, salt and pepper and simmer for 10 minutes. Preheat the oven to 225°C/435°F/gas mark 7 and grease a baking dish with olive oil.

Lay the prosciutto slices on the crespelle, roll them up and arrange side by side in the baking dish. Cover with the tomato sauce and sprinkle with the Parmesan and remaining olive oil. Bake for about 15 minutes.

Crespelle al forno
Crespelle Gratin

8 crespelle (see basic recipe)
300 g/11 oz assorted wild mushrooms
50 g/1¾ oz butter
1 small onion, finely chopped
100 g/3½ oz cooked ham,
cut into strips
2 tbsp chopped parsley
500 ml/18 fl oz béchamel sauce
100 g/3½ oz Gorgonzola, crumbled
salt
freshly ground pepper

Prepare the crespelle according to the basic recipe and cool slightly. Wash the mushrooms and cut into thin slices. Preheat the oven to 225°C/435°F/gas mark 7 and grease a baking dish with 1½ tablespoons of the butter.

Heat the remaining butter in a frying pan and sauté the onion until translucent, then add the ham and mushrooms. Stirring constantly, sauté for about 10 minutes until the liquid has thickened. Stir in the parsley and remove the pan from the stovetop.

Season the mushrooms with salt and pepper and place some on each crespelle. Roll them up and arrange side by side in the baking dish. Pour the béchamel sauce over the crespelle and sprinkle with crumbled Gorgonzola. Bake for about 15 minutes.

Truffles

The truffle is the uncrowned king of fungi. Right from the first taste of a fresh truffle, it is abundantly clear that this uncommon delicacy is worth its high price not only due to its rarity, but also because it is a culinary joy for both the nose and the palate.

In antiquity, the truffle was reputed to be an aphrodisiac, and the great composer Rossini dubbed it 'the Mozart among mushrooms'. But the truffle is also capricious: to this day, it has stubbornly resisted all attempts at cultivation.

When buying truffles, make sure they are clean and have no wormholes. Wrapped in a moist cloth, truffles can be stored in a tightly closed jar for three to four days without losing any of their flavour. Some people advocate storing truffles in rice, but this strips the succulent truffles of their moisture and aroma.

Frittata ai tartufi
Frittata with Black Truffles

2 small black truffles
5 eggs
3 tbsp double cream
1 pinch salt
2½ tbsp butter
2 tbsp finely chopped herbs, such as chervil, watercress or basil

Gently clean the truffles with a soft brush under warm running water. Dry, peel and finely slice them.

In a bowl, beat the eggs and cream and season with a pinch of salt. Melt the butter in a large frying pan. Add the truffle slices and, on low heat, gently shake the pan to move the truffles around the pan for several minutes. Then pour in the eggs, sprinkle with the herbs and stir briefly with a wooden spoon.

As soon as the surface solidifies, use a lid or plate to turn the frittata over gently and cook the other side until golden brown. Serve while hot.

White Truffles

Tuber magnatum pico – this is the botanical taxonomy of the best and most expensive of truffles, referred to colloquially as *tartufo bianco di Alba* (Alba truffle) or *tartufo bianco del Piemonte* (Piedmontese truffle). The name is misleading, however: this most delectable of truffles grows not only in Piedmontese Alba, but also in Emilia-Romagna, Marche, Umbria, Tuscany, Lazio and Abruzzo. It flourishes in symbiosis with oaks, chestnuts, poplars, willows and lime trees, growing under the ground at their base, and the type of tree determines the truffle's colour. Poplars and willows give the truffle a whitish hue, oaks light brown, and lime trees result in brown to reddish mushrooms. Regardless of the colour, the flesh is firm and compact and is traversed by many white veins. The harvest lasts from 1 October through 31 December. These truffles are always eaten raw, preferably fresh, cut with a specially designed truffle knife into paper-thin slices. Its incomparable aroma is best appreciated on thin, home-made noodles, in a frittata or risotto, or with a butter or cream sauce.

In Italy, dogs are used to sniff out truffles under the earth because hunting for truffles with pigs is illegal. The dogs, most of which are of the lagotto romagnolo *breed or mixed, are the pride and joy of truffle hunters.*

When sniffing out and finding truffles, dogs cause no damage to the root tips or the mycelia.

Another advantage: unlike pigs, the dogs do not eat the truffles they have located.

When the dogs detect a truffle, they bark and let their owner dig it out.

Expensive, black Norcia truffles are found primarily in the area around Norcia and Spoleto.

Formaggi

Cheeses

The moment when someone first noticed that curdled milk was in no way ruined, but could be used again, was surely one of the greatest moments in culinary history. According to legend, the first cheese maker was the shepherd Aristeus, son of the nymph Cyrene and the god Apollo. The fact is, cheese is one of the oldest and most versatile foodstuffs on earth, and the production of cheese is among humanity's oldest artisanal endeavours.

In the ancient world, cheese was a dietary staple. The Romans ate fresh and ripened cheeses made from the milk of cows, goats and sheep. They were the first to cultivate rennet cheese from milk that was thickened with the help of abomasum from young ruminants. Cheese was already mentioned in the Apicius, a collection of recipes dating from the Roman Empire. The Apicius includes a recipe for a sweet fresh cheese flavoured with honey, salt and pepper, oil and coriander. From Rome, the manufacture of cheese spread to every corner of the empire. During the Middle Ages, the art of cheese production was perfected by monks, especially the Cistercians and Benedictines.

From these early beginnings, the Italians' love of cheese has continued uninterrupted. Each region has its traditional specialities, many of which are still prepared according to the old recipes. Two types of cheese from the Campagna Romana, the plains surrounding Rome, were already being made during the Roman period: *pressato a mano* (literally, 'hand-pressed'), a soft sheep's milk cheese that is pressed and smoked over apple wood; and *cacio fiore*, a hard cheese also made from sheep's milk that is the ancestor of *Pecorino Romano*. Nowadays, the best-known varieties are DOP (*Denominazione d'Origine Protetta*), that is, certified according to the European Union's regulations controlling protected designations of origin. According to those regulations, foods bearing this label must be 'produced, processed and prepared within a particular geographical area, and with features and characteristics which must be due to the geographical area'. The seal is only granted to products that are made completely within the specified region. This rigid control also applies to all the raw materials – in this case, milk – necessary for production, and thereby recognizes the intense connection between the product and the region in which it originates.

Cheese and Wine

A ubiquitous culinary union at Italian tables is that of cheese and wine. Each cheese has its own history and particular taste qualities that must be taken into account when choosing the accompanying wine. The personal taste of each individual is also important, but there are certain criteria that help identify an ideal combination. The complexity of both should be emphasized without allowing one to overpower the

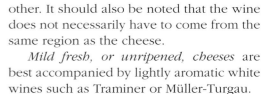

other. It should also be noted that the wine does not necessarily have to come from the same region as the cheese.

Mild fresh, or unripened, cheeses are best accompanied by lightly aromatic white wines such as Traminer or Müller-Turgau.

Briefly ripened firm or semi-soft cheeses made from raw milk harmonize well with structured white whines that have a higher alcohol content, or with rosés and young red wines with little tannin, which are served slightly chilled.

Hard, semi-fat and *full-fat cheeses of moderate ripeness* and made from pasteurized milk are ideally accompanied by a well-balanced red wine, full in body and with an accentuated bouquet.

Extensively aged hard cheeses are best enjoyed with tannin-rich red wines that have a high alcohol content.

Blue-veined and other piquant cheeses are the perfect accompaniment to fortified wines such as Marsala or to straw wines, for example Amarone.

Classification of Cheese

There are many methods for categorizing cheese. First of all, they can be distinguished according to the type of milk – cow, sheep, goat or buffalo – from which they were produced. Cheese is also frequently classified according to its fat content. Low fat cheese contains less than 20 per cent fat, semi-fat cheese 20 to 40 per cent, and full-fat cheese contains more than 42 per cent. Ripeness is also a criterion. Apart from fresh cheese, which is not aged at all and therefore does not keep long, there are medium-ripe *(mezzano)* and slow-ripened *(vecchio)* cheeses, often describing the same variety. Perhaps the best-known classification system is ordered according to water content. These groups are soft (containing more than 40 per cent water), semi-soft, semi-firm or semi-hard (these are equivalent), and hard cheeses.

*A selection of famous varieties
(from left to right):*
1. Parmigiano-Reggiano
2. Taleggio
3. Pecorino dolce
4. Fontina
5. Asiago
6. Pecorino spazzarello
7. Montasio
8. Marzolino
9. Pecorino misto
10. Pecorino Senese

Cheese Utensils

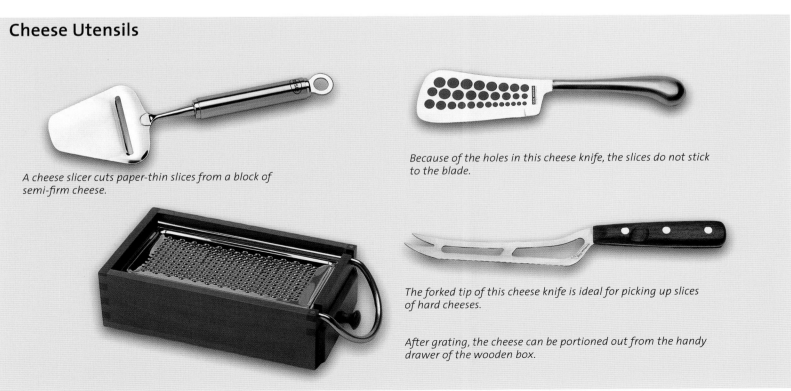

A cheese slicer cuts paper-thin slices from a block of semi-firm cheese.

Because of the holes in this cheese knife, the slices do not stick to the blade.

The forked tip of this cheese knife is ideal for picking up slices of hard cheeses.

After grating, the cheese can be portioned out from the handy drawer of the wooden box.

Favourite Cheeses

For hundreds of years, cheese was one of the most important parts of every meal in the Italian countryside, especially in poorer regions. Each district and almost every village had developed its own recipe and refined it over the course of time. In our era of globalization, there has been a marked return to the traditional cheeses.

Asiago
A traditional semi-hard cheese from Vicenza and Trento, formerly made with sheep's milk, but now with cow's milk. It has a yellow reddish rind and a ripening period of four months to two years. As the age increases, so do its hardness and aroma.

Bel Paese
The name Bel Paese means 'beautiful land'. This is a mild but aromatic semi-soft cheese from the region of Lombardy, and it is popular far beyond Italy's borders.

Pecorino 'foja de noce'
A type of cheese from the Marche region, the curd is wrapped in walnut leaves and left to ripen for several weeks. This process gives the cheese a special flavour.

Fontina
The most popular or most familiar cheese from the mountains of the Valle d'Aosta, it is semi-soft with a nutty flavour. It is an excellent melting cheese and is the basis for fonduta (cheese fondue).

Formaggio di fossa di Sogliano
A famous, flavourful sheep's milk cheese from the Sogliano area. It ripens in pits dug into the region's porous tuff, which are traditionally opened on 25 November, thus freeing the delicacy.

Caciotta
A semi-soft cheese made of unpasteurized sheep's milk and a little cow's milk that comes from Tuscany and Umbria. It has a subtle, floral aroma with hints of grass.

Caciocavallo
This is a pasta filata cheese, tied up in the shape of a gourd and ripened for at least six months. Its core is yellowish gold and it has a full, lightly sweet taste. It is also sold smoked.

Castelmagno
A traditional blue cheese from the Piedmont region. It is made with partially skimmed cow's milk with a little sheep's or goat's milk added, and aged in cellars for up to five months.

Gorgonzola piccante
One of the most famous Italian cheeses in the world, it is veined with greenish-blue mould. Its consistency is soft and creamy, its flavour sharp and savoury.

Gorgonzola dolce
The milder, spreadable version of Gorgonzola also comes from the city of the same name, and is made exclusively with cow's milk.

Bitto
An Alpine cheese from Valtellina, a region traversed by the river Bitto, is a spicy cow's milk cheese with a small proportion of goat's milk. This semi-hard cheese is sold young or aged.

Stracchino
This soft, spreadable cheese from the province of Bergamo has a soft, thin rind. Made from raw milk and without preservatives, it is intended to be consumed immediately.

Mascarpone
Mascarpone is made of aged cream that has been skimmed from milk during the cheese-making process. It has a wonderful, melting consistency and is the main ingredient of the well-loved dessert tiramisù.

Montasio
A speciality from the mountainous Friuli region, this is a small cow's milk cheese with a full aroma that tastes mild or sharp according to how long it is aged, and lends zest to the local dish frico.

Burrata
A delicacy from the region of Puglia, the outer shell of solid cheese hides a creamy interior imbued with pieces of mozzarella, all enveloped in lily leaves.

Mozzarella affumicata
When buffalo milk mozzarella is smoked, its consistency becomes drier and harder, it stays fresh longer, and it takes on a wonderfully spicy, lightly smoky taste.

Parmigiano-Reggiano
The most famous of Italian cheeses, which is prized throughout the world. A hard cheese originating in the Emilia-Romagna region, it is sold in varying degrees of ripeness.

Pecorino Romano
Pecorino Romano is made exclusively with sheep's milk. After ripening for five months it is enjoyed as a table cheese, and after eight months it is grated, giving dishes an inimitable flavour.

Mozzarella di bufala
Authentic buffalo mozzarella is produced in Campania from the milk of the water buffalo. It has an elastic texture and a pleasantly sour taste.

Provolone
A spicy pasta filata cheese from Campania with a long tradition, it is made with cow's milk and allowed to ripen for several months. The colour of the rind depends on the age.

Quartirolo
A young, square cow's milk cheese from Lombardy with a soft, thin rind, a lightly crumbly texture and a tart flavour.

Pecorino sardo
A semi-hard sheep's milk cheese with a less pronounced flavour, in riper forms it has a soft consistency beneath its hard rind, which is lightly boiled.

Pecorino Toscano
This cheese is produced in various parts of Tuscany from sheep's milk. It is sold at varying degrees of ripeness and is made with pure vegetable rennet.

Ricotta di pecora
This fresh cheese made with unsalted sheep's whey comes from Campania, and is enriched with milk or cream.

Ricotta stagionata
A Sardinian cheese made of sheep's whey, its practically liquid body develops a pleasantly sweet taste. It is usually eaten fresh.

Ragusano
A Sicilian cow's milk cheese sold in cubes, its rind is at first light yellow, but the colour darkens during the ageing process.

Scamorza
A southern Italian pasta filata cheese made from cow's milk, which is only briefly ripened and has a mild flavour and a soft texture. It is sold in its natural state or smoked.

Taleggio
This is a soft cheese from the Taleggio Valley in the Bergamo province. It has a soft, thin, light pink rind, a straw-coloured body and is aged for at least 35 days.

Tomino del boscaiolo
A Piedmontese fresh cheese made of whole cow's milk. It is roasted in a frying pan or grill, but the thin rind prevents the melting cheese running out.

Emilia-Romagna

Emilia-Romagna is a land of plenty for gourmets. This region actually consists of two parts: in the west is Emilia with its broad plains, and in the east Romagna, which stretches along the Adriatic coast. The famous university city of Bologna is situated in the middle, and is renowned as the birthplace of such things as tortellini and mortadella. Modena is also known for *zampone*, or stuffed pig's trotters, and its *aceto balsamico* is prized worldwide.

Simple, flavourful dishes made with excellent local produce typify the regional cuisine, whose landmark recipe is stuffed pasta: the saying that the inhabitants would wrap all their worldly possessions in pasta dough if they only could is not completely off the mark. Every town and city has its own distinctive specialities that have become classics of the Italian kitchen. Among the gastronomic treasures are *prosciutto* and *Parmigiano-Reggiano*, two products that are essentials in every Italian kitchen.

The medieval stone bridge Ponte Gobbo crosses the river Trebbia at Bobbio (Emilia-Romagna).

Emilia-Romagna

Parmigiano-Reggiano

'Parmesan' is synonymous the world over with an Italian hard cheese that is most often grated over pasta dishes. Many, however, do not differentiate between genuine Parmesan – Parmigiano-Reggiano (DOP) – and the numerous less expensive products that are simply called 'Parmesan'.

True Parmigiano is made from raw milk in the northern Italian provinces of Parma, Modena, Reggio Emilia, Bologna and Mantua. This milk comes exclusively from the red-and-black spotted Frisona-Italiana cow, a cross of Dutch and North American breeds fed only grass and alfalfa. It takes 16 litres of milk to produce 1 kilogram of cheese (or 1.6 gallons per pound), and production is strictly controlled by a consortium of 500 small and medium-sized dairies. The recipe, appearance and taste of this classic, world-famous cheese have remained unchanged for 800 years.

Parmigiano is mildly aromatic and has a fine-grained structure that breaks into flakes. Its incomparable flavour develops during the long ageing process. After a year of storage, each and every block of cheese undergoes a rigorous inspection, and if it passes, it receives an oval brand on the rind. Parmigiano is designated according to its age: *nuovo* or *fresco* indicates a ripening period of 12 to 18 months, *vecchio* from 18 to 24 months, and *stravecchio* from 24 to 36 months. Parmesan that has been aged for four years is a delicacy, expensive even in Italy. Connoisseurs do not slice this cheese with a knife, but rather break off small pieces with a special Parmesan blade and enjoy it straight from the hand, or accompanied with a hint of *aceto balsamico* or honey.

Soured milk is broken up into fine-grained curd.

Then the curd is heated and stirred.

The curd separates from the whey.

A linen cloth is pulled under the curd.

As the curd is removed, the first whey flows off.

Still in the cloth, the curd is put into a form.

The cloth is folded over the curd.

The remaining whey is gently pressed from the curd.

Ripe Parmigiano-Reggianos are packed into splint boxes.

After rigorous inspection, the cheese receives a seal of approval.

Grana Padano

Grana padano, which since 1996 has been a DOP cheese, is nowadays the best-selling cheese in the world. It is often confused with Parmigiano-Reggiano, but it differs significantly in several ways from its more expensive counterpart. Grana padano is a hard, semi-fat cheese made from the partially skimmed milk of cows that are fed dry fodder in addition to grass. The cheese is aged between 12 and 24 months. There are some excellent varieties of Grana padano that compare favourably with Parmigiano-Reggiano. Whether you are enjoying Grana padano or Parmigiano, in Italy, both cheeses are always grated just before eating.

Pecorino

Hardly any other Italian cheese is sold in as many different forms, flavours and stages of ripeness as *pecorino*. The name comes from the Italian word *pecora* (sheep). Every region has its own pecorino, and trying all the different varieties is a very rewarding endeavour, because although all are made from sheep's milk, each has a distinctive aroma. Some cheese makers rub their cheeses with charcoal, while others flavour them with green peppercorns or give them an intense smoky note.

Four types of pecorino carry the DOP seal and thereby enjoy protected designation of origin.

Pecorino Romano was a favourite already in antiquity, not only as a piquant delicacy for celebrations, but also as rations for Roman legionaries. Its taste is aromatic and pleasantly tangy. After five months' ageing, it is a popular table cheese served with fresh fruits, and after ripening for eight months it is suitable for grating, giving many Roman dishes their unmistakable flavour.

Pecorino Sardo has been produced on Sardinia since the eighteenth century. It is made from raw or semi-pasteurized milk. During production, the cheeses are briefly dipped into boiling brine in order to lengthen their shelf life. Young *Pecorino Sardo* is mild and aromatic, whereas the riper variants have a strong but pleasantly savoury flavour.

Pecorino Siciliano has its culinary roots in antiquity as well, and was described by Pliny as one of the best cheeses of his time. Young *Pecorino Siciliano* is also called *primo sale* and is used like mozzarella. Riper variations provide a delicious alternative to Parmesan.

Pecorino Toscano is delicious as a young cheese, but even as an aged, hard cheese it is significantly milder and softer than the other three varieties described above. It is most often sold as a young cheese with the name *pecorino tenero* after a ripening period of 20 days, or it is aged four months and sold as *pecorino a pasta dura*. Tuscan *pecorino* is often prepared with extra flavouring: the rind of *pepato*, for example, is rubbed with ground pepper; for *senese*, it is brushed with puréed tomatoes; fresh chillies are used for *peperoncini*; and *tartufato* is flavoured with black truffles.

Rennet and cultures containing bacteria are added to the milk.

The coagulated mass is cut into fine-grained curd.

Curd and whey are separated by kneading.

Then the curd is pressed into cylindrical forms.

It is left to stand for two days, so that the remaining whey can drain.

The pecorino is removed from the form and rubbed with salt.

The cheeses are aged in a cellar from two months to a year.

Pecorino is normally eaten as is, but it is also grated over other dishes.

Mascarpone and Ricotta

Outside of Italy, mascarpone is best known as a high-calorie ingredient of *tiramisù*. Made from heated cream to which citric acid or white wine vinegar is added, it is produced in almost every region of Italy. This voluptuous, spreadable fresh cheese has the colour and taste of milk and is primarily used in desserts, or in sauces as a substitute for butter or cream.

Ricotta is a fresh cheese made from the whey of buffalo, sheep or cow's milk that accumulates during the production of mozzarella, provolone and pecorino. This soft, crumbly cheese is customarily eaten fresh, either spread on bread or used to refine or enhance certain dishes, to fill pasta or as a basis for desserts. In Sicily, ricotta is packed into small forms and dried in the sun until it is hard enough to be grated. In the area around Norcia, dried ricotta is used as a substitute for Parmigiano, whereas in Puglia it gives local sauces an unmistakable flavour. Other varieties of ricotta are salted, smoked or baked, again acquiring very unique aromas.

The curdled mixture of whey and milk is poured into a cloth.

Then the cloth and its contents are placed in a sieve to drain.

Immediately after production, the ricotta has a mild flavour.

Before it is packed for sale, the cheese is cooled in baskets.

Ricotta di bufala is a unique speciality made from buffalo milk (right).

Gorgonzola

Gorgonzola, perhaps the most striking of the Italian cheeses, has an age-old tradition. It was produced as early as the eleventh century in the town of the same name, in the vicinity of Milan. It was originally called *stracchino di Gorgonzola* (literally, 'the tired one of Gorgonzola'), a reference to its origins. According to legend, the cheese was discovered when a dairy hand, after finishing an evening's milking, allowed himself to be distracted by a lovely milk-maid. When morning came, the exhausted young man accidentally mixed the fresh morning milk with the previous night's milk, which had soured.

Gorgonzola is made from cow's milk, but with unheated curd, and is infused with mould cultures. To encourage the growth of the fungus, the body of the cheese is pierced with copper or stainless steel needles so that oxygen reaches all parts of the cheese. The milder variant, *Gorgonzola dolce*, is mild, has few veins and ripens for two months. *Gorgonzola piccante*, the classic version, is aged for up to a year, is denser and is richly veined with blue mould that gives the cheese its emphatic spicy taste.

Depending on the variety, Gorgonzola ages in stone caves or ripening cellars for anywhere from two months to one year (above right).

After the milk is soured, the curd separates from the whey.

Spores of 'noble rot' (Penicillium gorgonzola) are added to the curd.

The curd is filled into forms that are lined with cloth.

The cheese rests in its form for a few days until the rest of the whey has drained off.

Then the raw cheese is removed from the form and rotated.

In order to encourage veining, holes are bored into the cheese with needles.

During the ripening process, a master cheese maker regularly inspects the product.

Samples are taken from the cheese to test the degree of ripeness.

Caprino in crosta
Goat's Cheese in Pastry

1 sachet easy-blend dried yeast

1 pinch sugar

200 g/7 oz flour, plus extra for dusting

½ tsp salt

2 tbsp olive oil, plus extra for greasing

1 tsp finely chopped oregano

300 g/11 oz fresh goat's cheese (log)

1 egg, separated

Dissolve the yeast and sugar in 100 ml/ 3½ fl oz warm water. Sift the flour into a bowl and make a well in the centre. Add the salt, olive oil and yeast-water mixture and knead everything into a smooth, silky dough. Form the dough into a ball, cover it and set it aside in a warm place for an hour or until doubled in size.

Grease a baking tray with olive oil and preheat the oven to 200°C/390°F/gas mark 6. Vigorously knead the dough once more, working in the oregano, then roll it out on a floured surface. Cut the goat's cheese into four equal slices. From the dough, cut eight circles slightly larger than the cheese slices. Place a slice of cheese on four of the dough circles and brush the edges of the dough with egg white. Cover with the remaining dough circles and press the edges together firmly.

Place the filled pockets on the baking tray and brush with whisked egg yolk. Bake for about 20 minutes.

Knead the finely chopped oregano into the dough and then roll it out.

From the dough, cut eight circles that are slightly larger than the pieces of goat's cheese.

Cover the cheese with the remaining dough circles and press the edges together firmly.

Brush the filled dough with whisked egg yolk and bake.

Pere con gorgonzola
Salad with Gorgonzola Pears

For the salad:

1 small radicchio
100 g/3½ oz lollo bionco
or other frilly leaf lettuce
100 g/3½ oz looseleaf lettuce
1 red onion
1 avocado, peeled
juice of 1 lime
4 tbsp fresh lentil sprouts
salt
freshly ground white pepper
sugar
4 tbsp walnut oil

For the Gorgonzola pears:

100 g/3½ oz Gorgonzola
2 tbsp crème fraîche
2 small pears
freshly ground white pepper

Tear the salad leaves into bite-sized pieces and combine them in a bowl. Peel the onion and cut into fine rings. Cut the avocado into narrow strips. Drizzle 2 tablespoons of lime juice over the avocado strips, and put the remaining juice in a small bowl. Rinse the lentil sprouts in cold water and set aside to drain. Season the lime juice with salt, white pepper and sugar, then whisk in the oil.

Pour the dressing over the salad, toss and distribute on to 4 salad plates. Top each serving with some of the onions, sprouts and avocado strips. Cut the Gorgonzola into small cubes. In a bowl, crush the cheese with a fork, then combine it with the crème fraîche. Stir until smooth, adding pepper. Transfer the Gorgonzola cream into a piping bag. Peel, halve and core the pears. Place half a pear on each plate and pipe some of the Gorgonzola cream on to each one.

Sfogliette al miele di castagno
Gorgonzola Tartlets
with Chestnut Honey

150 g/5 oz filo pastry, frozen
100 g/3½ oz Gorgonzola dolce
1 apple
1 tbsp chestnut honey
butter for greasing

Thaw the filo pastry and preheat the oven to 220°C/430°F/gas mark 7.

Grease four small tartlet forms with butter and line them with filo pastry. In a bowl, stir the Gorgonzola until smooth and then spoon it into the tartlet forms. Bake for 10 minutes or until golden brown.

Meanwhile, quarter the apple and remove the core. Cut the apple into thin slices. Remove the tartlets from the forms and insert apple slices into the cheese. Drizzle the honey over the tartlets and serve while hot.

Pere con gorgonzola

Dolci e Caffè

Desserts
and
Coffee

A seductive mousse, a fluffy soufflé, a delicately melting gelato, a successful composition of sweet fruits – in Italy, desserts are the crowning finish to a meal, and not just for those of us with a pronounced sweet tooth. The *dulce finale* demands the chef's undivided attention, because the conclusion remains fixed longest in one's culinary memory. Italian cooks are aware of this, and practise the high art of dessert with much imagination, love and care, whether in a restaurant or in their own kitchen. As a result, this small, sweet conclusion to a fine meal is often composed and prepared with uncommon thoughtfulness.

In Italian gastronomy, the north-south divide persists even among desserts: in the south, sweets are even sweeter, whereas in the north desserts are more elegant. In many northern Italian restaurants there is even a separate menu devoted solely to the *dolci*.

This love for the sweet life has ancient roots. In antiquity, honey was prized for sweetening not only wine, but also comestibles. When the Arabs arrived in Sicily in the ninth century, they brought more than pasta with them: marzipan, crystallized fruits and other titbits such as sugared almonds were also introduced. And they left much more than sugary traces behind. During their 250 years of dominance on the island, they contrived an elaborate irrigation system, thereby making possible the Sicilian fruit

garden, where today more than 'the lemon grows, where the bright orange midst the foliage glows', as Johann Wolfgang von Goethe once put it.

The first European confectioners, who adopted and further developed this art of the Orient, are mentioned around 1150 in Venice. During the Renaissance, the sweet life of the Tuscan nobility blossomed most splendidly in every respect. Sugared almonds and crystallized fruits were offered as gifts on special occasions. As *The Decameron* describes, beautiful women and rich young men allowed themselves pastry and sweets with wine between their sumptuous meals. Confections were then luxury items, and they remained unattainable for the common folk for several centuries.

Even the clergy were not immune to sweet temptation, and this was true for the pope, as well. At courts from Milan to Mantua, from Ferrara to Florence, confectioners competed with ever more extravagant creations for the reputation of being the very best. Showing off their sculptural abilities, they modelled entire hunting scenes, landscapes or the favourite animals of their patrons out of sugar.

Lorenzo 'the Magnificent' de' Medici ended all his banquets with a magnificent procession in which the remnants of the opulent foods – especially the desserts – were divided among the people of Florence. Catherine de' Medici took not only chefs, but also confectioners with her to Paris after her marriage, thereby captivating the French nobility with her sweets.

A high point in the history of sugar is undoubtedly the legendary banquet held in January 1574, given in honour of the French king, Henry III (a son of Catherine's), by the Republic of Venice. The tablecloth, plates and cutlery were all made of sugar, as were the table ornaments: two lions, an equestrian queen flanked by two tigers, and King David and Saint Mark surrounded by sculptures of kings and popes, animals, plants and fruits.

Nowadays in Italy, a simple meal is often rounded off with fresh fruits or a fruit salad. Thanks to the excellent quality of the produce, it probably tastes much better than the baroque sugar-bombs of the past.

Sweets have a long tradition in Italy, reaching back into antiquity. Pastry shops offer the finest confections for those who would rather not prepare them at home – to the right, a confectioner cuts a slice of cassata.

Macedonia Fruit Salad

5 large blue plums
2 nectarines
2 pears
juice of 1 lime
200 g/7 oz each, red and white grapes
2 tbsp caster sugar
2 tsp vanilla sugar
100 ml/3½ fl oz freshly squeezed orange juice
60 ml/2 fl oz amaretto
2 fresh figs

Stone the plums and nectarines and cut them into thin wedges. Peel and quarter the pears, remove the cores and chop the flesh into cubes. Place all the fruits in a bowl and sprinkle with the lime juice.

Halve the grapes and remove any seeds with the point of a knife. Combine the sugar and vanilla sugar with the orange juice and amaretto. Pour this over the fruits and gently toss so all the fruit is coated. Chill in the refrigerator for 1 hour.

Quarter the figs. Serve the fruit salad in glass bowls with the figs. Fruits may be varied according to what is in season.

Fruits of Italy

The Braeburn apple has juicy, firm flesh and a harmonious balance of sweet and tart flavours.

The Elstar is a relatively new breed of apple with tasty flesh and a thin peel.

The medium-sized Cox Orange winter apple is very popular due to its powerful sweet-and-sour taste.

Ripe Bartlett pears are juicy with sweet, delicate flesh, a thin peel and an intense aroma.

Ripe blackberries are sweet and delicious.

Wild raspberries have a more intense taste than their cultivated cousins.

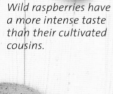

Among the most popular berries is the juicy, sweet strawberry.

The sweet-and-sour flesh of the prickly pear is eaten with its black seeds.

Due to its high concentration of sugar, the sweet fig is ideal for drying.

The Washington Navel, a juicy orange with few pips, was brought to Italy from Brazil about 60 years ago.

In Italy, sweet cherries are especially popular.

The edible seeds of the pomegranate are encased in aromatic flesh.

The lemon tree blossoms and bears fruit simultaneously. That means lemons can be harvested year-round.

Nectarines have white or yellow flesh.

Ripe apricots have a fine, sweet flavour and a delicate scent.

The lime has a thin, green rind and, in contrast to other citrus fruits, can only be peeled and segmented with difficulty.

The juicy peach is a true summer fruit. Different breeds have white or yellow flesh.

White and red table grapes are very popular in Italy.

The casaba melon has a white, creamy flesh, but is not as flavourful as the honeydew.

The cantaloupe, with its orange flesh, is a quintessentially Italian melon. Its name derives from Cantalupo, the summer residence of the popes, where it was cultivated from Armenian seeds about 300 years ago. Cantaloupes sold in the United States are actually muskmelons.

The Galia melon is very sweet and juicy. Its yellow or green rind is sheathed in a yellowish net.

The flesh of the oblong honeydew melon is juicy but firm, and its rind is yellow and smooth.

As its name suggests, the watermelon consists primarily of water. It is a cool, refreshing treat on hot summer days.

The sweet pepino, with its purple stripes, is typically 10 to 20 cm (4–8 inches) long. Its taste resembles a mixture of melons and pears. Ripe pepinos can be eaten whole, with the rind.

CALABRIA

The region of Calabria, surrounded by high mountain chains and caressed year-round by the sun, comprises the 'toe of the boot' at the southernmost point of the Italian Peninsula. Picturesque mountain villages, pine and olive groves, green forests and white sandy beaches dot the landscape between two seas, the Tyrrhenian and the Ionian. Citrus fruits, vegetables, olives and grapes thrive here. The Calabrian province of Cosenza is the most important centre of fig cultivation in Italy. This is the home of the Dottato fig, the principal ingredient of fig salami, a well-known southern Italian speciality. The fragrant, sweet figs are first baked, then chopped, enhanced with rum, spices and orange essence, rolled into a cylinder and covered with plain chocolate. After being tied up and dusted with icing sugar, it looks just like a real salami.

The inventiveness and creativity of Calabria's peasant cuisine is not limited to sweets. It is typified by two main ingredients: pasta and chillies. According to a Calabrian proverb, a woman is only ready to be married when she has mastered fifteen different ways of turning water and flour into pasta . . . and can make a perfect sauce to go with each of them. The native *peperoncino*, the spiciest chilli in all of southern Italy, lends a special sharpness to soups, vegetables, pulses, lamb and goat ragouts, and even stock- and swordfish. *Se non è piccante, non è calabrese* ('If it's not spicy, it's not Calabrian') is another noted saying. And in charge of preserving this local heritage is the *Accademia Italiana del Peperoncino*, or 'Peperoncino Academy', which maintains a small museum in the Tyrrhenian coastal town of Diamante and provides exhaustive information about the cultivation and uses of the spicy fruit.

The emblem of the Calabrian town of Tropea is the pilgrimage church of Santa Maria dell'Isola. This former Benedictine monastery was built on a great rock that was once completely surrounded by the sea. Today the church is accessible from the beach by way of a steep, narrow stairway.

Dolci e Caffè | 427

Favourite Desserts

The palette of Italian desserts is as colourful and multi-faceted as the land itself. One could simplify by distinguishing different categories of *dolci*: fruit desserts, creamy desserts and puddings (which are most often turned out of moulds), and frozen or semi-frozen treats. The scale of the recipes ranges from simple to complicated, from unostentatious to elegant – although complicated methods of preparation are no guarantee of a delicious dessert. As in all other areas of the culinary arts, the optimal quality of the products used is of primary importance. Fruits should have reached their full flavour, that is, they should be ripe but not over-ripe. Mousses should always be given enough time to chill, thereby allowing them to firm in the mould.

Most desserts are portioned and served on plates, decorated with herbs, nuts, cream, icing sugar or cocoa. If more than one dessert is served on a single plate, it is important that the flavours harmonize rather than overshadow one another. Neutral accompaniments include a fruit coulis, lady finger biscuits or ice cream, preferably home-made. Always valid is the dictum that a few select ingredients are often preferable to an abundance of unmanageable flavours.

Pere al vino rosso
Pears in Red Wine

750 ml/1⅓ pints full-bodied red wine
250 g/9 oz sugar
1 cinnamon stick
2 cloves
1 kg/2 lb 4 oz small, firm pears

Preheat the oven to 150°C/300°F/gas mark 2. Combine the wine and sugar in a saucepan, add the cinnamon stick and cloves, and bring to the boil.

Place the unpeeled pears, stems facing upwards, in a deep baking dish. Pour the hot spiced wine over the pears and bake for 1 hour or until soft but not falling apart. Remove the dish from the oven and leave the pears to cool in the wine. Slice and serve hot or cold. Cooking time may vary according to type of pear, so test them often.

Fragole all'aceto balsamico
Strawberries with
Balsamic Vinegar

500 g/1 lb 2 oz strawberries
2 tbsp caster sugar
2–3 tbsp high-quality balsamic vinegar
several mint leaves to decorate

Remove the stems from the strawberries and halve or quarter them, according to size. Sprinkle the sugar, then the vinegar over the berries and mix carefully. Cover with clingfilm and leave to rest for at least 1 hour. Before serving, gently mix again and garnish with mint leaves.

Pesche ripiene
Stuffed Peaches

4 firm yellow peaches
1 tbsp lemon juice
75 g/2½ oz crystallized lemon peel
75 g/2½ oz crumbled amaretti
3 tbsp sugar
1 egg yolk
50 ml/1½ fl oz Marsala
8 blanched almonds
250 ml/9 fl oz white wine
butter for greasing

Preheat the oven to 175°C/350°F/gas mark 4 and grease a baking dish with butter.

Cut the peaches in half and carefully twist the halves apart, removing the stones. Sprinkle with the lemon juice.

Finely chop the crystallized lemon peel. Combine it with the amaretti, sugar, egg yolk and Marsala. Fill the peach halves with the mixture and press one almond into the centre of each. Place the peach halves next to each other in the baking dish and pour on the white wine. Bake for 15 to 20 minutes. Serve hot or cold in the wine sauce.

Almonds

Native to the Middle East, the almond tree grows throughout the Mediterranean basin. In antiquity, its fragrant and slightly sweet seeds were already prized not only as a healthy food, but also for their medicinal properties. Almonds contain many valuable fatty acids, vitamins and minerals. In Italy, they are a popular ingredient for a wide range of confections, cakes and other baked goods.

Sugared almonds are traditionally associated with Italian weddings; newlyweds send little packets containing five sugar-covered almonds as a token of thanks for the gifts they receive. The nuts symbolize health, prosperity, fruitfulness, happiness and long life. Sugared almonds from Sulmona in Abruzzo are especially famous. Approximately 500 tons of their sugared almonds are sent throughout the world every year.

Pesche ripiene

Mele cotte al vino bianco
Apples in White Wine

1 kg/2 lb 4 oz apples
5 tbsp lemon juice
250 ml/ 9 fl oz white wine
200 g/7 oz sugar
1 cinnamon stick
2 cloves

Peel, quarter and core the apples. Cut them into narrow wedges and immediately sprinkle with the lemon juice.

Combine the wine, sugar, cinnamon stick and cloves in a saucepan and slowly bring to the boil. Add the apples and simmer on low heat for 10 minutes. Remove the apples with a slotted spoon and set them aside.

Bring the wine to the boil again and reduce to a thick syrup. Remove the cinnamon stick and cloves. Return the apple wedges to the pan and leave them to cool in the sauce.

Bianco mangiare
Blancmange

3 sheets leaf gelatine
or 1 sachet clear gelatine (7 g/¼ oz)
250 ml/9 fl oz milk
100 g/3½ oz ground almonds
75 g/2½ oz sugar
2 tsp vanilla sugar
1 tsp almond extract
250 ml/9 fl oz double cream

Soak the gelatine in cold water. Combine the milk, almonds and sugar in a saucepan and slowly bring to the boil. Drain or press the liquid from the gelatine. Remove the hot milk from the stovetop and dissolve the gelatine in it, then stir in the vanilla sugar and almond extract. Pour through a sieve into a bowl and leave to cool.

As soon as the mixture starts to become firm, whip the cream and fold it in. Rinse four small soufflé dishes with cold water and fill. Cover them and chill in the refrigerator for at least 3 hours. Before serving, dip the base of each dish briefly into hot water, then turn over on to plates.

Crema di marroni
Sweet Chestnut Mousse

500 g/1 lb 2 oz sweet chestnuts
50 g/1¾ oz sugar
2 tsp vanilla sugar
1 pinch cinnamon
200 ml/7 fl oz double cream
salt
amaretti to garnish

Preheat the oven to 200°C/390°F/gas mark 6. Cut an X into the rounded side of each chestnut, then place them on a baking tray, flat side down, and roast for about 20 minutes until the shells open. Peel the chestnuts and remove the brown membrane.

Put the chestnuts in a saucepan. Add water to cover them and a little salt. Simmer on low heat for about 40 minutes. Drain the chestnuts, then purée in a food processor. Mix in the sugar, vanilla sugar and cinnamon and leave to cool.

Whip the cream and fold it into the cooled chestnut purée. Portion into dessert bowls and garnish with amaretti.

Sweet Chestnuts

There are two types of edible chestnuts: marrons, or *marroni*, and sweet chestnuts, or *castagne*. The true marron is only found in Italy, the Swiss canton of Tessin, and certain regions of France and Spain. Their fruit is somewhat flatter than the common chestnut and is easier to shell. Because of this – and because their flavour is creamier and more intense than that of the common chestnut – they are preferred in the kitchen. At Italian markets, marrons are sold in autumn, fresh from the trees and still in the shell. In supermarkets, one can buy them in cans or jars, already shelled and cooked or puréed.

For centuries, marrons were considered a satisfying staple food – a poor man's potato. Italians said it grew on the *albero del pane*, or 'bread tree'. Due to the chestnut's high starch content, the nuts were ground into flour and used in bread baking. Today, flat loaves of chestnut bread – traditionally baked on hot stones – are sold in Italy as regional specialities. Crystallized or glazed chestnuts are a delicacy enjoyed throughout the country.

Cinnamon

Cinnamon is produced from the bark of thin branches of the evergreen cinnamon tree. The bark is freed of its outer mantel of cork, dried and then cut into pieces. Cinnamon is one of the oldest spices in the world and has its origins in Ceylon, today's Sri Lanka. As has always been the case, the best cinnamon still comes from this island. It is sold as true Ceylon cinnamon, or canela, in sticks or as powder and lends not only desserts, but also meat and vegetable dishes, a distinctive aroma.

Creme caramel
Crème Caramel

250 g/9 oz sugar
1 vanilla pod
300 ml/11 fl oz double cream
300 ml/11 fl oz milk
4 eggs
2 egg yolks

In a small saucepan, heat 150 g/5 oz sugar and 5 tablespoons of water until the sugar caramelizes. Pour the hot caramel into 4 small soufflé dishes and leave to cool. Preheat the oven to 150°C/300°F/gas mark 2.

Cut the vanilla pod lengthways and scrape out the seeds. Combine the cream and milk in a clean saucepan, add the vanilla pod and seeds, and slowly bring to the boil. Remove from the heat and take out the vanilla pod.

Beat the eggs and egg yolks with the remaining sugar. Stir in the warm vanilla milk, then pour into the soufflé dishes. Set the soufflés in a baking dish and add enough boiling water in the dish so that the soufflés are two thirds submerged. Place the water bath in the oven for about 40 minutes. Remove the soufflé dishes from the water bath, cool, and chill in the refrigerator overnight to firm.

Before serving, dip the base of each soufflé dish briefly into hot water, then turn over on to dessert plates.

Frutti di bosco con gelato
Forest Berries
with Vanilla Ice Cream

250 g/9 oz fresh red currants
250 g/9 oz fresh blackberries
250 g/9 oz fresh blueberries
2 tbsp icing sugar
juice of ½ lemon
juice of 1 orange
60 ml/2 fl oz amaretto
8 slices or scoops vanilla ice cream
fresh mint leaves to decorate

Sort the berries and place them in a bowl. Combine the icing sugar with the lemon and orange juices and amaretto, then pour over the berries. Mix carefully and set aside for 15 minutes.

Place the slices or scoops of ice cream on 4 plates, then top with the berry mixture. Decorate with mint leaves.

The Classics

Three famous desserts represent Italian cuisine throughout the world: *tiramisù*, *panna cotta* and *zabaione*. Their international reputation is well established – for many gourmets, without any one of these sinfully creamy delights, a Mediterranean menu is simply incomplete.

Tiramisù (literally, 'pull me up') most likely derives its name from the fact that this perfect mix of espresso, cocoa, sugar and liqueur has an invigorating effect. The original recipe probably has its roots in Tuscany. This dessert's first incarnation was reputedly created in Siena towards the end of the seventeenth century to honour Grand Duke Cosimo III de' Medici. For this famous connoisseur, the confectioners selected only the finest ingredients such as mascarpone made from pure buffalo milk and perfected their creation with the luxury items chocolate and coffee. The result greatly pleased the grand duke and his female coterie. *Tiramisù* immediately earned a reputation for being not only rich, but also stimulating in every respect.

Panna cotta (literally, 'baked cream') hails from the region of Emilia-Romagna.

This moulded custard numbers among the most delicate temptations northern Italy has to offer, where it is always served with a sauce made of fresh fruit, caramel or chocolate. In other regions, it is also served with marinated fruit.

Zabaione, a light, foamy cream originally made with dry white wine, is a traditional speciality of the Piedmont region. There it is served not only as a dessert, but there is also an unsweetened version that accompanies cooked mixed vegetables. The name of this delicate wine mousse supposedly derives from San Giovanni di Baylon, the patron saint of bakers. The name of its inventor remains just as mysterious as its age. While some sources honour Bartolomeo Scappi, an Italian cook who lived in the sixteenth century, with this distinction, others claim that it made its first appearance in the eighteenth century at the court of Duke Charles Emmanuel of Savoy.

Ingredients for tiramisù *are eggs, mascarpone, sponge fingers, grated chocolate, sugar and espresso.* Tiramisù *can be prepared in a rectangular form (as described in the recipe) or dome-shaped (as shown in the photo below).*

Tiramisù

3 egg yolks
4 tbsp amaretto
150 g/5 oz caster sugar
50 g/1¾ oz plain chocolate, finely grated
500 g/1 lb 2 oz mascarpone
200 ml/7 fl oz double cream
24 sponge fingers
500 ml/18 fl oz strong espresso
cocoa powder for dusting

Whisk together the egg yolks and amaretto. Gradually add the sugar and beat until the sugar has dissolved completely. Stir in the chocolate and mascarpone. Whip the cream and fold it in.

Dip the unsugared side of each sponge finger into the espresso. Arrange half of the sponge fingers on the base of a square or rectangular dish, then cover with half of the mascarpone cream. Layer the remaining sponge fingers and then the cream, spreading it evenly. Cover the dish and chill overnight in the refrigerator. Before serving, dust heavily with cocoa powder.

Fold the mascarpone and whipped cream into the mixture of eggs, sugar and grated chocolate.

Stir amaretto into the resulting cream and put half of it into a piping bag.

Arrange the sponge fingers on a round serving plate and squeeze some of the cream on top.

Spread the cream evenly. Repeat in several layers and finish with decorative mounds of cream.

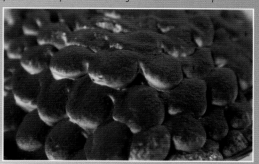

Chill the dessert overnight. Before serving, dust heavily with cocoa powder.

Zabaione

4 egg yolks

4 tbsp sugar

125 ml/4 fl oz Marsala

1 tsp grated lemon peel

Use a whisk to beat the egg yolks, sugar and 1 tablespoon of warm water in a metal bowl until they are thick and very pale.

Place the bowl in a hot water bath and continue to whisk, gradually adding the Marsala. Whisk until the mixture is thick and foamy. Remove the bowl from the water bath, add the lemon peel, and continue to beat until the Zabaione is warm but not hot. Pour into dessert bowls and serve immediately. Zabaione can be served with amaretti or lady finger biscuits, or poured over fresh berries.

For zabaione, *whisk the egg yolks with the sugar into a thick, pale cream.*

Beat the mixture in a hot water bath until foamy, gradually adding the Marsala.

Panna Cotta

1 vanilla pod

500 ml/18 fl oz double cream

60 g/2 oz sugar

4 sheets or 1½ sachets clear gelatine

500 g/1 lb 2 oz strawberries

3 tbsp icing sugar

Cut the vanilla pod lengthways and scrape out the seeds. In a saucepan, bring the cream to the boil with the pod and seeds. Stir in the sugar. Simmer on low heat for 15 minutes.

Soak the gelatine in cold water for about 10 minutes, then drain or press the liquid from the gelatine. Pour the hot cream through a strainer into a bowl, then dissolve the gelatine in it. Rinse four small soufflé dishes in cold water and fill with the cream. Chill overnight in the refrigerator.

Clean the strawberries, setting aside a few for decoration. Cook the remaining strawberries with the icing sugar. While hot, press the berries through a strainer into a bowl and then leave to cool.

To serve, unmould the soufflé dishes on to dessert plates, top with strawberry sauce and decorate with the reserved whole berries.

Frutta Martorana: Marzipan Fruits

Colorful, deceptively real-looking marzipan fruits are the jewels in the Sicilian confectioner's crown. *Frutta martorana* are named after the Monastero della Martorana in Palermo, a monastery whose nuns closely guarded the secret of creative marzipan modelling for generations. The dough, consisting of ground almonds, sugar, egg whites, vanilla seeds and lemon extract, is carefully moulded into astonishingly life-like fruit shapes, tinted with vegetable dyes, and finally coated with gum arabic to preserve their brilliant colours. Marzipan fruit is thought to have first been served in the year 1308 at a banquet that was held in honour of Pope Clement V. In the form of grapes, figs and apples, they adorned two trees.

Making Marzipan

Marzipan is made of almonds, icing sugar, egg whites, flavourings and water.

Boil the sugar and water into a syrup. Test the temperature by dipping a thumb and forefinger in ice water ...

... and rubbing a little of the syrup between them. The syrup should have a smooth texture.

Purée the almonds with water, add the cooled syrup and other ingredients and process into a smooth, supple mass.

Form the marzipan dough into a thick roll, cover with clingfilm and leave to rest overnight.

In Sicily, deceptively realistic fruits are modelled out of marzipan. They are tinted with vegetable dyes and covered in gum arabic to preserve their colours.

The White Gold of the Orient

While in other parts of Europe expensive cane sugar was primarily being used by apothecaries to make their bitter pills more palatable, for wealthy Italians it was already a treasured commodity for daily consumption. This state of affairs was made possible by the Venetian merchants, who for centuries controlled the European sugar trade. During the crusades of the twelfth and thirteenth centuries, to which they contributed money and ships, the Venetians learnt to appreciate and love the sweet world of the East – the crystallized fruits and almonds, marzipan and nougat, caramel and comfit. In 1204, the doge of Venice acquired suzerainty over three eighths of the Byzantine Empire, which meant that all trade routes into the East now stood open to Venetian merchants. Having grown wealthy from the salt from its lagoons, the city rapidly developed its sugar and spice trade into a monopoly.

Sugar was a product of sugarcane, which was native to India. But it was the Persians who first discovered the art of refining sugar in conical clay vessels (from which the sugarloaf, now rare, is descended). Arabs and Egyptians later achieved great wealth through their cultivation of sugarcane, and in the ninth century, in fact, the Arabs had tried – and failed – to grow sugarcane on a grand scale in Sicily. The Venetians had no better luck when they tried to cultivate this cash crop on Cyprus. Until the advent of plantation economies in the sixteenth century, therefore, the primary centres of production for the 'white gold', also called 'Indian salt', remained in the East. It was not until the middle of the eighteenth century that a German chemist discovered that sugar could be refined from the juice of the mangold, or 'sugar beet'. This breakthrough finally made sugar affordable for the common folk, and beet sugar gradually replaced honey as the most popular sweetening agent.

Cassata and Cannoli

In Sicily, there are lots of interesting legends associated with many different desserts. One of these describes the creation of the *cassata*, traditionally attributed to the court chef of an Arab emir ruling in Palermo. Several centuries later, in 1575, a document from the Synod of Mazara certified that this particular dessert was 'indispensable for Easter festivities'. For many years following, the *cassata* was only prepared for Easter, as a celebration of the end of the Lenten fasts. Nowadays this speciality adorns the display windows of Sicilian confectioners – as well as private parties – all year long.

The *cannoli siciliani*, another of the island's signature creations, has Arab roots and was supposedly invented in the harem of Caltanisetta. Crispy rolls of pastry, deep-fried in lard, are filled with a sweet ricotta cream flavoured with crystallized fruits, pistachio nuts or chocolate, and then dusted with icing sugar. In the past, this sweet temptation proved so seductive for the Benedictine monks that they spent fortunes acquiring them, growing ever rounder in the process. This predilection earned the monks the nickname *porci di Cristo* ('pigs of Christ') among the locals. At the end of the nineteenth century, the Benedictines were driven from the island – the *cannoli*, however, remained and still enjoy immense popularity – and not only in Sicily.

A Sicilian cassata *is certainly worth sinning for. The sweet tart, made of biscuits and ricotta, is often decorated so seductively that one simply cannot resist its allure.*

Cassata siciliana
Sicilian Cassata

600 g/1 lb 5 oz ricotta
2 tbsp orange blossom water
350 g/12 oz sugar
100 g/3½ oz plain chocolate
300 g/11 oz crystallized fruit
50 g/1¾ oz chopped pistachio nuts
4 tbsp maraschino liqueur
1 sponge cake base
2 tbsp lemon juice

Beat the ricotta and orange blossom water into a thick cream. Combine 200 g/7 oz sugar and 250 ml/9 fl oz water in a saucepan and boil into a clear syrup. Just before the syrup begins to brown, remove the pan from the stove, cool slightly, then stir the syrup into the ricotta mixture.

Chop the chocolate and half of the crystallized fruit as finely as possible. Stir into the cream along with the pistachio nuts.

Cut the sponge cake horizontally into two layers of equal thickness. Cut one layer into 12 pieces and place them in a round mould. Sprinkle the sponge cake with 2 tablespoons of the maraschino. Fill with the ricotta cream and smooth the surface. Place the second layer of sponge cake on top and press down lightly. Place in the refrigerator and chill for 5 hours. Then unmould the cassata on to a cake plate.

Boil the remaining sugar in the lemon juice, the rest of the maraschino liqueur and a little water, stirring constantly. Cover the cassata with the resulting glaze and decorate with the remaining crystallized fruit. Chill in the refrigerator for 1 hour before serving.

Frutta candita
Crystallized Fruit

500 g/1 lb 2 oz oranges

1 kg/2 lb 4 oz sugar

Wash the fruit in hot water, dry and cut into 1-cm/½-inch slices, complete with the peel.

In a large saucepan, stir the sugar into 1 litre/1¾ pints of water, heating until the sugar has fully dissolved.

Using a strainer that fits inside the pot, submerge the fruit in the hot syrup. Bring it to the boil, reduce the heat and simmer for 15 minutes. Remove from the stovetop.

Cover the pot and leave the fruit to marinate in the syrup for 24 hours. Do not move the pot or touch the fruit during this time.

Carefully remove the fruit with the strainer and drain for 1 hour. Lay it out on paper towels and leave it to dry for 4 to 5 hours.

Other fruits can also be crystallized by following this recipe, including strawberries, cherries, pineapples or lemons.

Wash the citrus fruits, dry them and cut into slices of equal size.

Immerse the sliced fruit in hot syrup and simmer on low heat.

Remove from stove and leave the fruit to soak overnight in syrup.

Gelato

Gelato, Italian ice cream: for many children and the young at heart who have had the pleasure of visiting Italy, this delicate frozen treat is the essence of Italy, sun, sand, sea and holiday. Like pizza, ice cream is known worldwide as a culinary ambassador of the *Bel Paese*, this beautiful Mediterranean land. Don't be fooled, though – outside of Italy, ice cream is made in myriad ways. In the United States, for example, it contains more air and has quite a different texture than genuine Italian *gelato*.

The Sicilians claim that ice cream was invented on their island, and indeed, it would seem that even more fantastically seductive frozen creations can be found here than anywhere else. But Sicilians are not the originators of ice cream – although they did invent *granita di limone*, an ice-cold refreshment made of water, sugar and lemon juice, to which wine, mint or orange juice are sometimes added. Even in the smallest bars in Sicily, one can find the giant mixers that keep the almost fluid sorbet fresh all day long.

The modern success story of Italian *gelato* begins in the sixteenth century, when it first became possible to generate cold artificially by adding saltpetre to water to make it freeze. Then a drum filled with chunks of ice was cooled to the extent that it was possible to freeze the necessary ingredients for ice cream. *Gelatiere*, or ice cream makers, spread their art not only throughout Italy, but also in other European countries. And of course, the well-travelled Catherine de' Medici took a *gelatiere* with her to the royal court in France when she became the bride of Henry II. For her wedding feast in Paris in 1533, her personal ice cream maker created a legendary dessert of frozen fruits.

The ice cream makers of the Veneto region, specifically those from the Val di Zoldo in the Dolomites, have established their reputation as the best *gelatiere* of the modern era. Every November, the town of Longarone hosts an ice cream trade show, the largest of its kind in the world. Specialists and enthusiasts come here from all over the world to obtain information about new flavours and trends – or simply to enjoy the delicious *gelato*.

Ice Cream Stories

A sweet frozen treat akin to ice cream was already known and popular in China some 5,000 years ago. The wise King Solomon is also said to have enjoyed ices made from fruit juice, snow and honey. On his journey into the Underworld, Orpheus refreshed himself with sorbet, as it is said that Alexander the Great did before every battle in the fourth century BCE. Even the emperor Nero, who lived in the first century CE, fell victim to this sweet temptation: specially chosen slaves running in relay brought him glacial ice from the Alps, which was flavoured with honey and fruit juice, ginger, coriander, cinnamon and rose or violet water.

it is not only children whose dreams come true when they visit an Italian ice cream shop. Nowhere else can one find home-made ice cream presented so creatively – or so temptingly.

Making Gelato

The basic ingredients for gelato are milk and cream, fresh eggs, sugar and flavourings.

First the egg yolks and sugar are beaten until they become thick, then the cream is added.

The remaining ingredients are blended in and the mixture is poured into the ice cream maker.

Granita di limone
Lemon Granita

2 lemons

*250 ml/9 fl oz freshly squeezed
lemon juice*

250 g/9 oz caster sugar

250 ml/9 fl oz dry white wine

4 large lemons

Wash the lemons in hot water, dry them and finely grate the peel. Remove the white skin completely, cube the flesh, remove the pips and purée. In a saucepan, combine the lemon purée, lemon juice and sugar. Add the white wine and 250 ml/9 fl oz water and heat, stirring until the sugar is completely dissolved. Pour the granita into a metal bowl, cool slightly, then place in the freezer for about 3 hours, periodically stirring with a fork or whisk to reduce ice crystals.

Cut off the tops of the lemons and scrape out the pulp (it is not used in this recipe). Freeze the lemons for 15 minutes. Purée the granita with a hand-held mixer and serve in the hollowed-out lemons.

The contents are frozen while being constantly stirred by the ice cream machine.

The higher the fat content and speed of stirring, the finer the ice cream.

For two centuries, Italian gelato has been a sweet ambassador to many lands.

Granita di cachi
Persimmon Granita with Chile

100 g/3½ oz unsalted pistachio nuts	
4 persimmons	
1 fresh chilli	
100 g/3½ oz sugar	
100 ml/3½ fl oz water	
juice and grated peel of 1 lemon	

Dry-roast the pistachio nuts in a frying pan without added fat, then chop and set aside.

Wash and dry the persimmons and discard the stems. Cut the fruit into small pieces. Halve the chilli lengthways, remove the seeds, and chop finely. Bring the sugar and water to the boil in a small saucepan and cook until the syrup begins to thicken. Cool slightly, then stir in the lemon juice, peel and the chilli.

Purée the fruit and syrup in a food processor. Stir in half the pistachio nuts, then transfer to a metal bowl and place in the freezer. When the mixture begins to harden, use a whisk to stir the frozen fruit from the side of the bowl towards the centre. Continue freezing in this manner until it has a creamy texture. When completely frozen, set the bowl in the refrigerator for 30 minutes to thaw slightly.

Serve portions in champagne glasses with pistachio nuts sprinkled on top.

Sorbetto sprizzetto
Sparkling Sorbet

500 ml/18 fl oz white wine	
peel of 1 lemon	
175 g/6 oz sugar	
juice of 1 orange	
100 ml/3½ fl oz Aperol	
200 ml/7 fl oz Prosecco	
fresh mint leaves to decorate	

Combine the wine, lemon peel and sugar in a saucepan and slowly bring to the boil. Simmer 1 to 2 minutes, remove from the stovetop, stir in the orange juice and leave to cool.

Pour the wine syrup through a fine sieve into a bowl and blend in the Aperol liqueur. Pour the mixtue into an ice cream machine and process to sorbet.

Serve the sorbet in long-stemmed cocktail glasses, pour on the Prosecco and garnish with mint leaves.

Chocolate and Confectionary

Have you had the pleasure of discovering the delicate chocolate-covered hazelnut kisses from Perugia? *Baci*, one of the most famous chocolate bonbons in the world, owes its global success to an ingenious and very Italian marketing idea. The silver wrappers were printed with romantic phrases, and these little chocolates quickly became the ideal present for smitten Italians to give to their loved ones.

Torrone

History has recognized the ancient Romans as gourmets with a penchant for sweets. Their name for *torrone*, the confection made of honey, egg whites and roasted nuts, was *cupedia* (literally, 'desire'), probably because of their insatiable predilection for this delicacy. In the seventeenth century, this white nougat reemerged in several incarnations, now called *il perfetto amore* ('the perfect love') or *torrone*. It is still produced according to a traditional recipe in the area around the Piedmontese city of Alba, its only ingredients being honey, white sugar, a dash of vanilla and the *Piemonte* hazelnut (IGP). This protected variety of hazelnut grows in the Langhe district and is widely regarded as the finest hazelnut in the world: a round, smooth nut with an intense fragrance and a mild flavour. They are carefully roasted and then, with the other ingredients, cooked for a long time in kettles. The raw *torrone* is still packed into wooden moulds completely by hand.

The triumphal procession of chocolate through Italy began in liquid form, however, in the southern part of the country, which at the time belonged to the Spanish Crown. The Spaniards had been introduced to a bitter drink made of cocoa beans by the Aztecs. But whereas the Spaniards spiced the hot, stimulating drink solely with ginger and chillies, as they had learnt to do in its native South America, the Italians instead tempered its bitterness with jasmine, ambergris and vanilla.

It was the Jesuits who first introduced this drink to monasteries, princely residences and royal courts. It was not long before faithful Catholics began to debate whether chocolate was a food or a beverage. If it were the former, then chocolate could no longer be enjoyed during the fasting period of Lent. The Jesuits, who did a fine business in the chocolate trade, insisted vehemently that it was without doubt a beverage, whereas the stricter Dominicans claimed it to be a food. Seven popes had to moderate this seemingly never-ending debate, and all seven declared it a beverage, therefore making it an indulgence that could be enjoyed year-round.

These days, two cities compete for first place in chocolate production: Perugia and Turin, which is especially known for its nougat specialities. In 1678, the first license in all of Italy to open a *bottega di cioccolateria* – a chocolate shop – was granted in Turin. Until that moment, the enjoyment of chocolate had been reserved for the clergy and the nobility, but within a very short time, dozens of chocolate shops appeared. By the end of the eighteenth century, almost 350 kg (800 lb) of chocolate were produced *daily* in Turin, much of which was exported to France, Germany, Austria and Switzerland.

When Napoleon's blockade made cacao beans a scarce commodity, the *cioccolatieri* of Turin responded to necessity by mixing the cacao with native hazelnuts, which were in abundant supply and much less expensive than the precious beans. Thus was the hazelnut praline born. Its form resembled the three-cornered hat of the Torinese carnival mask, the *guianduia*, and the confection was therefore called a *gianduiotti*. It is still sold in this form today, wrapped in elegant gold foil.

The Eurochocolate Trade Fair in Perugia

Since 1994, the international Eurochocolate Trade Fair has taken place every October in Perugia. For eight days, more than a hundred stalls are spread throughout the beautiful old town, offering the crowd of approximately 800,000 visitors samples of chocolate treats from all over the world. Apart from the tasting, visitors can also enjoy exhibitions, lectures, flavour seminars, musical performances, games and chocolate statuary. Here adoration of chocolate knows no bounds: even beauty spas offer aromatic baths, creams and masks incorporating chocolate.

Over the past centuries, northern Italy has established itself as a stronghold of chocolate production. The delectable creations, some of which are shown above, are manifold.

Through conching, the initially almost crumbly raw chocolate gradually becomes liquid.

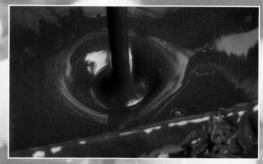

The raw chocolate is stirred, tempered and aired for several days, taking on a uniform texture.

For the production of fine truffle pralines, the moulds are first stamped.

Then the forms are filled with liquid chocolate by hand.

The truffles are coated with couverture and rolled on a chocolate grate.

Cakes and Pies

Cakes and pies are among the few foods that traditional Italian housewives sometimes buy ready-prepared. While they spare no time or effort preparing antipasti, pasta and complicated main courses themselves, and sometimes even grow their own vegetables, many enjoy buying cakes and especially fancier pastries in a *pasticceria*, or pastry shop. One look in the display window of an Italian *pasticceria* explains why. The selection of large and small works of the baker's art is simply overwhelming, and great self-control is required to resist the beguiling temptations.

Apart from the classic cakes and pies baked throughout Italy, every region has its own traditional specialities. In Emilia-Romagna and the eastern Alps, chestnut purée is used to produce a delicious chestnut cake, *torta alla mandorle* is popular in Sardinia, *zuccotto* comes from Tuscany and Lazio is the home of the cherry cake. The *torta della nonna*, or 'grandmother's cake', however, is adored everywhere. For this delectable dessert, there are almost as many recipes as there are grandmothers.

The crostata *(right) is a traditional Italian pie made with a crisp shortcrust base covered with fresh fruit, compote or preserves. It is often topped with a dough lattice.*

Panforte is a traditional fruitcake from Siena. Although it can be found in bakeries all over Tuscany, it tastes best in Siena.

Favourite Cakes and Pies

Crostata di limone
Lemon Pie

200 g/7 oz flour
250 g/9 oz sugar
5 egg yolks
grated peel and juice of 2 lemons
1 pinch salt
100 g/3½ oz chilled butter
3 eggs
150 ml/5 fl oz double cream
2 tbsp icing sugar
oil for greasing

Sift the flour on to a work surface, blend in 100 g/3½ oz sugar and make a well in the centre. Add 4 egg yolks, half the lemon peel, the salt and the butter cut into small pieces. Knead everything into a smooth, supple dough. Form the dough into a ball, cover it in clingfilm and chill for 1 hour in the refrigerator.

Grease a 26-cm/10-inch springform cake tin and preheat the oven to 175°C/350°F/gas mark 4.

On a floured surface, roll out the dough very thin and line the base and sides of the cake tin with it. Use a fork to prick several holes in the dough, then lay a sheet of baking paper over it. Fill the crust with dried beans to prevent buckling and bake for 15 minutes. Remove the dried beans and baking paper and leave the crust to cool.

Reduce the oven temperature to 160°C/320°F/gas mark 3. Beat the remaining egg yolk, the whole eggs and the rest of the sugar and lemon peel into a thick, pale cream. Stir in the lemon juice. Whip the cream and fold it into the egg mixture. Spread it in the crust and spread it evenly, then bake for 20 minutes. Dust the surface with icing sugar, then return to the oven until golden brown.

Torta di zucca
Pumpkin Cake

175 g/6 oz flour
125 g/4½ oz butter,
plus extra for greasing
200 g/7 oz sugar
1 pinch salt
250 ml/9 fl oz milk
125 g/4½ oz short-grain rice
500 g/1 lb 2 oz pumpkin flesh
2 eggs, whisked
100 g/3½ oz ricotta
2 tsp vanilla sugar
2 tbsp breadcrumbs
freshly ground pepper

Sift the flour on to a work surface and make a well in the centre. Add 75 g/2½ oz butter cut in small pieces, half of the sugar, the salt and 75–85 ml/2½–3 fl oz water. Knead everything into a smooth, supple dough. Form the dough into a ball, cover it in clingfilm and chill for 1 hour in the refrigerator.

Combine the milk, 250 ml/9 fl oz water and the rice in a saucepan and bring to the boil. Boil for 2 minutes, then remove from the stovetop and set aside, covered, to cool.

Melt the remaining butter in a second saucepan. Cut the pumpkin flesh into small cubes and cook in the butter until the liquid is absorbed. Purée the pumpkin and stir it into the rice. Stir in the eggs, ricotta, remaining sugar, vanilla sugar and a little pepper.

Grease a 24-cm/9½-inch springform tin and coat the inside of it with the breadcrumbs. Preheat the oven to 200°C/390°F/gas mark 6.

Roll out the dough on a floured surface and line the base and sides of the pan with it. Use a fork to prick several holes in the dough. Spread the rice and pumpkin mixture evenly in the pan and bake 35 to 40 minutes.

Crostata di limone

Crostata di visciole
Cherry Pie

500 g/1 lb 2 oz flour
150 g/5 oz caster sugar
1 pinch salt
2 eggs
grated peel of 1 orange
75 g/2½ oz cold butter
75 g/2½ oz fresh lard
400 g/14 oz sour cherry jam
1 egg yolk, whisked
2 tbsp icing sugar
oil for greasing

Sift the flour on to a work surface, blend in the sugar and make a well in the centre. Add the salt, eggs, orange peel, butter and lard and knead everything into a smooth, supple dough. Form the dough into a ball, cover it in clingfilm and chill for 1 hour in the refrigerator.

Grease a 28-cm/11-inch springform cake tin and preheat the oven to 175°C/350°F/gas mark 4.

On a floured surface, roll out two thirds of the dough very thin and line the base and sides of the pan with it. Spread the jam evenly over the dough.

Roll out the remaining dough and use a pastry wheel to cut it into strips about 2 cm/³/₄ inch wide. Use the strips to form a lattice over the jam. Brush the top of the pie with the whisked egg yolk, then bake for about 45 minutes.

Leave the pie to cool briefly in the tin, then transfer it to a cooling rack. Before serving, dust with icing sugar.

Zuccotto
Frozen Cream-filled Sponge Cake

1 sponge cake base
3 tbsp limoncello (lemon liqueur)
600 ml/1 pint double cream
150 g/5 oz icing sugar
100 g/3½ oz plain chocolate, finely grated
150 g/5 oz chopped almonds

Slice the sponge cake base horizontally into two equally thick layers. Cut one layer into 12 wedges and place them in a round mould. Sprinkle the cake with 2 tablespoons of the limoncello. Whip the cream, gradually adding 100 g/3½ oz of the icing sugar. Mix the grated chocolate into half of the whipped cream and spread in the cake mould. Blend the remaining whipped cream with the almonds and spread on top of the chocolate layer. Top with the second layer of cake, press down lightly and sprinkle with the remaining limoncello. Chill in the freezer for 6 hours or longer before serving.

To serve, turn the cake out of the mould on to a plate and dust with the remaining icing sugar.

Cut the sponge cake into 12 wedges and press them into a round cake mould.

Sprinkle the cake wedges with 2 tablespoons of limoncello liqueur.

Parozzo
Abruzzan Chocolate Cake

5 eggs
100 g/3½ oz caster sugar
75 g/2½ oz butter, plus some for greasing
100 g/3½ oz flour
2 tbsp cornflour
100 g/3½ oz ground almonds
200 g/7 oz chocolate coating, melted

Grease an 28-cm/11-inch springform cake tin with a little butter and preheat the oven to 200°C/390°F/gas mark 6.

Separate the eggs. Beat the egg yolks with the sugar until foamy. Melt the butter in a saucepan, then remove from the stovetop. Combine the flour, cornflour and ground almonds, then stir into the yolks a spoonful at a time. Mix in the melted butter.

Beat the egg whites until stiff and fold them into the dough. Turn the dough into the springform tin and smooth the surface. Bake for 25 minutes, cover the top with aluminium foil and bake an additonal 10 minutes.

Turn the cake out of the tin and cool on a wire rack, then coat with the chocolate, using a fork to make wave patterns in the coating.

Spread first chocolate cream, then almond cream on top of the cake wedges, smoothing it evenly.

Cover with the second cake layer and sprinkle with limoncello, then freeze.

Crostata con i fichi freschi
Fresh Fig Pie

200 g/7 oz flour
150 g/5 oz sugar
6 egg yolks
1 pinch salt
grated peel of 1 lemon
100 g/3½ oz chilled butter
200 ml/7 fl oz milk
1 tbsp cornflour
200 ml/7 fl oz double cream
6–8 large fresh figs
oil for greasing

Sift the flour on to a work surface, blend in 100 g/3½ oz of the sugar, and make a well in the centre. Add 4 of the egg yolks, the salt, lemon peel and butter (cut into small pieces) and quickly knead everything into a smooth dough. Form the dough into a ball, cover it in clingfilm and chill for 1 hour in the refrigerator.

Grease a 24-cm/9½-inch springform cake tin and preheat the oven to 175°C/350°F/gas mark 4. On a floured surface, roll out the dough very thin and line the base and sides of the cake tin with it. Use a fork to prick several holes in the dough, then lay a sheet of baking paper over it. Fill the crust with dried beans to prevent buckling and bake it for 15 minutes. Remove the dried beans and baking paper and bake another 10 minutes. Leave the crust to cool in the tin and then set it on a wire rack.

In a saucepan, bring the milk and 1 table-spoon of sugar to the boil. Beat the remaining 2 egg yolks with the rest of the sugar and the cornflour. Use a whisk to stir them into the hot milk and simmer on low heat for several minutes. Pour into a bowl and leave the custard to cool, whisking occasionally to prevent a skin forming.

Whip the cream, fold it into the cooled custard and fill the crust with the mixture. Wash the figs, pat dry and cut into slices. Arrange fig slices on top of the pie.

Torta della nonna
Grandmother's Cake

300 g/11 oz flour
100 g/3½ oz chilled butter,
plus extra for greasing
2 eggs
1 pinch salt
175 g/6 oz sugar
4 egg yolks
seeds of 1 vanilla pod
2 tbsp cornflour
400 ml/14 fl oz milk
icing sugar for dusting
50 g/1¾ oz pine kernels, chopped

Place all the ingredients for the torta della nonna *within arm's length.*

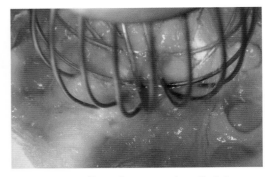

Beat the egg yolks with sugar and vanilla into a thick cream.

Sift the flour on to a work surface and make a well in the centre. Add the butter (cut into small pieces), eggs, salt and 100 g/3½ oz of the sugar. Knead everything into a smooth, supple dough, adding 2–3 tablespoons of water if needed. Form the dough into a ball, cover it in clingfilm and chill for about 1 hour in the refrigerator.

Grease a 26-cm/10-inch springform cake tin and preheat the oven to 175°C/350°F/gas mark 4.

In a bowl, beat the egg yolks with the remaining sugar, vanilla seeds and cornflour into a thick cream. Place the bowl in a hot water bath and continue to beat, gradually adding the milk. Beat until the cream mixture thickens again. Remove from the stove and place in a cold water bath, stirring until cool.

On a floured surface, roll out the dough and cut out two circles the size of the springform tin. Place one circle in the base and use scraps of dough to line the sides of the pan. Spread the cream in the pan and cover with the second circle. Press the edges together firmly. Bake on the lower rack of the oven for 45 minutes.

Set the cake on a wire rack to cool. Before cutting, coat heavily with icing sugar and sprinkle pine kernels on top.

Every Italian household has its own family recipe for the torta della nonna.

Mix in the cornflour and beat the cream in a hot water bath.

In a bakery, the vanilla cream is distributed among the cake tins already lined with a crust.

When baking without a second layer of dough, the pine kernels are sprinkled on the vanilla cream.

After baking, the cake is left to cool and then dusted with icing sugar.

Biscotti

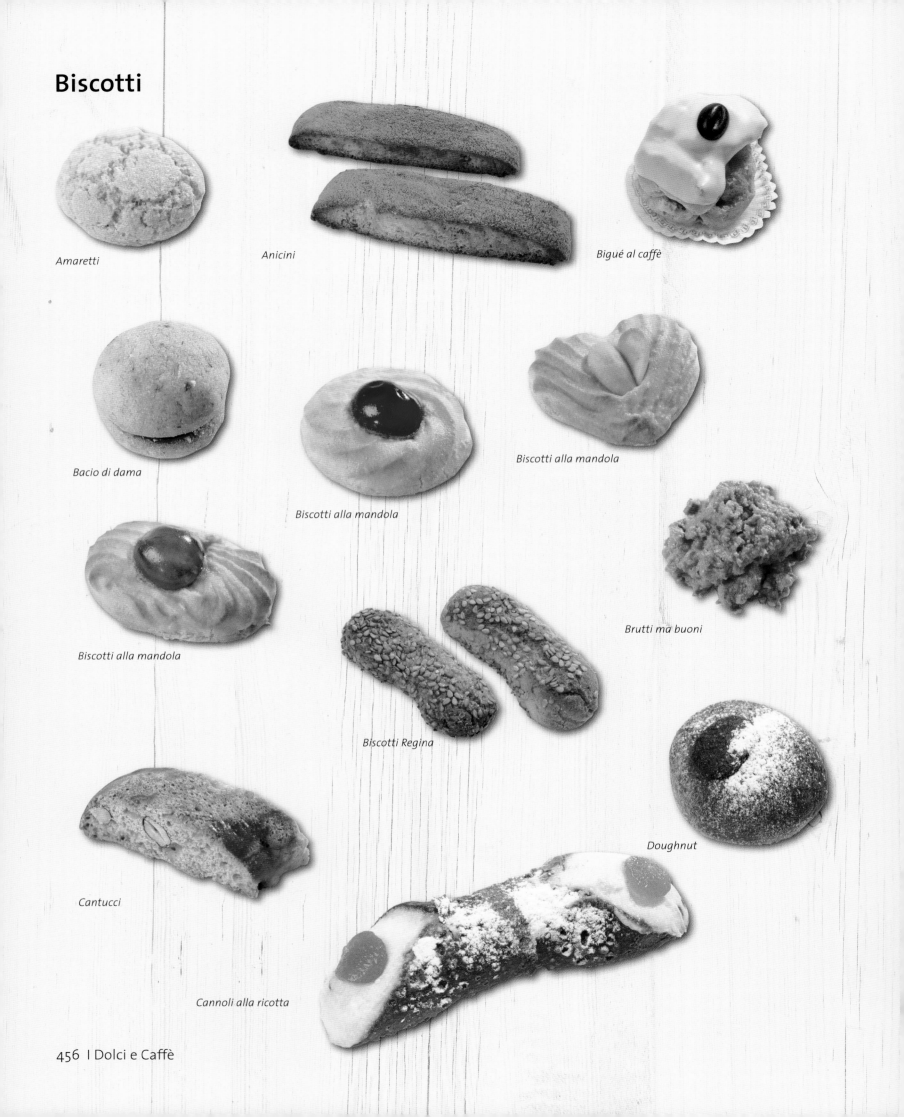

Amaretti

Anicini

Bigué al caffè

Bacio di dama

Biscotti alla mandola

Biscotti alla mandola

Biscotti alla mandola

Brutti ma buoni

Biscotti Regina

Doughnut

Cantucci

Cannoli alla ricotta

Cakes and Pastries

Pan di arancia

Pastine all'anguria

Pastine con fragoline

Torta bigué e frutta

Stola alla ricotta

Cassata

Dolci di Carnevale: Carnival Pastries

Every year, in the days leading up to Ash Wednesday, costume balls, historical processions, fireworks and artistic performances transform many Italian cities into colourful, turbulent fortresses of fools. For days, historical masks and flamboyant costumes mark the cities' appearances. The origins of this fancy-dress festival lie in the Roman holiday of Saturnalia, a massive masquerade that heralded the coming of the new year. With Christianity came the name carnival. *Carne vale* (literally, 'farewell flesh') referred to the last meal of meat before the long meatless period of Lent, and was later extended to include all the festivities occurring in the week before Ash Wednesday. During the Middle Ages, *il carnevale* was the only time of the year in which everyone, rich and poor, could behave freely, without respect and without fear of class-related reprisals.

The most famous carnival in the world takes place in Venice. In the eighteenth century, it lasted for months, but during the Austrian occupation in the nineteenth century, it was forgotten. In 1980, artists 'rediscovered' the lost carnival festival and breathed new life into it. But the joyous carnivals of Bagnolino and Viareggio, San Giovanni Bianco and Fano, Arezzo and Putignano, Sciacca and Misterbianco are also renowned. At this time of year, special, traditional confections are baked all over Italy: crullers and doughnuts, fried *cenci* and sweet ravioli.

Frappe
Roman Carnival Pastries

400 g/14 oz flour
2 tbsp cornflour
1 tbsp easy-blend dried yeast
250 ml/9 fl oz white wine
60 g/2 oz butter
1 tsp grated lemon peel
1 tsp grated orange peel
1 tbsp cinnamon
oil for deep-frying
icing sugar for dusting

Sift the flour and cornflour into a bowl. Dissolve the yeast in 2 tablespoons of warm water. In a large saucepan, heat the wine and melt the butter in it. Remove from the stovetop and slowly stir in the flour. Finally,

Work all the ingredients for the Tuscan *cenci* into a smooth dough.

Divide the dough into four portions and roll each as thin as possible (1–2 mm/less than 1/8 inch).

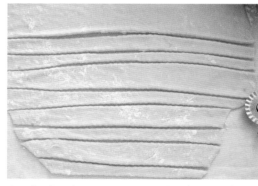
Cut the dough into strips 3–4 inches (8–10 cm) long of varying widths.

Then deep-fry the strips in hot oil until they are golden brown.

add the dissolved yeast. Cover the dough and set it in a warm place for 1 hour, or until its volume has doubled.

Knead the orange and lemon peels and cinnamon into the dough, then roll it out on a floured surface to a thickness of 2 cm/³/₄ inch. Cover a baking tray with baking paper. Cut out 5-cm/2-inch circles from the dough and place them on the baking tray, leaving some space between them. Cover and leave them to rise for about 1 hour.

Heat oil to 175°C/350°F and fry the dough circles until they are golden brown. Set them on paper towels to drain, then dust with icing sugar and serve while hot.

Cenci
Tuscan Dough Strips

500 g/1 lb 2 oz flour
1½ tsp baking powder
50 g/1¾ oz sugar
2 tsp vanilla sugar
1 pinch salt
50 g/1¾ oz softened butter, *in small pieces*
2 eggs
1 tbsp grated orange peel
100 ml/3½ fl oz Vin Santo
oil for deep-frying
icing sugar for dusting

Sift the flour and baking powder into a bowl and make a well in the centre. Add all the remaining ingredients and knead everything into a smooth, supple dough. Form the dough into a ball and set it aside, covered with a moist tea towel, to rise for 30 minutes.

Divide the dough into four portions and roll out each of them on baking paper as thin as possible (1–2 mm/less than ¹/₈ inch). Use a pastry wheel to cut irregular strips that are about 8–10 cm/3–4 inches long. Separate the strips and twist the ends slightly.

Heat oil in a deep-fryer to 175°C/350°F and fry the dough strips, in portions, until they are golden brown. Set on paper towels to drain, then on a cooling rack. Before serving, dust with icing sugar.

The Venetian carnival is world-renowned. For days, historical masks and flamboyant costumes add colour to the Lagoon City.

Castagnole fritte
Venetian Doughnuts

2 eggs
3 tbsp sugar
2 tsp vanilla sugar
1 pinch salt
200 g/7 oz flour
4 tbsp olive oil
2 tbsp brandy
1 tsp grated lemon peel
oil for deep-frying
icing sugar for dusting

Beat the eggs with the sugar, vanilla sugar and salt until foamy. Gradually stir in the flour, olive oil, brandy and lemon peel. Leave the dough to rest for 30 minutes, then beat it vigorously once more, adding a little water or flour as needed. Heat oil to 175°C/350°F in a deep frying pan or a deep-fryer. Use two teaspoons to scoop little balls of dough and drop them in the hot oil. Fry until golden brown. Place on paper towels to drain, and dust with icing sugar before serving.

Easter

In predominantly Catholic Italy, *Pasqua*, or Easter, is the most important Church holiday of the year. After the great, mournful processions held on Good Friday, Easter Eve is marked by the beginning of a joyful series of feasts. *Natale con i tuoi, Pasqua con chi vuoi!* ('Christmas with your family, Easter with anyone you like!') is the Italian maxim, and thus is Easter joyously and abundantly celebrated. Unlike in northern Europe or North America, there is no tradition of an Easter Bunny hiding chocolate eggs in Italy. There *are* eggs – always an odd number of them – which are an important part of Easter cakes. But the true symbol of Easter is the dove, which adorns the Easter displays of bakeries and confectioneries from one end of Italy to the other. These doves are made of fine yeast dough with almonds, dried fruits and sugar crystals.

The *colomba pasquale*, or Easter dove, has its origins in Lombardy. The dreaded Lombard king, Alboin, had conquered the city of Pavia and wanted to exact a terrible revenge on its citizens for their bitter resistance. In their moment of need, the Pavians prayed for divine assistance, and Alboin was thrown from his rearing horse. This enraged the king even further, and it wasn't until a local girl fed the horse a dove-shaped cake that it returned to its usual docile nature. The king gave the citizens of Pavia their freedom back and made their city his capital. Ever since, dove-shaped cakes have been baked and eaten on Easter as a symbol of peace.

Apart from sweet cakes, the *torta di Pasquetta* is baked throughout Italy. This is a savoury cake that formerly consisted of thirty-three layers of crisp dough, each layer representing a year in the life of Jesus. Between the layers of dough was a filling made of spinach, ricotta, eggs and Parmesan. Nowadays, the cake has only twelve layers.

Throughout Italy, traditional Easter processions are held on Good Friday. In the Sicilian town of Modica, the faithful carry statues of Jesus and Mary through the late baroque city to the Cathedral of San Giorgio.

To make the Easter Plait, first sift the flour on to a work surface.

Make a well in the middle of the flour and add the remaining ingredients.

Divide the dough into three equal portions and roll them into long strands.

Plait the strands of dough and press the ends together to make a ring.

Brush the crown with beaten egg and bake until golden brown.

Scarcedda
Easter Plait

500 g/1 lb 2 oz flour
1 pinch salt
1 tsp baking powder
100 g/3½ oz sugar
2 tsp vanilla sugar
grated peel of ½ lemon
100 ml/3½ fl oz olive oil,
plus extra for greasing
2 egg yolks
4 eggs

Sift the flour on to a work surface. Mix in the salt, baking powder, sugar, vanilla sugar and lemon peel, then mound up the dry ingredients and make a well in the centre. Add the olive oil and egg yolks and knead everything into a smooth, supple dough.

Preheat the oven to 200°C/390°F/gas mark 6 and grease a baking tray. Divide the dough into three equal portions and roll them into long strands. Plait the strands together, then bring the ends together to form a ring. Place the ring on the baking tray.

Clean 3 whole eggs and press them into the dough. Whisk the remaining egg and brush it on the ring. Bake 30 minutes or until golden brown. Set on a cooling rack to cool.

Christmas

The classic Christmas cake is the *panettone*, which comes from Milan. In the past, it was prepared in the form of loaves of bread, and the lord of the house oversaw its baking personally. To show his approval, he carved a cross into every loaf before it went in the oven, and today one still finds a cross on every *panettone*. Every family member gets a slice of Christmas cake, because it brings luck and wealth in the coming year.

The origin of the name *panettone* is the subject of many legends. According to one of them, over time the Christmas bread came to be baked only with expensive white flour, so as to emphasize its special nature. Therefore it was called *pan del ton*, or 'luxury bread'. Another legend claims that a kitchen servant named Toni threw together this delicious bread – *pan del Toni* – out of butter, crystallized fruit and scraps of dough after a court chef had burnt the dessert for his prince's Christmas banquet.

Panforte

The Tuscan city of Siena is the birthplace of *panforte*, a traditional cake originating in the kitchens of medieval peasants. The dough originally consisted of nothing more than flour, water, nuts and dried fruit – ingredients that could be found in every peasant kitchen of that era. *Panforte* (literally, 'strong bread') was no delicacy at the time, however, but a nutritious and long-keeping provision for the winter, with a very intense and rather tart flavour.

Later, monastery kitchens further developed the recipe, adding honey, sugar and spices. The cake became expensive to make, and eventually was only baked for the Christmas feast. According to the traditional recipe, the dried fruits are cut into dice and then boiled in honey and sugar at 112°C (235°F) so that they remain hard even after baking. Later, almonds, crystallized citrus peel and spices such as nutmeg and cinnamon are added to the dried fruits. This mixture, after cooling somewhat, is then kneaded in with flour.

Ossa di mortu
Bones of the Dead

5 eggs
200 g/7 oz sugar, plus extra for dusting
150 g/5 oz flour
1 tbsp baking powder
100 g/3½ oz ground almonds
1 tsp ground cloves

Beat the eggs with 2 tablespoons of warm water until foamy. Gradually mix in the sugar and beat until very pale and creamy.

Combine the flour, baking powder, ground almonds and cloves, then fold the dry ingredients into the eggs. Preheat the oven to 170°C/340°F/gas mark 3.

Cover a baking tray with baking paper. Spoon the dough into a piping bag with a large tip and squeeze 10-cm/4-inch strips of dough on to the paper. Sprinkle with sugar and bake for 15 to 20 minutes.

Panforte

150 g/5 oz sugar
150 g/5 oz honey
2 tbsp lemon juice
250 g/9 oz crystallized fruit, finely chopped
175 g/6 oz flour
150 g/5 oz chopped walnuts
150 g/5 oz chopped almonds
1 tsp cinnamon
1 tsp ground allspice
½ tsp ground coriander
1 pinch freshly ground nutmeg
15 large wafers (or baking paper)
2 tbsp icing sugar

In a small saucepan, stir together the sugar, honey and lemon juice over low heat until bubbling. Remove from the stovetop and stir in the crystallized fruit.

Thoroughly blend 140 g/5 oz of the flour with the chopped nuts and spices. Gradually add to the fruit and honey, and stir until smooth. Preheat the oven to 170°C/340°F/gas mark 3.

Line the base of a 26-cm/10-inch springform cake tin with wafers or a ring of baking paper. Fill with the dough and smooth the top. Mix the icing sugar and remaining flour and sprinkle over the top, then bake for 30 to 40 minutes. Cool in the pan before serving.

Gather all the ingredients for the panettone on the work surface.

In bakeries, softened butter is included with the other ingredients.

Knead lemon peel and crystallized orange and lemon peel into the dough.

Then cover the dough and set it in a warm place to rise.

Fill portions of the dough into paper forms and bake until golden brown.

Panettone are sold in paper wraps, which help keep them moist.

Panettone

200 ml/7 fl oz milk
40 g/1½ oz compressed fresh yeast or
2 sachets easy-blend dried yeast
125 g/4½ oz sugar
125 g/4½ oz butter,
plus extra for greasing
2 eggs
2 egg yolks
1 pinch freshly grated nutmeg
1 pinch salt
500 g/1 lb 2 oz flour
100 g/3½ oz raisins
60 ml/2 fl oz rum
1 tsp grated lemon peel
50 g/1¾ oz crystallized lemon peel, diced
50 g/1¾ oz crystallized orange peel, diced

Heat the milk and crumble the yeast into it. Stir in 1 teaspoon of sugar, cover and leave it to rest for 15 minutes.

Melt the butter, then stir in the eggs and egg yolks. Add the nutmeg and salt.

Sift the flour on to a work surface and make a well in the centre. Add the remaining sugar, the yeast-milk mixture and the butter-egg mixture, and knead everything into a smooth, supple dough. Place it in a bowl, cover and set aside in a warm place to rise for 1 hour.

Soak the raisins in rum for 20 minutes, then knead them into the dough along with the lemon peel and crystallized orange and lemon peels. Cover the dough and leave it to rise for another 30 minutes.

Preheat the oven to 175°C/350°F/gas mark 4 and grease a 22-cm/8½-inch springform cake tin with butter. Fold a piece of baking paper into a strip 45 cm long and 25 cm wide (18 x 10 inches). Use the strip to form a collar for the springform tin, extending the height of its sides. Fill the tin with dough and bake for 30 minutes. Cut a cross into the surface of the panettone and bake another 20 minutes. Leave it to cool in the cake tin before serving.

Panettone was once the classic Christmas cake in Milan. Nowadays it is baked all over Italy and traditionally eaten on Christmas day.

Caffè

Once again it was the Venetians who laid the cornerstone of this national passion. G.F. Morosini, a member of one of Venice's oldest noble families, told the Venetian senate in 1585 of a peculiar custom of the Arabs: 'From the simplest commoner to the loftiest lord, they sit at taverns and in the street, and they drink publicly a black, very hot water made from a seed that they call *cavèe*, and which, they say, keeps one awake.'

Thirty years later, in 1615, the Venetian Pietro della Valle introduced the coffee bean to the Lagoon City, and after another thirty years, the first coffeehouse – *bottega del caffè* – in Europe opened on Saint Mark's Square in Venice. By the end of the century, there were more than two hundred coffeehouses. One of the most renowned, most beautiful, and most expensive coffeehouses in the world is the Caffè Florian, founded in 1720. Purple satin, golden mirrors and intimate niches and tables take visitors back in time to the days when Giacomo Girolamo Casanova sat here and dedicated himself – wide awake – to the world of women.

From Venice, coffeehouses soon spread throughout Italy and much of Europe. They became more than places where one bought coffee. They became synonymous with the cosmopolitan Venetian lifestyle, a meeting place for artists and merchants, where pleasure mingled with business, and culture with politics. Coffeehouses provided a stage for social communication, which, as one eyewitness described, 'stood for progress, contemporaneity and ultimately for humanity'.

The most historically significant coffeehouse in Rome is in the Via Condotti, just a stone's throw from the Spanish Steps. A Greek by the name of Nicola della Maddalena founded the Caffè Greco here in 1760, which soon became the nerve centre of the 'German artists' colony', and a place for artists of all nationalities to meet. Goethe and Wagner, Liszt and Mendelssohn appreciated the stimulating effects of the Greco's coffee on their creative work, and they valued the conversations they had there with like-minded people, beyond the constraints of social hierarchy and other limiting forces.

For the Italians, coffee remains to this day a symbol of conviviality and friendship. And coffee accompanies the Italians in many variations throughout their day, from a morning cappuccino (which is only enjoyed at breakfast) to the evening espresso, taken before bed. Most Italians have two or three favourite bars in the vicinity of their home and office where they typically take their espresso – normally while standing – several times a day. *Prendiamo il caffè!* ('Let's have a coffee!') is the friendly invitation to a short conversation, a brief pause from the day's stress, heard in the street at every time of day.

The social significance of coffee is most beautifully demonstrated in the old Neapolitan custom of the *sospeso* (literally, 'suspended', or 'in suspense'). If someone has successfully completed a business transaction, or has simply had an unusually good day, she or he orders a *sospeso*, an espresso for a worthy cause. One espresso is drunk, but two are paid for. The second espresso is intended for guests who cannot afford their own coffee. If someone comes into a coffee bar and asks, *C'è un sospeso?* ('Is there one in suspense?'), he is given a coffee free of charge.

The historical Caffè Florian on Saint Mark's Square in Venice (opposite) is not only one of the most beautiful coffeehouses in the world, but also one of the most expensive.

The Art of Espresso

Hot as hell, black as the devil, pure as an angel and sweet as love – that is a perfect espresso. There are many details to attend to in the quest for the perfect *caffè*: precise proportions of coffee and water, pressure, water temperature, brewing time and more. The water cannot contain too much calcium, the coffee must be freshly ground every time, the espresso machine must be the correct temperature, the cups must be preheated and they have to have a rounded shape and cannot be too thick or too thin.

The quality of an espresso is immediately apparent in the *crema*, or the light foam floating on its surface. If the golden brown *crema* has a consistency firm enough to support the sugar that is spooned on to it, and if this covering remains intact even after stirring, then there is nothing left to stand in the way of a cup of perfect pleasure.

Italian Coffee Variety

In Italy, *caffè* means first and foremost an espresso. In spite of the intense flavour, a *caffè* contains only 40 per cent of the caffeine of an average cup of 'normal', filtered coffee. The Italian Roast is the darkest of the five classic roast levels, yielding coffees that have bitter or lightly sweet flavours, less caffeine and less acidity, which makes them easier on our stomachs.

Slight but important differences distinguish the most popular Italian coffee specialities.

Caffè, Espresso: a small, highly concentrated cup of coffee
Espresso doppio: a double espresso
Ristretto: highly concentrated espresso made with only half the usual amount of water
Caffè corretto (literally, 'corrected coffee'): espresso with spirits or liqueur
Caffè latte: a double espresso in hot milk (without foam)
Caffè macchiato (literally, 'speckled coffee'): espresso with a small dash of milk and a little foam
Caffè lungo: espresso with additional water
Caffè americano: espresso with a lot of hot water
Cappuccino: espresso with hot, foamy milk, ideally in equal proportions
Latte macchiato: hot milk with a cap of foam, into which an espresso is carefully poured
Bicerin: espresso with cocoa, sugar, cinnamon and foamy milk
Caffè freddo: an iced and sweetened espresso with a lot of water
Granita di caffè: frozen espresso

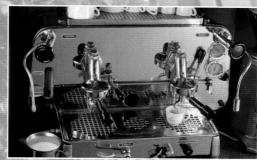

The pride and joy of every Italian bar is the large, gleaming espresso machine.

Hot water under high pressure shoots through the ground coffee and into the waiting heated cup.

The interaction of man and machine makes the perfect espresso.

The quality of an espresso can be judged by its golden brown, solid crema.

A good baristo tops off a cappuccino with foamy milk in the form of a heart.

Digestivi

Digestifs

D*igestivi* – or 'digestive aids' – with this prosaic word, Italians describe drinks that are typically enjoyed at the end of a meal. Whereas the *aperitivi* open the palate to pleasure and stimulate the appetite, and whereas wine heightens the enjoyment of a fine meal, the role of the liqueurs, brandies and bitters is to ensure that this enjoyment is what remains in the memory, and not any difficulty with digestion. Bitters especially, but also strong alcohols, are reputed to aid in the digestion of rich and fatty foods, and not without reason. The active ingredients in herbs, fruits and vegetables such as the artichoke support the functions of the liver and gall bladder and help break down fatty acids. And, of course, they should also be a pleasure in themselves, and not simply a bitter medicine.

As a rule, Italians do not drink wine after a meal is over. The finale to a fine meal is punctuated by beverages that are more intense in both flavour and alcohol content such as liqueurs or brandies. Only in southern Italy are these stronger drinks not enjoyed so often, a preference attributable to the region's climate. Several of the classic liqueurs come from the south, however – a result, perhaps, of the strong Arab influence on the region, especially Sicily.

Whether before or after a meal, Italians love to stop by their favourite bar to enjoy an aromatic herbal or bitter liqueur (right).

The selection of aromatic liqueurs is enormous. Many are still produced according to centuries-old recipes (below).

Liqueurs

The flavoured wines that were already produced by the Greeks and Romans of antiquity could be considered the prototypes for today's liqueurs. Wine laced with herbal extracts was a well-known component of Greek and Roman medicines. But the story of liqueur as we know it – a strong, sugared concentrate – began in the herb gardens and apothecaries of the European monasteries, a development that was only possible after the art of distillation had been learnt from the Arabs. Choice herbs were soaked in strong alcohol to release their active ingredients (this process is called maceration). The herbed wine was distilled several times and then mixed with honey to make it more palatable. To this day, such herbal distillates are still available in European pharmacies.

In the fourteenth century, liqueurs began to be produced for enjoyment. Their ingredients – alcohol, sweeteners and flavouring agents – as well as their expensive production made them the exclusive domain of the wealthy. When Catherine de' Medici married the future French king Henry II, she also brought specialists in the distillation of liqueurs with her. After sugar became affordable to all levels of society, liqueur production spread rapidly .

Liqueur is defined as a beverage with a high sugar content (at least 100 grams/litre in the European Union) and an alcohol level between 15 and 40 per cent. There are

Amaretto and limoncello are the most famous Italian liqueurs. Sambuca is often served con la mosca, or with three coffee beans that are chewed while drinking.

exceptions, however, with alcohol levels over 50 per cent. Nowadays, many inexpensive liqueurs are sold in concentrated form, but the best are still made by hand and have an especially fine flavour – they are not too sweet and sticky, but full-bodied and well-rounded.

The most famous Italian liqueur is the widely imitated *Amaretto di Saronna*, which hails from the Lombard city of Saronno, north-west of Milan. World-renowned by now, it is made from almonds and apricot kernels and refined with vanilla, among

To produce limoncello, the first step is to wash the lemons.

The fruit is scrubbed thoroughly with a hard brush.

The yellow part of the rind is cut from the lemons by hand.

Water and sugar in just the right proportion are cooked into a clear syrup.

The sugar syrup is added to the soaking lemon peels.

This mixture steeps for a week in high-proof alcohol.

Then the lemon liqueur is filtered in special bottling machines.

Now the finished limoncello can be bottled.

other things. Its flavour is highly reminiscent of marzipan. Amaretto is used for delicious desserts, and also as the basis of many cocktails. It is enjoyed in Amaretto Sours or simply over ice.

From the area around Naples, the Amalfi Coast, and Sicily comes *limoncello*, an extremely popular lemon liqueur. It is produced through the maceration of the especially thick, fragrant peels of a special variety of lemons in pure alcohol. A similar liqueur is produced in Liguria under the name of *limoncino*.

Mirto is a Sardinian speciality. The white variant of this liqueur is made from the leaves and blossoms of myrtle, an evergreen bush, and the red version is made from the berries of the same plant. Its flavour is tartly aromatic, velvety and spicy, with gentle, ethereal bitter notes.

Frangelico is a nut liqueur invented around three hundred years ago by a monk, and comes from the Piedmont region. The production process involves five steps that must be carried out to the letter in order to guarantee the quality of the resulting product. Selected Piedmontese hazelnuts are shelled, roasted and ground, and then steeped in a solution of water and alcohol. A portion of this mixture is then distilled. Naturally aromatic ingredients such as cacao, coffee, vanilla, rhubarb or orange blossoms are added to the distillate, and this mixture is blended into a concentrate. The concentrate is then aged in oaken barrels. After the ageing process is complete, it is diluted with water to drinking strength and stored for a further four months for the flavour to develop its final nuances.

Amari and Bitters

Italy produces a great variety of the drinks called bitters, which are normally taken as digestifs. They are collectively identified by the term *amaro*. *Amari* succeed through their perfect balance between bitterness and sweetness. The bitter note is sometimes the result of cinchona, a natural flavouring agent. The most famous amari are *Averna*, *Fernet-Branca* and *Ramazzotti*.

In the nineteenth century, a Franciscan friar, Fra Girolamo, developed a herbal liqueur, and shortly before his death he passed on the recipe for it to his friend Salvatore Averna. Thus began the production of *Amaro Siciliano*. Averna's son, Francesco, took charge of the business and designed a label that, with only slight modifications, is still in use today. The headquarters of this family business are still located in Salvatore's hometown of Caltanissetta, Sicily. The basis of Averna consists of sixty different herbs, roots and fruit peels. The raw materials are carefully selected, chopped and pulverized with mortars and pestles. The mixture, to this day a family secret, steeps for thirty to forty days in pure alcohol. Then it is filtered several times and enriched with sugar syrup and burnt sugar. The most important steps in the production process are still carried out exclusively by hand. After two months' storage, the Averna is finally bottled. In Italy, Averna is normally enjoyed neat, but

Alchermes, Herbal Elixir of the Medicis

The *Farmacia di Santa Maria Novella*, founded in Florence in the fourteenth century, is one of the most famous pharmacies in Italy, and it rests on a tradition that is hundreds of years old. In the age of the Medicis, the monks served their customers – predominantly nobles, of course – self-made herbal elixirs such as *alchermes*, which stems from an Arab recipe. Apart from the main ingredients of alcohol, sugar, rose water, orange peel and vanilla, it contains such spices as cinnamon, coriander, mace, cloves, anise blossoms and cardamom. Its radiant red hue is the product of the cochineal, a scale insect that was dried and ground to give the mixture its tint. The Spanish name for this insect is *alquermes*, which comes from the Arabic *al-qirmiz* (literally,

'scarlet-coloured'). These days, cochineals are primarily used in the production of Campari (see *Aperitivi*).

Alchermes – both as a liqueur and as an ingredient in many desserts – was not only enjoyed at the court of the Medicis. It was dubbed the 'elixir of long life' and, like so many other culinary specialities, was introduced in France by Catherine de' Medici, where it came to be known as '*Liquore de' Medici*'. Due to its heavy viscosity and intense colour, it is nowadays used primarily in the making of certain desserts, including *Zuppa inglese*. The special flavour resulting from the numerous spices in the recipe makes it live on in the memory of those who have been fortunate enough to taste it, and makes its almost complete disappearance most regrettable. But in the *Farmacia di Santa Maria Novella* in Florence, *alchermes* is still for sale.

the addition of ice, lemon or blood orange juice is also popular.

Fernet-Branca has been produced in Milan since 1845 by the Fratelli Branca Distillery S.r.L. The recipe, which also remains a family secret, incorporates forty different herbs. According to the distillery, Fernet-Branca contains – among other ingredients – gentian, saffron, chamomile, myrrh and elder blossoms. The alcohol content reaches 40 per cent (43 per cent in Italy). Fernet-Branca is aged for more than a year in oaken vats so that its flavour can fully develop. It is drunk straight, on ice or as a cocktail.

Ramazzotti was first produced in Milan in 1815 according to another closely guarded recipe developed by Ausano Ramazzotti. This recipe contains thirty-three especially aromatic herbs and plants, including sweet and bitter orange peels, cinchona, angelica, masterwort, rosebuds, vanilla and star anise. Ramazzotti contains no artificial colours or flavours, and its alcohol content is about 30 per cent. It is imbibed as a digestif or bitter, usually on ice and with a small wedge of lemon, although it can also be mixed with ginger ale or soda water. Adding a portion of mint results in the mixed drink *Ramazzotti Menta*.

The Farmacia di Santa Maria Novella *in Florence (left) is one of the most famous pharmacies in Italy.*

Fernet Branca, *the world-famous bitter, is sold in its classic form, or with mint as* Fernet Branca Menta.

Grappa

For many Italians, a fine meal is not complete unless a *grappa* accompanies the customary espresso that rounds it off. Grappa is a brandy made from pomace, which is the pressed and distilled grape pulp, peel, seeds and stalks left over after winemaking.

What many today consider to be one of the noblest products of distillation – and in recent times, correctly so – has its origins in making use of leftovers, that is, the art of producing something valuable and enjoyable out of something that seems worthless. The method of distillation was already being used to make brandy in the eleventh century. In the process of making wine, grapes are typically only pressed to about 70 per cent of capacity. With the idea to mash the grape remnants again and then to distill them, a soon-to-be national drink was born.

Grappa as such is first mentioned in documents dating from the middle of the fifteenth century, when a Piedmontese notary left a distillery and large quantities of aqua vitae and '*grape*' to his heirs. By this time, there was already an independent trade in this spirit. Farmers were allowed to produce enough for their own needs, which contributed to grappa's image as a poor man's drink.

As the Italian nation was founded in the nineteenth century, this pomace brandy became a national symbol, as it were, and during World War I, Italian soldiers received a daily ration of grappa to lessen the horrors of their ordeal. But even these patriotic associations did not help boost grappa's reputation. Its profile first improved in the middle of the twentieth century, through the great efforts of distillers. What was required – apart from refinements in the

A good grappa deserves an elegant bottle and an appropriate label.

distillation process – was a higher quality of raw materials, and this was made possible by a general improvement in wine production. Nowadays, almost every region of Italy has its own grappa specialities, most of which are produced from certain grape varieties. Also in terms of refinement – for example, through a longer ageing process in wooden vats, or multiple distillations – quality and taste have markedly improved.

The requirements for a quality grappa are high. The pomace must be as fresh as possible and the distillation process must be very closely monitored. A grappa depends on its fruitiness. It should ultimately have a delicate yet powerfully fruity flavour and it must – in spite of its strong character – softly caress the gums.

Among the most famous distillers who produce greatly desired and accordingly steeply priced grappa are Nonino, Sardini and Jacopo Poli. One can also visit gourmet conventions such as the *Salone del Gusto* in Italy or the *Vinitaly*, where excellent small-scale producers are often discovered. Their only shortcoming is that their production is not on a large enough scale to reach a greater audience.

The distillation process for a quality grappa must be supervised with utmost care and knowledge.

Most grappas are clear, colourless and light.

To make good grappa, you have to start with the pomace of high-quality wines.

During the distillation process, the alcohol content is measured with an aerometer.

The finished grappa is bottled and labelled.

Vini e Acque

Wines and Waters

WINE

It can be said without exaggeration that Italy is the most diverse wine-producing country in the world. More than two thousand different types of grapes grow there, a number much greater than in most other countries. Some of these grapes were already cultivated by the Greeks and Romans. The land's soil is also very diverse, but the climate has a unifying influence. The Alps act as a screen, keeping the cold northern winds at bay, and the Apennines create a weather divide stretching from the Piedmont down to Sicily. The Mediterranean in the east and the Tyrrhenian Sea in the west, together with numerous rivers and lakes, also influence the climate. In the best regions, the average temperature lies between 12°C and 15°C (54–60°F). Sufficient snow and rainfall in the winter and warm to hot summers with sunshine lasting well into autumn produce excellent grapes. Vineyards are planted both at sea level and at altitudes of up to 1,000 metres (3,250 ft).

Although some varieties had been renowned for centuries, well into the twentieth century Italian wine was considered a cheap thirst quencher and mood lifter. In addition, some wines had earned acclaim locally, but remained largely unknown to connoisseurs outside of Italy. In the wine-producing rival France, things were not actually so different. Only the world-famous wine regions such as Bordeaux, Burgundy and Champagne outshone the inexpensive but generally below-average, run-of-the-mill wines from their neighbour to the south.

But the image of Italian wine underwent a facelift when traditionally recognized producers such as Antinori or Frescobaldi took a new path and garnered attention with new, premium grape varieties. Showing the way were wine experts, oenologists, who focused their interests on internationally renowned winemakers and imitated their practices. Improved cellar conditions and informational tours abroad contributed to a rapid increase in quality.

The 1970s witnessed the appearance of the 'Super Tuscans', red wines from Tuscany but produced with international grape varieties such as Cabernet Sauvignon and Merlot, made by winemakers who focused on the coveted large grapes of the Bordelais. Because these wines do not meet the strict criteria of geographically protected cultivation (DOC or DOCG) – also

Varieties of Grapes

Four hundred varieties of grapes are officially registered in Italy. The 'greats' are found almost exclusively among the red wines, but there are nevertheless excellent and original Italian white wines. The most widely grown varieties include:

Trebbiano (white)
Sangiovese (red)
Cataratto Bianco
        (diverse varieties, white)
Malvasia (diverse varieties,
        white and red)
Barbera (red)
Merlot (red)
Montepulciano (red)
Negroamaro (red)
Primitivo (red)
Nero d'Avola = Calabrese (red)

because the grapes from which they were made did not qualify for the region – they were originally identified simply as 'table wines'. The most famous of these are the *Tignanello*, the *Ornellaia* and the *Sassicaia*. Their success led to modification of Italian law and the creation of the designation 'IGT' (*Indicazione Geografica Tipica*) for exclusive, yet non-DOC wines. This turn of events also affected other regions such as Umbria and Marche, which were originally not so highly regarded. In the meantime, the great names in Italian wine are in great demand worldwide, and are correspondingly expensive. Crucial to this success was a return to quality and a more critical selection of grape varieties.

The focus on international varieties, however, has led to something of a counter-movement. Today, the traditional, 'autochthonous' varieties are once again highly regarded. These are grapes that only grow in a clearly delineated geographic area. They are primarily older varieties that had gone out of fashion because they did not appeal to mainstream tastes. Italy has one of the highest numbers of autochthonous varieties, about three hundred and fifty,

Many people associate Tuscany with a very special quality of life – including romantic landscapes, good food and excellent wine.

The riper the blue grapes are, the more easily soluble their colouring pigments. The pigments are also more stable during the later stages of the red wine's ripening.

and many of these have been favoured by connoisseurs for some time. The prestigious wine guide *Gambero Rosso*, which is published in Italy under the aegis of Slow Food, and which rates about 18,000 wines every year, has lately been awarding its coveted 'Three Glasses' to more and more wines made from autochthonous varieties.

Italy, Wine Country

In quantity of wine produced and area cultivated, Italy ranks at the top with France and Spain. Grapes are grown and wine produced from the northernmost (Trentino, South Tyrol) to the southernmost (Sicily) of Italy's regions, as well as on the Mediterranean islands: two million winegrowers, 340,000 cellars and 45,000 bottlers produce wine for the market. More than half of all Italian farms include vineyards, and 80 per cent of them encompass less than 5 hectares (12 acres).

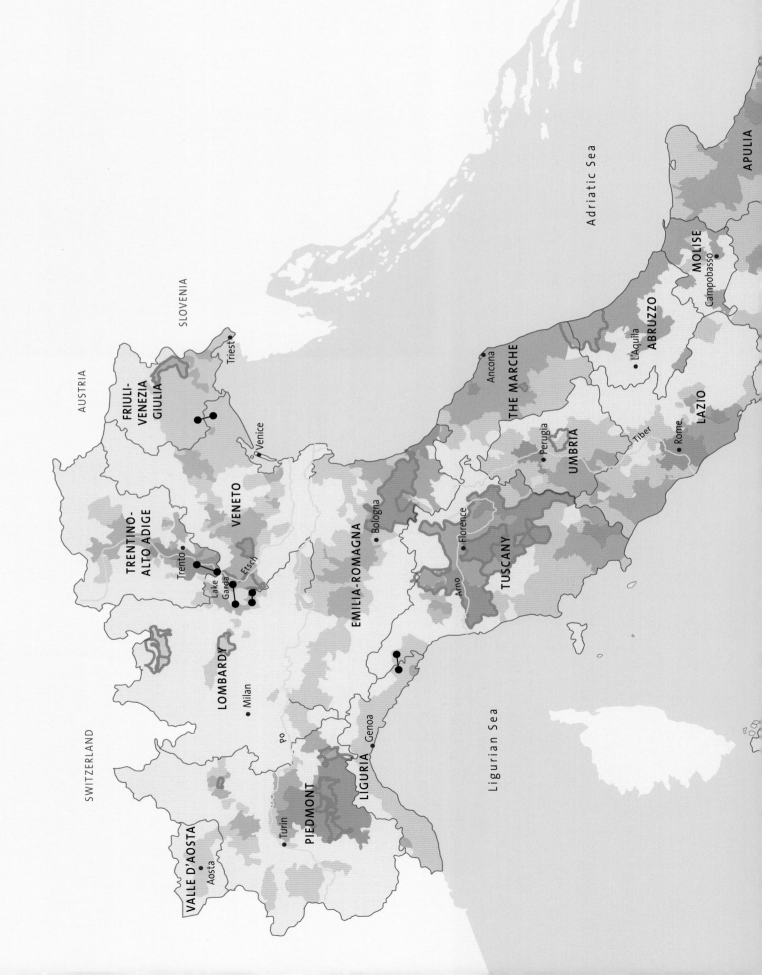

Italy's Great Wines

N

SWITZERLAND

AUSTRIA

SLOVENIA

FRIULI-
VENEZIA
GIULIA

Triest

TRENTINO-
ALTO ADIGE

Trento

VENETO

Lake
Garda   Etsch

Venice

Adriatic Sea

LOMBARDY

Milan

Po

EMILIA-ROMAGNA

Bologna

THE MARCHE

Ancona

MOLISE

Campobasso

APULIA

ABRUZZO

L'Aquila

Perugia

UMBRIA

Tiber

LAZIO

Rome

VALLE D'AOSTA

Aosta

Turin

PIEDMONT

Genoa

LIGURIA

Florence

Arno

TUSCANY

Ligurian Sea

Naples

BASILICATA
Potenza

CALABRIA
Catanzaro

Ionian Sea

Tyrrhenian Sea

SICILY
Palermo

SARDINIA
Cagliari

Mediterranean Sea

DOC (Denominazione d'Origine Controllata) and
DOCG (Denominazione d'Origine Controllata e Garantita) are
abbreviations for the official seals signifying controlled or
controlled and guaranteed origins of Italian wines.

DOC area

Area con 2 o 3 D.O.C. che insistino sullo stesso territorio =
Region with two or three independent DOC areas

Area con 4, 5 o piu D.O.C. che insistino sullo stesso territorio =
Region with four, five, or more independent DOC areas

DOCG area

DOC interregionale = interregional DOC area

A Diversity of Wines

Italy can offer just the right wine for every occasion and for every budget – from light, bubbly whites known as *spumante* and *frizzante* and uncomplicated reds such as *Bardolino*, *Valpolicella* or *Lambrusco* to impressive, bold red varieties and voluminous sweet wines that compare favourably to wines from Germany and France.

The various climate zones also offer numerous styles. Some of the most sought-after white wines – not only in Italy, but the world over – grow in Friuli and the Alto Adige area, one speciality being *Picolit*, a legendary, beguiling sweet dessert wine that is produced in disappointingly small quantities. The Piedmont boasts *Barolo* and *Barbaresco*, two giants that belong to the 'Champions' League'.

Venice is represented not only by sparkling *Prosecco* and smooth *Valpolicella*, but also by the powerful *Amarone* and *Recioto*. Tuscany offers *Brunello* and *Nobile di Montepulciano* alongside its well-loved *Chianti* (not forgetting the aforementioned 'Super Tuscans'), all of which are worthy of gracing the finest tables in the world. Central and southern Italy also present imposing wines. Campania, Sardinia and Apulia are home to fiery vintages such as *Aglianico di Vulture*, *Cannonau* and *Negroamaro*.

Wine should be stored on its side, in a dark, humid space, and at a constant temperature of 12–15°C (50–60°F). That allows the wine to mature slowly, and its flavour to develop to the fullest extent.

PINOT NERO
1988

PRINO
ARRIQUE
'87

COMPRI
BARRIQUE

Classifications

In Italy, wine is an everyday drink. The great wines are rare and expensive, and are thus reserved for special occasions – and, of course, for a small group of well-funded aficianados whose members are located not just in Italy, but all over the world. It is therefore no surprise that the majority of Italian wine is simply identified as 'table wine'. *Vino da tavola* (or *vin de table* in French) accounts for about 40 per cent of Italian wine production. According to law, no information regarding its geographical origin or grape variety may not be displayed on the label of such wines – they are simply identified as *bianco* (white) or *rosso* (red).

The reformation of the category *Vino da Tavola Indicazione Geografica*, which was replaced by the current classification *Indicazione Geografica Tipica* (IGT), has led to a revival, since many excellent wines that had previously been classified simply as table wines have become models for new wines with registered geographic origins. IGT wines must follow stricter requirements regarding alcohol content and vineyard output than normal table wines, but they are less stringent than those governing the next status: *Denominazione d'Origine Controllata* (DOC – controlled origin) and *Denominazione d'Origine Controllata e Garantita* (DOCG – controlled and guaranteed origin). These two categories account for approximately 30 per cent of the wine produced in Italy, whereas there are currently about one hundred and thirty IGT wines on the market.

DOC and DOCG wines are produced from registered grape varieties, according to precise methods and in specifically designated geographic areas. The permitted yield per hectare is also prescribed. DOC wines account for approximately 25 per cent of the annual production in Italy, and the remaining 5 per cent of those so labelled are DOCG. All in all, there are about three hundred and twenty different designations of origin. Some regions only produce one such wine, whereas some make reds and whites and more (such as Piedmont). The terms *Riserva* and *Gran Riserva* can be used when wines have a longer ageing process (normally two to four years).

Prosecco, Frizzante and Spumante

Sparkling wine is nothing new: the ancient Romans had already mastered the art of temporarily interrupting fermentation. As far as Italian wine is concerned, *Prosecco* has practically become a synonym for all bubblies. There is hardly any region whose sparkling wine's name does not end in '-*secco*'. This is actually misleading, because Prosecco merely identifies a grape variety native to Veneto that yields not only a light, sparkling wine, but also a still wine.

The truly accurate labels for most sparkling wines are *frizzante* when the carbon dioxide pressure is less than two and a half bar, and *spumante* if the pressure is greater. Wines with added carbon dioxide are required to be labelled *gassificato* or *vino addizionato di andride carbonica*. Spumante wines are produced either by the Charmat process or according to the classic *méthode champenoise*.

The classifications *extra brut, brut, extra dry, secco* (or *asciutto*), *abboccato* and *dolce* refer to the sweetness of sparkling wine. Among the most famous are *Asti* (DOCG, Piedmont), *Franciacorta* (DOCG, Lombardy) and *Conegliano-Valdobiaddene* (DOC, Veneto). *Asti Spumante*, which is most often medium sweet to sweet, is pressed from the Moscano Bianco grape. *Moscato d'Asti* has been a widely known and highly regarded sparkling wine since the Middle Ages.

The *méthode champenois*, or *metodo classico*, was introduced in the nineteenth century and helped establish the reputation of Asti sparkling wine. The Moscato d'Asti – normally regarded as one of the better varieties – has a very low alcohol content of 4.5 to 5.5 per cent. Asti Spumante, on the other hand, has almost 11 per cent. In terms of production, with its 80 million bottles a year, Asti Spumante ranks second worldwide – behind Champagne.

Italy produces a large variety of quality sparkling wines, produced according to the classical méthode champenois *of in-bottle fermentation. They are without question just as good as their French relatives.*

Franciacorta

Almost 1,000 hectares (2,500 acres) of vineyard yield what many aficionados consider to be the best sparkling wine made in Italy. Twenty-three communities on the southern shore of Lago d'Iseo, in the Lombard province of Brescia, produce *Franciacorta*. The name is derived from the Latin *francae curtes*, or the tax exemption enjoyed by the local monasteries and convents. The district is affectionately known as 'Italy's Champagne'.

The young vintner Franco Ziliani, who had learnt his trade from the makers of Moët et Chandon in Champagne, France, began producing sparkling wine at the vineyards of Guido Berlucchi in 1961. It was not long before connoisseurs began to take note of the quality of his product, and many other vineyards followed his example. In 1995, his wine received the DOCG designation as the first Spumante in Italy to be fermented in the bottle.

The straw-coloured to greenish wine is made from Chardonnay, Pinot Nero, Pinot Bianco and no more than 15 per cent Pinot Grigio grapes according to the *metodo classico*. A storage period in the bottle of eighteen months – or thirty months for vintages – is required, and the minimum alcohol content is 11.5 per cent. The base wine is often barrel-aged. The variant now known as *Satèn* (previously *Crémant*) is only made as a *brut*, and only from Chardonnay and/or Pinot Bianco ('*blanc de blancs*'). Other requirements include smaller yields and longer fermentation.

Rosé wines must contain at least 15 per cent Pinot Nero. This and the *brut* both have DOCG status. Famous producers include Belavista, Berlucchi, Ca' del Bosco, Cavalleri, Faccoli and Monte Rossa. Since 1995, when the sparkling wine was admitted to the most stringently controlled category (DOCG), the still wine has been classified as DOC *terre di Franciacorta* (recently renamed *Curtefranca*).

Light White Wines

The lightest Italian white wines are often made from the variety Trebbiano, a grape with relatively high acidity and little extract, but high yields. The numerous versions of this ancient variety that were mentioned by Pliny the Elder (23–79 CE) – including Trebbiano d'Abruzzo, Trebbiano Toscano, Trebbiano Romagnolo and Trebbiano di Soave – reflect the diversity of styles produced from this grape, as well as its amazing adaptability.

The popular *Soave* wine, which comes from Veneto, is primarily made from the Garganega grape, but usually with a variable proportion of Trebbiano di Soave as well as Chardonnay and Pinot Bianco. Especially when in the form of *Soave Classico* and *Soave Classico Superiore* – all of which come from a narrowly defined area of 1,500 hectares (3,700 acres) – it is an ideal accompaniment to any meal, because it goes with any dish. There is also a Spumante version of Soave, as well as a heavier, sweet version called *Recioto di Soave*.

The *frizzante* wines made from Prosecco grapes are also among the refreshing, stimulating vintages from the Veneto region. People enjoy drinking a glass already in the morning hours in one of the multitude of bars. Although Tuscany is most renowned for its red wines, it also produces the white *Vernaccia di San Gimignano*, which has an alcohol content of at least 11 per cent. This was reputed to be the favourite wine of the famous painter and sculptor Michelangelo Buonarroti (1475–1564).

Growing Areas

The most important growing areas for white wines are in the northern provinces, including Alto Adige, Friuli, Veneto, Lombardy and Piedmont. But local specialities abound all the way down the peninsula to the southern reaches of Italy such as *Vermentino* from Sardinia or *Verdicchio* from the Marche region. Vermentino is a distinctive wine that is well-suited to the powerful tastes of Sardinian cuisine. The Marche, with its bountiful fishing grounds in the Adriatic Sea, is the home of *Verdicchio dei Castelli di Jesi*, which many consider to provide the best accompaniment to any fish or seafood dish. This area and the

somewhat smaller *Verdicchio di Matelica* belong to the DOC category.

However, the modern white wines of Italy, for the most part, are made from the 'global players' – grapes of the Chardonnay and Sauvignon Blanc varieties. The Alto Adige, especially, attracts attention with its high-quality wines. Apart from these two varieties, Riesling and Müller-Thurgau are cultivated, as well as White Burgundy (Pinot Bianco) and Gewürztraminer, which actually originated here, in Termeno (called 'Tramin' in German).

In Friuli, which many aficionados consider to be one of the finest wine regions on the planet, two regional specialities are grown: the *Ribola Gialla* and *Friulano* (previously *Tocai friulano*). The Slow Food organization regularly posts information about the best white wines of Friuli-Venezia Giulia on their 'Super Whites' website (www.superwhites.it). They also put on SuperWhites events, which showcase the very best regional wines in order to increase public awareness of them.

The Arneis grape comes from Piedmont, where it is flatteringly called *Barolo Bianco*. This name should not be construed as an attempt to compare its quality to that of the renowned variety Nebbiolo, from which the world-famous red wines *Barolo* and *Barbaresco* are made. The Arneis grape, to which the Nebbiolo is not related, yields a wine with exceptionally low acidity and a fragrance that betrays a hint of almond when the wine is young. This wine does not age well, though, and should be enjoyed while young.

The town of Ruttars in Friuli-Venezia Giulia, situated on a hill of the same name, is known for its superior wines and lovely trattorias.

Red Wines

With all due respect to the quality of the white wines mentioned in the previous section, Italy's reputation rests mainly on its red wines, of which there are also a number of different styles. The home of light, uncomplicated reds such as *Bardolino* or *Valpolicella* is, of course, northern Italy. But it is hardly the case that northern vineyards only produce light wines.

With its *Amarone* and *Recioto di Valpolicella*, Veneto proves that strong, impressive wines can also be produced in northern regions. A decisive factor is the trick of drying the grapes before they are pressed. But Amarone wines – unlike Recioto – are not sweet. They always have an impressive alcohol content of at least 15 per cent, which almost causes them to assume the appearance of a liqueur.

Among the lighter wines from the north are *Marzemino* from Trentino and *Vernatsch* (*Trollinger*) from Alto Adige. Also native to this region, however, are the classic varieties Merlot, Pinot Nero and Cabernet Franc. Many of these grapes simply flesh out Italy's 'sea of wine' and aspire to be little more than pleasant, uncomplicated thirst quenchers. Some, however, can display an astonishing level of quality. This is especially true of the wines made from autochthonous grape varieties – and Italy is very well endowed in this regard.

One of Italy's most important and most common red grapes is the Sangiovese. This variety was already cultivated by the Etruscans, and is a main ingredient of Chianti today.

Harvesting Red Grapes

The ripe grapes used in the best wines are still picked by hand.

It takes thirty harvesters one day to pick 1 hectare (2.5 acres) of vineyard.

The grapes are collected and placed in larger containers for transport.

Autochthonous Varieties

The term 'autochthonous' (from the Greek *autós,* or 'self' + *chthón,* or 'earth') refers in geology and biology (flora and fauna) to 'species native to or originating in their location'. The oenologist designates as autochthonous grape varieties that originated in the area where they are traditionally grown. Even if the cultivation of a variety has spread further afield geographically, it can still be typical of its region of origin.

The cultivation of many varieties of grapes has spread to such an extent, however, that it is no longer possible to determine where they originated. The current amount of cultivation in any one place is therefore no indicator of whether or not a grape variety is autochthonous. If an uncommon variety appears even today in only one area – for example on Sardinia – and nowhere else, then one can assume that it is most likely autochthonous to that region.

Among the older varieties, cultivation of which has spread widely, mutations have brought about local and regional variants that are considered autochthonous to the regions in which they are now grown. Every region in Italy has such varieties. Over the last few years, more and more southern Italian wines, especially, have been produced from autochthonous grapes. Impressive red wines grown from autochthonous varieties are made in Apulia, Calabria, Campania and Sicily – *Primitivo* and *Negroamaro* in Apulia, for example, *Aglianico* in Campania and Calabria, and *Nero d'Avola* on Sicily.

In the winery, the grapes are first separated from their thick acidic stalks.

Then the grapes are mashed together with their skin, that is, split open and crushed.

Then they are fermented, during which the pigment and aromas in the skin dissolve.

Barolo and Barbaresco

The hilly district of Langhe in Piedmont is the home of two of the best and most sought-after red wines in the world: *Barolo* and *Barbaresco*. This small geographical area provides optimal growing conditions for the late-ripening Nebbiolo grape, which is the basis of both wines. The communes of Ghemme and Gattinara, also situated in the Piedmont, are recognized as well, but neither can approach the quality inherent in the two *grands crus* (a term that designates vineyards with superb qualities) in Langhe. Until the middle of the nineteenth century, these wines could not be made dry. Due to the late ripening and the resulting fermentation in the colder months of November and December, the fermentation of the must could only be accomplished with inadequate yeast. Consequently, the wines always had a relatively level of residual sweetness.

In 1850, the French oenologist Louis Oudart was the first person to succeed in creating a dry version of this wine. And thus began Barolo's steady climb to the pinacles of the wine world. Characteristics held in common by all Barolo wines include a garnet red hue; relatively high levels of alcohol, tannin and acidity; and a complex aroma with accents of plum, roses, pine resin and licorice. To soften the tannin, the wine requires a long ageing process of up to ten years, during which the colour develops from ruby to brick red. Barolo wines have a shelf life of at least twenty-five years.

Among connoisseurs, Barolo wines enjoy cult status: the Italians have dubbed it 'the king of wines and the wine of kings' (a title that Louis XIV admittedly granted to Tokaji, and which is also claimed by the Burgundian *Grand Cru Chambertin*). Barolo is sold after three years at the earliest, two of which must have spent ageing in the barrel. If the label displays the word '*Riserva*', then the wine is at least five years old. A speciality known as *Barolo Chinato*, which is enhanced with cinchona and other spices, has an alcohol content of about 16 per cent and is classified as a DOCG. In the last few years, younger vintners have begun trying out new techniques of wine production such as barrel-ageing.

Barbaresco could be considered the twin brother of the Barolo, although its area of cultivation amounts to just over a third of the Barolo's. The French oenologist Oudart was also instrumental in developing the dry Barbaresco, which is the only type still being produced today. Starting in the 1960s, the vintner Angelo Gaja has been most responsible for the immense improvement in the wine's quality.

Old, ripened wines are the pride and joy of every wine collector and connoisseur.

Angelo Gaja

Angelo Gaja (born 1940) is one of the most influential of Italy's winemakers. Since 1969, he has overseen the vineyard in Cuneo, founded in 1859, south of the Piedmontese city of Alba. The measures he and his oenologists have taken to improve quality – including rigorous limitation of output – as well as his willingness to experiment with the newly introduced grape varieties Cabernet Sauvignon and Chardonnay, have made him a leading figure in the region.

Another of Gaja's innovations is a red wine in the style of a Beaujolais. With a *Barbaresco*, a wine made solely from the grapes of the three vineyards Costa Russi, Sori Tildin and Sori San Lorenzo, Gaja attracted much international attention. Since 1996, however, he has stopped labelling it as such. Today his vineyards encompass 90 hectares (225 acres) in the Piedmont and 114 hectares (280 acres) in Tuscany. Gaja is also very active in other undertakings such as importing wine glasses and the French sweet wine *Château d' Yquem*, and even as a hotel owner. A living legend, Angelo Gaja has been granted the honourary title of *Angelo nazionale* ('National Angel'). As of 2008, the famous Italian wine guide *Gambero Rosso* has given Gaja's wines the highest honour – a rating of three glasses – over forty times.

Wine Degustation

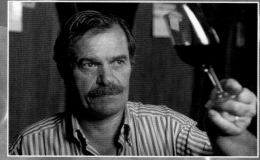

First, one examines the clarity as well as the deepness and tone of the wine's colour.

Then one sniffs the wine to investigate its bouquet.

To heighten the bouquet's impression, the wine is swirled in the glass.

Finally, the wine is sipped and allowed to run over the palate.

The Grands Crus

Brunello di Montalcino

Brunello is produced in the area surrounding the picturesque hill town of Montalcino, 40 km (25 miles) south of Siena. It is made exclusively from the Brunello grape, a variant of the Chianti varietal Sangiovese, which was developed and has been grown since 1870 in the vineyard of the Biondi-Santi family. Clemente Santi produced the first wine made from this grape in 1865 under the name *Vino Rosso Scelto.*

Ferruccio Biondi-Santi, the grandson of the 'inventor', furthered its cultivation and dedicated the majority of his vineyard to this grape. In 1888 and 1891, he produced the first wines designated as a Brunello (although this name appears in documents from as early as the fourteenth century). He left it to age for years in large barrels made of Slavonian oak. There are still a few bottles of these two legendary vintages in the vineyard's cellars. Under the next two generations of the family (Ferruccio's son Tancredi, and his son Franco), this wine became world famous. Until 1945, only four vintages of Brunello had ever been produced: 1888, 1891, 1925 and 1945. The limited production, together with its singular quality, were reason enough to justify its exorbitant price. For decades, the vineyard possessed the exclusive right

Tuscany is home to two world-famous wines, namely Brunello di Montalcino *and* Nobile di Montepulciano.

to produce this wine, and until the end of World War II, the name Brunello was only used by the Biondi-Santi family. Even into the 1970s, most Brunello came from their vineyard, because there were only twenty-five producers.

Nowadays, *Brunello di Montalcino* is made by around two hundred vineyards. In 1960, the total area of cultivation was only about 60 hectares (150 acres); by 1980, this number had increased to just 700 hectares (1,700 acres), and today it is grown on approximately 1,500 hectares (3,700 acres). Unfortunately, this expansion in production has also affected the overall range of quality. In 1980, Brunello was designated *Vino Nobile di Montepulciano,* thus becoming the first wine in Italy to receive the DOCG classification.

One important aspect of Brunello's quality is the microclimate in which it is grown, which is warmer and drier than the neighbouring Chianti zones, but with cooler nights. The alcohol content must be at least 12.5 per cent, but most vintages are about 13.5 per cent. The total ageing process – in barrel and bottle – must be at least forty-eight months. That means the wine is first released on the market on 1 January of the fourth (formerly the sixth) year following the harvest, and in the case of the *Riserva,* it is the fifth (formerly seventh) year.

With the reduced production time, the trend is following an increase in barrel-ageing, a condition that is not contested. The intense, ruby red wine has a dry, tannic flavour with a bouquet of aromatic woods, fruits, vanilla and jam. When young, the

Meditation Wine

An Italian dinner is almost always accompanied by wine. Or the other way around: wine is almost exclusively enjoyed at meal-times, at the very least with a snack. There are some wines, however, that demand our undivided attention while drinking them. The enjoyment of such wines would be disturbed by anything edible, even if nothing more than cheese and bread. Italian food critic Luigi Veronelli (1926–2004) baptized wines such as these *vini da meditazione,* or 'meditation wines'. Veronelli described them as 'especially complex, not everyday wines; they lend themselves to slow, sip for sip enjoyment on long winter evenings by the fire, and every sip should arouse a renewed sensation of surprise, happy warmth and contentedness'. Popular meditation wines include first and foremost the extraordinary Barolo and Brunello from top vineyards, Amarone or Recioto di Valpolicella (e.g., from Romano dal Forno), but also sweet wines such as Vin Santo or liqueur wines.

Grands crus wines are also among the meditation wines, because their enjoyment requires time and attention.

wine is hard and inaccessible; it first develops after a few years. It has an exceptionally long shelf life – in the case of *Riserva*, it often requires twenty-five years to mature.

Nobile di Montepulciano

Montepulciano, situated 120 km (75 miles) south-east of Florence in the upper Chiana Valley, is among the most beautiful cities in Tuscany. Every August, this 'pearl of the Renaissance' hosts the wine barrel race known as the *Bravio delle Botti*, in which representatives of eight arch-rival neighbourhoods roll wine barrels weighing well over 450 kg (1,000 lb) through the steep, narrow streets.

As early as the Middle Ages, wine from Montepulciano – today referred to as the 'doyen of all Tuscan wines' – was renowned and sought-after throughout Europe. Many poets have sung its praises. Traditionally, the very best wine was always reserved for the pope and the Vatican clergy, an arrangement probably not unrelated to the fact that two popes have hailed from Montepulciano. One of them, Pope Paul III (1468–1549), was particularly fond of the wine from his hometown. The title *vino nobile* ('wine for the nobility'), as it has been called since the eighteenth century, originated in this custom.

Wine from Montepulciano has a violet bouquet, ages for at least two years in oak or chestnut barrels, must have an alcohol content of at least 12.5 per cent, and has a long shelf life. It can only be produced in its region of origin, and can only be sold in Bordeaux bottles. After ageing for three years – of which six months are spent in the bottle – the label can bear the designation *Riserva*. Red wines from the same community, but with less stringent requirements, are classified as DOC *Rosso di Montepulciano*.

Both Brunello and *Nobile di Montepulciano* are outstanding accompaniments to a meal, whether it is a well-known barbecued speciality, for example a *bisteca fiorentina*, a popular game dish, or with hard cheeses such as pecorino. Like its great rival Barolo from Piedmont, the very best Brunello from the top producers is enjoyed as a 'meditation wine'.

Among the most famous producers of Brunello are Biondi-Santi, Castello Banfi, Castelgiocondo, Poggio di Sotto, Poggione, Salvioni, Talenti, Tenuta La Fuga, Tenute Silvio Nardi, Valdicava and Vasco Sassetti.

Dessert Wines

Sweet wines are not terribly fashionable these days. In antiquity, as well as from the Middle Ages to the early modern era, however, this was not the case at all. Italy has a long tradition of producing sweet wines using a diverse assortment of grapes, especially Malvasia. Dessert wines are popular in combination with *cantuccini*, an almond cake, or paired with strong blue cheeses such as Gorgonzola.

The now rare Picolit grape comes from Friuli. One family alone has been responsible for this grape's continued cultivation and refinement. A very expensive dessert wine called *Colli Orientali* is produced all over central Italy and the Trentino from the dried grapes of this variety. The most famous vintages, however, come from Tuscany in many variations. There, Picolit is produced in almost all of the DOC zones, and beyond. In April 2006, *Colli Orientali del Friuli Picolit* was classified as a DOCG wine. Up until the middle of the eighteenth century, it was a favourite at the nobility's tables, but was then forgotten.

In the three DOC zones of Chianti, Chianti Classico and Montepulciano, Vin Santo has its own DOC zones: *Vin Santo del Chianti, Vin Santo del Chianti Classico* and *Vin Santo di Montepulciano.* Most Vin Santo, however, is produced and sold without the DOC classification. Meaning 'holy wine', the name of this famous Italian wine stems from its frequent use as the consecrated wine for communion. Almost every farm produces its own version of it, mainly for personal use and special occasions such as weddings and christenings. These home-made wines are usually sweet (*dolce*), but half-sweet (*amabile*) and dry (*secco*), with variable alcohol content and residual sweetness, are also made.

To make Vin Santo, select grapes are picked – often by hand – from the preferred white varieties such as Malvasia Bianca, Trebbiano or Grechetto, as well as the reds Sangiovese and Malvasia Nera. They are air-dried, predominantly in barn lofts, hanging from shelves or laid out on reed or straw mats (*passito* technique). By the end of December at the earliest, the grapes have shrivelled. Any mouldy fruits are discarded and the grapes are gently pressed.

For centuries, the Benedictine Abbey of Rosazzo in the Colli Orientali (Friuli) played an important role in the preservation of viniculture. There is still a vineyard there today.

The viscous must is fermented to yield a wine with about 16 per cent alcohol content and much residual sugar. After fermentation, the wine is traditionally stored in small, half-full oaken or chestnut barrels that hold 70 to 200 litres (15–44 gallons). Some *Madre del Vin Santo* ('Mother of the Holy Wine') – a portion of a previous round of wine used to start a second fermentation – is often added as well. Then the barrels are sealed and stored, usually in an airy attic, so that they are exposed to the changes from cold winter to hot summer.

After no less than two to six years, the barrels are reopened. The result is a rich, powerful and sweet wine with the typical aroma of nuts, apricots, honey and spice. Rosé, red and white Vin Santos are produced, ranging from dry to sweet.

In the approximately 140-hectare (350-acre) Cinque Terre growing zone in Liguria, semi-dry to sweet *Cinqueterre Sciacchetrà* is made from dried grapes. The grape varieties used to make this wine are Bosco, Albarola and Vermentino, as well as several other white varieties that are permitted to account for up to 20 per cent of the finished product. There is also a *Cinqueterre Sciacchetrà Riserva*.

Malvasia

There are an especially large number of varietals of the Malvasia grape, which are grown on about 50,000 hectares (125,000 acres) in Italy. The most common are the white Malvasia Bianco (Lazio, Umbria, Tuscany), Malvasia di Sardegna (Sardinia) and Malvasia Istriana (Friuli), as well as the red Malvasia Nera (Apulia, Tuscany), Malvasia Nera di Casorzo and Malvasia Schierano (Piedmont). Malvasia varieties are often used to produce Vin Santo, as well.

MINERAL WATER

At meal-time, a jug of fresh water or a bottle of mineral water belongs on every Italian table, whether in a restaurant or at home. People carrying heavy crates of water bottles through the streets is an everyday sight, from the Valle d'Aosta to Sicily, and tourists making their first visit to a supermarket on the Adriatic coast or in Apulia may marvel at the mountains of mineral water bottles stacked next to the entrance.

Mineral water has a long tradition in Italy, and not only because it is a volcanic land with countless natural springs, fed by networks of subterranean channels. The ancient Romans' love of hot and cold mineral springs is legendary, both for bathing and drinking. Spas and thermal baths including Abano, Salsomaggiore and Fiuggi still attract health-conscious visitors today. Because Italy boasts countless regional and local varieties of mineral water – aside from the internationally recognized brands – it has long been customary to order not just *acqua minerale con* or *senza gas* (mineral water with or without carbon dioxide bubbles), but also to request a specific brand.

The most famous Italian mineral water is *San Pellegrino*. Originating at a depth of 700 metres (2,300 ft) in the Lombard Alps, its flavour is the result of its long passage through thick layers of limestone and igneous rock to the surface, a journey that filters, purifies and enriches the water with valuable minerals and trace elements.

This largest of Italy's bottlers exports its water to over a hundred different countries. In the thirteenth century, sparkling water from Bergamo in Lombardy was already famous, and Leonardo da Vinci was a devoted adherent of this spring.

Not far from the winter resort of Bormio, also in Lombardy, is the *Levissima* spring. Water from this spring is multi-purpose – it contains few minerals and is practically sodium-free. *San Benedetto* comes from Veneto. This pure water from the Dolomites originates 200 metres (660 ft) below

Water is an important staple item in Italy. A jug of fresh water or a bottle of mineral water accompanies every meal.

the earth's surface, and is popular throughout Italy. It has an extremely low mineral content and is almost free of sodium as well. *Acqua panna* – a telling name, as *panna* means 'cream' – is bottled in Tuscany, originating in the hills south of Florence.

Lauretana advertises itself as the 'lightest water in Europe', and is named after Saint Mary of Loreto. The source is located in the Monte Rosa Massif, which is more than 4,600 metres (15,000 ft) high. It flows through twisting subterranean, crystalline channels to the spring, situated at an altitude of some 1,050 metres (3,450 ft), and is bottled in Graglia (Piedmont). This spring is what is called an artesian well, from which the water gushes by its own pressure; it is bottled without pumps or mechanical pressurization. Its exceptionally low mineral content makes it a highly versatile water, and it is often offered between glasses at wine tastings, because it does not burden the palate with its own flavour.

Apart from the internationally famous brands, there are a multitude of regional and local mineral waters in Italy.

Water and Wine

Although wine is the customary accompaniment to an Italian meal, water is equally indispensable at the table. Wine – in combination with food – should please the palate, rather than quench one's thirst. That is water's purpose. The ancient Romans did not drink their wine pure, but mixed it with water, a practice that remained common into the modern era.

Although this custom is not so often observed nowadays (except in the case of wine drinks such as spritzers), since the enjoyment of wine – especially expensive wine – should not be diluted or lessened, the habit of drinking water and wine simultaneously has remained. With regard to the palatability of wine, it is a practice that can be recommended. To moderate the consequences of immoderate wine consumption, it is advised to drink at least the same quantity of water as of wine.

Appendix

Cooking Methods

Blanch
Briefly immersing foods into boiling water in order to loosen the skin or peel, or to preserve the colour and flavour of vegetables before further steps in a recipe.

Dry-roast
Quickly browning food in a non-stick frying pan without any added fat, for example pine kernels.

Fry, deep-fry
Cooking and browning food in hot fat at approximately 180–200°C (360–390°F). When deep-frying, food is submerged in sufficient hot oil to cover it completely; the food rises to the surface as it cooks.

Grill
Cooking food through direct radiant heat, for example under an oven grill or over an outdoor barbecue.

Refresh
Immersing hot food in icy cold water immediately after cooking to prevent further cooking.

Roast
Cooking and browning food, especially meat, in the hot air of an oven. The food is not covered and may or may not be in a small amount of fat or liquid.

Sauté
Cooking food in a small quantity of hot fat (usually oil or butter) while stirring frequently. The fat is heated before the food is put in the pan so that it cooks quickly.

Simmer
Cooking food submerged in hot liquid just below the boiling point, at approximately 85°C (185°F).

Steam
Cooking food in a perforated insert set in a saucepan of hot water just at the boiling point. The food should not come into contact with the hot water.

Stew
Cooking food in liquid in a covered pot or pan, at a moderate temperature, over a long period of time.

Abbreviations and Quantities

1 g =	1 gram =	1/1,000 kilogram
1 kg =	1 kilogram =	1,000 gram
1 tbsp =	1 level tablespoon =	3 tsp
1 tsp =	1 level teaspoon	

Mass and Weight of Ingredients

Weight of frequently used ingredients in grams	1 tbsp	1 tsp
Baking powder	10	3
Breadcrumbs	6	2
Butter	15	5
Cheese, grated	8	3
Cocoa	6	2
Cornflour	9	3
Cream, double	15	5
Flour	9	3
Honey	20	6
Icing sugar	8	3
Mayonnaise	15	5
Mustard	9	3
Nuts, ground	8	3
Oil	12	4
Raisins	9	3
Rice, uncooked	12	4
Salt	15	5
Soured cream	16	5
Sugar	15	5
Tomato purée	18	6
Water, milk, juice	15	5
Yogurt	16	5

Bibliography

Asselle, Maria Grazia and Yarvin, Brian. *Cucina Piemontese: Cooking from Italy's Piedmont*. Hippocrene Press, 2005.

Bardi, Carla. *Prosciutto*. The Wine Appreciation Guild, 2004.

Batali, Mario and DePalma, Gina. *Dolce Italiano: Desserts from the Babbo Kitchen*. W. W. Norton, 2007.

Boudin, Ove. *Grappa: Italy Bottled*. PianoForte Publishing, 2008.

Bugialli, Giuliano and Dominis, John. *Foods of Sicily & Sardinia and the Smaller Islands*. Rizzoli, 2002.

Caggiano, Biba. *Italy Al Dente: Pasta, Risotto, Gnocchi, Polenta, Soup*. William Morrow Books, 1998.

Callen, Anna Teresa. *Food and Memories of Abruzzo: Italy's Pastoral Land*. Wiley, 2004.

Capetti, Alberto and Montanari, Massimo. *Italian Cuisine: A Cultural History*. Columbia University Press, 2003.

Cipriani, Arrigo. *Harry's Bar: The Life and Times of the Legendary Venice Landmark*. Arcade Publishing, 1996.

Clark, Maxine. *Italian Salads*. Ryland, Peters & Small, 2006.

—— . *Italian Vegetables: Delicious Recipes for Appetizers and Sides*. Ryland, Peters & Small, 2005.

Davids, Kenneth. *Espresso: Ultimate Coffee*. St. Martin's Griffin, 2001.

Del Conte, Anna. *Gastronomy of Italy*. Pavilion Books, 2004.

Della Croce, Julia. *Veneto: Authentic Recipes from Venice and the Italian Northeast*. Chronicle Books, 2003.

Dettore, Mariapaloa. *Pizza Pane Focaccia! Pizza, Bread and Focaccia the Italian Way*. McRae Books, 2005.

Dettore, Mariapaola, Gioffe, Rosalba, Bardi, Carla and Vignozzi, Sara. *Carne! Meat the Italian Way*. McCrae Books, 2001.

—— . *Pesce! Fish the Italian Way*. McCrae Books, 2006.

—— . *Verdure! Vegetables the Italian Way*. McCrae Books, 1997.

Dewitt, Dave. *Da Vinci's Kitchen: A Secret History of Italian Food*. Benbella Books, 2007.

Dickie, John. *Deliza! The Epic History of Italians and their Food*. Free Press, 2008.

Downie, David and Harris, Alison. *Enchanted Liguria: A Celebration of the Culture, Lifestyle and Food of the Italian Riviera*. Rizzoli, 1997.

Esposito, Mary Ann. *Ciao Italia in Tuscany: Traditional Recipes from One of Italy's Most Famous Regions*. St. Martin's Press, 2003.

—— . *Ciao Italia Slow and Easy: Casseroles, Braises, Lasagna, and Stews from an Italian Kitchen*. St. Martin's Press, 2007.

Essa, Sharon and Edenbaum, Ruth. *Chow Venice: Savoring the Food and Wine of La Serenissima*. Wine Appreciation Guild, 2006.

Faas, Patrick. *Around the Roman Table: Food and Feasting in Ancient Rome*. University of Chicago Press, 2005.

Ferrigno, Ursula and Yorke, Francesca. *La Dolce Vita: Sweet Things from the Italian Home Kitchen*. Mitchell Beazley Food, 2006.

Field, Carol. *Focaccia*. Chronicle Books, 2003.

Ganugi, Gabriella. *Cheese: An Italian Pantry*. Wine Appreciation Guild, 2003.

Ganugi, Gabriella and Romanelli, Leonardo. *Olive Oil: An Italian Pantry*. Wine Appreciation Guild, 2003.

Guy, Patricia. *Wines of Italy: Il Gusto Italiano del Vino*. Tide-Mark Press, 2003.

Hazan, Marcella. *Essentials of Classic Italian Cooking*. Knopf, 1992.

Irvine, Sian. *Mozzarella: Inventive Recipes from Leading Chefs with Buffalo Mozzarella*. Periplus Editions, 1999.

Johns, Pamela Sheldon. *Balsamico: A Balsamic Vinegar Cookbook*. Ten Speed Press, 1999.

Kasper, Lynne Rossetto. *The Splendid Table: Recipes from Emilia-Romagna, the Heartland of Northern Italian Food*. William Morrow Cookbooks, 1992.

Kramer, Matt. *Matt Kramer's Making Sense Of Italian Wine*. Touring Press, 2006.

La Marca, Giovanna Bellia. *Sicilian Feasts*. Hippocrene Press, 2003.

La Place, Viana. *Panini, Burschetta, Crostini: Sandwiches, Italian Style*. William Morrow Cookbooks, 2002.

Marchetti, Domenica. *The Glorious Soups and Stews of Italy*. Chronicle Books, 2006.

Menghi , Umberto. *Umberto's Kitchen: The Flavours of Tuscany*. Douglas & McIntyre, 2003.

Orsini, Guiuseppe. *Italian Baking Secrets*. Thomas Dunne Books, 2007.

Palmer, Mary Amabile. *Cucina Di Calabria: Treasured Recipes and Family Traditions from Southern Italy*. Hippocrene Books, 2004.

Parkinson, Anthony. *Traditional Italian Seafood Cuisine*. Lulu.com, 2006.

Pellegrino, Vittorio. *Simply Bruschetta*. Maui Arthoughts Company, 2001.

Petrini, Carlo. *Slow: The Magazine of the Slow Food Movement*.

Petrini, Carlo, McCuaig, William and Waters, Alice. *Slow Food: The Case For Taste*. Columbia University Press, 2004.

Piras, Claudia. *Culinaria Italy: Pasta – Pesto – Passion*. Ullmann, 2008.

Plotkin, Fred. *La Terra Fortunata: The Splendid Food and Wine of Friuli Venezia-Giulia, Italy's Great Undiscovered Region*. Broadway, 2001.

Riley, Gillian. *The Oxford Companion to Italian Food*. Oxford University Press, 2007.

Romer, Elizabeth. *Italian Pizzas and Hearth Breads*. Clarkson Potter, 1988.

Rubino, Roberto, Sardo, Piero, and Surrusca, Angelo, eds. *Italian Cheese: A Guide to Its Discovery and Appreciation*. Slow Food Editore, 2006.

Salavadore, Jean Govani and Parolari, Luciano. *Tales of Risotto: 50 Recipes: Culinary Adventures from Villa d'Este*. Glitterati Press, 2006.

Schwartz, Arthur. *Naples at the Table: Cooking in Campania*. William Morrow Cookbooks, 2007.

Scicolone, Michele. *The Antipasto Table*. Ecco, 1998.

Seibert, Lou. *Biscotti*. Chronicle Books, 1992.

Simon, Susan. *Contorni: Authentic Italian Side Dishes for All Seasons*. Diane Publishing, 2003.

—— . *Insalate: Authentic Italian Salads for All Seasons*. Chronicle Books, 2001.

Slow Food Editore. *Osterie & Locande D'Italia: A Guide to Traditional Places to Eat and Stay in Italy*. Slow Food Editore, 2007.

Soletti, Francesco, ed. *The Italian Food Guide: The Ultimate Guide to the Regional Foods of Italy*. Touring Club Italiano, 2002.

Stellino, Nick. *Cucina Amore: Sausage stuffing and sausage* (DVD), Film Ideas, Inc, 2008.

Trabocchi, Fabio. *Cucina of Le Marche: A Chef's Treasury of Recipes from Italy's Last Culinary Frontier*. Ecco, 2006.

Ungaro, Fabrizio. *Pasta: An Italian Pantry*. Wine Appreciation Guild, 2003.

Verkaar, Desiree. *Carpaccio! 80 Wafer-Thin Recipes*. Miller Books, 2008.

Acknowledgments

The publisher, the authors and the photographer wish to thank the following people and institutions for their helpful support and collaboration in bringing this project to fruition.

The authors are especially grateful to Monika Sodomann, who for many months provided us with pasta, espresso and cheerful encouragement.

Dr Alessandro Marino, Italian Chamber of Commerce Munich
Antica Marcelleria Falorni, Greve
Artigian Salumi, Torremaggiore
Azienda Agricola e Frantoio, Vitiano, Arezzo
Camera di Commercio Industria Artigianato e Agricoltura
    di Verona, Verona
Christian Valentini, Italian State Tourist Board E.N.I.T.,
    Munich
Cipressi Deutschland, Gersthofen
De Cecco, Fara San Martino S.p.A.
Farris, Industria Agroalimentare, Troia
Federico Pierazzi, Villa Rigacci, Reggello
Giardinetto, Soc. Coop. Agricola, Orsara di Puglia
Gundula Dietrich, Food Marketing,
    Italian Chamber of Commerce Munich
Chamber of Commerce South Tyrol, Bozen
Konstanze Nimis, Orsara di Puglia
LaSelva, San Donato, Ortobello
Mazzetti, Mirandola, Modena
Raimondo Cusmano, Slow Food International, Bra
Regionale Associazioni Toscane, Florence

Regione Marche, Assessorato al Turismo, Ancona
Riseria Ferron, Isola della Scala
Slow Food International Office, Bra
Veronica Veneziano, Slow Food International, Bra

The photographer's special thanks to the following for their enthusiastic support:

Germany: Catrin Wagner, Alessandra Agliata

Italy:
La Pasticceria ALBA Enzo Costa, Palermo
Ercoli, Rome
Tamborini, Bologna
Pietro Prandini e figli, Modena
Mulino Sobrino, Piedmont
Le Baladin, Piedmont
La Cambusa Baldo, Positano
Pasticceria Nanini, Siena
Adelfio, Sicily
G. Cova & C, Milan
Panificio Paolo Atti e Figli, Bologna
Canta Napoli, Naples
Zafferano purissimo dell'Aquila, Aquila
C.A.T.A., Amalfi

We would also like to include in our appreciation all those who, without being known to us by name, supported and contributed to our project.

Picture Credits

All product photographs and cutouts: Martin Kurtenbach, Jürgen Schulzki, Ruprecht Stempell

All other photographs: Martin Kurtenbach

Except the following:

Günter Beer: all wood backgrounds, 8, 44, 46, 47 (t.), 51 (b.), 54 (t. l., t. c.), 55, 60/61 (steps, large), 62/63 (except cutout), 64/65, 68/69 (steps, large), 70, 72/73 (large), 74, 89 (r.), 94, 95 (t.), 96, 97, 101, 102, 103, 104, 105, 114, 115, 116, 117, 120 (t. l.), 121, 125, 131 (t.), 134, 135, 137, 142, 147, 151, 154 (large), 160, 162, 163, 169 (r.), 171 (t.), 172 (t.), 176, 177, 180/181, 184, 185, 186 (t. r.), 187, 189, 191, 205, 206, 207, 208, 209, 220, 221, 226, 227, 229, 231, 233, 237, 238, 239, 242, 244, 246, 247, 260, 266, 267, 268, 273, 274 (steps), 275, 278–279 (large), 285, 287, 289, 290/291, 292 (steps), 293, 299, 300, 301, 302 (b.), 303, 305, 306 (steps), 307, 308, 309, 313, 314 (t.), 315 (steps), 316 (steps), 317, 319, 320, 321, 323, 325, 327 (t.), 329, 330 (t. c., t. r.), 331, 335, 336, 338, 339, 341, 343, 346, 349, 350, 352, 355 (b.), 358 (c., r.), 359, 367, 368–374, 376, 377 (t.), 379 (t.), 380, 381 (steps), (t. r.), 382 (steps), 383 (t. l.), 385, 387, 388, 390, 391 (t.), 392/393, 398, 399 (large), 400, 401 (r.), 418/419, 429, 430, 432, 433, 440, 444, 445, 450–452, 453 (large), 458, 459, 461, 462 (steps), 463

Botanik Bildarchiv Laux: 188

Corbis: 2 J. Hall/photocuisine, 8 Colin McPherson, 10/11 Ingolf Hatz/zefa (large), 12/13 Envision, 13 Atlantide Phototravel, 15 Atlantide Phototravel (b.), 16 Historical Picture Archive (l.), 16/17 Bettmann (large), 17 Gustavo Tomsich (r.), 20/21 Atlantide Phototravel, 22 Atlantide Phototravel (b.), 23 Owen Franken (t. r.), 24/25 Marco Cristofori (large), 26 Atlantide Phototravel, 29 Atlantide Phototravel, 30 Sergio Pitamitz, 36 Atlantide Phototravel, 38 Image Source (large), 38 Swim Ink 2, LLC (t.), 39 Roulier/Turiot/photocuisine (t.), 40/41 Guido Baviera/Grand Tour (large), 42 Jose Fuste Raga (t. r.), 45 Mark Bolton, 47 Todd Gipstein (b.), 48 Austrian Archives (Kasten), 48/49 Atlantide Phototravel (large), 50/51 Atlantide Phototravel (gr), 52/53 Atlantide Phototravel (large), 56 (t.), 57 Sandro Vannini (t.), 58 Enzo & Paolo Ragazzini (b.), 76/77 Robert Harding World Imagery (large), 78/79 Atlantide Phototravel, 81 Jean-Bernard Vernier (box), 86 Atlantide Phototravel (box r.), 98/99 (large) Cultura, 106/107 Sandra Ivany/Brand X, 118 Poisson d'Avril/photocuisine, 122 Sebastiano Scattolin/Grand Tour, 124/125 Hussenot/photocuisine (large), 126/127 Hulton-Deutsch Collection, 129 Atlantide Phototravel (t.), 132/133 Atlantide Phototravel, 138 Massimo Ripani/Grand Tour, 140/141 Vittoriano Rastelli (large), 141 Roy Morsch (t.), 149 Atlantide Phototravel, 152/153 Grand Tour, 155 (b.) Mascarucci, 158 Puku/Grand Tour, 158/159 Sergio Pitamitz (large), 164/165 Grand Tour (large), 168/169 Grand Tour (large), 174/175 Guido Baviera/Grand Tour, 182/183 Massimo Ripani/Grand Tour (large), 190/191 Hussenot/photocuisine (large), 192/193 Angelo Giampiccolo/Grand Tour, 193 Max Power, 194 Mimmo Jodice, 194/195 The Art Archive (large), 198 Y. Bagros/photocuisine, 210/211 Dale Spartas (large), 212/213 H. Taillard/photocuisine, 214/215 (large) Walter Bibikow/JAI, 219 Elio Ciol, 230 Grand Tour (t. l.), 232/233 (large), 234/235 (large) Atlantide Phototravel, 240/241 P. Hussenot/photocuisine (large), 248 Riccardo Spila/Grand Tour (l.), 248/249 Angelo Cavalli/Robert Harding World Imagery (large), 252/253 (large) Hall/photocuisine, 258 Riccardo Spila/Grand Tour (large), 270/271 Grand Tour (large), 276/277 Bob Krist, 280 Peter Adams/JAI (t.), 294 Tom Bean, 295 Gunter Marx Photography (t.), Giraud Phillippe/Corbis Sygma (b.), 297 Atlantide Phototravel (large), 311 Atlantide Phototravel (small), 312 Robbie Jack, 315 Guido Baviera/Grand Tour (large), 316 Ted Spiegel (b.), 326/327 Atlantide Phototravel (large), 332 Roger Tidman (b.), 340 Ryman Cabannes/PhotoCuisine (t.), Frank Lukasseck (b.), 347 Stefan Meyers/zefa (b.), 348 P. Kettenhofen/photocuisine (t.r.), 354/355 Sara Danielsson/Etsa (large), 364/365 Atlantide Phototravel (large), 382 Atlantide Phototravel (b. l.), 386 Peter Adams, 396/397 Atlantide Phototravel (large), 410/411 Guido Baviera/Grand Tour, 420/421 C. Fleurent/photocuisine (large), 423 image100 (t.), 426/427 Richard Broadwell/Beateworks, 442/443 (large) Michael Jenner, 446/447 Atlantide Phototravel (large), 462 Bob Sacha (l.), 466/467 Sergio Pitamitz/zefa (large), 470/471 Gary Houlder (large), 474/475 Alinari Archives (large), 478/479 SPS (large), 479 Stefano Scata/Grand Tour (r.), 488/489 Grand Tour, 496/497 Grand Tour (large)

Michael Ditter: 364 (l.)

ditter.projektagentur GmbH: 37 (b. r.), 172, 188, 282/283 (large), 460, 469 (r.)

Burga Fillery: 22/23 (menus)

Jo Kirchherr: 41 (b.), 225, 268, 291 (r.), 367

Jürgen Schulzki: 81 (r.), 95 (box), 200/201 (except 2nd row), 203/203 (except b. r.), 219 (b. r.), 269, 272 (steps), 278 (steps), 296/297 (steps), 302, 304, 312 (t.), 324 (t. l.), 333, 342 (steps), 353 (steps b.), 377 (steps), 438 (steps)

Slow Food: 18/19

Ruprecht Stempell: 54 (t. l.), 57 (steps r.), 58 (t. l.), 66 (b.), 66/67 (large photo), 86 Salametto, 110 (step 1, 3–5), 154, 156 (t. l.), 161 (box), 178/79 (large), 204, 218 (b.), 230 (t. r.), 243, 253 (t.), 257, 262 (l.), 262/263 (large), 262 (step l.), 264 (t.), 265, 279 (r.), 284 (t.), 286, 322 (b.), 327 (b.), 330 (t. l.), 332 (b.), 337 (t. l.), 340 (b.), 342 (t.), 345 (t. r.), 351 (b. r.), 353 (t. l.), 361 (t. r.), 365 (t.), 378 (large), 384 (l.), 389, 447 (steps), 479 (small), 481 (t.), 495 (large)

Index of Recipes: English

Index of Recipes: Italian

Aperitivi

Antipasti

Topical Index